BASIC BY DESIGN
Structured Computer Programming
in BASIC

BASIC BY DESIGN
Structured Computer
Programming in BASIC

ANDREW KITCHEN

St. John Fisher College

Rochester, N.Y.

Prentice-Hall, Inc.

Englewood Cliffs, New Jersey 07632

Library of Congress Cataloging in Publication Data

Kitchen, Andrew.
    BASIC by design.

    Includes index.
    1. Basic (Computer program language)   2. Structured
programming.   I. Title.
QA76.73.B3K55 1983   001.64'24   82-21562
ISBN 0-13-060269-8

Editorial/production supervision: *Aliza Greenblatt/Barbara Palumbo*

Interior design: *Aliza Greenblatt*

Cover design: *Ray Lundgren*

Manufacturing buyer: *Gordon Osbourne*

Printed in the United States of America

10 9 8 7 6 5 4 3 2 1

ISBN 0-13-060269-8

PRENTICE-HALL INTERNATIONAL, INC., *London*
PRENTICE-HALL OF AUSTRALIA PTY. LIMITED, *Sydney*
EDITORA PRENTICE-HALL DO BRASIL, LTDA., *Rio de Janeiro*
PRENTICE-HALL CANADA INC., *Toronto*
PRENTICE-HALL OF INDIA PRIVATE LIMITED, *New Delhi*
PRENTICE-HALL OF JAPAN, INC., *Tokyo*
PRENTICE-HALL OF SOUTHEAST ASIA PTE. LTD., *Singapore*
WHITEHALL BOOKS LIMITED, *Wellington, New Zealand*

To Judith

Contents

Preface

There are two major pitfalls on the way to writing an introduction to BASIC programming.

The first is the difficulty of deciding which features of the language should be covered, for the truth is that BASIC is not just one language but numerous dialects, all of which lay claim to the name "BASIC." There is a national standard for the language, the ANSI standard for minimal BASIC.†
Unfortunately, this does not cover character string manipulation and file handling, two important areas of computer programming. Although most recent versions of BASIC provide facilities for handling these operations, the approaches taken vary widely from one dialect to another. This situation is made worse by the fact that some BASIC dialects do not conform to the ANSI standard, even where it does apply. This problem is resolved in *BASIC by Design* by discussing a particular version of BASIC, Digital Equipment Corporation's BASIC-PLUS, which observes the national standard wherever it applies, and by using the minimum extensions necessary to give a solid introduction to character strings and files. The discussion is kept general enough, and sufficient guidelines are provided, to make the conversion from this BASIC to any other relatively painless. Comparison of certain features of selected dialects are presented in the appendices.

The second pitfall surrounds the emphasis of the presentation. The beginning programmer does not want to be faced with a heavy treatise on programming style, particularly at a stage when his major concern is "How on earth do I get this *!?**? machine to do anything useful and not just sit there spitting error messages at me?" On the other hand, it does the student no service to introduce the features of the language one after another, cookbook style, without providing some instruction on how to write programs—clear, readable, error-free, working programs!

†Standard specifications for the syntax and semantics of a minimal core of BASIC statement types approved by the American National Standards Institute in 1978.

Like well-written prose, clearly organized programs are easier to understand and therefore easier to check and debug. The ramifications, however, go deeper than this because the structure of a program is intimately related to the approach that is taken in writing it. One cannot graft good style onto a badly planned program. So the question becomes: Does one tell the student about BASIC or teach him how to program? The bias of this text is, not surprisingly, toward the latter.

Initially, a sufficient number of statement types (PRINT, LET, INPUT) are discussed to allow the reader to write simple straight-line programs. Subsequently, new statement types (READ, DATA, IF-THEN, etc.) are introduced progressively as tools for solving the problems that arise as more sophisticated projects are attempted. The elementary building blocks (REPEAT loops and IF blocks), are introduced, first informally and later as part of a structured programming approach. In the interests of laying a solid foundation of good programming habits, the logical constructions introduced are kept as few and as simple as possible. For example, the IF-THEN-ELSE structure is not discussed nor is the ON-GO TO statement, both of which add extra power at the cost of confusing the beginning student just when he is coming to terms with REPEAT loops and IF blocks. Once the foundations are laid, other topics are tackled: the processing of lists and tables of data, text manipulation, the use of subroutines and data files and the application of the random number generator, RND.

The approach is kept on an elementary level. For example, a knowledge of high school algebra is the extent of the mathematical background required for all but a handful of the exercises, and the formalism of structured programming is kept to the bare essentials. However, this is not to say that the book will not challenge the more sophisticated reader. The exercises play an important role. Those in the early chapters lead the reader in easy steps through the process of program development, but he is increasingly left on his own in the later chapters. There are many extensions of the material in the book which would provide interesting classroom discussion or could be pursued independently by the reader (e.g., sorting and searching techniques; numerical methods; other program structures, IF-THEN-ELSE, CASE blocks, etc.; extensions to BASIC, PRINT-USING, MAT statements, etc.). Chapters 2 through 6 represent the core of the book. They should, as far as possible, be read in sequence, as each one builds on the one before. The second half of the book is more loosely organized, as each chapter covers a separate topic. Here are a few comments on the contents of some of the chapters.

Chapters 1 and 2 provide a leisurely introduction to communication with the computer. Their purpose is to help the beginning user to see the computer as a nonthreatening tool.

Chapter 3 introduces a principal theme of the book: the production of clear and readable programs, both as far as the output is concerned as well as in the structure of the code. The INT function is introduced in this chapter. It appears this early primarily because it is such a useful tool; it appears repeatedly in the examples and exercises of later chapters. Furthermore, it is needed here to provide some control over output format (the PRINT USING statement gives better results but is system dependent). The semicolon, as used in the PRINT statement, is also introduced here. The use of the comma to produce columns is deferred until Chapter 4, where the printing of tables is discussed. For the more sophisticated reader, Chapters 1 through 3 will be easy reading and can be covered quite rapidly.

In Chapters 4 and 5, the two major program structures, loops (REPEAT loops) and conditional blocks (IF blocks), are introduced informally. The nonstandard form of the IF statement,

IF condition THEN statement

is used to a limited extent in Chapter 5. It is restricted to a few examples and alternative approaches are discussed at length. The reason for discussing it all, apart from the fact that it is available in most popular versions of BASIC, is that it provides a simple introduction to conditional statements and blocks. By contrasting its use with the traditional "jump around" approach, the action of the latter can be clarified.

Chapter 6 summarizes the presentation of the earlier chapters. A structured approach to program development is formally introduced and is illustrated with worked examples.

In Chapter 9, the operators required for character string manipulation are introduced. Many versions of BASIC use functions almost identical to those discussed here. Examples of other approaches are illustrated in Appendix III.

As mentioned above, file handling in BASIC has not been standardized. Chapter 11 attempts to address this problem by emphasizing general concepts of sequential file handling, those common to all systems. The examples given are written in BASIC-PLUS. However, guidelines for file handling are discussed which should enable the reader to convert these examples to run on different systems without much difficulty. Again, a survey of other approaches is provided in Appendix IV.

BASIC by Design is intended for use in a wide range of introductory courses, from a semester-long introduction to programming to an intensive (perhaps, self-study) course for graduate students in the social sciences and management. However, it is not aimed solely at the college student. Any person who has a microcomputer at home and would like to learn how to control the little monster should find this book a solid and, hopefully, entertaining introduction to programming in BASIC.

Andrew Kitchen

Acknowledgements

Many people have contributed to the form and content of this book. Unfortunately, the complete list far exceeds the capacity of my rather unreliable memory and so my thanks and apologies go to all those not mentioned.

I am most grateful for the careful analysis and suggestions provided by each of my reviewers, Drs. Brian Kernighan, Kenneth Long, Philip Raymond, and Spotswood Stoddard, and the comments of my colleagues, Nancy Watts and Marjorie Schmieder, as well as the response of my students to classroom presentation of this material. Dr. Larry Coon corrected erroneous information in the appendices and Karen Lattierre and her word processor lightened the load of writing letters to numerous software companies. The editorial staff at Prentice-Hall was always helpful and efficient. Particular thanks go to editors Stephen Cline, James Fegen, Aliza Greenblatt, and Barbara Palumbo as well as to Paulette Christie.

However, the one person who deserves the major credit for the completion of this book is my wife, Judith. Not only did she take time away from her own writing career to type the manuscript, but, also, her watchful eye helped to keep my style relatively pure. Her cynical view of the world of computers and computerese has eliminated much meaningless verbiage from the text and helped to make the book, as they say in the trade, user-friendly.

Finally, I wish to thank my sons, William and Matthew, for being prepared, at times, to turn down their stereo so that I could think.

BASIC BY DESIGN
Structured Computer Programming in BASIC

Chapter

1

Starting Out

1.1 THE COMPUTER

A popular way to begin an introductory programming text is to give a brief
history of the computer and a survey of the present situation in the field,
with descriptions of the machines available and the uses to which they are
put. Such discussions will be more fruitful when you have a better grasp of
the nature of the beast. So we will dive right into the practical problem
of communicating with it. Later we will return to discuss computers in more
general terms and to remove some of the mystery that surrounds their
operation.

There are many different makes of computer available and each manufacturer tries to design its machine to be different, and a little more attrac-
tive than those of its competitors. Specifically, every system has its own set
of procedures which must be followed before the computer can be used. The
computing system that you are using is likely to fall into one of two categories: either a personal microcomputer or one of a number of video or typewriter terminals serviced by a larger computer. Detailed instructions on how
to use your system will be available in the manufacturer's manuals or at the
installation where you are doing your computing.

This chapter describes the sign-on procedure for one time-sharing system, that provided by Digital Equipment Corporation on their PDP-11 series
of minicomputers, a system popular with colleges and universities. If you are
using a system of this type rather than a microcomputer, your sign-on procedure will be similar, although probably not identical. Rather than being
upset by this lack of uniformity, always be prepared to ask for help if you

are having trouble. Even an expert cannot know everything about every available system. On the other hand, if you are using a microcomputer, starting up the machine may consist of little more than switching it on and typing a single command. Because of this wide variation, you may find it helpful to read Appendix I, where the procedures for two small systems are discussed.

A word of reassurance before you start: Please do not be afraid to experiment, no matter how little you feel you know. The modern computer is a relatively robust piece of equipment. It may not always respond the way you wish it would, but you cannot make it go up in smoke just by pressing the wrong key.

We used the term **time sharing** above. Let's clarify this. If you are using a microcomputer, you will have all that computing power to yourself. However, it is wasteful to devote an entire large computer to one user. The fact is that a computer operates so fast that most of the time it is idling, waiting for data to be typed in or printed out or waiting for instructions. Ingenious use is made of this fact to enable the computer to service more than one user at a time. A number of users are linked to the machine by means of video display or typewriter terminals. The machine processes instructions or data from each terminal in turn, cycling rapidly through all the users currently signed on. It spends no more than a fraction of a second with each one. Every user has all the power of the computer at his disposal, and because of the extraordinary speed of the machine, is unable to detect that this process is taking place. This technique is called **time sharing** and the system is referred to as a **multiuser** system.

If you are using such a system, it is quite possible that you will never see the computer. You will communicate with it through a **terminal,** a device similar to a typewriter, which will, in general, be in a different room from the machine itself. In fact, it is quite possible for the computer to be in a different building or even in another town.

Two types of terminal are in common use. A **printing terminal** is very much like an electric typewriter. You communicate by typing instructions at the keyboard. These are printed out for your convenience, as well as being transmitted to the machine. Responses from the computer are sent to the terminal to be printed so that you can read them. The other popular design is the **video display** or **CRT terminal** (CRT stands for cathode ray tube). This device has a typewriter keyboard but the printer is replaced by a television screen. No printed output can be produced; instead, the instructions and responses are displayed on the screen. The usefulness of such devices is limited by the fact that the user has no printed record of his work. On the other hand, they are fast and quiet and often cheaper than **hard-copy** (i.e., printing) devices.

One device you are less likely to see today is the **keypunch.** Most computer input was, until quite recently, punched onto cards in a coded form.

The cards were then fed into a **card reader,** which sensed the holes in each card electrically and transmitted the coded information to the computer. Many organizations still use such equipment, but more efficient methods have begun to supersede it.

1.2 SIGNING ON

Your terminal may be wired directly to the computer. However, if the machine is an appreciable distance from the terminal, communication will probably take place via a telephone line. Contact with the machine is made by first placing the telephone receiver face down on a device called a **modem** (modulator-demodulator) or **coupler** and then dialing the computer's number. In many installations, the dialing occurs automatically. Incidentally, the **modem** is a unit which translates the electronic code of the terminal into a code of sounds that can be transmitted by telephone, and vice versa.

Once you have made contact with the computer, the computer may respond with a message or by printing some sort of prompting character to indicate that it is ready. If you are using a small microcomputer, you are now ready to start playing with the machine, so you can skip the rest of this chapter. Larger multiuser systems require more elaborate sign-on procedures. If you are using one of these, you will now have to establish your right to use the computer. This is usually done by typing an account number and a password. So, before you attempt to use the machine, find out what the protocol is for your installation and also make sure that you have been issued an account number and have chosen a password.

All this may seem like an inconvenience, but it allows for some control over the users of the system. Also, as you will see later, it provides individual users with protection if they have private material to which they wish to restrict access.

1.3 A TYPICAL SIGN-ON PROCEDURE

Here is the **sign-on** procedure (also referred to as **log-in**) used on the PDP-11 RSTS-E time-sharing system. Switch on the terminal and, if necessary, dial the computer. Then type

    HELLO ●

and press the **RETURN** key (on some keyboards this key is referred to as **ENTER**). The machine responds with (for example)

    RSTS V7.0-07 **SJFC** Job 7 KB14 11-Feb-80 15:00

and continues on the next line with

    #

Then it stops. It is waiting for your account number. Type it right after the # symbol:

    #202,1 ●

The symbol ●   indicates that you should press the RETURN (or ENTER) key. This key must be pressed after every message or command that you type. The machine responds with

    password: ●

and stops again, this time waiting for your password. Type this on the same line and press RETURN. As you type, the system will hide the password by suppressing the printout, so that nothing appears on the paper. Some systems allow the password to be printed and then print over it with X's to obliterate it. The machine may now respond with a message. In any case, it ends by printing

    Ready

The sign-on procedure is complete. Now you can use the system.

Just to give you a better idea of the procedure and to introduce some notation, here is the complete example as it appears at the terminal. Everything you type has been **underlined** to distinguish it from what is printed by the computer. We will continue this convention throughout the book in order to clarify the examples, whenever there is interaction between the machine and the user.

Example

The complete sign-on procedure may look something like this:

    HELLO ●
    RSTS V7.0-07 ** SJFC ** Job 5 KB20 02-Feb-82 08:48
    #202,1 ●
    Password: ●   (machine suppresses the printing of your secret
                            password)

    WELCOME TO RSTS/E V7.0 TIME SHARING

```
THE USER  ROOM HOURS ARE:
---------------------------------------------

    MON-FRI  7:00 A.M.  TO 12:00 MIDNIGHT
    SAT     10:00 A.M.  TO 12:00 MIDNIGHT
    SUN     12:00 NOON  TO 12:00 MIDNIGHT

THE DECWRITERS ARE SET TO A BAUD RATE OF 300
AND A WIDTH OF 80 CHARACTERS.

TIMESHARING WILL BE DOWN FROM 4:30 P.M. TO 5:15 P.M.
EVERY FRIDAY NIGHT TO ALLOW FOR SYSTEM BACKUP...



HOPE YOU HAD A GOOD VACATION!!!!!!!!!!!!!!!!!!!!!!!


                            THANK YOU!!!!




Ready                                                   ∎
```

You will notice that almost all the printing is in uppercase letters. Computer output devices were traditionally limited to printing uppercase characters and now, although most systems will accept and print both upper- and lowercase, it is still common practice to use only capital letters in computer programming. In fact, most terminals have a key labeled **CAPS LOCK** which selects uppercase letters without affecting the other keys. Uppercase symbols such as !, (,), and * over the numbers must still be selected by holding down the **SHIFT** key.

Don't forget that, when typing data or instructions into the machine, you must always (well, almost always) follow your input by pressing the RETURN key, ● . This tells the machine that you are done and that it can start to process whatever you have typed in. On the other hand, the machine itself will indicate to you that it has finished the current task, and is ready to accept further instructions, by printing a word such as **Ready** (or **Done** or **OK**).

1.4 SIGNING OFF

When you learn to drive a car, learning to stop the thing is at least as important as starting it. The same is true for the computer. After you have finished working at the machine, resist the temptation to just switch it off and leave. Usually, the procedures to be followed before leaving the machine are a little more involved than that. They vary from machine to machine but the principles are the same. Here is the procedure for the RSTS-E time-sharing system. Type

>   BYE ●

The machine responds with

>   Confirm:

and waits on the same line for your response. Type the letter F followed by ● , meaning "Fast Sign-off!". The machine hesitates a moment and then advances the paper a few lines. This indicates that it is done. Now you can switch off the power and breathe a sigh of relief.

Example

>   BYE ●
>   Confirm: F ●   ■

There are usually other options for the sign-off procedure. Descriptions of these are given in all computer manuals.

It is most important to become completely familiar with the procedures for signing on and off your system. Before you start learning to program, you should practice signing on and off a few times until you are absolutely comfortable with all the steps. It is a little embarrassing to set out to do some work on the computer and find that you have forgotten how to sign on.

Chapter 1: EXERCISES

Section 1.1

1. Read as much as you can of the introductory and nontechnical parts of the manual(s) for your system.
2. Be on the alert for articles in the popular press on computers and computing.
3. Browse through copies of computing magazines, such as *Creative Computing* and *Byte*, at your local library or newsstand.

[*Note: The process of learning about a new field need not be painful if you are prepared to be receptive to the gratuitous information that drifts by you every day. When reading or browsing through a technical article, keep going until you get lost, then drop that article and go on to another. Constantly reading to the limit of your knowledge in this way will extend it surprisingly fast. Don't, however, read uncritically. If an article seems silly or pointless, as some of them are, don't torture yourself.*]

Section 1.2

No exercises.

Section 1.3

No exercises.

Section 1.4

1. Learn the sign-on and sign-off procedures for your system. Practice signing on and off repeatedly until it becomes second nature. Be persistent. Some people find their first contact with the computer rather daunting. Don't be awed by the machine. Nothing terrible can happen, even if you mess things up completely.

Chapter 2

The Basic Idea

2.1 THE $64,000 CALCULATOR

A simple description of the computer might state that it is nothing more than an elaborate and expensive calculator. We shall see later that it is very much more than this, and, in fact, that arithmetic calculations are only a minor part of most computer applications. However, there is enough truth in the description for us to use it as a starting point. We'll begin by solving a short arithmetic problem with a hand calculator and then we'll solve the same problem on the computer.

Suppose that you wish to calculate a 7% sales tax on a $2.49 item, using a hand calculator. The arithmetic is as follows:

$$\text{Sales tax} = 2.49 \times \frac{7}{100}$$

To get the answer, you do the following:

		Display Shows
Enter	2 . 4 9	2.49
Press	×	2.49
Enter	7	7
Press	=	17.43 (2.49 × 7)
Press	÷	17.43
Enter	1 0 0	100
Press	=	.1743 (2.49 × 7 ÷ 100)

So the tax is $0.17, to the nearest cent. Notice that each operation is performed as it is entered and the result is displayed immediately. Think of each entry as an instruction to the calculator, which is performed as the key is pressed.

On the computer we have a little more flexibility. First, we can enter a sequence of operations without any calculations taking place. We can review the instructions and then, when we are sure there are no errors, we can order the machine to perform the calculations and display the answer, or even save the answer to be used in further calculations. For instance, the instructions for the tax problem, when entered in the computer, would look like this:

```
10  PRINT 2.49*7/100
20  END
```

The symbols * and / indicate multiplication and division, respectively. We will talk about the numbers 10 and 20 and the word END later, but first just follow the mechanics of entering these instructions. Type

<u>10 PRINT 2.49*7/100</u> ● [†]

The **print head** of the terminal (or the **cursor** if you are using a video terminal) will move to the beginning of the next line, but nothing else will happen. Now type

<u>20 END</u> ●

Again the print head will perform a **carriage return** (a move to the beginning of the line) and a **line feed** (a move to the next line) and once again, nothing else will happen. All you have done is to store a copy of these instructions in the computer, in an electronic storage area called the **memory.** You have not yet ordered the machine to execute them; in fact, they could be changed or added to at any time. We will come to that later. Meanwhile, let's command the machine to perform these calculations. Type

<u>RUN</u> ●

The machine responds with something like this:

```
NONAME  15:05  11-Feb-80
0.1743
Ready
```

[†]Remember, the underlining is included to distinguish your typing from the machine's printing. When **you** use the machine, don't underline your input.

This is a rather baroque response for such a simple calculation. On the system we have been discussing, one can suppress the heading by typing **RUNNH** (RUN with No Heading) instead. Your computer may produce no such heading at all. So, for simplicity, we will use the word RUN but omit the heading. This example shows the complete calculation as it appears at the terminal:

Example

```
10  PRINT 2.49*7/100  ●
20  END  ●
RUN  ●
0.1743
Ready                                                                       ■
```

Now, suppose that we want to do more than one calculation, say, the sales tax on $2.49, $1.30, and $6.95. Remembering that the previous instructions are still stored in memory, we type the following:

```
20  PRINT 1.30*7/100  ●
30  PRINT 6.95*7/100  ●
40  END  ●
```

Let's find out what instructions are now stored in the machine. To do this, type

```
LIST  ●
```

to which the machine will respond:

```
NONAME  15:11  11-Feb-80
10  PRINT 2.49*7/100
20  PRINT 1.30*7/100
30  PRINT 6.95*7/100
40  END
Ready
```

Notice that the original instruction, number 10, is still there but "20 END" has been replaced by "20 PRINT 1.30*7/100", which we just typed, and the instructions 30 and 40 have been added to the list of stored instructions. The command **LIST** can be used at any time to print out a listing of the instructions currently stored in memory. As with RUN, the system provides the command **LISTNH** to suppress the heading. In the text we will use LIST, but will leave out the heading. Incidentally, the numbered instructions that we typed into the machine remain stored until we command it to erase them or until we sign off.

If we type RUN again, the machine will now follow this new list of instructions, starting at 10 and continuing until it reaches the instruction "40 END."

Example

```
RUN  ●
0.1743
0.091
0.4865
Ready
```

Thus the sales tax on each item is $0.17, $0.09, and $0.49, respectively, to the nearest cent.

This is not the most efficient solution to the tax problem and it certainly lacks a little finesse. After all, it would not be unreasonable to expect an expensive machine to be able to round to the nearest cent. However, before we turn to these questions, let's step back and analyze what it is we are doing.

2.2 PROGRAMMING LANGUAGES

The list of instructions

```
10  PRINT 2.49*7/100
20  PRINT 1.30*7/100
30  PRINT 6.95*7/100
40  END
```

is an example of what is called a **program** or **routine.** This particular program is written in a **programming language** called BASIC. BASIC stands for "Beginner's All-purpose Symbolic Instruction Code" and was developed about 1965 by John Kemeny† and Thomas Kurtz of Dartmouth University, specifically for the teaching of computer programming. It is also used now in computer systems designed for small businesses and is the *lingua franca* of the recreational computer world. It provides a means of transmitting instruc-

---

†Kemeny has since gone on to bigger and better things, having become president of Dartmouth and, more recently, chairman of the President's Commission on Three Mile Island.

tions to a computer in a form that is relatively easy for a human being to comprehend. The computer does not understand these instructions directly. By a procedure that we will discuss later, they are translated into sequences of switching patterns for the electronic circuits inside the machine.

There are many other programming languages that are in common, and uncommon, use. Two of the most popular in the United States are FORTRAN and COBOL. FORTRAN (FORmula TRANslation) was designed as a language for scientific calculation and COBOL (COmmon Business Orientated Language) for business data processing. Incidentally, in the time scale of the history of computing, which in the modern sense only reaches back to World War II, these are relatively old languages. However, the hard work and expense involved in developing **software**—that is, the programs required in business, science, and other applications—lead to a reluctance to abandon the old reliables and to rewrite programs in some new language, however powerful and sophisticated it is. In fact, old languages do not die, or break down, or become unreliable. **Programmers,** that is, professional program writers, get used to their weaknesses and learn to program around them. So BASIC, FORTRAN, and COBOL will be with us for some time to come. However, just for the fun of it, here is a list of other programming languages that have been, and are being, used:

> ALGOL, Pascal, PL/1, SP/k, LISP, SNOBOL, FORTH, URTH, MAD, SYMSCRIPT, GPSS, QUICKTRAN, C, TINYC, JOVIAL, RPG, APL, XPL, PILOT, MUMPS, BASEX, SPARKS, FOCAL, BLISS, DIBOL, Ada, SMALLTALK, LOGO, DYNAMO, GASP

As its name indicates, BASIC was designed to be easy to understand and to learn, but just as important, it was designed so that writing and running programs on the computer would be a simple process. The procedures we will follow are much simpler than they usually are, say, for FORTRAN or COBOL.

2.3   WRITING PROGRAMS

Let's begin again and discuss in more detail the procedures to be followed. You will notice that these are a little more involved than was indicated at the beginning of the chapter. However, the extra complication has its advantages. Your system may differ from the one discussed here, so check before you try anything!

To understand certain concepts more clearly, you will often find it helpful to imagine that, when you sign on, you are provided with an area of computer memory that is exclusively yours to write programs in, and to which no other user has access. In reality, the situation is more complicated;

however, we will find this a convenient fiction. This reserved memory area is called your **workspace.** It is rather like a blackboard on which you, and the computer, can write and erase at will. It is important not to clutter your workspace with old programs and other garbage. So before you write a new program, the workspace must be wiped clean. Incidentally, you may be wondering what you should do with programs that you wish to save for further use. These cannot be kept in your workspace—that would be like writing your last will and testament on a blackboard. We'll return to this question in Chapter 4.

We will represent the workspace by a large box like this:

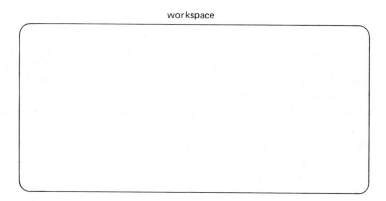

workspace

and we'll use this diagram whenever it is necessary to show exactly what is stored in memory at a given moment.

After you have signed on, or *at any time that you wish to erase your workspace and start a new program,* just type

NEW ●

The system will respond with something like

New file name - -

Type the name you have chosen for your program. This can be almost any string of letters and/or numbers. Many systems, however, have the restriction that the name be six characters or less. The effect of all this is to erase anything currently stored in your workspace and to establish a name for the program you are about to write. This name will be useful later if you decide that you wish to save a permanent copy of the program.

When the machine responds with

Ready

you can start typing in the instructions that make up your program.

Example

```
NEW  ●
New file name - - TAX  ●
Ready
```

You can get to the point faster by typing the name on the same line as NEW: that is,

```
NEW TAX ●
Ready
```
■

(Please remember that the procedures discussed here are those that work for a particular system. Some systems use the command **SCRATCH** instead of **NEW**. This clears the workspace but does not allow for the naming of a program. That may be handled by a separate command, such as **NAME-**.)

Two facts about BASIC language programs should already be apparent. The first is that the final statement always consists of the word END. Although many systems are more tolerant, some just won't run programs that do not include the END statement. The second involves the numbers that precede every statement that we have entered. Every line beginning with a number is interpreted by the machine as being part of a program, to be stored in memory for processing at a later time. These **line numbers**, therefore, distinguish **program instructions**, such as

```
10   PRINT 2.49*7/100
```

from **commands**, such as

```
RUN
```

which are executed immediately. To summarize: Program instructions are preceded by line numbers and are stored in memory for later use; commands, which are **not** preceded by line numbers, are executed immediately and are **not** saved in memory. Furthermore, the line numbers indicate to the computer the order in which the stored instructions are to be followed.

Example

If you type

```
10   PRINT 2.49*7/100  ●
30   END  ●
20   PRINT 1.30*7/100  ●
```

the computer will follow the instructions in numerical order by line number (i.e., 10, 20, 30), not in the order in which you typed them. In fact, if you now type LIST, the machine will print them in increasing order:

```
LIST  ●
10   PRINT 2.49*7/100
20   PRINT 1.30*7/100
30   END
Ready                                                    ■
```

2.4 EDITING BASIC PROGRAMS

No one can avoid an occasional typing mistake and, quite frankly, many people who use computers regularly are lousy typists. Furthermore, it is good practice to test a preliminary version of a program before adding refinements. Thus a requirement of any computer system is that it should provide the means for correcting amd modifying program instructions.

The most straightforward way to correct an error in a BASIC instruction is to retype the instruction.

Example

Suppose that you have typed

```
20   PRIMT 1.30*7/100  ●
```

The machine will respond with a message such as

```
?illegal verb in line 20
```

To make the correction, retype the entire line:

```
20   PRINT 1.30*7/100  ●
```

This replaces the erroneous line 20 previously entered.   ■

Thus, for any given line number, only the latest version of that instruction is stored in your workspace. Beware: This does not mean that a new version of a program, when typed in, will automatically replace an earlier one. New lines replace old ones individually, according to their numbers.

An instruction can be deleted, without replacing it with a new one, by typing just its line number.

Example

To erase this instruction, stored in your workspace:

```
20   PRINT 1.30*7/100
```

type

<u>20</u> ●   ■

Most systems provide commands, such as the word **DELETE** or **SCRATCH,** which allow the user to delete blocks of one or more lines from a program. However, the method above suffices for most purposes.

Suppose, on the other hand, that you wish to insert extra lines into your program. This can be done provided that you have planned ahead for it. If a new line is to be inserted between two existing lines, say 20 and 30, the only requirement is that its number lie between theirs; that is, it should carry one of the numbers 21 through 29.

Example

Currently, your workspace contains

```
10   PRINT 2.49*7/100
20   PRINT 1.30*7/100
30   END
```

To insert PRINT 6.95*7/100 between lines 20 and 30, type

<u>25   PRINT 6.95*7/100</u> ●

On listing the program again, you will find line 25 in its correct place:

```
LIST  ●
10   PRINT 2.49*7/100
20   PRINT 1.30*7/100
25   PRINT 6.95*7/100
30   END
Ready
```
                                                                              ■

It is a good practice, when writing programs in BASIC, to increase your line numbers in steps of 10 or even 100, so as to leave room in case you need to add lines to the program at a later time. I can guarantee that sooner or later you will find yourself having to do that, either to refine a program or to patch up one that is not working properly. Some systems provide a command, **RENUMBER,** which will automatically renumber all the lines of your program according to your instructions. This eliminates the need for such care. Incidentally, many programming languages do not require line numbers (e.g., FORTRAN and Pascal) or have a more flexible numbering system (e.g., APL). The problem is, in general, peculiar to BASIC.

Occasionally, one hits a wrong key. It is tiresome to have to retype a line to correct one little mistake, so all terminals are provided with a special key by means of which the character or characters just typed can be erased and retyped. Depending on the terminal and the computer system, this key may be called, variously, **RUB-OUT, DELETE** (not to be confused with the DELETE command mentioned above), or ←.[†] The response to this key will also vary widely according to the type of terminal and computer system. Here is an illustration of the approach taken by the RSTS-E time-sharing system.

Example

On the terminal we are using, the DELETE key erases characters. Suppose that you type the following:

```
10  PRGNT
```

but realize, before you press RETURN, that you have made a mistake. Press the DELETE key three times. This produces the following printout:

```
10  PRGNT\TNG
```

Then type INT 5.33*7/100 and press RETURN. The complete line looks like this:

```
10  PRGNT\TNG\INT 5.33*7/100
```

but is stored in the workspace like this:

```
10  PRINT 5.33*7/100
```

The backslashes are produced automatically by the system to enclose a list of the characters that have been deleted.   ■

[†]The key ← is referred to as the backspace key by some manufacturers. If it is used as a delete key, this terminology is incorrect. A true backspace key does not erase characters. In fact, it is used for overprinting (the printing of one character on top of another, e.g., ⊗). Beware of using any key labeled BACKSPACE for erasing unless the manual expressly says that it is OK.

Your system may have a similar procedure. However, if you are working with a video terminal, the process will be much simpler, as the offending characters can actually be erased from the screen.

The editing techniques we have discussed are adequate for all but the largest programming problems. However, most systems provide other commands and techniques which make the programmer's life a little easier. I urge you to learn all you can about your system that will simplify the job of typing and correcting programs.

2.5   MATHEMATICAL OPERATORS

The range of characters available on a standard computer terminal is a fairly limited one. We have already seen that * and / replace × and ÷, which are not normally part of this set. Here is a complete table of the characters used to indicate the elementary mathematical operations:

Operation	Character	Example
Addition	+	2+3
Subtraction	–	14–5
Multiplication	*	3*7
Division	/	15/4
Exponentiation ("raising to a power")	^ or ↑	$2\char`\^3$ and $2{\uparrow}3$ both mean $2^3 = 2 \times 2 \times 2$

Exponentiation cannot easily be represented by a superscript (e.g., 2^3) on a typewriter, so the problem is solved by introducing a new symbol. The standard symbol in BASIC is the "up arrow". However, its actual representation, ^ or ↑, will depend on the type of terminal you are using. With a little experimentation, you can easily discover what you should use.

Perhaps this is a good time to make an important point. If you are unable to find out information about a particular procedure by any other means, don't hesitate to experiment at the terminal to see if you can discover the answer yourself. Many people have a tendency to lose their natural curiosity and all their self-will on coming face to face with a computer. The fact is that most computer systems are relatively indestructible and quite forgiving.

On the whole, calculations using the mathematical operators are handled in a straightforward way.

Example

```
10 PRINT 1+2+3+4+5
20 PRINT 1*2*3*4*5
30 PRINT 3^2 + 4^2
40 PRINT 7*(-13)
50 END
```

RUN ●

```
 15
120
 25
-91
```

Ready

In line 40 we have written 7*(-13) rather than 7*-13. BASIC does not allow operators to be placed next to one another.   ■

However, statements such as

```
PRINT 30/3*5
```

are open to more than one interpretation. For example, the expression 30/3*5 could mean either

$$\frac{30}{3 \times 5} \quad \text{or} \quad \frac{30}{3} \times 5$$

In fact, the computer interprets this unambiguously, on the basis of a well-defined set of rules. They follow, fairly closely, the conventions one is taught to follow when evaluating mathematical expressions by hand.

Examples

1.
```
10 PRINT 30/3*5
20 END
RUN ●
50
Ready
```

This is calculated from left to right, that is, first the division and then the multiplication, so that 30/3*5 becomes 10*5, which is 50.

2. The same left-to-right rule applies to addition and subtraction.

```
10  PRINT 5 – 3 + 1
20  END
RUN
3
Ready
```

The subtraction is done first: 5 – 3 + 1 becomes 2 + 1, so the result is 3.

3.
```
10  PRINT 14 – 3*4
20  END
RUN  ●
2
Ready
```

Multiplication and division are always performed before addition and subtraction. So 14 – 3*4 is calculated to be 14 – 12, that is, 2.

4. Exponentiation is the cock-of-the-roost. It is performed before any of the other four operations:

```
10  PRINT 5 – 4*3^2
20  END
RUN  ●
– 31
Ready
```

The computer evaluates this as follows:

	5 – 4*3^2
becomes	5 – 4*9
which becomes	5 – 36
and, finally	–31

These rules are explained more systematically in Appendix II. However, in most cases it is almost as simple and much clearer to use parentheses to indicate the order in which operations are to be carried out. Remember, all operations within a pair of parentheses are performed before those outside.

Examples

1. The expression in

```
PRINT (5 – (2–3))*(2+1)
```

is evaluated in the following order:

$$(5 - (2-3))*(2+1)$$

step 1 $(5 - (-1))*(3)$

step 2 $(5+1)*3$

step 3 $6*3$

step 4 18

2. The expression $\dfrac{30}{3 \times 5}$ is written as 30/(3*5) and $\dfrac{30}{3} \times 5$ as (30/3)*5.

3. Be careful of this one, $(6 - 4)^{2 \times 3}$ must be written as (6 – 4)^(2*3), not as (6 – 4)^2*3.

4. The expression $\dfrac{15 - 3}{2 \times 3} \times 7$ can be written in two different ways:

$$((15 - 3)/(2*3))*7 \quad \text{and} \quad ((15 -3)*7)/(2*3)$$

These are equally valid and give rise to the same result.   ■

2.6 SCIENTIFIC NOTATION

The computer uses a special technique for representing very large and very small numbers. Here is an example:

```
10 PRINT 2000^5
20 PRINT 1/(3000*2000)
30 END
```

```
RUN ●
 .32E 17
 .166667E-6
```

```
Ready
```

This looks strange but is in fact just a variation of a notation that you are probably familiar with. The first calculation is $(2000)^5$, that is, 32,000,000,-000,000,000. This is rather unwieldy, so in scientific calculations, such a number is often written in an abbreviated form, 32×10^{15}. A typical convention is to rewrite the 32 as a decimal fraction so that the number becomes 0.32×10^{17}. (Multiply this out and you'll see that it is the same value.) The second calculation is 1/(3000*2000), or 0.0000001666 . . . . A similar approach gives

$$0.0000001666 \ldots = (0.1666 \ldots) \times 10^{-6}$$

or if we round the first part to, say, six decimal places,

$$0.166667 \times 10^{-6}$$

This should give you some clues about the strange output above. The numbers

$$0.32E\ 17 \quad \text{and} \quad 0.166667E\text{-}6$$

are just the computer's way of printing

$$0.32 \times 10^{17} \quad \text{and} \quad 0.166667 \times 10^{-6}$$

This is a standard notation and is used by most computer languages. As in the example above, the number of digits in the fractional part is usually limited to six or so, depending on the type of machine. This has to do with limitations in the size of the storage locations for numbers.

Although we will not make much use of **scientific notation,** as it is called, you should be familiar with it because, occasionally, programs you write will produce output in this form.

2.7 VARIABLES AND THE LET STATEMENT

If you analyze the arithmetic in the tax program that we wrote, you will see that its form is the same no matter what the item costs. The tax calculation can be described as follows:

$$\text{Tax} = \text{price} \times \frac{7}{100} \qquad\qquad (*)$$

and this description does not depend on our knowing the actual price.

We ought to be able to describe the calculation to the computer without specifying the numbers (in our case, prices) on which the calculation is to be performed and then, when we want to do the calculation, be able to provide the data to the machine to have it processed. We need a symbolic notation, similar to that in (*) above, to describe the tax calculation to the computer. In BASIC this can be done as follows:

```
20   LET T = P*7/100
```

This line uses P and T as symbols, to stand for "price" and "tax." However, in BASIC, as in other computer languages, the characters P and T are also names of storage locations in the workspace, into which numbers can be placed when the completed program is run. These characters are examples of **variable names,** about which we'll have more to say in a moment.

To make use of statement 20 above, we need to be able to assign a value to P, say 2.49. This can be done quite simply by typing

```
10   LET P = 2.49
```

Both 10 and 20 are examples of what is called an **assignment statement.**

To see how this works, let's look at a complete program that does more or less what we want. We will assume that the program is stored in the workspace and we will follow it step by step as it is run. Here is the workspace as we start:

```
10   LET P = 2.49
20   LET T = P*7/100
30   PRINT T
40   END
```

Now we type RUN and the computer starts to translate the instructions in the program and follow them in sequence. On reading the first part of statement 10, that is,

```
LET P =
```

it interprets P to be the name of a variable and automatically reserves a storage location in the workspace, to hold any value given to P. We will denote this as follows:

P ☐

The number on the right-hand side of the equals sign is stored in this location, that is,

P ☐ 2.49

and this completes the execution of the statement. Line 20 is handled similarly. The first part of the statement causes the computer to reserve a location for T. The next step is a little more involved; the machine must evaluate P*7/100. The current contents of P are 2.49, so P*7/100 is interpreted as 2.49*7/100. This expression is evaluated and the result placed in location T. The next statement prints the current value of T at the terminal and, finally, execution stops at line 40. Here are the contents of the workspace as the program finishes:

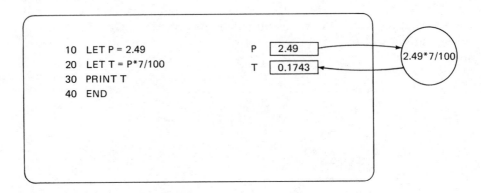

The result of this run looks like this:

```
RUN  ●
0.1743
Ready
```

The important thing to understand about variables is that they are locations in the workspace, reserved for the storage of values during the execution of a program. Each variable is identified by a **variable name** (the symbol associated with it) and at any particular time it has a **value** (the number currently stored in it).

This concept of a variable is slightly different from the traditional one used in mathematics and the sciences. In the traditional view, a variable is a place marker in a formula. It indicates the position at which a given value is to be substituted. For example, in the formula

$$area = \frac{bh}{2}$$

for the area of a triangle, the variables b and h mark the places where the actual values of the base and height of the figure are to be substituted. That is, to calculate the area of this triangle:

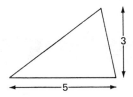

We replace b by 5 and h by 3 to get

$$\text{area} = \frac{5 \times 3}{2} = 7.5$$

In computer programming, a variable is more than just a marker. It is an actual location in the memory of the computer, where a number can be stored for later use. A variable is like a mailbox. It has a name,

which doesn't change, but its contents can, and do, change.

Example

Here is a rather silly program that illustrates the principle:

```
10   LET P = 9.5
20   LET P = 23.2
30   PRINT P
40   END
```

When we run it we get

RUN ●
23.2
Ready

These snapshots of the workspace tell the story behind the run.

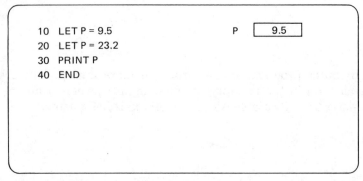

After line 10

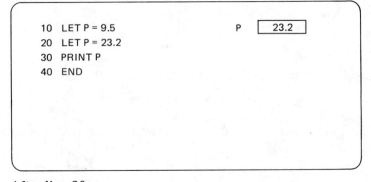

After line 20

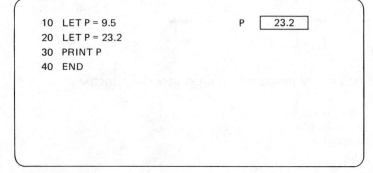

After line 30

The values stored in the location P change during the course of the run. When the name P is used in the PRINT statement, the value stored in P at that particular moment is printed. Notice that this does not erase the contents of P.   ∎

In most versions of the BASIC language a variable name consists of a single letter (e.g., P) or a letter followed by a single digit (e.g., A1).

Example

Some legal variable names:

   Z, J3, P, N, K2, A9

Some illegal variable names:

   AA, 3B, J19, C*

(Although the letter O is a legal variable name, it is a good idea to avoid using it, as it is easily confused with the digit 0.)   ∎

The **assignment statement** (or **LET statement**) has the general form

   line number   LET   *variable = expression*

The expression on the right may be a number or a variable, or it may be a formula consisting of constants and variables combined with mathematical operators +, −, *, /, and ^ .

Examples

1.   LET N = 100
2.   LET Y = (X–1)^2+3*(X–1)+2
3.   LET B4 = A*F*T*E*R
4.   LET C = C+1   ∎

An assignment statement evaluates the expression on the **right-hand side** of the equals sign, using the current values of all the variables in the expression, and stores the result in the variable whose name appears on the **left**. This variable may or may not have a value already stored in it. If it does, the old value is erased and replaced by the new one.

It is most important to understand that the equals sign in the LET statement is not "equals" in the sense of, say, the mathematical equation

$$3 + 5 = 8$$

It should instead be read as an instruction: "Place the value of the expression on the right in the variable on the left."

Examples

1. In

    LET G = (12 – 7)*4

    the expression $(12 - 7)*4$ is evaluated and the result, 20, is stored in the location named G.

2. Suppose that, during the running of a program, A and B have been assigned the values 13 and 10, respectively, and that K currently has the value 5. Also suppose that the next statement to be executed is

    40   LET K = (A – 2)*B

    Then the right-hand side is evaluated by retrieving the current values stored in A and B, namely 13 and 10, and putting them into the expression in place of A and B. This becomes $(13 - 2)*10$ and the result, 110, is stored in K, replacing the value 5 previously stored there. The following diagrams[†] of the workspace before and after line 40 illustrate the effect of the LET statement.

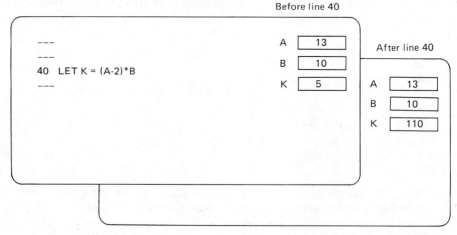

[†] I have overlapped the two diagrams to save space and to show the time sequence. Notice that although the program cannot be seen in the second diagram, it is still there.

Using the values of A and B did not erase them. K is the only location whose contents were changed.

3.   This little program:

```
10  LET X = 3
20  LET Y = X + 1
30  LET X = Y + 1
40  PRINT X
50  END
```

when executed produces this:

RUN
5
Ready

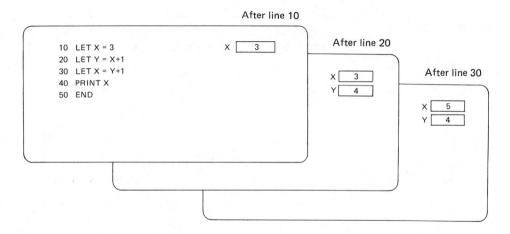

In line 20, the current contents of X, namely 3, are substituted in the expression X + 1, so that 3 + 1, or 4, is stored in Y. In line 30, the Y in Y + 1 is replaced by 4 and the value currently stored in X is replaced by the value of Y + 1, that is, 5.   ∎

Translating mathematical expressions into BASIC can cause a little trouble until you get used to the rather clumsy appearance of BASIC expressions.

Example

Translate

$$y = \sqrt{\frac{a(x-1)}{b}}$$

into BASIC! Remember that

$$\sqrt{\frac{a(x-1)}{b}} = \left(\frac{a(x-1)}{b}\right)^{\frac{1}{2}} = \left(\frac{a(x-1)}{b}\right)^{0.5}$$

Using the variables Y, A, B, and X, the inside becomes

$$(A*(X-1))/B$$

so that the whole expression is

$$Y = ((A*(X-1))/B)^{\wedge}0.5$$

Can the number of parentheses in this expression be reduced?   ■

By using the assignment statement in our tax program, we have gained a little more flexibility—not much it is true, but it is a small step forward. If we want to calculate the tax on a different amount, all we have to do now is retype statement 10, with a different value of P.

Example

```
10   LET P = 8.50
20   LET T = P*7/100
30   PRINT T
40   END
RUN†
0.595
Ready
```
                                                                              ■

To be honest, this is a rather inflexible way of changing the value of a variable. We need some way of getting data into the machine that does not require that one be a programmer to do it.

2.8   INTERACTING WITH THE PROGRAM: THE INPUT STATEMENT

One of the goals of programming is to produce programs that are useful tools for people who are not, themselves, programmers. For example, the program that handles inventory control for a modern department store is a relatively

---

†From now on, the RETURN key, ●, will not be mentioned in situations where its use is obvious: for example, after typing RUN and LIST and after entering BASIC instructions.

complicated thing, yet salesclerks use it every day when making sales. In fact, every time a clerk uses the cash register (or point-of-sale terminal, to use the current jargon) he or she communicates with this program, and it is clear that salesclerks are not required to be programmers to do their job successfully.

To pursue this argument further, the program controlling the cash registers may include a short segment that calculates the sales tax, much like our example. Now, as the programmer who writes the program has no idea ahead of time what items will be purchased, he or she must design the program so that it will accept the data on an item being sold, at the time of the sale. Let us see how this problem can be handled in BASIC. Here is a rather crude program to do this:

```
10  INPUT P
20  LET T = P*7/100
30  PRINT T
40  END
```

The only change from our previous program is in statement 10. Suppose that this program is run; what does the computer do when it reads "INPUT P"? Quite simply, it stops and waits for the person running the program to type a number at the keyboard. When this is done, it stores that number in the variable P and proceeds to the next statement.

In fact, of course, it is rather difficult to tell the difference between a machine that is busy calculating and one that is just waiting for a number to be typed in, so the machine prints a question mark to indicate that it requires data. Let's run the program to illustrate the procedure. Type RUN. The machine responds with a question mark:

```
?
```

Now, type a number immediately after the question mark and press RETURN:

```
? 8.50  ●
```

The machine responds with

```
0.595
Ready
```

That is, the complete run looks like this:

```
RUN
? 8.50
0.595
Ready
```

In this case, the action of "INPUT P" is similar to that of "LET P = 8.50."
A location named P is established in the workspace and the value 8.50 is
stored in it. The only difference is that the value stored is read from the
keyboard rather than from the statement itself. These diagrams of the workspace illustrate the process:

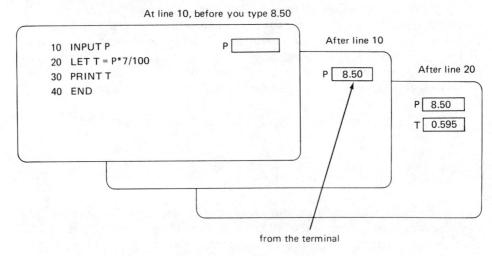

The program can be run again and different data entered. Each time
that the first statement, 10 INPUT P, is executed, the computer stops and
waits for the user to type in a number. This value is then stored in location P
before the machine continues to statement 20.

Example

```
RUN
? 32.40
2.268
Ready
```

Finally, we have a flexible program, a little gaunt and cryptic perhaps, but
we will correct that shortly.

Section 2.1

1. Sign on to your system and try the examples in this section on the computer. This is a useful thing to do after reading any section of the book.
2. Write a set of instructions to calculate a 4% sales tax on the amounts $37.40, $0.73, and $18.99. [*Hint: Don't worry if your answers have more than two decimal places.*]
3. This set of instructions calculates the Celsius temperature corresponding to 83° F [*Hint: The general pattern is* $°C = (°F - 32)*5/9$]:

    ```
    10  PRINT (83 - 32)*5/9
    20  END
    ```

    Write instructions to convert 25°F, 113°F, 98.6°F, and –40°F to Celsius temperatures.
4. Write instructions to convert a set of Celsius temperatures into Fahrenheit.
5. Write instructions that will print out the total payments for items costing $5.95, $27.80, and $1.99 if a 7% sales tax is levied. For example, the tax on $9.00 is $0.63, so the total payment is $9.63.

Section 2.2

1. By looking through books and journals in your college or public library, make a list of programming languages that have been used at one time or another. There are some strange names among them and the reasons behind some of the names are quite entertaining.

Section 2.3

1. Read your system manuals for the procedures required to name a program.

Section 2.4

1. Learn the commands for deleting and correcting BASIC code on your system.

Section 2.5

    If you are unsure about the legality of a BASIC statement or do not know how the machine will interpret it, incorporate the statement into a short test program and run the program on the machine. For example, Exercise 1(a) below can be tested in the following program:

```
10  PRINT (15/2)*3
20  END
```

1.　What is printed by each of the following instructions?
   (a)　PRINT (15/2)*3　　　　　　(b)　PRINT 15/(2*3)
   (c)　PRINT 15/2*3　　　　　　　(d)　PRINT (3*17)-5
   (e)　PRINT 3*(17 – 5)　　　　　(f)　PRINT 3*17 – 5
   (g)　PRINT (2^3)*3　　　　　　(h)　PRINT 2^(3*3)
   (i)　PRINT 2^3*3　　　　　　　(j)　PRINT (12 – 2*4)^(0.5)
   (k)　PRINT 5*7/5*7　　　　　　(l)　PRINT – 4 + 2 – 3 + 1
   (m)　PRINT 100^6　　　　　　　(n)　PRINT 1/(2^15)

2.　Identify which of these statements contain errors. Describe the errors.
   (a)　PRINT 12 + -3.33　　　　　(b)　PRINT 12 + (-3.33)
   (c)　PRINT 2*3*　　　　　　　(d)　PRINT ((0.72)/4)
   (e)　PRINT ((7)(18))　　　　　(f)　PRINT (4+)/3
   (g)　PRINT 9(3 + 5)　　　　　(h)　PRINT (1.02*(0.93 – 0.11)

3.　Write PRINT statements to evaluate these arithmetic expressions:

   (a)　$2(14 – 8.25)$　　　　　　(b)　$\left(\dfrac{2}{3}\right)\left(\dfrac{4}{5}\right)\left(\dfrac{6}{7}\right)$

   (c)　$(3.5 \div 2) \div 7$　　　　　(d)　$\dfrac{23 + 16}{11 - 5}$

   (e)　$7^2 + (1 + 2^7)$　　　　　(f)　$10^{1/3}$

   (g)　$\sqrt{1 + 3^3}$

Section 2.6

1.　Write the following numbers in scientific notation.
   (a)　0.0025　　　　　　　　　(b)　2,500
   (c)　140,000　　　　　　　　(d)　79,434.5
   (e)　0.000001

2.　Convert the following numbers to standard notation.
   (a)　0.125E13　　　　　　　　(b)　0.125E-7
   (c)　0.34343E3　　　　　　　(d)　0.142857E-3

Section 2.7

1. Evaluate these LET statements, using the values given.

$$A = 3, \quad B = 7, \quad C = 2, \quad K1 = 1.6, \quad K2 = 1.1, \quad Q = 6.95$$

(a) LET S = Q*0.07   (b) LET K3 = (K1+K2)/(K1–K2)
(c) LET A2 = A*B - B   (d) LET W = B^(1/3)
(e) LET F = A^2 + B^2   (f) LET H = (A^2 + B^2)^(0.5)
(g) LET X = (-B + (B*B - 4*A*C)^0.5)/(2*A)

2. Describe any errors that appear in the following statements.
   (a) LET X = 2B + 1   (b) Z3 = 4.9*Y
   (c) LET 5Y = X^X   (d) LET M12 = M3^4
   (e) I + J = K1   (f) LET 2 = 2
   (g) LET B = XY   (h) LET A*Y*3
   (i) A9 = B9   (j) LET TAX = PRICE*13/100

3. Write LET statements to perform these calculations:

   (a) $T = \left(\dfrac{h_1 + h_2}{2}\right)b$
   (b) $c = \dfrac{x}{\sqrt{(T - r)^2 + x^2}}$

   (c) $I = 100\left[\left(\dfrac{F}{P}\right)^{1/n} - 1\right]$
   (d) $S = a\left(\dfrac{1 - r^n}{1 - r}\right)$

   (e) $A = \dfrac{h}{3}(v_1 + 4v_2 + v_3)$

4. Choosing appropriate variables, write LET statements to:
   (a) Convert Celsius temperatures to Fahrenheit.
   (b) Calculate average miles per gallon, given miles traveled and gallons of gas consumed.
   (c) Convert kilometers to miles using the approximate relation: 5 miles = 8 kilometers.
   (d) Calculate the hypotenuse of a right triangle given the other two sides.
   (e) Calculate the final balance after the principal is deposited in a savings account for n years at an interest rate of I% compounded quarterly, using

   $$\text{final balance} = \text{principal} \times \left(1 + \frac{I}{400}\right)^{4n}$$

5. Show what is printed by the following programs. You can help yourself understand the action of a program by making a table to one side of it

to show the values of the variables after each statement is executed; for example:

	X	Y	Z
10 LET X = 3	3	–*	–*
20 LET Y = 2	3	2	–*
30 LET Y = 2*X	3	6	–*
40 LET Z = X*Y	3	6	18
50 PRINT Z	3	6	18
60 END			

Some systems automatically set variables to zero initially. In others, the variables may initially contain unpredictable values. Beware!

The table shows that the value 18 is printed.

(a)
```
10  LET A = 3
20  LET B = 12
30  LET C = (A + B)*0.5
40  LET D = (A*B)^0.5
50  PRINT C
60  PRINT D
70  PRINT C – D†
80  END
```

(b)
```
10  LET A = 2
20  PRINT A
30  LET B = A + 1
40  PRINT B
50  LET B = 2*A
60  PRINT B
70  END
```

(c)
```
10  LET A = 2
20  PRINT A
30  LET A = A + 1
40  PRINT A
50  LET A = 2*A
60  PRINT A
70  END
```

(d)
```
10  LET A = 5
20  LET B = 7
30  LET A = B
40  LET B = A
50  PRINT A
60  PRINT B
70  END
```

(e)
```
10  LET A = 5
20  LET B = 7
30  LET T = A
40  LET A = B
50  LET B = T
60  PRINT A
70  PRINT B
80  END
```

†*This has the same effect as*
```
70  LET E = C – D
75  PRINT E
```

Section 2.8

1. Show what is printed by typical runs of each of these programs.

   (a)
   ```
   10  LET X = 1
   20  INPUT X
   30  PRINT X
   40  END
   ```
   [*Hint: What if the value typed is not 1?*]

   (b)
   ```
   10  INPUT X
   20  LET X = 1
   30  PRINT X
   40  END
   ```
   [*What if the value typed is not 1?*]

   (c)
   ```
   10  INPUT A
   20  INPUT B
   30  PRINT A + B
   40  END
   ```

   (d)
   ```
   10  INPUT A
   20  INPUT A
   30  PRINT A + A
   40  END
   ```
   [*Hint: What if two different values are typed in?*]

   BASIC allows a more streamlined version of Exercise 1(c):

   ```
   10  INPUT A,B
   20  PRINT A + B
   30  END
   ```

   The variables for which values are to be entered follow the word IN-PUT and are separated by commas. When the program is run, the values are entered on one line, separated by commas:

   ```
   RUN
   ? 3,5  ●
   8
   Ready
   ```

   (e)
   ```
   10  INPUT A,B,C
   20  INPUT D,E
   30  INPUT F
   40  LET M = (A + B + C + D + E + F)/6
   50  PRINT M
   60  END
   ```

2. Write programs to solve the following problems, using INPUT statements to supply the data.
   (a) Convert Fahrenheit temperatures to Celsius.
   (b) Convert miles to kilometers (see Section 2.7, Exercise 4).
   (c) Calculate a 4% sales tax on an item and print the total payment required for the item.

3. Write programs to solve these. In each exercise more than one value is required by the program.
   (a) Calculate average miles per gallon, given miles traveled and gas consumed.

(b) Calculate the final balance, after n years, if a given amount is deposited in a savings account paying $I\%$ per year compounded quarterly (see Section 2.7, Exercise 4).

(c) Calculate the length of the hypotenuse of a right triangle, given the lengths of the other two sides.

(d) Calculate the two solutions, x_1 and x_2, of a quadratic equation $ax^2 + bx + c = 0$, where

$$x_1 = \frac{-b + \sqrt{b^2 - 4ac}}{2a}$$

$$x_2 = \frac{-b - \sqrt{b^2 - 4ac}}{2a}$$

Use your program to solve the following equations.

(i) $x^2 + 3x + 2 = 0$

(ii) $x^2 + 2x + 1 = 0$

(iii) $x^2 - x - 1 = 0$

(iv) $x^2 + 2x + 3 = 0$

Can you explain what happens in case (iv)?

Chapter

3

Polishing
the Program

3.1 CONSTRUCTING UNDERSTANDABLE PROGRAMS

Most useful computer programs are very large. It is easy to lose sight of this fact when, as a beginning programmer, the largest program that you write is never more than 50 lines or so. For example, in business data processing, programs to handle inventory control or payroll may run to many pages of code. Furthermore, the person who designs such a program is often **not** the one who runs it or who later modifies or corrects it.

Much of the programming that is done today, particularly for small business applications, is written by companies that specialize in software development. These companies design programs for businesses which do not want to invest their time in such development or do not have the expertise for it. The programs are often used for years and are, consequently, modified repeatedly in response to the changing demands of the companies that use them. This is a very different situation from that of an individual who writes short programs for entertainment or to solve small problems. The printed output and the requirements for the input of data must be as clear as possible, so that an operator with little or no understanding of the internal workings of the program can feed it the correct data at the correct time and can understand the output. Thus explanations of how to run the program and how to interpret its output must be provided to the user. In large software systems, such as the operating system of the computer you are using, these explanations are usually provided in the form of separate manuals. In smaller programs the alternative is to have the program itself print out instructions. This is the course we will take.

There is another aspect to the design of understandable programs. I mentioned above that a large program may go through many modifications during its lifetime, often at the hands of many different programmers. Incidentally, such a program is usually the work of a team of programmers rather than just one person, in the first place. A program of, say, 500 statements or more is hard to read and, as a program must be understood before it can be modified, difficulty in understanding it will lead to delays and expense in its modification. For this reason all programming languages make provision for the inclusion of descriptive comments or remarks in the program code. These are ignored by the machine, but help programmers to understand the action of the program.

In this chapter we discuss some tools for producing understandable programs. I should warn you that good programming style is a topic that will be emphasized throughout the book. It is not enough to be able to write programs that are correct. Programs must, among other things, be readable.

3.2 PRINTING TEXT

At the end of Chapter 2, we saw that when the program

```
10  INPUT P
20  LET T = P*7/100
30  PRINT T
40  END
```

was typed in and then RUN was typed, the machine responded with

```
?
```

Now we happen to know that this is caused by statement 10, but it is hardly self-explanatory. A person who didn't know anything about BASIC would be completely baffled and even one who did would have to read the program first in order to understand what it was supposed to do. This is no problem with a four-line program but is much harder with one of 40 or 400 lines. The program is an example of bad programming practice and, once you have read this chapter, you should make a vow never to write one like it. A program must contain sufficient explanation to indicate to the operator how it is to be used and what data are required. However, we will continue to discuss examples that do not satisfy these requirements. The examples will often be kept very short, to focus your attention on their message. Therefore, to emphasize their incompleteness, and to avoid leading you astray, we will refer to them as **program segments**.

Here is the kind of printout that a user should expect from a program. I will not give a listing of the program yet, as I want to emphasize the goal first and then work toward it. When the user types

    RUN

the machine responds with

    7% SALES TAX.
    TYPE IN SALES AMOUNT (IN DOLLARS, BUT
    OMITTING THE $ SIGN) THEN PRESS RETURN.
    AMOUNT?

The user then enters, say, 13.35:

    AMOUNT? 13.35

to which the machine responds:

    THE TAX IS $ 0.93
    Ready

This may look complicated but, in fact, is quite easy. Let's look at some shorter examples first, to find out what techniques are available to us. This:

    10   PRINT "HI! I'M A COMPUTER."
    20   END

produces the following printout:

    RUN
    HI! I'M A COMPUTER.
    Ready

The segment

    10   PRINT "HI! I'M A COMPUTER."
    20   PRINT "I PRESUME YOU ARE NOT."
    30   END

not surprisingly gives

    RUN
    HI! I'M A COMPUTER.
    I PRESUME YOU ARE NOT.
    Ready

The pieces of text enclosed in quotes (e.g., "HI! I'M A COMPUTER.") are referred to as **character strings**. Any string of characters, including letters, numbers, punctuation symbols, mathematical symbols, and special symbols such as the dollar sign, as well as the space or blank, will be printed as typed when enclosed in quotes. Note that the quotation marks themselves are not printed. The job of investigating how one persuades the computer to print quotes, as in "HI!" SHE BURBLED is left to you. Computer languages, like natural languages, have dialects and the question we have raised concerns a part of the BASIC language that varies from one brand of computer to another.

If we want to put a space between two lines, we instruct the computer to print a blank line, like this:

```
10  PRINT "HI! I'M A DUCK."
20  PRINT
30  PRINT "I PRESUME YOU ARE NOT."
40  END
```

That is, we include a statement that consists of just the word PRINT. Running this, we get

```
RUN
HI! I'M A DUCK.

I PRESUME YOU ARE NOT.
Ready
```

If you look at the "ideal" printout for the tax program, you will notice that the last two lines are a little more complicated. One involves the printing of text and then the input of a number:

```
AMOUNT? 13.35
```

The other involves the printing of text followed by a number:

```
THE TAX IS $ 0.93
```

Both of these situations are handled by one simple operator, the **semicolon** (;). In the BASIC language, when any item in a PRINT statement is followed by a semicolon, the next item to be printed by the computer will be placed on the same line immediately after the preceding one.

Example

```
10  PRINT "YOU BROKE MY HE";"ART!"
20  END
```

produces

```
RUN
YOU BROKE MY HEART!
Ready
```

and this program segment:

```
10   PRINT "I ALWAYS TRY TO GET";
20   PRINT " AS MANY WORDS ONTO ONE LINE";
30   PRINT " AS I POSSIBLY CAN."
40   END
```

produces

```
RUN
I ALWAYS TRY TO GET AS MANY WORDS ONTO ONE LINE AS I POSSIBLY CAN.
Ready
```

By the way, did you notice the extra blank spaces inside the quotes before
AS MANY . . . and AS I . . . ? Why are those necessary? Here are a few more
questions about the use of the semicolon that you might try to answer by
experimenting on the computer. What happens if the semicolon is put inside
the quotes instead of outside? What if a semicolon is placed before the first
item in a PRINT statement? What if a PRINT statement ending in a semicolon is followed by the statement that prints a blank line? Why the semicolon? In fact, the comma is used in PRINT statements, too. We won't
discuss this until a later chapter but, meanwhile, you can experiment with
statements such as PRINT A,B.

The use of the semicolon is not limited to the printing of text. For example, this:

```
10   LET A = 3
20   LET B = 5
30   PRINT A;B
40   END
```

when run, produces this:

```
RUN
 3  5
Ready
```

Here is a slightly more complicated example.

Example

```
10  LET A = 3
20  LET B = 5
30  LET S = A+B
40  PRINT "THE SUM OF";A;"AND";B;"IS";S;"."
50  END
RUN
THE SUM OF 3 AND 5 IS 8.
Ready
```

■

Notice that in this example no extra spaces were included in the character strings, yet the output was correctly spaced. This is due to a peculiarity of numerical output in BASIC. Individual numbers are surrounded by blank spaces; they are not compressed together the way text is. The exact spacing will vary from system to system. However, at least one space is usually inserted on each side of a positive number. If the number is negative, the space in front of it is filled with a minus sign. Some versions of BASIC vary the spacing according to the size of the number printed, so the best thing to do is to experiment with your computer until you understand the way in which it handles this problem. But remember that this applies only to numbers. Spaces are not inserted on either side of a character string.

Let's return to the tax program and write the program code necessary to produce the output we have planned. Here is the modified program:

```
10 PRINT "7% SALES TAX."
20 PRINT "TYPE IN SALES AMOUNT (IN DOLLARS, BUT"
30 PRINT "OMITTING THE $ SIGN) THEN PRESS RETURN."
40 PRINT
50 PRINT "AMOUNT";
60 INPUT P
70 LET T = P*7/100
80 PRINT
90 PRINT "THE TAX IS $";T
100 END
```

The original program is still there, embedded in statements 60–100. What has been added is descriptive text to aid the user. When the program is run, the description is printed; then the pair of statements

```
50  PRINT "AMOUNT";
60  INPUT P
```

produces the printout

```
AMOUNT?
```

and causes the machine to wait for the user to type a number after the question mark. This is another example of the effect of the semicolon. The next item to be printed after the word AMOUNT is the question mark produced by the INPUT statement. The semicolon forces it to be printed on the same line.

Here is a complete run of the program, for the case where the user types the value 23.45:

```
RUN

7% SALES TAX.
TYPE IN SALES AMOUNT (IN DOLLARS, BUT
OMITTING THE $ SIGN) THEN PRESS RETURN.

AMOUNT? 23.45

THE TAX IS $ 1.6415

Ready
```

Perhaps this is a little overdone for such an insignificant program. Although it is not unusual for program code to be dominated by PRINT statements, it is possible to print so much description that you bore and even confuse the user. Your own good taste and sense of style must be your guide here. Try to design each program so that its output is appropriate for the needs of the people who will be using it. For example, if you had to run the tax program repeatedly while a line of your customers grew murderously impatient, you might wish the programmer had been a little less lavish with the explanation. The following output would be easier to live with:

```
RUN
7% SALES TAX
SALE AMOUNT? 27.50
TAX IS $ 1.925
Ready
```

Even that might be too much if you had to handle a large volume of traffic. Under these circumstances a harried salesclerk would be grateful for

```
RUN
AMT? 1.50
TAX $ 0.105
Ready
```

Bear in mind, however, that "brief" can quickly become "incomprehensible." If you are keeping the output short in the interests of efficiency, you must also provide an explanation of the program for the person who is using it for the first time. This can be handled in two ways: A separate manual for the program can be written or the program itself can provide instructions to the user who requests them. Unfortunately, the techniques required for the latter are beyond our programming ability at the moment.

If you look at the final line of the program, you will see that the output is still not entirely satisfactory. Although it is true that 1.6415 is exactly 7% of 23.45, the fact is that if we are attempting to do calculations involving dollars and cents, we don't normally deal in fractions of a cent. The answer we really want is 1.64, that is, 1.6415 rounded to the nearest cent. We could do this step in our head, but it would make more sense to put the power of the machine to work for us.

3.3 ROUNDING NUMERICAL RESULTS

As the tax program shows, the business of designing appropriate output for a program is not just a matter of printing the "right" instructions. The data must be beaten into shape as well. This process usually consists of chopping, or rounding off, extra digits. On some systems, the PRINT statement itself can handle this for us, but as those facilities are not available in many dialects of BASIC, we will opt for a more cumbersome method. I strongly urge you not to skip this section, even though its contents may seem a little too "mathematical" for your taste. The techniques we learn here will see wider application than just the polishing of numerical output.

We will discuss the problems of truncating and rounding numerical data to a given number of decimal places. Our primary tool for this will be the function INT.

If you run the following little program segment

```
10  PRINT INT(3.25)
20  END
```

the output will look like this:

```
RUN
3
Ready
```

To investigate the effect of placing different numbers in the parentheses after INT, you can retype line 10.

Example

```
10  PRINT INT(4.999)
20  END
```

RUN
4
Ready   ■

You can make the experiment easier by using a slightly more elaborate version.

Example

```
10  PRINT "NUMBER";
20  INPUT X
30  PRINT "INT APPLIED TO ";X;"GIVES ";INT(X)
40  END
RUN
NUMBER? 7.612
INT APPLIED TO   7.612 GIVES   7
Ready
RUN
NUMBER? –4.33
INT APPLIED TO –4.33 GIVES –5
Ready
etc.
```
      ■

The function INT is followed by a number or a variable (or even, as we shall see, a mathematical expression) enclosed in parentheses. It performs some operation on that quantity to produce a numerical value. Here is a table of some numbers, X, that were typed into the program above and the corresponding output, INT(X) :

X	INT(X)
4.999	4
3.25	3
2	2
1.13	1
0.9	0
–0.9	–1
–1.13	–2
–2	–2
–3.25	–4
–4.999	–5

Before reading the next paragraph, try to deduce for yourself what it is that INT does to a number.

On the real number line, drawn in the normal way with positive numbers to the right and negative to the left, INT(X) is that integer (whole number) lying immediately to the left of X. Of course, if X is already an integer, then INT(X) will be the same as X. The following diagram should clarify the picture:

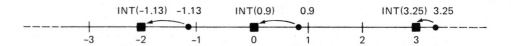

A mathematically precise definition of the action of INT goes like this. INT(X) is the greatest integer that is less than or equal to X. However, if we restrict our attention to *positive* numbers, the rule for INT can be stated more simply as "INT chops off the decimal fraction."

Example

Using the program segment above:

```
RUN
NUMBER? 8.76
INT APPLIED TO  8.76 GIVES  8
Ready
```

That is, the effect of INT is to strike off the .76. This does not work for negative numbers:

```
RUN
NUMBER? -8.76
INT APPLIED TO -8.76 GIVES -9
Ready
```

The value of this function to us in solving the rounding problem will not yet be clear to you. To understand its usefulness, we will temporarily restrict our discussion to the case of positive numbers.

If we view INT as chopping off the fractional part of a number, we can think of it as a scalpel with which to perform mathematical surgery. The decimal point acts as a marker to indicate where INT is to make its cut. In the tax program we want to drop off everything to the right of the second decimal place. The solution to this problem is to move the decimal point two places to the right, perform surgery using INT, and then return the decimal point to its original position. We can shift the point two steps to the right by multiplying by 100 and return it later by dividing by 100.

Example

Here is the sequence of steps applied to X, where X contains the value 1.6415:

Operation	Value
X	1.6415
X*100	164.15
INT(X*100)	164.
(INT(X*100))/100	1.64

Note that each operation is applied to the result of the previous one. ■

The complete expression, which performs what we will call *truncation to two decimal places* on the number X, is

(INT(X*100))/100

You can use the following lines of code to experiment with the formula until you understand its action completely:

```
10  PRINT "NUMBER";
20  INPUT X
30  LET Y = (INT(X*100))/100
40  PRINT X; "TRUNCATED TO TWO DECIMAL PLACES IS";Y
50  END
```

Example

```
RUN
NUMBER? 4.758
4.758 TRUNCATED TO TWO DECIMAL PLACES IS 4.75
Ready
```
■

If the formula still confuses you, try following the steps used in the table above with different values for X. Remember, the computer always calculates formulas from the inside out; that is, the operations inside the innermost parentheses are performed first.

We are close to our goal, but the result is still not perfect. After all, 4.758 to the nearest cent is 4.76, not 4.75. We have to *round* to the nearest cent, not just chop off the extra decimal places.

This may seem to be a picayune distinction. However, such subtleties have been put to use in embezzlement schemes involving computers. Here is a typical story. A computer programmer, who is employed by a bank, modifies the program that calculates the interest on savings accounts so that the interest that is paid each customer is *truncated* to two decimal places, but the corresponding charge made to the bank is *rounded* to two decimal places. In roughly half the transactions there will be no difference, but in the remaining ones there will be an extra one cent charged to the bank which is not paid to the customer. This the programmer diverts to his own account. He makes an average of half a cent on every interest calculation—not much, but when you consider the number of such calculations that must be performed in a year, you can see that he could accumulate quite a nest egg. In fact, in at least one case the amount involved was in the hundreds of thousands of dollars. Clearly, the success of the scheme depends on the high volume of business that can be handled by a computer. Such an operation is hard to uncover. The evidence of the crime is often embedded deep in complex programming code and the individual amounts of money involved are small enough to escape notice. In fact, it is suspected that much computer crime goes undetected because, in those cases that have been solved, suspicions were more often aroused by the unusually lavish life-style of the person involved than by any direct evidence of the crime. In many cases, the crime itself would probably not have been discovered if the suspect had not decided to own up, in order to "get it off his chest."

Returning to the task in hand, we need a procedure to handle "rounding to the nearest . . . . " First we'll look at the problem of rounding to the nearest integer. The number 3.25, when rounded to the nearest integer, should be 3. On the other hand, 3.9 should give 4. Clearly, a number below the halfway point between two integers rounds to the lower and anything above to the higher of the two.

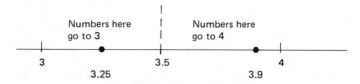

Compare this with a similar picture for the action of INT on numbers one-half step to the right:

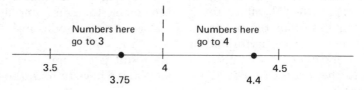

The similarities between these two diagrams suggest the following approach: To round to the nearest integer, add 0.5 to the number and then apply INT. Experiment with this program segment to verify that the idea works:

```
10  PRINT "NUMBER";
20  INPUT X
30  LET R = INT(X+0.5)
40  PRINT X;"ROUNDED TO NEAREST INTEGER IS";R
50  END
```

Rather than printing a run of this program, here instead is a table showing the effect of INT(X+0.5) on various numbers, X:

			Case		
	1	**2**	**3***	**4***	**5**
X	3.25	3.9	–5.12	–5.7	6.50
X+0.5	3.75	4.4	–4.62	–5.2	7.00
INT(X+0.5)	3	4	–5	–6	7

*Remember the effect of INT on negative numbers.

The function INT(X+0.5) does in fact round any number X, even a negative one, to the nearest integer. Note that when X ends in 0.5 it is always rounded up to the next integer.

   To handle "rounding to the nearest cent" we need to combine the truncation technique, which we discussed earlier, with this rounding process. Some experimentation will show that the formula we need is

    (INT(X*100+0.5))/100

To understand its action, we can use the table technique to break it down into simple steps.

		Case	
	1	**2**	**3**
X	2.532	2.539	–2.532
X*100	253.2	253.9	–253.2
X*100+0.5	253.7	254.4	–252.7
INT(X*100+0.5)	253.	254.	–253.
(INT(X*100+0.5))/100	2.53	2.54	–2.53

To satisfy yourself that this formula always rounds to the nearest cent, you should write a short program to test it.

Here is a summary of the functions we have developed. They are useful formulas to have at your fingertips.

INT(X)	truncation of X to an integer†
INT(X+0.5)	rounding of X to an integer
(INT(X*100)/100	truncation of X to two decimal places†
(INT(X*100+0.5))/100	rounding of X to two decimal places

I leave to you the problem of designing functions that will perform rounding to, say, one or three decimal places or, at the other extreme, to the nearest 10, 100, or 1000.

3.4 DOCUMENTING THE PROGRAM

Before we write out the final form of the tax program there is one point, made at the beginning of this chapter, which we should take up in more detail.

We discussed how it is just as important to provide comments in a program, to explain its internal workings to other programmers, as it is to provide instructions to the user when it is run. Comments can be included in a BASIC program by using the **REMARK** statement. Any line beginning with the word REMARK or its abbreviation REM is ignored by the computer when it is executing the program.

Example

```
10  REM  THIS PROGRAM ACCEPTS A NUMBER
20  INPUT N
30  REM  AND PRINTS ITS SQUARE.
40  PRINT N*N
50  END
RUN
? 7
 49
Ready
```

■

The text in lines 10 and 30 of this example is not printed when the program is run. Thus it is **not** a substitute for printed explanations. The REM statements are helpful only to a person reading a listing of the program, not to

---

†Beware, these descriptions are strictly true only when X is not negative.

someone running it. They should clarify the internal structure of the program. Beginning programmers tend to be confused about this point and often include instructions for running a program in the REMARK statements. A program should contain REMARKS, *as well as* instructions in PRINT statements.

Your first programs will be so simple that they will hardly seem to need internal documentation. However, it is best to start developing good habits right at the beginning. The following is the minimum that you should include:

1. Program title
2. Programmer name and date of creation
3. Description of variables used

Beyond this minimum, it is often useful to include a paragraph giving a general description of the program and, also, to use remarks to break the program listing visually into sections, as well as to provide explanations of difficult pieces of code.

I'll illustrate what I consider minimum documentation with the final form of the tax program. Here is the program, complete with operating instructions and rounding, as well as REMARKS.

```
100 REM TITLE: 7% TAX CALCULATION WITH ROUNDING
110 REM PROGRAMMER: A. KITCHEN        DATE:4-JUN-80
120 REM
130 REM VARIABLES:
140 REM           P = PRICE OF ITEM
150 REM           T = 7% TAX ON PRICE
160 REM
170 REM PROGRAM:
180 PRINT "7% SALES TAX."
190 PRINT "TYPE IN SALES AMOUNT (IN DOLLARS, BUT"
200 PRINT "OMITTING THE $ SIGN) THEN PRESS RETURN."
210 PRINT
220 PRINT "AMOUNT";
230 INPUT P
240 LET T = P*7/100
250 PRINT
260 PRINT "THE TAX IS $";(INT(T*100 + 0.5))/100
270 END
```

A run of the program looks like this:

```
RUN

7% SALES TAX.
TYPE IN SALES AMOUNT (IN DOLLARS, BUT
OMITTING THE $ SIGN) THEN PRESS RETURN.

AMOUNT? 38.95

THE TAX IS $ 2.73

Ready
```

3.5 CHARACTER STRING VARIABLES†

In this chapter we have discussed how the machine can be programmed to print text. We will see in Chapter 9 that the manipulation of character strings is as much a part of computing as is mathematical calculation. Although we will not get into those details yet, the little we do discuss here will enable us to use more interesting examples in the chapters that follow.

A tool that has proved useful for increasing the flexibility of our programming is the concept of a variable. Together with the numeric variables already introduced, most versions of the BASIC language provide variables for storing character strings. Typical **character string variables** are denoted as follows:

```
A$, B$, P$, X$, etc.
```

a letter followed by a dollar sign.

Values can be assigned to character string variables by means of the LET statement:

Example

```
LET N$ = "THEDA BARA"
```

stores the characters T,H,E,D,A, blank, B,A,R,A in the variable N$:

```
N$   | THEDA BARA |
```                                                         ∎

The value of a variable can be printed.

Example

```
10   LET N$ = "THEDA BARA"
20   PRINT N$
30   END
RUN
THEDA BARA
Ready
```                                                         ∎

Character strings are (almost!) always enclosed in quotes. This is necessary

---

†The way in which character string variables are handled varies widely from one version of BASIC to another. If these examples do not work on your system, check your manuals. See also Appendix III.

to avoid confusion between strings that are to be processed by a program and parts of the program itself.

Example

```
10  LET K$ = "SOME DAY MY PRINTS WILL COME!"
20  LET A$ = K$
30  LET B$ = "K$"
40  PRINT A$
50  PRINT B$
60  END
RUN
SOME DAY MY PRINTS WILL COME!
K$
Ready
```

■

Any collection of characters enclosed in quotes is considered to be a character string and can be stored and printed. For example:

```
LET E$ = "***"
LET N$ = "13.75"
LET G$ = "1 2 3 KABOOM!!!?*?**!??"
```

are all valid. The middle example stores the string 13.75 in the variable N$. However, don't be deceived into thinking that this is a number. It is just a string of characters and cannot be used to do arithmetic.

Example

Try running:

```
10  LET N$ = "2.5"
20  LET A = 3*N$
30  PRINT A
40  END
```

You should get an error message. In which line do you get it?
Does this help? . . . or this?

```
10  LET N$ = "2.5"              10  LET N$ = "2.5"
20  LET A$ = 3*N$              20  LET A$ = "3"*N$
30  PRINT A$                    30  PRINT A$
40  END                        40  END
```

The moral is: Don't mix mathematical operations with character strings. ■

The INPUT statement can be used with strings, too. By the way, this is one of the few situations in which quotes are not required around strings of characters. It would be rather inconvenient to demand that a user enclose his responses to the computer in quotes; therefore, BASIC does not require them around strings typed in response to an INPUT statement.

Example

```
10  PRINT "WHAT'S YOUR NAME M'DEAR";
20  INPUT G$
30  PRINT "COME UP AND SEE MY ETCHINGS";G$;"."
40  END
RUN
WHAT'S YOUR NAME M'DEAR? PHYLLIS
COME UP AND SEE MY ETCHINGSPHYLLIS.
Ready
```

At line 20 of this program the name that was typed in, PHYLLIS, is stored in the variable G$:

G$ | PHYLLIS

By the way, notice the use of the semicolon to control the output. What would you do to improve the spacing in the computer's response? What happens if you put quotes around PHYLLIS? ■

This is all you need to know about character string variables until we come to Chapter 9. We'll end with two program segments which illustrate the difference between the way BASIC handles character strings and its manipulation of numbers:

```
10  INPUT A$                    10  INPUT A
20  INPUT B$                    20  INPUT B
30  PRINT A$+B$                 30  PRINT A+B
40  END                         40  END
```

Try these on various pairs of character strings, including pairs of numbers.

Chapter 3: EXERCISES

Section 3.1

No exercises.

Section 3.2

1. What is printed by each of the following instructions? Assume that the variable F has the value 5.
   - (a) PRINT "A GOOD 5-CENT";"CIGAR."
   - (b) PRINT "A GOOD 5-CENT CIGAR."
   - (c) PRINT "A GOOD";5;"-CENT CIGAR."
   - (d) PRINT "A GOOD"; "5";"-CENT CIGAR."
   - (e) PRINT "A GOOD;5;-CENT CIGAR."
   - (f) PRINT "A GOOD";F;"-CENT CIGAR."
   - (g) PRINT "A GOOD";"F";"-CENT CIGAR."

2. Identify which of these statements contain errors. Describe the errors.
   - (a) PRINT "PLOFFSKIN, PLUFFSKIN, PELICAN JEE!
   - (b) PRINT HE SAID: "MY NAME IS JAN JANSEN."
   - (c) PRINT "HE SAID: "MY NAME IS JAN JANSEN." "

   [*Hint: Find out how your system handles the printing of quotes.*]
   - (d) PRINT "THE";3"MUSKETEERS
   - (e) PRINT "LET T = P*7/100"
   - (f) INPUT A;
   - (g) LET N = "JAN JANSEN"

   [*Hint: Systems vary in their tolerance of irregularities, particularly in the handling of strings. What is an error on one system may be acceptable to another. For example, part (a) contains an error but would, in fact, be accepted by my system without complaint.*]

3. Show exactly what is printed by a typical run of each of the following.
   - (a)
     ```
     10  PRINT "HOW OLD ARE YOU"
     20  INPUT A
     30  PRINT "YOU HAVE LIVED ABOUT"
     40  PRINT A*365
     50  PRINT "DAYS."
     60  END
     ```
   - (b)
     ```
     10  PRINT "HOW OLD ARE YOU";
     20  INPUT A
     30  PRINT "YOU HAVE LIVED ABOUT";
     ```

```
40  PRINT A*365;
50  PRINT "DAYS."
60  END
```

(c)
```
10  PRINT "BEGINNING";
20  PRINT " MIDDLE "
30  PRINT "END"
40  END
```

(d)
```
10  PRINT BEGINNING";
20  PRINT
30  PRINT " MIDDLE "
40  PRINT
50  PRINT "END"
60  END
```

Section 3.3

1.   Show what will be printed by each of these instructions.

```
PRINT INT(X)              PRINT INT(X+0.5)
PRINT INT(X*10)           PRINT INT(X*10+0.5)
PRINT INT(X*10)/10        PRINT INT((X+0.5)*10)
PRINT INT(X*10+0.5)/10    PRINT INT(X*1000)/1000
PRINT INT(X/100)*100
```

if X equals

(a) 0.8642   (b) –3.4567   (c) 7777.77

2.   By experimentation (on the computer or by hand), determine what this function does:

```
INT(X*2+0.5)/2
```

3.   Construct a function that
   (a) Sets all digits below the "tens" column to zero, in any positive number. [*Hint: 759.3 should become 750.*]
   (b) Rounds numbers to the nearest 10. [*Hint: 759.3 becomes 760, whereas 753.9 becomes 750.*]

4.   What does this code do when it is executed?

```
10  INPUT X,D
20  LET P = 10^D
30  LET Y = INT(X*P+0.5)/P
40  PRINT Y
50  END
```

Section 3.4

1. Comment on the remarks and printed output of these programs.

    (a)
```
10  REM  CALCULATION OF CUBE ROOTS
20  PRINT
30  PRINT "X = NUMBER ENTERED"
40  PRINT "R = ITS CUBE ROOT"
50      INPUT X
60      LET R = X^(1/3)
70      PRINT R
80      END
```

    (b)
```
10  PRINT "TYPE VALUE FOR P"
20  INPUT P
30  LET T = P*7/100
40  PRINT "VALUE OF T IS"; T
50  END
```

    (c)
```
10  REM  B IS ACCEPTED FROM TERMINAL
20      INPUT B
30  REM  C IS ACCEPTED FROM TERMINAL
40      INPUT C
50  REM  A IS THE SUM OF B AND C
60      LET A = B + C
70  REM  PRINT THE VALUE OF A
80      PRINT A
90      END
```

2. Add complete documentation to one of the programs in Section 2.8, Exercises 2 and 3.

In the following exercises, write completely documented programs to solve the given problems. Plan the output of the programs carefully. Write them for a first-time user, then modify for repeated use by a more experienced operator.

3. The area of any triangle can be calculated from the lengths of its sides using the following formula:

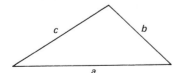

$$\text{Area} = \sqrt{s(s-a)(s-b)(s-c)}$$

$$\text{where } s = \frac{a+b+c}{2}$$

Calculate the area of a triangle given the lengths of its sides. [*Hint: Test your program on "well-known" triangles (e.g., the 3–4–5 triangle). What happens if you use, say, the dimensions 2, 3, 6? Why does this happen?*]

4. Calculate the monthly deposits, D, to a savings account, which are required in order to accrue $B after Y years. If the annual interest rate is $I\%$, D is given by

$$D = B \frac{\left(\dfrac{I}{1200}\right)}{\left(1 + \dfrac{I}{1200}\right)^{12Y} - 1}$$

   [Hint: This program is designed to answer such questions as: My savings account pays 7.25%. I wish to accumulate $100,000 over the next 25 years. How much must I deposit each month in order to achieve this goal?]

5. There is an interesting phenomenon, predicted by Einstein's theory of relativity, known as time dilation. Time passes more slowly for someone who is traveling. This is not caused by boredom; the rate of all natural processes actually slows down and this phenomenon becomes more noticeable as the rate of travel increases. As a consequence of this, a space traveler does not age as fast as those of us who remain on earth. In fact, if one were to travel at $P\%$ of the speed of light for Y years, one would only age y years, where

$$y = Y \sqrt{1 - \left(\frac{P}{100}\right)^2}$$

   You are to embark on a space voyage. Given your age at departure, your speed of travel (as a percentage of the speed of light), and the length of your journey (in years), calculate your biological age on return. *[Hint: The speed of light is about 670,000,000 mph, so it is easier to work with percentages than actual velocities. What happens if you attempt to travel over the speed of light? Can you make any conclusions about time travel, forward or backward, from this formula?]*

6. Write a program to calculate the quotient and remainder when a positive integer A is divided by a positive integer B. *[Hint: If $A = 29$ and $B = 8$, then $A/B = 3.625$. So the quotient = 3. The remainder = 5, that is, $29 = 3*8+5$. You will need to use the function INT.]*

Section 3.5

1. Identify which of these statements contain errors. Describe the errors.

   (a) PRINT A$ B$ C (b) LET N$ = 5
   (c) INPUT "HELLO" (d) C$ = "MY NAME IS ";N$
   (e) LET X = INT(X$) (f) LET X = INT(X)
   (g) PRINT "WHERE WAS M$;" WHEN THE LIGHTS WENT OUT";

2. What is produced when these are run?

(a)
```
10 LET A = 1
20 LET B = 2
30 LET C$ = "3"
40 LET D$ = "4"
50 PRINT A;B;C$;D$;
60 PRINT A
70 END
```

(b)
```
10 LET G$ = "GOOD"
20 LET A$ = "AS"
30 LET S$ = "GOLD"
40 LET B$ = " "
50 PRINT G$;A$;S$
60 PRINT G$;B$;A$;B$;S$
70 END
```

(c)
```
10 LET B$ = "A"
20 LET C$ = B$
30 LET D$ = C$
40 PRINT D$
50 END
```

(d) Experiment with this one:
```
10 INPUT X$;Y$
20 PRINT X$;Y$
30 PRINT X$+Y$
40 END
```

3. Write a program to produce output similar to this (the names are to be typed by the user):

FIRST NAME, PLEASE? ALICE
FAMILY NAME? BRAITHWAITE
DEAR MR/MS BRAITHWAITE:
IF I MAY CALL YOU BY YOUR FIRST NAME
I LOVE YOU, ALICE!!
Ready

Chapter

4

Loops and Data Processing

4.1 PROGRAM LOOPS

If you have attempted to use the tax program of Chapter 3 to calculate the sales tax on a large number of different items, I'm sure that you will have found it a decidedly irritating process. Each new calculation requires that the program be rerun and this entails having to suffer through the printing of the same instructions over and over again. We discussed ways to avoid this inconvenience by shortening or eliminating the instructions but, unfortunately, this just introduced other problems. Another solution might be to design the program so as to print the instructions just once and then to accept a price, calculate the tax, and print it out—doing this repeatedly for as long as was needed.

Here are some other situations where such an approach would be useful: calculating and printing numerical tables, printing out payroll or inventory data, and calculating sums and averages of lists of numbers. Each one of these involves the repetition of an identical calculation, where only the data change. We cannot immediately tackle all these problems, but here is a small beginning.

Example

```
10 PRINT "HUMPTY DUMPED HIS HAT ON A WALL."
20 GO TO 10
```

```
30 END
```

```
RUN
```

```
HUMPTY DUMPED HIS HAT ON A WALL.
HUMPTY DUMPED HIS HAT ON A WALL.
HUMPTY DUMPED HIS HAT ON A WALL.
HUMPTY DUMPED HIS HAT ON A WALL.
HUMPTY DUMPED HIS HAT ON A WALL.
HUMPTY DUMPED HIS HAT ON A WALL.
. . .
. . .
```

for ever!   ■

You'd better not try this example until we discuss how to stop a runaway machine! Before we do that, however, let's find out what is happening.

When the program is executed it starts processing, as usual, with the first statement, which causes

HUMPTY DUMPED HIS HAT ON A WALL.

to be printed. Control then passes to statement 20, which immediately sends the machine back to statement 10 again. This happens repeatedly. In fact, there is nothing in the program to stop this process from continuing forever. A statement of the form

GO TO *line-number*

causes the computer to branch to the statement in the program with that line number and to continue processing at that point. Remember that, although we have learned that the statements in a program are executed in order of increasing line number, the GO TO statement breaks this sequence. However, once a GO TO has been executed, processing returns to its normal flow, starting at the destination of the GO TO statement. If the destination of the GO TO statement is earlier in the program, the intervening statements are repeated endlessly. This is what is referred to as a **loop** or, more graphically, an **infinite loop**. What happens if the destination is later in the program? For example, what does this program do?

```
10  PRINT "I LOVE";
20  GO TO 40
30  PRINT "NEW YORK"
40  PRINT "NEWARK"
50  END
```

Here is another example of a loop.

Example

```
10 LET N = 1
20 PRINT N
30 LET N = N+1
40 GO TO 20
50 END
```

RUN

```
1
2
3
4
5
6
7
8
9
10
11
12
13
14
15
16
```

for ever!   ∎

This example introduces another useful concept, that of a counter. The
statement

```
LET N = N+1
```

is a peculiar one by the standards of ordinary algebra. After all, the equation
$x = x + 1$ simplifies to $0 = 1$, which is a bit of foolish nonsense. Clearly, LET
N = N+1 is not to be interpreted this way. Remember that in the LET statement "=" means "calculate the expression on the right-hand side and store
its value in the variable on the left." To see its action we'll follow the example above through one cycle of its loop.

Initially, after line 10, N has the value 1. This value is printed by
line 20, after which control passes to statement 30. First, the right-hand
expression

```
N+1
```

is calculated, using the current value of N, which is 1. The result of this calculation, 2, is then placed back in N, so that N now has the value 2. In the
next cycle N is increased from 2 to 3 by the same process, and so on.

The variable N is a **counter,** that is, a variable which is increased by 1
periodically to keep a count of some repetitive process within a program. In

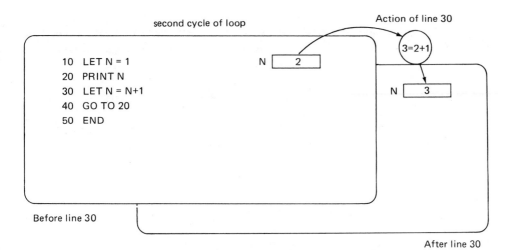

this case it keeps track of the number of repetitions of the loop. There are really two parts to the concept:

1. An initial value must be established (e.g., LET N = 1).
2. The value must be changed periodically (e.g., LET N = N+1).

Incidentally, there is no reason why counters should be restricted to counting up in steps of 1. One can have counters that count up in larger or smaller steps

Example

```
LET M = M+2
LET X = X+0.1
```
∎

or which count down.

Example

```
LET N = N–1
LET F = F–5
```
∎

Counters are useful in many applications of computing. In fact, almost every program of any consequence includes at least one counter, often many of them.

Before we go any further, let's discuss how to stop a program that is caught in an infinite loop; then you can try some of these examples. The approach varies from one machine to another, but the following is generally true. Every terminal has one key or a combination of keys which, when pressed, will cause the computer to stop whatever it is doing and immediately return control to you. On many systems there are two options: one can press the **BREAK** key or one can hold down the **CONTROL** key (usually labeled CTRL) and type the letter **C** (referred to as CTRL-C). Either of these causes the system to stop what it is currently involved in and to print the message **Ready,** or a similar response.

Example

The following is typical:

```
RUN
HUMPTY DUMPED HIS HAT ON A WALL.
HUMPTY DUMPED HIS HAT ON A WALL.
HUMPTY DUMPED HIS HA ^C
Ready
```

The BREAK key or CTRL-C was pressed at this point. It caused the program to stop immediately and printed ^C.

Here is another typical response to the BREAK key: The system stops the program and prints the message BREAK AT LINE 10.   ∎

Before you continue, find out what the procedure is on your system. Run the HUMPTY example and then try to stop it. This advice is not as irresponsible as it sounds. It is most important to be familiar with these procedures. Any time that you get yourself in a bind or cannot get a response from the computer, pressing BREAK, or whatever works on your system, will return control to you.

The use of loops introduces a problem which has a tendency to grow more oppressive and intractable as programs become larger and more complex: namely, that because the normal top-to-bottom flow is disturbed by GO TO statements, programs become harder to read the more loops they contain. The main reason for this is that it is difficult to see the physical boundaries of a loop within the program code. Here is one solution to this problem, applied to the counting program:

```
10        LET N = 1
20   REM   REPEAT
30             PRINT N
```

```
40          LET N = N+1
50          GO TO 20
60          END
```

Begin the loop with the remark REPEAT and end it with a GO TO statement, which sends the machine back to the REM REPEAT statement. The statements that do the actual processing within the loop, what is called the **body of the loop,** are inset a little to emphasize the extent of the loop (this can be done conveniently by means of the TAB key if your terminal has one[†]).

All this helps anyone reading the program to identify exactly which segment of the program is repeated. This technique of indenting statements to improve readability goes by the rather coy name of **prettyprinting.** We will refer to REPEAT and GO TO as **control statements,** as they are devoted to controlling the flow of the program and do not actually process data themselves. (This is rather loose terminology in the case of REPEAT, which is just a remark and actually does nothing other than identify the beginning of the loop.)

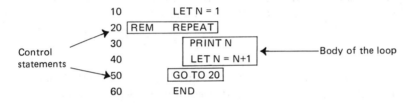

The structure of a loop

4.2 PROCESSING LARGE AMOUNTS OF DATA: READ AND DATA

Loops come into their own in programs designed to process large quantities of data, where each data item or group of items is treated in a similar fashion. However, we need some way of supplying data to such a program which is flexible enough to allow us to change and add to the data, when this is required, and yet provides us with a means of reviewing and proofreading it before a run. The LET statement is too inflexible and the INPUT statement does not allow one to correct errors in data once it has been typed in.

[†]Unfortunately, some older systems automatically erase any extra spaces typed into a BASIC statement by the user. This is a deplorable situation and severely hampers one's ability to write readable programs.

Here are three program segments with almost identical output:

(1)	(2)	(3)
10 LET A = 13	10 INPUT A	10 READ A
20 LET B = 27	20 INPUT B	20 READ B
30 PRINT A*B	30 PRINT A*B	30 PRINT A*B
40 END	40 END	40 DATA 13,27
RUN	RUN	50 END
351	?13	RUN
Ready	?27	351
	351	Ready
	Ready	

The first is simple, the second has flexibility, the third is neither as simple as the first nor as flexible as the second, but we will see that it does have its own subtle advantages. Let's discuss how it works.

When program (3) is run, the first statement to be processed is READ A. As with the instructions LET A = 13 and INPUT A in the other programs, a storage location is first set aside with the name A:

Then the machine attempts to find a value for A. The READ instruction causes the computer to search for the statement beginning with the word DATA. The first of the list of numbers in this statement, 13, is then placed in A. The next READ statement causes the remaining number, 27, to be read from the DATA statement into B.

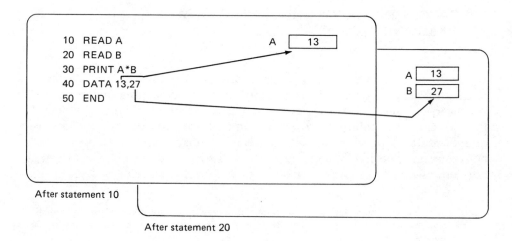

After statement 10

After statement 20

Thus, as each READ statement is executed, the next item from the list in the DATA statement is placed in the variable appearing in the READ statement. There is, in fact, a lot of flexibility in the way that this can be written. READ statements can be combined and the list of data can be spread over more than one DATA statement. Here are some variations on program (3).

Example

10 READ A	10 READ A,B	10 READ A,B
20 READ B	20 PRINT A*B	20 PRINT A*B
30 PRINT A*B	30 DATA 13	30 DATA 13,27
40 DATA 13	40 DATA 27	40 END
50 DATA 27	50 END	
60 END		∎

The DATA statements can appear anywhere in the program, even before the READ statements. The program does not actually process a DATA statement. Such a statement is just a repository for constants to be accepted by READ statements at the appropriate time. In spite of this, it is good practice always to place DATA statements at the end of the program, just before the END statement. This makes the program more readable and flexible, particularly if one plans to add to the data or modify them in any way.

As we just mentioned, the values in the DATA statements are read in strict succession so that when the list of data has been completely read, any attempt to read more values will cause an error message.

Examples

1.
```
10 READ A
20 PRINT A
30 READ A
40 PRINT A
50 READ A
60 PRINT A
70 DATA 3579,2468
80 END
```

```
RUN

 3579
 2468
?Out of data at line 50

Ready
```

2.
```
10 REM    REPEAT
20                READ X
30                PRINT X
40           GO TO 10
50           DATA 5,4,3,2,1
60           END
```

```
RUN

  5
  4
  3
  2
  1
?Out of data at line 20

Ready
```

Situations do arise where it is necessary to reread a data list. This is handled by the RESTORE statement.

Example

```
10 READ A
20 PRINT A
30 READ A
40 PRINT A
50 RESTORE
60 READ A
70 PRINT A
80 DATA 3579,2468
90 END
```

```
RUN

  3579
  2468
  3579

Ready
```

The statement RESTORE causes the READ statements following it to reread the values in the DATA statements, beginning with the **first** item in the **first** DATA statement.

Example

```
10 READ A,B,C
20 PRINT A;B;C
30 READ X,Y,Z
40 PRINT X,Y,Z
50 DATA 111,222,333
60 END
```

```
10 READ A,B,C
20 PRINT A;B;C
30 RESTORE
40 READ X,Y,Z
50 PRINT X;Y;Z
60 DATA 111,222,333
70 END
```

Compare the runs of these two program segments:

```
RUN                                  RUN

 111   222   333                      111   222   333
?Out of data at line 30               111   222   333

Ready                                Ready                          ■
```

Beware: Every time that a RESTORE statement is executed, it has the effect of restoring the data list, even if the list has not been completely read.

Example

```
10 REM   REPEAT
20                  READ X
30                  PRINT X
40                  RESTORE
50        GO TO 10
60        DATA 5,4,3,2,1
70        END
```

```
RUN

   5
   5
   5
   5
   5
   5
   5
   5
   .
   .
```

forever !   ■

Here is a program that shows how the READ/DATA statements and loops can be combined to process large amounts of data.

Example

```
100 REM TITLE: TABLE OF ROOM DIMENSIONS AND AREAS
110 REM PROGRAMMER: A. KITCHEN          DATE:15-JUN-80
120 REM VARIABLES:
130 REM          W = WIDTH OF ROOM
140 REM          L = LENGTH OF ROOM
150 REM          A = AREA OF ROOM
160 REM
170 REM PROGRAM:
180     PRINT "WIDTH";" LENGTH ";"AREA"
190 REM REPEAT
200                READ W,L
210                LET A = W*L
220                PRINT W;L;A
230     GO TO 190
240 REM
```

```
250       DATA 5,5,5,10,5,25,5,50,5
260       DATA 100,10,10,10,25,10,50,10,100
270       DATA 25,25,25,50,25,100
280       END
```

```
RUN

WIDTH LENGTH AREA
  5    5    25
  5   10    50
  5   25   125
  5   50   250
  5  100   500
 10   10   100
 10   25   250
 10   50   500
 10  100  1000
 25   25   625
 25   50  1250
 25  100  2500
?Out of data at line 200

Ready
```

Before we discuss what is obviously unsatisfactory about this program, notice how the READ/DATA statements behave in a loop. The statement

```
READ W,L
```

is executed over and over. Each time, it takes the next two items from the data list in statements 250, 260, and 270 and places them in the variables W and L (first 5,5, next 5,10, etc.). This continues until all the data have been processed.

One advantage of handling a large amount of data this way is that the data can be entered ahead of time and checked for accuracy before the program is run. Try writing this program using either LET or INPUT statements. With LET statements you will not be able to take advantage of looping, so the program will be impossibly long. Using INPUT you will not be able to print the table; furthermore, mistakes made when typing in the data cannot be eliminated unless they are caught immediately.

Having said all that, it is quite clear that the program is far from satisfactory. Let's look at its weaknesses. First, the table printed by the program is rather ragged. The headings and numbers in each column are not aligned properly and the table ends untidily with the message **Out of data at line 200.** Second, the data in this program have a definite structure. That is, each repetition of the loop reads two numbers from the data list, a width and a length, but the organization of the DATA statements does not honor this division into pairs.

The column alignment and data organization are easily taken care of, but the out-of-data message is a more serious problem and requires a major addition to our knowledge of BASIC.

4.3 PRINTING TABLES

In the print statements of the program above we used the semicolon to separate the items to be printed. Clearly, this is unsatisfactory for printing tables of items arranged in regular columns. For that purpose BASIC provides another punctuation symbol, the **comma.** To understand the action of the comma, imagine that each page of your computer printout paper is divided into a number of columns or fields of fixed width. Each comma in a PRINT statement causes the print head of the terminal to advance from its current position to the beginning of the next field. The actual width of these fields will vary from one computer system to another. On mine each field is 14 characters wide. The number of fields on your page or screen will depend on the number of characters your terminal prints per line.

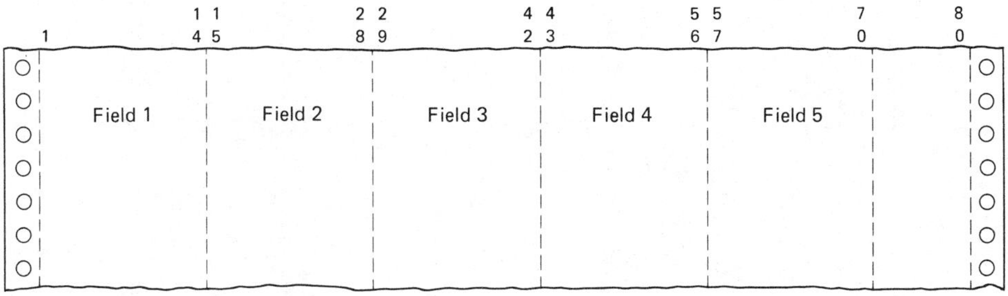

Five 14 character fields on 80 character width paper

Here are some examples of the action of the comma.

Examples

In each case, the diagram shows the printout produced by the given PRINT statement.

1.   30   PRINT "A","B","C"

2.   70   LET A = 6
      80   PRINT A,A*A,A*A*A,A*A*A*A

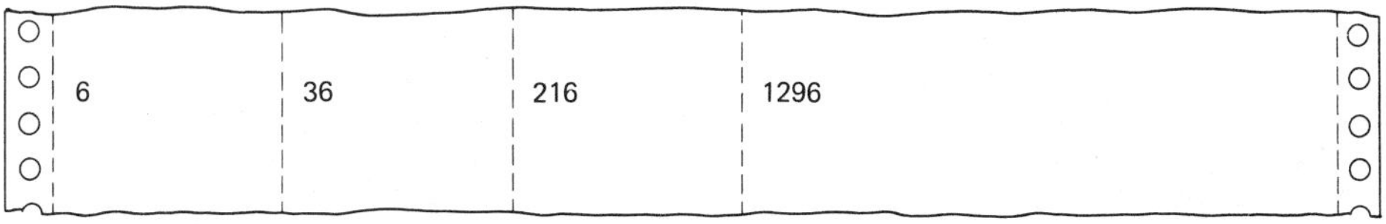

3.   100 PRINT "FELIX LOPE DE VEGA CARPIO","JEAN NICOT"

```
FELIX LOPE DE VEGA CARPIO  JEAN NICOT
```

Notice that JEAN NICOT appears in the third field, because FELIX LOPE DE VEGA CARPIO took up the whole of the first field and part of the second.

4.   10   LET N = 1
        20   REM REPEAT
        30   PRINT N,
        40   LET N = N+1
        50   GO TO 20
        60   END

```
 1        2        3        4        5
 6        7        8        9        10
11       12       13       14       15
16       17       18       19       20
21       22       23       24       25
26       27       28       29       30
31       32       33       34       35
36       37       38       39       40
41       42       43       44       45
```

If the number of available fields is exceeded, the print head moves to the next line and starts over again.

5.   90 PRINT "NAME"," ","DATE"

```
NAME                    DATE
```

We'll end this section by tidying up the table printed by the room dimensions program. If we change statements 180 and 220 to

    PRINT "WIDTH","LENGTH","AREA"

and

    PRINT W,L,A

the run will look like this:

```
RUN

WIDTH           LENGTH          AREA
  5               5               25
  5              10               50
  5              25              125
  5              50              250
  5             100              500
 10              10              100
 10              25              250
 10              50              500
 10             100             1000
 25              25              625
 25              50             1250
 25             100             2500
?Out of data at line 200

Ready
```

4.4 DATA RECORDS

Most computing in the business world, and much of the work done in other fields as well, consists of relatively straightforward calculations. For example, payroll calculations will consist of such things as:

WAGES = REGULAR HOURS*HOURLY RATE+OVERTIME HOURS*OVERTIME RATE

plus percentage calculations for various deductions, and other items. What complicates business computing is not the complexity of the calculations so much as the amount of data to be processed. For a large corporation the calculations mentioned above will be performed on thousands of employees. The sheer quantity of data becomes even more oppressive in the case of programs to handle the billing for a utility or telephone company. This kind of computing is referred to as **data processing**. The data in such applications invariably have a structure of their own. For example, in the case of a payroll program, at the very least the following items will have to be read for each employee: name, social security number, hourly rate, overtime rate, regular hours, and overtime hours. In fact, there will certainly be more data required for each employee: tax information (such as number of deductions, etc.); information on savings, medical, and retirement plans; and many other things. Thus the complete data stream for such a program naturally divides into groups of items, where each group applies to a single individual or business transaction. Such a group is referred to as a **record**.

When using READ/DATA statements in data processing, the structure of your programs will be clarified if you organize the DATA statements to show the record structure. For example, in the room dimension program we could do this:

```
240 REM
250 REM DATA: RECORD = WIDTH,LENGTH
260     DATA 5,5
270     DATA 5,10
280     DATA 5,25
290     DATA 5,50
300     DATA 5,100
310     DATA 10,10
320     DATA 10,25
330     DATA 10,50
340     DATA 10,100
350     DATA 25,25
360     DATA 25,50
370     DATA 25,100
9999    END
```

I have used a large line number for the END statement to allow for the insertion of extra DATA statements if they are needed. In fact, to be systematic, we will consistently use the number 9999 with END. This way DATA statements can be added and programs modified without having to worry about the fate of the poor END statement. The organization in this example is, perhaps, a case of overkill. However, when the individual records are any larger, follow these guidelines:

1.   Begin the data section with a remark describing the record structure.
2.   Store each record in a separate DATA statement.

Here is an example of a simple data processing program.

Example

A program to print a table of names, account numbers, and balances for a company's charge account customers.

```
100 REM TITLE: TABLE OF CUSTOMER NAMES, ACCOUNT NUMBERS, BALANCES
110 REM PROGRAMMER: A. KITCHEN        DATE: 12-DEC-81
120 REM
130 REM VARIABLES:
140 REM         N$ = CUSTOMER NAME
150 REM         A = CUSTOMER ACCOUNT NUMBER
160 REM         B = BALANCE
170 REM
180 REM PROGRAM:
190     PRINT
200     PRINT "NAME","ACCOUNT","BALANCE"
210     PRINT
220 REM REPEAT
230             READ N$,A,B
240             PRINT N$,A,B
250     GO TO 220
260 REM
270 REM DATA: RECORD = NAME, ACCT. #, BALANCE
280     DATA "B. ADLER",3419,39.45
```

```
290      DATA "L. BEAM",7266,8.16
300      DATA "M. BERLE",1045,95.33
310      DATA "J. DONNE",3861,121.01
320      DATA "K. JANSKY",5482,25.25
330      DATA "A. MURRAY",9295,54.65
340      DATA "J. OORT",7334,15.75
350      DATA "G. RIPLEY",2710,170.99
360      DATA "N. WEBSTER",4527,105.06
9999     END


RUN


NAME            ACCOUNT        BALANCE

B. ADLER        3419           39.45
L. BEAM         7266           8.16
M. BERLE        1045           95.33
J. DONNE        3861           121.01
K. JANSKY       5482           25.25
A. MURRAY       9295           54.65
J. OORT         7334           15.75
G. RIPLEY       2710           170.99
N. WEBSTER      4527           105.06
?Out of data at line 230

Ready
```

Notice how the blank PRINT statement in line 210 separates the column headings from the rest of the table. ∎

When printing in columns like this, try to keep the length of each data item small enough to fit within its column field (to be safe, keep it less than 14 characters). Names, particularly, have a tendency to creep over the limit. There are techniques for handling this but, for the moment, try to avoid the problem by using abbreviations, for example by printing initials rather than first names. If you have to print a table that contains names of widely differing lengths and you do not want to abbreviate them, fill out the shorter ones with blank spaces so that, at least as character strings, they are all the same length. You may lose the use of one field, but the data will be printed in columns.

Examples

1.
```
10 REM   REPEAT
20               READ N$,W
30               PRINT N$,W
40       GO TO 10
50       DATA "SOLOMON",700
60       DATA "AUGUSTUS THE STRONG",365
70       DATA "JOSEPH SMITH",49
80       DATA "IKE WARD",16
9999     END
```

```
RUN

SOLOMON          700
AUGUSTUS THE STRONG            365
JOSEPH SMITH    49
IKE WARD        16
?Out of data at line 20

Ready
```

2.
```
10 REM    REPEAT
20                READ N$,W
30                PRINT N$,W
40        GO TO 10
50        DATA "SOLOMON           ",700
60        DATA "AUGUSTUS THE STRONG",365
70        DATA "JOSEPH SMITH       ",49
80        DATA "IKE WARD           ",16
9999      END
```

```
RUN

SOLOMON                700
AUGUSTUS THE STRONG    365
JOSEPH SMITH           49
IKE WARD               16
?Out of data at line 20

Ready
```

The second approach has the added advantage of making the DATA statements more readable.   ∎

4.5 STOPPING A LOOP: THE IF-THEN STATEMENT

The "out of data" message in the customer accounts program is a little untidy. However, there are many situations in which our inability to terminate the repetition of a program loop gracefully is a more serious problem.

Look at this program to keep a running total of numbers entered at the keyboard:

```
100 REM TITLE: SUBTOTALS FOR A LIST OF NUMBERS
110 REM PROGRAMMER: A. KITCHEN          DATE: 20-NOV-81
120 REM
130 REM VARIABLES:
140 REM         A = VALUE ENTERED
150 REM         S = SUBTOTAL OF VALUES ENTERED
160 REM
170 REM PROGRAM:
180     PRINT "TO CALCULATE SUBTOTALS, ENTER A"
190     PRINT "NUMBER AFTER EACH QUESTION MARK."
200     LET S = 0
```

```
210 REM REPEAT
220             PRINT "NUMBER";
230             INPUT A
240             LET S = S+A
250             PRINT "SUBTOTAL =";S
260      GO TO 210
9999     END
```

RUN

```
TO CALCULATE SUBTOTALS, ENTER A
NUMBER AFTER EACH QUESTION MARK.
NUMBER? 3
SUBTOTAL = 3
NUMBER? 115
SUBTOTAL = 118
NUMBER? 27
SUBTOTAL = 145
NUMBER? 93
SUBTOTAL = 238
NUMBER? ^C†
```

Ready

There is one slightly confusing step in this program. The statement

LET S = S+A

is the one that does all the work. Compare it with the counter discussed earlier in the chapter:

LET N = N+1

The principle is similar. Line 230 causes a question mark to be printed, after which the machine waits for the user to type a number. This is then stored in the variable A. Statement 240 now takes over: The right-hand side, S+A, causes the number in A to be added to the current value of S; then the rest of the statement places this new sum back in S. This is repeated indefinitely. Thus S keeps a record of the current subtotal as each number is entered at the keyboard. Before any numbers are entered from the terminal, the subtotal will be zero. This is, of course, the purpose of the first statement:

LET S = 0

Some systems automatically set all variables to zero at the beginning of a program but, whatever the case, it is a good precaution to include such a statement.

The program certainly works, but if we were using such a program to

---

†The BREAK key was pressed. This immediately terminated execution of the program.

sum a list of numbers, it would be more convenient and clearer if the intermediate subtotals were not printed: that is, if a run of the program looked
more like this:

```
RUN
TO CALCULATE TOTAL ENTER A
NUMBER AFTER EACH QUESTION MARK.
NUMBER? 3
NUMBER? 115
NUMBER? 27
NUMBER? 93
NUMBER? ^C
TOTAL IS 238
Ready
```

A naive solution to this problem might go as follows: Just move the PRINT
statement outside the REPEAT loop.

```
- - -             - - -
200           LET S = 0
210    REM  REPEAT
220            PRINT "NUMBER";
230            INPUT A
240            LET S = S+A
250           GO TO 210
260           PRINT "TOTAL IS";S
9999          END
```

BAD PROGRAM

Unfortunately, this doesn't work. The machine will continue to cycle
through the loop until BREAK is typed. At that point the computer will
stop execution of the program immediately. It never reaches statement 260,
so the total is not printed:

```
RUN
TO CALCULATE TOTAL, ENTER A
NUMBER AFTER EACH QUESTION MARK.
NUMBER? 3
NUMBER? 115
NUMBER? 27
NUMBER? 93
NUMBER? ^C
Ready
```

The solution we require cannot be produced with the statements that
we have at our disposal. We need to be able to signal to the system that we
have finished entering the data and would like it to print out the total. We
must decide on a signal and we also have to provide the means, within the

program, for the computer to be able to check for that signal and terminate the loop when it receives it.

When summing a list of numbers, one does not bother to include zero values in the list, as they contribute nothing to the sum. Thus we might consider using zero as the signal. That is, we could arrange that, when the digit 0 is typed in, the machine will stop accepting numbers and will print out the total, like this:

```
RUN
ENTER A NUMBER AFTER EACH QUESTION
MARK. TO GET TOTAL, ENTER ZERO.
NUMBER? 3
NUMBER? 115
NUMBER? 27
NUMBER? 93
NUMBER? 0
TOTAL IS 238
Ready
```

How can we instruct the machine to do this? Well, all that is necessary, beyond changing the instructions to the user, is to add one extra statement to the program that didn't work, as follows:

```
- - -            - - -
200        LET S = 0
210   REM  REPEAT
220            PRINT "NUMBER";
230            INPUT A
235            IF A = 0 THEN 260
240            LET S = S + A
250        GO TO 210
260        PRINT "TOTAL IS";S
9999       END
```

The new statement is, of course, in line 235. Read this statement as "If A = 0, then go to line 260." It works as follows. Each time through the loop, statements 220 and 230 print NUMBER? and the computer waits for a response from the terminal. Suppose that we type the value 35. The number 35 is stored in A and control moves to line 235, where the first part of the statement:

```
IF A = 0 THEN 260
```

compares the value of A with 0. Clearly, in this case it is not true that A = 0, so the second part is ignored: the machine does not go to 260. Instead, control passes to the next statement, line 240, where the contents of A are added to the subtotal. After this the statement GO TO 210 starts the process over again. On the other hand, if we type 0 in response to NUMBER?, the value 0 is stored in A. This time the relation A = 0 holds true, so control passes to line 260. As this jumps out beyond the statement

```
GO TO 210
```

the looping ends, the total is printed, and the program comes to a stop.

The number 0, which we type in to stop the loop, is an example of a **flag**, a special value which is used to signal to the machine that a change of control is to take place. We are free to choose the value for our flag; in fact, there may be situations in which 0 is not an appropriate one. Another approach is to pick a number that is unlikely to occur in the data and which looks distinctive, say 9999. If we were to use 9999 as a flag in the program, instead of 0, line 235 would have to be rewritten as

```
IF A = 9999 THEN 260
```

and, of course, the instructions would have to be changed, too. A typical run would look like this:

```
RUN
ENTER A NUMBER AFTER EACH QUESTION
MARK. TO GET TOTAL, ENTER 9999.
NUMBER? 71
NUMBER? 25
NUMBER? 149
NUMBER? 331
NUMBER? 9999
TOTAL IS 576
Ready
```

Each time through the REPEAT loop, after having executed statement 230 and transferred a number from the terminal to the variable A, statement 235 causes the contents of A to be compared with the number 9999. If they equal this value, the machine jumps to statement 260. Otherwise, control passes to the line following 235, that is, to statement 240. So the "GO TO 260" at line 235 implied by . . . THEN 260 is ignored and the loop repeated *until 9999 is typed in.* At that point, the machine executes the . . . THEN 260 and jumps out of the loop to print the sum and end the program.

This new statement is a special case of a general class of statements, which are referred to in BASIC as IF statements. We discuss this family in Chapter 5, but for the moment, the special case will be sufficient for our purposes. It has the form

```
IF variable = value THEN line-number
```

It behaves like a GO TO statement that switches on or off, depending on whether the variable in the statement has the given value or not.

You may have noticed that the equals sign in the IF statement plays a different role from the one in the LET statement. Its meaning is much closer to that of the equals sign in mathematics. For example, the statement IF A = 9999 THEN 260 does not store 9999 in A. It compares the value 9999 with the contents of A and takes action on the basis of this. The relation A = 9999 is either true or false: true when the two sides are equal; false when they are not.

The IF-THEN statement can be used with character string variables; however, in that case, the value to be tested must also be a character string.

Example

```
100  - - -
110  IF D$ = "DONE" THEN 350
120  - - -
```

In this program segment, if the variable D$ contains the string DONE when the computer executes line 110, the next statement to be processed will be at line 350. If D$ contains any other character string, the THEN part will be ignored and control will pass to line 120. ∎

We'll end by using the IF-THEN statement to put the finishing touch to the data processing program discussed earlier.

```
100 REM TITLE: TABLE OF CUSTOMER NAMES, ACCOUNT NUMBERS, BALANCES
110 REM PROGRAMMER: A. KITCHEN          DATE: 12-DEC-81
120 REM
130 REM VARIABLES:
140 REM          N$ = CUSTOMER NAME
150 REM          A = CUSTOMER ACCOUNT NUMBER
160 REM          B = BALANCE
170 REM
180 REM PROGRAM:
190      PRINT
200      PRINT "NAME","ACCOUNT","BALANCE"
210      PRINT
220 REM REPEAT
230            READ N$,A,B
235            IF N$ = "****" THEN 260
240            PRINT N$,A,B
250      GO TO 220
260 REM
270 REM DATA: RECORD = NAME, ACCT. #, BALANCE
280      DATA "B. ADLER",3419,39.45
290      DATA "L. BEAM",7266,8.16
300      DATA "M. BERLE",1045,95.33
310      DATA "J. DONNE",3861,121.01
320      DATA "K. JANSKY",5482,25.25
330      DATA "A. MURRAY",9295,54.65
```

```
340      DATA "J. OORT",7334,15.75
350      DATA "G. RIPLEY",2710,170.99
360      DATA "N. WEBSTER",4527,105.06
370      DATA "****",9999,9999
9999     END


RUN

NAME            ACCOUNT        BALANCE

B. ADLER         3419           39.45
L. BEAM          7266            8.16
M. BERLE         1045           95.33
J. DONNE         3861          121.01
K. JANSKY        5482           25.25
A. MURRAY        9295           54.65
J. OORT          7334           15.75
G. RIPLEY        2710          170.99
N. WEBSTER       4527          105.06

Ready
```

The last data record is obviously a dummy. The value ****, in the name field of this record, is used as a flag to terminate the REPEAT loop. Notice that, although we do not need the account number and balance fields for the IF-THEN statement, something has to be read into the variables A and B; otherwise, the computer will print an error message. It is natural to use obviously phoney data here, too, as that will make this final record stand out from the others.

Just one last comment on what we have developed. We introduced the IF-THEN statement so that we could stop a REPEAT loop in an orderly fashion. In each case that we have used it, the modification has had a similar form.

Examples

The path followed by the computer during execution is shown alongside each loop:

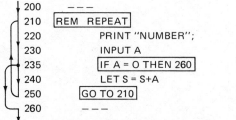

Exit from this loop when A = 0.

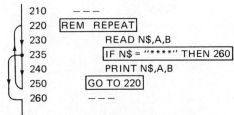

Exit from this loop when N$ = "****".

In each case we have added a statement that controls the order in which processing is done, that is, another **control statement.** These REPEAT loops are no longer endless; they can be stopped!

We will have more to say about this new form of the REPEAT loop in the next two chapters. I point it out now only to show the kinds of standardized logical structures that can occur in programming. We will take advantage of such patterns to help us develop a systematic method for designing and writing programs, but more than this, we will use them to organize the final written form of our programs for readability. The single most important lesson to learn in programming is that there is a monstrous difference between a program that just works and one that works *and* has the form and structure which makes it understandable to others. It is essential to keep in mind that a program must communicate with two audiences: computers and people. Computers require only that the logical flow of statements be correct. People demand an overall organization of structure, something to make the bare logic digestible.

The readability of a program can be improved by grouping its statements into blocks, each of which handles a well-defined task, rather in the way that a book is divided into chapters, paragraphs, and sentences. We will see that this analogy is better than it might, at first, appear because the blocks into which a program is divided may themselves be subdivided into yet smaller blocks for greater clarity.

4.6 SAVING A PROGRAM

This section is in the nature of an appendix. It doesn't really deal with programming so much as with the housekeeping that surrounds the writing of a program.

By now our programs are getting rather long. So that to have to retype a program each time one needs to use it is fast becoming an onerous chore. Yet you will already have noticed that when you sign off from the computer, your program is automatically erased. The same thing happens when you type the command NEW (or whatever your system requires, e.g., SCRATCH) before typing in a new program. The reason for this has to do with the design of the computer system.

Data and programs, currently being processed, are stored in the user's workspace in memory. Information can be transferred in and out of memory very fast. This is necessary to produce the speed and power that we associate with computers. However, this fast memory is expensive, so it is not economical to provide large amounts of it just for the long-term storage of programs and data. This job is handled by cheaper and slower storage media.

Two common forms of long-term storage are provided by **magnetic tape** and **magnetic disks.** A tape storage system is similar in principle to a tape deck for sound recording. In fact, many microcomputers use a regular cassette tape recorder. A disk storage system consists of a set of magnetic disks, which look a little like phonograph records but actually work on the same principle as magnetic tape. The capacity of such peripheral storage is usually thousands of times larger than that of main memory. The characters that form the program to be stored are coded as patterns of magnetic charges on the surface of the tape or disk. To retrieve this information, the electrical patterns are read and decoded into the characters they represent.

When you have finished working on a program but wish to save it for further use, you must transfer a copy of it to long-term storage. Later, when you want to run it again, you will be able to copy it from this storage area back into your workspace.

One way to understand the difference between memory and long-term storage is to think of memory as like a blackboard. It is used by everyone who uses the computer. Information stored there is constantly erased and rewritten by the system, as different programs are run. Long-term storage, on the other hand, is more like a file cabinet in which information is stored when it is not needed and from which it is retrieved when it is to be used or updated.

The procedures for transferring programs from one storage medium to another are not part of the BASIC language. The specific commands vary from machine to machine, but the principles are the same. We will illustrate the process with some of the commands available on the RSTS-E time-sharing system. Consult your manuals for details about yours.

Suppose that you have a program currently sitting in your workspace and you wish to save a copy of it in long-term storage (disk storage, say). Type

SAVE ●

This can be done at any time after you have written the program and before you log off or start to write another program.

Example

We wish to save a program called BEER. The following diagrams illustrate the procedure:

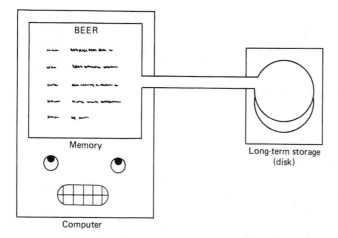

The program BEER in the workspace, before SAVE is typed.

<u>SAVE</u> ●

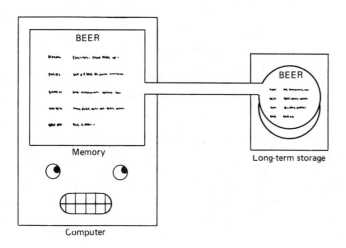

The situation after SAVE is typed.   ■

Notice that the command SAVE does not require the name of the program, because only a single program can fit in one's workspace at a time. The situation is different when it comes to retrieving a program from long-term storage. One may have a number of programs that have been saved at various times. To retrieve one of them, you must mention it by name.

Suppose that you wish to transfer a program called DOODLE from long-term storage to your workspace. Type

OLD DOODLE ●   (on some systems, GET DOODLE, on others, LOAD DOODLE)

The machine, after performing the transfer, prints

Ready

DOODLE is now in your workspace and you can list, run, and make changes to it, as you wish.

It is often necessary to save an unfinished program so that one can return to complete it at a later time. This can be handled in the way we have just discussed and, when the time comes to finish the project, the partially completed program can be retrieved for further editing by means of the OLD command. However, a problem arises on many systems when one attempts to save the updated program.

Example

OLD MESSY ●   The incomplete program, MESSY, is retrieved from your file space.
Ready
- - -   This represents an editing session in which additions and corrections
- - -   are made to the copy of MESSY in your workspace.
- - -
- - -
SAVE ●   The new version is saved.
File exists - - Rename/Replace

This message is warning you that there is already a program called MESSY in your file space (the old version of MESSY), so that you must either rename the program you are trying to save, or replace the one in your file space with the updated version. In any case, the new version has not been saved.   ■

To replace a program with an updated version, the old one must first be eliminated. On the RSTS-E time-sharing system the command for the deletion of a program is UNSAVE[†] (on many systems it is KILL). This example shows one technique.

[†]You don't have to be a poet to hate this one! . . . his wife.

Example

After the editing session on MESSY, type

<u>UNSAVE MESSY</u> ●	(or, perhaps, <u>KILL MESSY</u>)
Ready	This deletes the old version of MESSY from the disk.
<u>SAVE</u> ●	This transfers a copy of the updated version of
Ready	MESSY from the workspace to the disk. ■

Note that, although SAVE is the standard command on most systems for copying a BASIC program onto the disk, it may be interpreted in different ways by different systems. For example, on some, the command SAVE will automatically erase from the disk any program with the same name as the one to be saved, before saving the latter.

We have only covered the bare essentials here. Most systems provide many other useful commands for file management and housekeeping. Read your manuals.

Chapter 4: EXERCISES

Section 4.1

1.   What is printed when these programs are run?

(a)
```
10   PRINT "A"
20   GO TO 40
30   PRINT "B"
40   GO TO 70
50   PRINT "C"
60   GO TO 30
70   PRINT "D"
80   PRINT "E"
90   GO TO 60
999  END
```

(b)
```
10       LET N = 1
20       LET N = N+1
30  REM  REPEAT
40           PRINT N
50       GO TO 30
99       END
```

(c)
```
10       LET N = 1
20       LET E = 2
30  REM  REPEAT
40           PRINT N
50           LET N = N+E
60       GO TO 30
99  END
```

(d)
```
10       LET E$ = "*"
20  REM  REPEAT
30           PRINT E$
40           LET E$ = E$ + "*"
50       GO TO 20
99       END
```

(e)
```
10       LET N = 2
20  REM  REPEAT
30           PRINT N
40           LET N = N*2
50       GO TO 20
99       END
```

(f)
```
10       LET N = 2
20  REM  REPEAT
30           PRINT N
40           LET N = N*N
50       GO TO 20
99       END
```

(g)
```
10       PRINT "SHE LOVES ME"
20  REM  REPEAT
30           PRINT "SHE LOVES ME NOT"
40           PRINT "SHE LOVES ME"
50       GO TO 20
60       PRINT "HALLELUJAH!"
99       END
```

2.   (a)   Write a program that will print the phrase

THE LEITH POLICE DISMISSETH US

repeatedly, forever.

(b)   Write a program to print numbers, starting at 0 and increasing by 0.5. [*Hint: 0, 0.5, 1, 1.5, 2, etc.*]

(c)   Write a program to count down by tens from 1000. [*Hint: 1000, 990, 980, etc.*]

(d)   Write a program to print the square roots of the integers, 1, 2, 3, 4, and so on.

(e)   Here are two traditional ways of counting seconds:

1 CATERPILLAR	1 LITTLE SECOND
2 CATERPILLAR	2 LITTLE SECONDS
3 CATERPILLAR	3 LITTLE SECONDS
etc.	etc.

Write programs that count in each of these ways. The second will have to be a little more complicated. Why?

3.   Modify one of the programs in Exercise 2, 3, 4, or 5 of Section 3.4 so that they will repeatedly request and process new data, until stopped, say, by pressing the BREAK key. Your program should print some instructions, similar to those in the tax program in Chapter 3. However, these should not be repeated; that is, they should not be inside the RE-PEAT loop.

Section 4.2

1.   Identify which of these statements contain errors. Describe the errors.

(a)   READ A;B;C   (b)   GO TO END

(c)   INPUT A*B   (d)   READ 1.3,1.4,1.5,1.6

(e)   READ A,B,   (f)   DATA A,4.95,B,3.05

(g)   LET 3 = B   (h)   READ A = 7.9

(i)   INPUT X;Y   (j)   DATA: 7,9,24,6,

2.   What do these program segments do? Trace them by showing the contents of every variable after each instruction is processed. Show the printout as well.

(a)
```
10  DATA 3
20  READ A
30  DATA 6
40  READ B
50  DATA 18
60  PRINT A+B
99  END
```

(b)
```
10  READ A
20  READ B,C
30  DATA 2,3
40  PRINT A;B;C
50  DATA 1,4,5
99  END
```

(c)
```
10  REM  REPEAT
20           READ A,A
30           PRINT A;A
40       GO TO 10
```

(d)
```
10    READ A,B
20    PRINT A;B
30    RESTORE
40    READ C,D,E
```

```
50        DATA 1,2,3,5,7,11              50  PRINT C;D;E
60        DATA 13,17,19,23,29,31         60  RESTORE
99        END                           70  READ F,G,H,I
                                        80  PRINT F;G;H;I
                                        90    DATA 1.2, 3.4, 5.6
                                        999 END
```

3.   (a) Write a program to read the following dimensions of triangles from DATA statements and then to print the areas of the triangles.

Sides		
a	b	c
1	2	3
2	3	4
3	4	5
4	5	6
	etc.	

Use the formula

$$\text{Area} = \sqrt{s(s-a)(s-b)(s-c)}, \quad \text{where } s = \frac{a+b+c}{2}$$

(b) Modify the program in part (a) so that it accepts the data through an INPUT statement.

(c) Rewrite this program so that it uses neither READ nor INPUT statements. [*Hint: The performance of each of these three programs will be slightly different. In part (a) the program will stop when it runs out of DATA statements; in parts (b) and (c) it will only stop when the user types the BREAK key.*]

Section 4.3

1.   Show, exactly, the printout from these program segments.

(a)
```
10  PRINT 3,4;5
20  PRINT "3","4";"5"
30  PRINT "3";"4","5"
40  PRINT "3",,"4";;"5"
99  END
```

(b)
```
10  PRINT "MERELY","CORROBORATIVE","DETAIL"
20  PRINT "GIVING","ARTISTIC";"VERISIMILITUDE"
30  PRINT "TO AN OTHERWISE BALD","AND"
```

```
       40  PRINT "UNCONVINCING",
       50  PRINT "NARRATIVE"
       99  END
(c)    10        LET N = 1
       20  REM  REPEAT
       30            PRINT N," ",
       40            LET N=N+1
       50        GO TO 20
       99        END
(d)    100 REM  REPEAT
       110           READ A,B,C,D
       120           PRINT A,B,C
       130       GO TO 100
       140 REM  DATA:
       150       DATA 1,5,9
       160       DATA 2,6,10
       170       DATA 3,7,11
       180       DATA 4,8,12
       999       END
```

2. (a) The following are dates, in the given calendars, corresponding to A.D. 1900.

Calendar	Year Corresponding to A.D. 1900
Jewish	5660
Japanese	2560
Indian	1822
Mohammedan	1320

Write a program to print a five-column table of correspondences for the years from A.D. 1900 on. Do not use DATA statements.

(b) Write a program to print a conversion table from meters to feet, arshine (USSR), and ch'ih (China). The table should go from 0 to 1 in steps of 0.1 meter, from 1 to 10 in steps of 1 meter and from 10 to 100 in steps of 10 meters. These values will have to be read from DATA statements.

1 meter = 39.37 inches   1 arshine = 28 inches   1 ch'ih = 12.60 inches

Section 4.4

1. Write a program to print a table of student/teacher ratios for the colleges listed here.

College	Students	Faculty
Abilene Christian	4,372	175
Alma	1,250	75
Chadron State	1,954	90
DePaul	12,857	365
Edinboro State	5,596	384
Free Will Baptist Bible	600	26
Holy Names	654	48
Humbolt State	7,500	400
Johnson C. Smith	1,473	68
Lenoir-Rhyne	1,139	96
Peru State	765	52
St. Mary-in-the-Woods	350	50
Sul Ross State	2,161	81
Tennessee Temple	4,004	140
Walla Walla	2,010	125

[*Hint: The student/teacher ratio is the number of students divided by the number of teachers rounded to the nearest integer. As the names of these colleges are variable in length and some are very long, you will find that it is hard to get the columns to line up properly. One solution is to fill out the shorter names with blanks in the DATA statements. With very little modification this program could be used for other ratio calculations: for example, the calculation of population densities for the states, given their populations and areas.*]

2. Print a table of final grades for the following students, using this formula:

$$\text{Final grade} = \left[\frac{(\text{homework}/2) + \text{exam 1} + \text{exam 2} + 2*\text{final exam}}{\text{maximum possible grade}} \right] * 100$$

Round grades to the nearest 1%.

Student	Homework (150 pts.)	Exam 1 (100 pts.)	Exam 2 (100 pts.)	Final (100 pts.)
Baker, Norma J.	106	52	69	41
Crosby, Harry	112	75	36	62
Dukenfield, Claude W.	90	98	52	88
Gumm, Frances	129	86	84	91
King, Leslie L.	120	76	69	42
Konigsberg, Allen S.	113	74	83	94

Student	Homework (150 pts.)	Exam 1 (100 pts.)	Exam 2 (100 pts.)	Final (100 pts.)
Morrison, Marion	121	72	74	77
Pratt, William H.	143	95	100	97
Smith, Gladys	95	72	68	46
Sanford, John E.	133	99	80	78

[See the hint to Exercise 1.]

Section 4.5

1. What is wrong with this program, apart from its pitiful lack of documentation?

```
10            LET S = 0
20    REM  REPEAT
30            INPUT A
40            LET S = S+A
45            IF A = 9999 THEN 60
50         GO TO 20
60         PRINT "SUM=";S
9999       END
```

2. Describe exactly what each of these segments does when it is run. If in doubt, trace them by showing the value of N after each statement.

(a)
```
10         LET N = 1
20    REM  REPEAT
30            PRINT N
40            IF N = 5 THEN 9999
50            LET N = N+1
60         GO TO 20
9999       END
```

(b)
```
10         LET N = 1
20    REM  REPEAT
30            PRINT N
40            IF N = 1 THEN 9999
50            LET N = N+1
60         GO TO 20
9999       END
```

(c)
```
10         LET N = 1
20    REM  REPEAT
30            PRINT N
40            LET N = N+1
50            IF N = 5 THEN 9999
60         GO TO 20
9999       END
```

(d)
```
10         LET N = 1
20    REM  REPEAT
30            PRINT N
40            LET N = N+1
50            IF N = 1 THEN 9999
60         GO TO 20
9999       END
```

(e)
```
10         LET N = 1
20    REM  REPEAT
30            IF N = 5 THEN 9999
40            PRINT N
50            LET N = N+1
```

(f)
```
10         LET N = 1
20    REM  REPEAT
30            IF N = 1 THEN 9999
40            PRINT N
50            LET N = N+1
```

```
        60           GO TO 20              60         GO TO 20
        9999         END                  9999       END
(g)     10           LET N = 1
        20     REM   REPEAT
        30              LET N = N+1
        40              IF N = 5 THEN 9999
        50              PRINT N
        60           GO TO 20
        9999         END
```

3. Rewrite the summation program of this section to read numbers from DATA statements.

4. Write a program to accept numbers and to calculate their average.

5. The Greek mathematicians (notably the followers of Pythagoras) were interested in the geometric form of numbers. They were particularly intrigued by the squares:

and the triangular numbers:

Print a table of the first 50 square and triangular numbers. [*Hint: A very much more challenging exercise is to print the diagrams of these numbers. By the way, can you see any relationship between the two classes?*]

6. Print a table of the first 10 factorials:

$$1!, 2!, 3!, \ldots . 10!$$

[*Hint: Factorial n, written n!, is the product of the first n whole numbers; for example, 4! = 1 × 2 × 3 × 4.*]

7. There were 10 in the bed
And the little one said:
'Roll over, roll over!'
So they all rolled over
And one fell out.
There were 9 in the bed
And the little one said:

.

.

.

.

.

.

And one fell out.
There were none in the bed!

Write a program to print the whole of this rhyme (watch out for the last verse). Other simple counting songs (e.g., "99 bottles of beer") can be handled similarly. However, "Old MacDonald's Farm" and "The Twelve Days of Christmas" are a little more challenging (see Section 8.2, Exercise 12).

8. Print an amortization table showing the monthly installments required to pay off (liquidate or amortize) a mortgage over various time periods and at various percentage rates. The table should show the payments on a $1000 loan. Here is a suggested format for the table:

Years	Number of Payments	Monthly Payments per $1000 at:		
		9.75%	10%	10.25%
45				
40				
35				
30				
.				
.				
.				

If your terminal allows more columns, you can include a greater range of interest rates. [*Hint: The monthly payment is given by*

$$M = 1000 \left[\frac{I}{1 - (1 + I)^{-n}} \right]$$

where n = the total number of payments and I = the interest rate per payment period, written as a fraction = percentage interest rate/1200.]

9. Write a program to calculate the average (A) and the standard deviation (D) of a list of numbers. In a sense, the average measures the center of a range of values. The standard deviation is a measure of the spread of the data. For example, the value of A for each of the lists (7, 50, 96) and (49, 50, 54) is 51. However, D = 36.34 for the first and 2.16 for the second.

The formula for the standard deviation of a list of values is

$$D = \sqrt{\text{average of squared values} - \text{square of average value}}$$

[*Hint: Two quantities required for calculating A and D are (1) the sum of the values and (2) the sum of the squares. These can be calculated* *in the same REPEAT loop. Incidentally, in most statistical applications a slightly larger number is used as the standard deviation, namely $\sqrt{n/(n-1)}\ D$, where n is the number of values in the list.]*

Section 4.6

1.   Read your system manuals for information on other commands that aid in the editing and saving of programs.

Chapter

5

Decisions, Decisions

5.1 MAKING DECISIONS: THE RETURN OF IF-THEN

The greatest advantage that the computer enjoys over a simple hand calculator is its ability to make decisions. Put this way, it sounds impressive and
rather mysterious, as though we had trapped some kind of demon in a box.
The reality is more mundane. We have already seen some indication of this
ability in the IF-THEN statement discussed in Chapter 4. In this chapter we
expand on that introduction. Although the process we discuss is quite
simple, it is the one property of computers which, together with their speed,
gives them their unique abilities.

Here are a couple of runs of a little program:

```
RUN
I AM THINKING OF A NUMBER BETWEEN 1 AND 20
GUESS WHAT IT IS? 17
SORRY, BETTER LUCK NEXT TIME
Ready

RUN
I AM THINKING OF A NUMBER BETWEEN 1 AND 20
GUESS WHAT IT IS? 13
WELL DONE, YOU GOT IT!
Ready
```

Notice how the response depends on the number typed in. Here is a listing of the program:

```
100    REM  TITLE: GUESSING GAME
110    REM  PROGRAMMER: A. KITCHEN        DATE: 1-AUG-80
120    REM
130    REM  VARIABLES:
140    REM                 G = NUMBER GUESSED BY PLAYER
150    REM
160    REM  PROGRAM:
170         PRINT "I AM THINKING OF A NUMBER BETWEEN 1 AND 20"
180         PRINT "GUESS WHAT IT IS";
190         INPUT G
200    REM  THE SECRET NUMBER IS 13!!!
210         IF G = 13 THEN PRINT "WELL DONE, YOU GOT IT!"
220         IF G <> 13 THEN PRINT "SORRY, BETTER LUCK NEXT TIME."
9999        END
```

Apart from the symbols $<>$, which are used to denote **not equal**, the program is pretty easy to understand. Lines 210 and 220 involve another version of the IF statement. The way in which they are executed is very similar to that of the IF-THEN statement of Chapter 4. For example, if the value of G is 13, then the PRINT statement

```
PRINT "WELL DONE, YOU GOT IT!"
```

in line 210 is processed; otherwise, it is ignored by the computer. The PRINT statement in line 220 is processed under the opposite condition, namely if G takes any value *but* 13.

This is really a very dull little game, particularly when you realize that the number, 13, had to be decided upon beforehand and written into the program. I'm afraid we'll have to wait until later to see how to design more challenging games.

Here is another example; what does it do?

```
10    INPUT X
20    IF X < 0 THEN LET X = -X
30    PRINT X
9999  END
```

("$X < 0$" is read "X is less than zero.")

This segment, line 20 specifically, may seem a bit confusing, but remember, the machine has no innate ability to think. It just follows orders, one at a time. Intellectually, you are by far its superior, even if a little on the slow side, and you should have no trouble putting yourself in its shoes. The secret to understanding a program is to take it one step at a time, keeping a record of any changes that occur in the variables as you go. Let's try.

Imagine that you have typed RUN. The machine begins at statement 10, prints a question mark, and waits for your response. You now type in a number, suppose that it is 27, which is then stored in the variable X. Next, the machine processes line 20 and tests X to see if its contents are less than zero. They are not, so the rest of the statement is skipped. Finally, line 30 causes the value of X (i.e., 27) to be printed.

The process of following a program through, statement by statement, is called **tracing** the program. It is a useful technique when it is necessary to **debug** a program, that is, to search for errors or **bugs**.

Well, nothing much happened in the run we just completed. Clearly, the interesting case occurs when X is less than zero. Here is a more systematic trace:

Program	Trace
10 INPUT X	Machine prints "?"\user types –5\X $\boxed{-5}$ *
20 IF X < 0 THEN LET X = –X	Is X < 0? yes\LET X = –(–5)\X $\boxed{5}$
30 PRINT X	Machine prints 5
9999 END	

*The backslash, \, separates the steps in the processing of each statement.

Thus, when the value typed by the user is positive, the program just prints that same value. When the value typed in is negative, the program first changes its sign, then prints the resulting positive value. To summarize, the program prints the **absolute value**[†] of the number typed in. What would the program do if statement 20 read

    IF X < 0 THEN LET X = +X?

There is just one thing wrong with our discussion so far. Many systems do not support this new kind of IF statement. We will have more to say on this subject very soon but, meanwhile, study the following two program segments. Their performance is identical to the ones above and, although they are rather clumsy looking, they are guaranteed to work on any system that supports BASIC.

[†]Incidentally, BASIC provides a function, ABS(X), which performs the same operation. Try this:

    10   INPUT X
    20   PRINT ABS(X)
    9999 END

Examples

1.
```
170        PRINT "I AM THINKING OF A NUMBER BETWEEN 1 AND 20"
180        PRINT "GUESS WHAT IT IS";
190        INPUT G
200   REM  THE SECRET NUMBER IS 13!!!
210        IF G <> 13 THEN 220
215        PRINT "WELL DONE, YOU GOT IT!"
220        IF G = 13 THEN 9999
225        PRINT "SORRY, BETTER LUCK NEXT TIME."
9999       END
```

2.
```
10    INPUT X
20    IF X >= 0 THEN 30
25    LET X = –X
30    PRINT X
9999  END
```

("X > =0" is read "X is greater than or equal to zero.")   ∎

Try to trace their execution for a couple of different values of G (X, respectively). The IF statements used are very simple extensions of the statement introduced in Chapter 4.

5.2 RELATIONS

It is time that you were given all the details on the IF statements. First, here is the general pattern for the new IF-THEN statement:

IF *relation* THEN *any-legal-statement*

and here is the general pattern for the IF-THEN statement introduced in Chapter 4:

IF *relation* THEN *line-number*

These are some examples of what is meant by a **relation**:

$$A = 999, \quad X < 0, \quad G <> 13, \quad R = A*B,$$
$$N^2 < = 1000, \quad A+B > C+D, \quad Q\$ = "YES", \quad INT(A) < N$$

A relation consists of two **expressions** separated by one of the following:

=	meaning	"is equal to"
<	meaning	"is less than"

>	meaning	"is greater than"
< =	meaning	"is less than or equal to"
> =	meaning	"is greater than or equal to"
<>	meaning	"is not equal to"

An **expression** is any legal variable or value, or any legal combination of these using operators and functions. In fact, anything that is permissible on the right-hand side of a LET statement is legal on either side of a relation. This includes expressions involving character strings and string variables, but you'll get the full story on that situation in Chapter 9. Here are some examples of valid IF-THEN statements:

```
IF X < 0 THEN LET X = -X
IF R = A*B THEN PRINT "JOLLY GOOD SHOW."
IF Q$ = "YES" THEN GO TO 20
IF 10 < = N THEN IF N < 100 PRINT N;"IS A TWO DIGIT NUMBER."
```

The last one is a bit of a mouthful, but they all follow the rules. In each case, the statement following the IF-THEN clause is a legal BASIC statement in its own right. If the relation in the IF-THEN clause is true for the current values of the variables in it, then the statement in **boldface** is executed; otherwise, the statement is skipped. Test the last example with different values of N, say 5, 50, 500, to make sure that you understand the process. I personally don't like to use IF-THEN statements nested in this way. Here is another approach that has the same effect, and, I think, reads more clearly.

```
IF (10 < = N) and (N < 100) THEN PRINT N; "IS A TWO DIGIT NUMBER,"†
```

One can combine and modify relations by means of the three logical operators:

```
AND    OR    NOT
```

For example, $(10 <= N)$ AND $(N < 100)$ is true if N is both greater than equal to 10 and less than 100. The operator OR is used similarly and NOT is used to negate a relation. For example, NOT(Q$ = "YES") is the same as Q$ <> "YES".†

Examples

1.   IF G*G < 4 THEN PRINT G

Suppose that G is 1.5; then G*G = 2.25, so that "G * G < 4" is true. In this case the value of G is printed.

---

†Read the relation as "ten is less than or equal to N and N is less than one hundred."
†For more on AND, OR, and NOT, see Appendix II.

If G is 2, then G*G = 4 and "G*G < 4" is false. The value of G is not printed.

2.   IF (10 < =N) AND (N < 100) THEN PRINT N;"IS A TWO DIGIT NUMBER".

Imagine that N is 7. This means that "10 <= N" is false, so it is not true that "(10 <= N) AND (N < 100)"; therefore, nothing is printed.

On the other hand, suppose that N = 41.5. Notice that both "10 <= N" and "N < 100" are true. That is, "(10 <= N) AND (N < 100)" is true, so the sentence

41.5 IS A TWO DIGIT NUMBER.

is printed. Beware: The fact that this assertion is actually false is quite beside the point. That is the fault of the programmer for not designing the test (relation) carefully enough.   ∎

The discussion applies equally well to the more elementary form of IF-THEN. The following are also valid IF-THEN statements:

```
IF B > INT(B) THEN 750
IF (A >= 0) OR (B >= 0) THEN 510
IF NOT (R = A*B) THEN 320
IF R$ = "NO" THEN 9999
```

In this case the IF-THEN clause is followed by a line number. Control jumps to this line of the program if the relation holds; otherwise, control passes to the next line of the program following the IF-THEN statement.

Example

```
- - -
480   IF (A >= 0) OR (B >= 0) THEN 510
490   PRINT "THEY ARE BOTH NEGATIVE."
- - -
```

If A = 3.5 and B = –1.5, then "A >= 0" is true and "B >= 0" is false. Because at least one of them is true, "(A >= 0) OR (B >= 0)" is also true, so control jumps to line 510 and all the statements between lines 480 and 510 are skipped.

On the other hand, if A = –3.5 and B = –1.5, then neither "A >= 0" nor "B >= 0" is true; therefore, "(A >= 0) OR (B >= 0)" is false. This time control passes to line 490 and

THEY ARE BOTH NEGATIVE.

is printed.   ∎

5.3 THE THREE IFS

Here is an historical summary of the whole IF business. The earliest versions of BASIC had only one form of the IF statement:

1.   IF *relation* THEN *line-number*

Your system may only allow this one. We will see that actually this suffices for all applications. It does, however, lead to less readable code in some situations. In later versions of the language a more general form of the statement was introduced:

2.   IF *relation* THEN *statement*

Finally, some systems have added a variant of (1), namely:

3.   IF *relation* GO TO *line-number*

The forms (1) and (3) are interchangeable on a system that provides both. In fact, forms 1 to 3 give us three ways of doing exactly the same thing.

Example

These are all identical in action:

```
IF A = 999 THEN 70
IF A = 999 THEN GO TO 70
IF A = 999 GO TO 70
```
                                                                                     ∎

When I need a conditional jump in one of my own programs, I tend to use type 3. It is distinctive just because it doesn't use THEN. I feel it is helpful to alert a reader to any jumps that do take place in a program, because jumping out of the normal order of things is what makes a program hard to understand. It is often at such points that errors creep in. However, my wife, who typed this manuscript, hates IF-GO TO and says that the IF-THEN forms are much better aesthetically. She is a poet and I accept her judgment in such matters, so in this text no further mention will be made of IF-GO TO.

On a more serious note: You should be aware that only type 1, the "jumping" IF-THEN, is available in **all** versions of BASIC. So although there are many good arguments for the use of the others, if you want to become a versatile BASIC programmer, and if you want your programs to be **transportable,**[†] you should make a practice of using only this form of the IF statement.

In commenting on the first form of the IF statement I mentioned that it is powerful enough to handle all situations for which IF statements are required. Let's look at how the "nonjumping" IF can be replaced by the jumping IF. We touched on this briefly in Section 5.1. Here is another example:

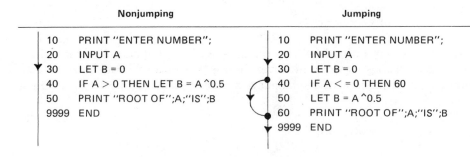

Nonjumping		Jumping	
10	PRINT "ENTER NUMBER";	10	PRINT "ENTER NUMBER";
20	INPUT A	20	INPUT A
30	LET B = 0	30	LET B = 0
40	IF A > 0 THEN LET B = A^0.5	40	IF A < = 0 THEN 60
50	PRINT "ROOT OF";A;"IS";B	50	LET B = A^0.5
9999	END	60	PRINT "ROOT OF";A;"IS";B
		9999	END

In both segments, if A is positive, then B is calculated to be the square root of A. If A is negative or zero, then B is set to zero. In the nonjumping version, LET B = A ^ 0.5 is executed only if A > 0, so it is skipped if A < = 0. In the jumping version, we have to program an active leap over the statement LET B = A ^ 0.5 when A < = 0. Alongside each segment is drawn the path (or paths) that the machine takes through it.

Thus, in translating a nonjumping IF, in other words, the pattern

```
---
---
IF relation THEN statement
---
---
```

we have to reverse our viewpoint. We now want to jump over the statement if the relation is not true. Roughly speaking:

```
---
---
IF NOT (relation) THEN skip next statement
statement
---
---
```

[†]Capable of being run on any system that can execute BASIC programs.

Example

```
310   IF R = A*B THEN PRINT "JOLLY GOOD SHOW."
```

becomes

```
310   IF R <> A*B THEN 320
315   PRINT "JOLLY GOOD SHOW."
```

or, equivalently,

```
310   IF NOT (R = A*B) THEN 320
315   PRINT "JOLLY GOOD SHOW."
```
■

As with the REPEAT loop this is a situation in which the straight-line flow through the program is disturbed and, again, this can be confusing to anyone trying to read the BASIC code (possibly even you, the programmer). So when we use the jumping IF to translate the nonjumping form, we will signal its presence with a little decoration, like this:

```
10            PRINT "ENTER NUMBER";
20            INPUT A
30            LET B = 0
40            IF NOT (A > 0) THEN 60
50                LET B = A^0.5
60    REM   ENDIF
70            PRINT "ROOT OF";A;"IS";B
9999          END
```

We indent the statement that is to be executed if the relation holds and we add the remark

```
REM   ENDIF
```

The computer jumps to this statement if the relation in the IF statement is false. In other words, this:

```
mm            IF relation THEN statement
```

translates into this:

```
mm            IF NOT (relation) THEN pp
nn                statement
pp    REM   ENDIF
```

where mm, nn, and pp stand for line numbers. As in the case of the REPEAT loop, we'll refer to the IF statement and ENDIF as control statements to emphasize that they handle the flow of the program as opposed to calculation.

Example

```
310         IF NOT (R = A*B) THEN 317
315                 PRINT "JOLLY GOOD SHOW."
317 REM  ENDIF
```

If this seems a long-winded approach to you, don't judge it by the effort involved in writing it. After some experience with writing longer programs, you won't begrudge the few extra seconds it takes to indent and add REM ENDIF. Programs can be very difficult to read and yet they MUST be read.[†] They have to be proofread and corrected and later, perhaps, updated. All this requires a complete understanding of the code: therefore, every effort must be made to clarify the logical structure. Indenting and the use of appropriate remarks can help alert the reader to disturbances in the flow (leaps and loops).

5.4 A PROGRAMMING PROJECT

The programming examples that we have tackled so far have hardly challenged the capabilities of the BASIC language. Let's look at a slightly more ambitious programming project. This will lead us close to some of the problems that arise as such projects get more complex. As programs get longer and more involved, they become harder to write and, what is perhaps even more important, harder to read. We must study the whole business of program development and train ourselves to take care over every step in this process.

Suppose that we have data on a college class stored in the computer. By the way, we will have to handle this by putting the data into DATA statements. In the long run, this is not very efficient or flexible and, in practice, the data would be stored in a file. However, that is the subject of Chapter 11. We'll assume that the data look like this:

```
REM  DATA: RECORD = STUDENT NAME, GRADE (111 = WITHDRAWN)
     DATA "ADAMS, H.", 97
     DATA "BENTHAM, J.", 63
     DATA "DISRAELI, B.", 111
```

[†]If God hadn't wanted us to read them, He wouldn't have given us words like PRINT, LET, IF, THEN, and END.

```
DATA "FOX, U.", 78
• • •
• • •
DATA "***", 999
```

The code 111 is used to indicate a student who has withdrawn from the class and a dummy record ("***", 999) is used to flag the end of the data.

We are to write a program that prints a list of those currently enrolled in the class, with their grades, and prints out the class average at the end. Thus the program must cause the computer to read each record in turn and determine whether the student is enrolled or withdrawn. If the student has withdrawn, nothing is done. If the student is still enrolled, the data must be printed and the appropriate calculations made in order to determine the average. Now:

$$\text{Average grade} = \frac{\text{sum of grades of students enrolled}}{\text{number of students enrolled}}$$

The top line of the quotient is evaluated by a summing procedure like the one discussed in Chapter 4. As the data do not include the number of students enrolled, a counter will be required in order to calculate the bottom line. Here is a more precise description of the steps required:

Repeat (A) and (B) until student's name = "***".
(A)   Read a record consisting of student's name and grade.
(B)   If grade is not 111 then do (B1), (B2), (B3).
    (B1)   Add grade to grade total.
    (B2)   Add one to student counter, to count this student.
    (B3)   Print out student's name and grade.

When finished with all student records, divide grade total by student counter to give average grade.
Print average grade.
Stop.

We have missed a couple of steps: for example, setting the grade total and student counter to zero, initially, and printing a heading for the table. It might also be a good idea to round the average grade to, say, one decimal place. Here is a more formal version of the description. I have spruced it up a bit and underlined those parts of the description that seem to refer to variables. Notice how the boxes divide the description into pieces which are roughly equivalent to BASIC statements. For greater clarity the parts of the program that are subject to the "repeat" and "if" clauses are indented.

Documentation
Print "Grade list for students enrolled in MTH 115"
Print "Name", "Grade"
Set grade total and student counter to zero
Repeat (A) and (B) until student's name = "****"
(A) Read student's name, grade
(B) If grade <> 111 then do (B1), (B2), (B3)
(B1) Add grade to grade total
(B2) Add one to student counter
(B3) Print student's name, grade
Divide grade total by student counter to give average grade
Print average grade rounded to one decimal place
Data
Stop

From this format it is quite easy to translate the description into a BASIC program. We will use the following names for the variables:

T = grade total
S = student counter
$N\$$ = student's name
G = grade
A = average grade = T/S

The instruction for adding a grade to the grade total will be LET $T = T+G$ and the student counter will be increased by the statement LET $S = S+1$. Here is an unpolished and undocumented translation of the description into BASIC. I have left room for documentation at the beginning.

```
200     PRINT "GRADE LIST FOR STUDENTS ENROLLED IN MTH 115"
210     PRINT "NAME","GRADE"
220     PRINT
230     LET T = 0
240     LET S = 0
250 REM REPEAT
```

```
260              READ N$,G
270              IF N$ = "***" THEN 320
280              IF G <> 111 THEN LET T = T+G
290              IF G <> 111 THEN LET S = S+1
300              IF G <> 111 THEN PRINT N$,G
310       GO TO 250
320       LET A = T/S
330       PRINT
340       PRINT "CLASS AVERAGE IS"; INT(A*10 + 0.5)/10
350 REM
1000 REM DATA: RECORD = STUDENT NUMBER,GRADE (111=WITHDRAWN)
1010      DATA "ADAMS, H.",97
1020      DATA "BENTHAM, J.",63
1030      DATA "DISRAELI, B.",111
1040      DATA "FOX, U.",78
1050      DATA "MUNRO, H.",71
1060      DATA "FAIRFIELD, C.",85
1070      DATA "BRONSTEIN, L.",82
1080      DATA "BURKE, M.",68
1090      DATA "GRAHAM, F.",71
1100      DATA "KAPELHOFF, D.",74
2000      DATA "***",999
9999      END
```

The control statements in the REPEAT loop are underlined to emphasize the steps that must be taken from the informal instruction:

Repeat (A) and (B) until student's name = "***"

to its interpretation in BASIC. In writing the BASIC program from the description, the only decision that had to be made concerned where to put the statement

IF N$ = "***" THEN 320

In this case the only reasonable place was right after the READ statement, so that the dummy record ("***", 999) would be caught before it did any damage.

The block of IF statements 280, 290, and 300 reads quite clearly. However, this approach could become rather clumsy if there were many more than three statements to be processed conditionally. The solution to such a problem is to use the jumping form of the IF statement. In this case:

```
280  IF G <> 111 THEN LET T = T+G
290  IF G <> 111 THEN LET S = S+1
300  IF G <> 111 THEN PRINT N$, G
```

would be rewritten as

```
275              IF G = 111 THEN 305
280                  LET T = T+G
```

```
290                LET S = S+1
300                PRINT N$,G
305  REM  ENDIF
```

Either way, the computer skips 280, 290, and 300 if G = 111, and executes them if G <> 111. Notice the use of indentation and the remark REM ENDIF to give a visual clue as to which statements are to be skipped. Make sure that you line up ENDIF directly below the initial IF. This is a straightforward extension of the technique introduced in the preceding section. The statements will look like this when inserted in the REPEAT loop:

```
250  REM  REPEAT
260            READ N$,G
270            IF N$ = "***" THEN 320
275            IF G = 111 THEN 305
280                LET T = T+G†
290                LET S = S+1†
300                PRINT N$, G†
305  REM      ENDIF
310            GO TO 250
```

This segment illustrates an important point. Notice that it contains two separate IF statements. This one:

```
IF G = 111 THEN 305
```

controls the execution of the block consisting of the lines 280, 290, and 300, and to show this we have indented these statements. On the other hand, the statement

```
IF N$ = "***" THEN 320
```

is not part of an IF block. It controls the REPEAT loop, stopping the looping process when N$ = "***". It is important to understand the difference in the roles played by these two IF statements. Notice, in particular, that the statements following

```
IF N$ = "***" THEN 320
```

are not indented.

---

†These statements are double indented because they are part of an IF block which is, itself, part of a REPEAT loop.

To complete this section we'll sketch the run of this program.

```
RUN
NAME              GRADE

ADAMS, H.         97
BENTHAM, J.       63
FOX, U.           78
- - -             - - -
CLASS AVERAGE IS 79.3
Ready
```

5.5 IF BLOCKS

The decision on how to write a block of statements which are to be processed when a certain condition holds is one of style. If the **IF block** is small, say just a couple of statements, each statement in the block can be written as a nonjumping IF. Otherwise, a jumping IF statement, which skips the block when the condition is not satisfied, is preferable. Of course, if your system does not support the nonjumping form, you have no choice.

The translation from an informal IF block to the final BASIC code is quite automatic. Suppose that we have the following segment:

```
If (relation) then do (A), (B), (C), (D)
    (A) Statement A
    (B) Statement B
    (C) Statement C
    (D) Statement D
```

This can be translated as:

```
mm          IF NOT (relation) THEN ss
nn              Statement A
pp              Statement B
qq              Statement C
rr              Statement D
ss    REM  ENDIF
```

where mm, nn, pp. qq, rr, and ss are line numbers. All we have done is to skip the statements if the condition is false. In the example in the preceding section, the instruction

```
IF NOT (G < > 111) THEN 305
```

was rather hard to read, so I chose to write it as

```
IF G = 111 THEN 305
```

instead. However, in many cases, the NOT version may emphasize more clearly that the given statements are to be skipped if the condition fails to hold.

Example

```
- - -
200   IF A > 0 THEN LET B = A ^0.5
210   IF A > 0 THEN LET S = S+B
- - -
```

is equivalent to:

```
- - -
200          IF NOT (A > 0) THEN 230
210                LET B = A ^0.5
220                LET S = S+B
230  REM  ENDIF
- - -
```

◼

The next example shows a simple but useful type of IF block. As we have already seen, a recurring problem in program design concerns the inclusion of documentation for the user. The first time a person uses a given program, an explanation of what to enter as well as a clear description of the output is required. However, after a couple of runs this explanation becomes unnecessary and irritating. We can solve this problem now by using an IF block to allow the user to skip the instructions.

Example

```
- - -
200          PRINT "INSTRUCTIONS (Y OR N)";
210          INPUT R$
```

```
220        IF R$ = "N" THEN 270
230                PRINT "ENTER EACH NUMBER AFTER"
240                PRINT "THE QUESTION MARK AND PRESS"
250                PRINT "RETURN.  WHEN DONE, ENTER"
260                PRINT "9999."
270  REM   END IF
- - -
```

RUN
INSTRUCTIONS (Y OR N)? Y
ENTER EACH NUMBER AFTER
THE QUESTION MARK AND PRESS
RETURN. WHEN DONE, ENTER
9999.
? 17.3
? 29.25
- - -
etc.

RUN
INSTRUCTIONS (Y OR N)? N
? 93.72
? 58
- - -
etc.   ■

Chapter 5: EXERCISES

Section 5.1

1. Trace the following program segments when each of the given values is typed in. You don't have to describe every detail. It is enough to show the contents of the variables after each statement, the results of the decisions (IF statements), and the printout.

(a)
```
10    INPUT X
20    IF X < 0 THEN LET X = +X
30    PRINT X
9999  END
```
for X = 5, –5

(b)
```
10    INPUT N
20    PRINT "THIS NUMBER IS";
30    IF N = 0 THEN PRINT " ZERO."
40    IF N = 1 THEN PRINT " ONE."
9999  END
```
for N = 0, 0.5, 1, 2

(c)
```
10    INPUT N
20    PRINT "THIS NUMBER IS";
30    IF N = 1 THEN 50
40    PRINT " ZERO."
50    IF N = 0 THEN 9999
60    PRINT " ONE."
9999 END
```
for N = 0, 0.5, 1, 2

(d)
```
10    INPUT N
20    PRINT "THIS NUMBER IS";
30    IF N = 0 THEN LET N = N+1
40    IF N = 1 THEN PRINT " ONE."
9999  END
```
for N = –1, 0, 1, 2

(e)
```
10    INPUT N
20    IF N = 1 THEN LET N = N+1
30    IF N = 2 THEN LET N = N+1
40    IF N = 3 THEN LET N = N+1
50    PRINT N
9999  END
```
for N = 0, 1, 2, 2.5, 3, 4, 5

(f)
```
10    INPUT N
20    IF N <> 1 THEN 60
30    IF N <> 2 THEN 60
40    IF N <> 3 THEN 60
50    LET N = N+1
60    PRINT N
9999  END
```
for N = 0, 1, 2, 2.5, 3, 4, 5

What happens if you reverse the order of the three IF statements in part (e)?

2. Write a program that will accept two numbers and then print SAME if they are equal, and DIFFERENT if they are not.

3. (a) Write a program that will accept a single-digit number and then print its name: for example, a typical RUN:

```
RUN
TYPE A DIGIT? 3
THIS IS THREE
Ready
```

(b) Write a program that will accept a positive three-digit whole number and will print the names of its digits: for example, a typical RUN:

RUN
TYPE AN INTEGER? 294
ITS DIGITS ARE: TWO NINE FOUR
Ready

[Hint: This is appreciably harder than 3(a). You will need functions to truncate to the 100s and to the 10s; see Section 3.3, Exercises 1 and 3(a). Then you will have to extract the digits from these (e.g., from 294, 94, 4 you must extract 2, 9, 4). Once your program is running correctly, try entering one- and two-digit numbers. What happens when you enter a negative number?]

(c) Modify the program in part (b) to handle positive and negative numbers by printing MINUS in front of the digits of a negative number.

Section 5.2

1. Identify which of these statements contain errors. Describe the errors.
   (a) IF Z4 > B PRINT "ZEE FOUR IS BIG"
   (b) IF "END" THEN GO TO 990
   (c) GO TO B
   (d) IF 10 <= N < 100 THEN PRINT N;"IS A TWO DIGIT NUMBER."
   (e) IF INPUT A = 999 THEN 990
   (f) IF X < 0 THEN X = 0
   (g) IF X < 0 THEN X < 0
   (h) REPEAT UNTIL A = 0
   (i) PRINT Y <> 0
   (j) DATA "P"," > ","Q"
   (k) IF N = 0 OR 1 THEN N = N+1

2. (a) Describe the output of this program segment when the given values are typed in for A, B, and C.

   ```
   10    INPUT A,B,C
   20    IF A < B THEN IF B < C THEN PRINT "FI"
   30    IF A < B THEN IF A < C THEN PRINT "FO"
   40    IF A < B THEN IF A > C THEN PRINT "FUM"
   9999  END
   ```

   (i) 5, 3, 7   (ii) 5, 7, 3   (iii) 3, 7, 5   (iv) 3, 5, 7

   (b) Rewrite this segment without using IF statements "nested" in this way.

   (c) Rewrite it using IF statements of the form: IF relation THEN line number.

3. Describe the output of the following segment when the given values are typed in for X, Y, and R.

```
10    INPUT X,Y,R
20    LET L = R^2
30    LET D = X^2 + Y^2
40    IF L <> D THEN 9999
50    PRINT "CONTACT"
9999  END
```

(a) 4, 11, 12   (b) 5, 12, 13   (c) 6, 13, 14

[*Hint: We could get the same effect if we replaced lines 20, 30 and 40 with*

```
20   IF R^2 <> X^2 + Y^2 THEN 9999
```

However, in the interests of readability, it is better to evaluate long expressions in LET statements and to keep the relations in the IF statements as simple as possible.]

4. Describe the output of each of the following when the given values are typed in for A and B.

```
(a)   10    INPUT A,B
      20    IF (A = 1) AND (B = 1) THEN PRINT "AMBOS"
      9999  END

(b)   10    INPUT A,B
      20    IF (A = 1) OR (B = 1) THEN PRINT "ALGUM"
      9999  END

(c)   10    INPUT A,B
      20    IF NOT ((A = 1) OR (B = 1)) THEN PRINT "NENHUM"
      9999  END
```

```
(d)   10    INPUT A,B          (e)   10    INPUT A,B
      20    IF A <> 1 THEN 9999       20    IF A = 1 THEN 40
      30    IF B <> 1 THEN 9999       30    IF B = 1 THEN 40
      40    PRINT "AMBOS"             40    PRINT "SEMPRE"
      9999  END                       9999  END
```

(i) 0, 0   (ii) 0, 1   (iii) 1, 0   (iv) 1, 1

Can you write a simpler IF statement with the same effect as the one in part (c)? [*Hint: You must experiment with the operators AND, OR, and NOT. I have not provided much information on them in this chapter.*]

5. Discuss the performance of these program segments and compare them with the one in Section 5.1, Exercise 1(e).

```
10    INPUT N
20    IF (N=1) OR (N=2) OR (N=3) THEN LET N = N+1
30    PRINT N
9999  END
```

```
10    INPUT N
```

```
20    IF (1<=N) AND (N<=3) THEN LET N = N+1
30    PRINT N
9999  END
```

6. (a) Write a program that accepts any two distinct numbers and prints them in increasing order.

   (b) Write a program that accepts any three distinct numbers and prints them in increasing order. [*Hint: You may find you have to use as many as six IF statements in part (b). It is possible that if you extended your solution to handle 10 numbers, it would require up to 3,628,800 IFs. There are better ways. The sorting of data into some standard order is a major concern of computer scientists. It is difficult to design programs that sort efficiently. Consequently, the methods that have been developed are quite complicated.*]

   (c) Design a solution to part (b) which uses as few IF statements as possible. The minimum is three jumping IF statements; see Section 5.3. [*Hint: This is not trivial. However, the resulting program should be quite a simple one.*]

Section 5.3

1. Rewrite these segments using only the jumping form of the IF statement, that is, IF relation THEN line number.

   (a)
```
10    INPUT X,Y
20    IF X > Y THEN PRINT Y;X
9999  END
```

   (b)
```
10    INPUT N
20    PRINT "THIS NUMBER IS ";
30    IF N = 0 THEN PRINT "ZERO."
40    IF N = 1 THEN PRINT "ONE."
9999  END
```

   (c)
```
10    INPUT N
20    IF N = 1 THEN LET N = N+1
30    IF N = 2 THEN LET N = N+1
40    IF N = 3 THEN LET N = N+1
50    PRINT N
9999  END
```

   In each case, check that the performance of your translation is identical to that of the original.

2. Rewrite these using the jumping form of the IF statement and without using the operators NOT, AND, and OR.

   (a)
```
10    INPUT A,B
20    IF (A=1) AND (B=1) THEN PRINT "AMBOS"
9999  END
```

   (b)
```
10    INPUT A,B
20    IF (A=1) OR (B=1) THEN PRINT "ALGUM"
9999  END
```

(c)   10   INPUT N
       20   IF (N=1) OR (N=2) OR (N=3) THEN LET N = N+1
       30   PRINT N
       9999 END

[*Hint: You will need more than one IF statement and perhaps a GO TO statement.*]

Section 5.4

The structure of these programs is similar to the example discussed in this section. Each consists principally of a REPEAT loop which controls the reading, or input, of data. Inside this, a group of IF statements (IF block) performs operations that depend on the values of the data.

1.   Salesmen for the Ceausescu Calliope Company receive a base salary of $1000 per month. In addition, they earn a 4.75% commission on the amount of sales above $5000 per month. For the following salesmen, print a table showing their individual earnings for November 1981.

C.C.C. Sales for November 1981

Salesman	Sales ($)
Thibault, A.	4,250
Peshkov, A.	7,185
Ulyanov, V.	6,010
Poquelin, J.	6,530
Slye, L.	5,500
Beyle, M.	3,900
Cream, A.	15,895
Robusti, J.	9,415
Scicolone, S.	5,950
Herzog, E.	4,995

2.   Write a program that reads the following data on Vermont towns and prints a table of those whose populations have decreased from 1970 to 1980, together with their percentage decreases over that period, rounded to 1/10 of 1 percent.

Town	Population	
	1970	1980
Barre	10,209	10,004
Bennington	14,586	15,772
Brattleboro	12,239	11,880

	Population	
Town	**1970**	**1980**
Burlington	38,633	37,135
Colchester	8,776	12,624
Essex	10,951	14,418
Essex Junction	6,511	7,770
Montpelier	8,609	8,059
Rutland	19,293	18,427
St. Albans	8,082	7,392
South Burlington	10,032	10,690
Springfield	10,063	10,180
Winooski	7,309	7,300

3. Here is a table describing a selection of harpsichords, virginals, and otta-vinos built by Hans Ruckers the Younger.

Date	Type	Keyboards	Range (Octaves)	Present Location
1599	H	2	5	Halle
1604	V	1	4	Brussels
1610	VO	2	4.5	Brussels
1614(?)	V	1	4	Brussels
1614	H	2	5	Destroyed (WW II)
ND	V	1	4	Brussels
ND	H	2	5	South America(?)
1618	O	1	4	Paris
1619	HO	3	4.5	Brussels
1622	V	1	4.5	New York
1627	H	2	5	New Haven
1629	H	1	4.75	Antwerp
1636	H	2	5	Geneva
1637	H	1	4.75	Edinburgh
1642	V	1	4	Stockholm
1642	H	2	4.5	New York
ND	HO	2	4	Berlin

Write a program that will print a table of all instruments with a given number of keyboards and with a range less than or equal to a specified value. Both these values are to be typed in by the user. [*Note: The Ruckers family, of Antwerp, were famous Belgian harpsichord makers of the early seventeenth century. The virginal was a small, usually rectangular, harpsichord. The ottavino was smaller and was pitched an octave higher. The double-letter codes, HO and VO, refer to "Mother and child" instruments; it was common to incorporate an ottavino into the side of a larger instrument.*]

4. Write a program to give a student a mathematics quiz, consisting of a fixed number of questions of a given type (say, multiplication problems). The program will print each question and accept the student's answer. It will keep track of the number of correct responses (also printing RIGHT or WRONG as appropriate) and will print a percentage grade at the end. The data for the questions should be stored in DATA statements. [*Hint: By the way, this program need not be restricted to math problems. Any kind of "objective" quiz can be given in this way. For simplicity, it is best to restrict the student's responses to yes/no, multiple choice, or one-word answers. Later we will see how we can program the machine to generate its own questions or to retrieve them from data files stored in magnetic disk storage.*]

Section 5.5

1. Translate each of these groups of statements into IF blocks, each controlled by a jumping IF statement.

    (a) 200 IF P > 0 THEN LET T = T+P
         210 IF P > 0 THEN LET S = S+P*P
         220 IF P > 0 THEN PRINT S/T

    (b) 200 IF X > T THEN PRINT "THIS VALUE IS TOO LARGE,"
         210 IF X > T THEN PRINT "PLEASE TYPE ANOTHER VALUE."
         220 IF X <= T THEN LET L = X/T
         230 IF X <= T THEN INPUT Y,Z
         240 IF X <= T THEN LET P = Y*(1–L)+Z*L

    (c) 200 IF A < B THEN INPUT C
         210 IF A < B THEN IF B < C THEN L = (B–A)*(B–A)
         220 IF A < B THEN IF B < C THEN C = L/(C–A)+A
         230 IF A < B THEN PRINT C

2. Modify Exercise 3 or 4 of Section 5.4 to include optional instructions to the user.

Chapter

6

Program Design

6.1   THE IMPORTANCE OF GOOD DESIGN

The bane of the computing world today is the proliferation of badly designed software. Programs that have been poorly written in the first place
are often modified and patched until any understanding or analysis of their
code is nearly impossible. The greatest danger in all of this is that, in a given
program, a well-hidden **bug** (programming error) could, at any time, rear its
ugly head and cause the program to come to a sudden halt, or **crash**, as it is
referred to in the computing business. Perhaps what is worse, in such circumstances, is that the program may not crash at all but may instead print out
erroneous information. The trouble is that in any program that is constantly
being used, no matter how badly written, the obvious bugs will have been
ironed out. The errors which are left are those that become evident only
when an unusual sequence of data values is entered. One might say, "Well,
so what! If the program does what it is supposed to do 99.99% of the time,
that 0.01% is a small price to pay." However, to take an extreme example, a
hidden error in an air-traffic control program, which comes to light in an
emergency, might mean the loss of two or three hundred lives. That price is
too high.

    Correcting errors in a badly written program is an expensive and time-
consuming job. It is much better if the program is clearly written and
completely free of errors in the first place. The latter may sound like an unreasonable demand, but in fact, it is possible to come very close to this ideal
if one is careful and systematic when developing programs.

6.2 SPAGHETTI LOGIC

One rather obvious lesson that has been learned over the years is that the better written a program is, the easier it will be to find and correct any errors that do arise. Here is an example of an outrageously lousy program. It is intended to produce output identical to that of the one in Chapter 5. By the way, it has some errors. Can you find them?

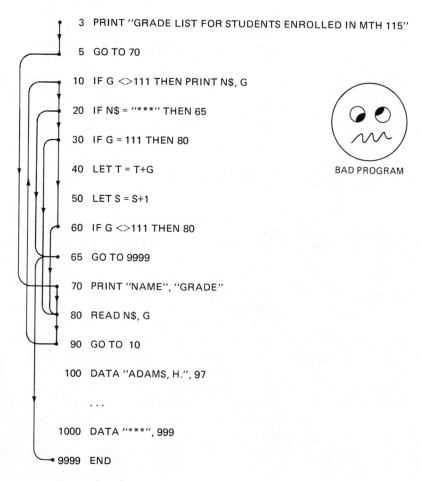

```
  3  PRINT "GRADE LIST FOR STUDENTS ENROLLED IN MTH 115"

  5  GO TO 70

 10  IF G <>111 THEN PRINT N$, G

 20  IF N$ = "***" THEN 65

 30  IF G = 111 THEN 80

 40  LET T = T+G

 50  LET S = S+1

 60  IF G <>111 THEN 80

 65  GO TO 9999

 70  PRINT "NAME", "GRADE"

 80  READ N$, G

 90  GO TO 10

100  DATA "ADAMS, H.", 97

     . . .

1000  DATA "***", 999

9999  END
```

BAD PROGRAM

This is awful, of course, and very difficult to read. No experienced programmer should produce such a mess. In fact, it is quite clear that many of the problems here arose from bad planning: the patching in of pieces of code that were initially forgotten. I have indicated to the left of the program the paths that the computer follows through it. Notice that what makes it hard to read is the way in which the flow hops around haphazardly. This type of programming is called, appropriately, **spaghetti logic.** Our goal is to avoid such excesses at all costs. This program is extreme but it is important to understand that, once programming applications become complex, such problems can creep into any program unless one guards against them by careful planning and a systematic approach to the development of the code.

You have seen the beginning of such an approach in Chapter 5. In this chapter we formalize the ideas we have already touched on.

6.3   THE BUILDING BLOCKS OF PROGRAM DESIGN

The problems that we are battling have little to do with the complexity of individual statements or the calculations done by a program. They usually arise out of the way that the flow of the program is controlled: its logical structure, what is done, in what order, under what conditions, and how often. All of this is handled by the GO TO and IF statements. Now, up to this point, we have been careful to use these statements in very controlled ways, in REPEAT loops and IF blocks. I have good news: What we have developed so far is adequate for any programming project, no matter how complex. A fairly recent development in the theory of programming is the realization that any program can be built using just three types of logical building block:

1. **SEQUENTIAL block:** a block of statements that is executed once under all circumstances
2. **REPEAT block (or REPEAT loop):** a block of statements that is executed repeatedly until a specified condition occurs
3. **IF block:** a block of statements that is executed if a specified condition holds and is ignored otherwise

Of course, items 2 and 3 are just the REPEAT loop and IF block that we have already discussed. SEQUENTIAL blocks are, quite simply, those segments of a program that do not contain GO TO or IF statements.

All is not simplicity, even so. A program may be constructed from such building blocks in a fairly complex way. Here is an analysis of the logical structure of the program from Chapter 5.

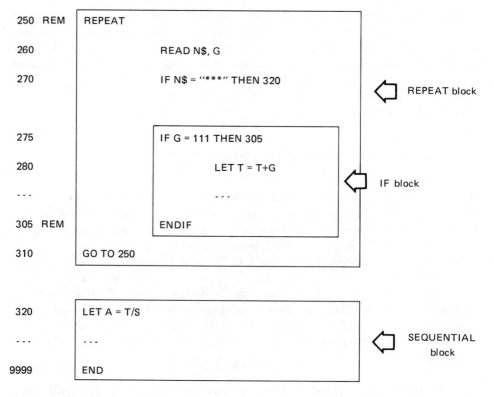

250 REM | REPEAT
260 | READ N$, G
270 | IF N$ = "***" THEN 320   ⇐ REPEAT block
275 | IF G = 111 THEN 305
280 | LET T = T+G   ⇐ IF block
- - - | - - -
305 REM | ENDIF
310 | GO TO 250

320 | LET A = T/S
- - - | - - -   ⇐ SEQUENTIAL block
9999 | END

The overall structure is

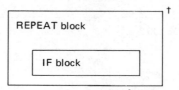

SEQUENTIAL block

REPEAT block

SEQUENTIAL block

but within the REPEAT block, certain statements are skipped if G = 111. That is, an IF block is **nested** inside the REPEAT block:

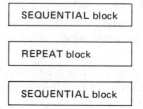

REPEAT block

IF block

This illustrates the general pattern. Blocks of various types may follow one another in sequence and they may also be nested one within the other, often to many levels. For example, the following pattern is not unreasonable:

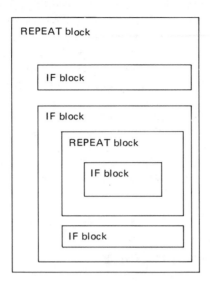

Of course, the way in which the various blocks are used will depend on what the program in question is designed to do.

When you are designing a program, your job will be a lot easier if you attempt to describe the project in terms of these three building blocks as early as possible in the development. To make this more systematic we will introduce a technique called **structured flowcharting.** We have already used the technique in Chapter 5 without naming it. It provides a fairly painless way of moving from the description of a problem to be solved to the final

---

†In fact, if we want to be really picky, the structure of the REPEAT block is as follows:

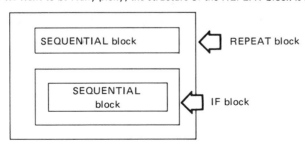

Can you identify which statements belong in each of these blocks?

program. Most people find it hard to take the informal statement of a problem and then to develop from it a formal solution. Whether this occurs in word problems in algebra or calculus, or in programming, it gives rise to similar difficulties and for many people tends to produce symptoms of what is often referred to as "math anxiety." The method we are developing is not a panacea. So do not feel depressed if when you first attempt a major programming project, you feel confused and lost. Program design is a challenging process and requires some experience. Knowing the principles is only a first step and not a guarantee of success. I hate to use the cliché, but practice does (at least help to) make perfect.

In the remainder of this chapter we will follow the development of a couple of programs from beginning to end, to illustrate good techniques. The details of the steps by which a programmer develops a program depend very much on that individual's train of thought at the time. However, the techniques we develop in this chapter will give you a framework on which to hang your ideas.

6.4   A SIMPLE PROJECT: AN UNUSUAL SALARY SCALE

Let's take a rather simple example and go through its development in some detail. Here is the problem to be solved. Suppose that I talk to the administration of the college where I work and tell them that I would like to renegotiate my salary. I say I am prepared to work for $1 during the coming year and, in fact, the only requirement I make is that my salary be doubled in each subsequent year: $2 in the following year, $4 the year after that, and so on. If this arrangement is accepted by the college, how long will it be before my annual salary reaches $1 million?

It is a good idea to write down, first, what you think a run of the final program should look like. Deciding what input will be required and what is to be printed before you necessarily have any idea of how the program will be written will help you focus on what you do and don't know and what you need to calculate. Here is my idea of how this program should run:

```
RUN

IF MY SALARY IN THE FIRST YEAR IS $1
IT WILL TAKE 364† YEARS OF SUCCESSIVE
DOUBLING FOR IT TO REACH $1 MILLION

Ready
```

†Of course we don't know the answer yet.

This problem does not demand that any data be typed in at run time. We are interested only in one specific case: an initial salary of $1. We could tackle a more general problem and make the program more interesting, but we won't, for simplicity's sake.

There is certainly more than one way to skin a cat. However, in this case the simplest approach is, figuratively, to send the computer into the future: counting off the years and doubling my salary until it tops $1 million. At that point the computer can print out the year it has reached. Let's start refining this into a more precise description. There are no prizes in this game for the fewest steps from problem to program, so we will proceed carefully and methodically.

Step 1

> The machine must first set up variables to keep track of the salary and the year count. It must then increase the year count in steps of 1 and double the salary, for each year counted, repeating this until the salary reaches or exceeds $1 million. At this point the year count should be printed out and the program stopped.

Read this description carefully. You will see that the second sentence describes a REPEAT loop. There are other familiar things hiding in this description: a counter and a PRINT statement. Let's rearrange this description so that it follows the form of a program more closely. If possible, we'll try to put boxes around parts of the description that appear to correspond to single BASIC statements. However, we shall not agonize over whether the division is strictly accurate.

Step 2

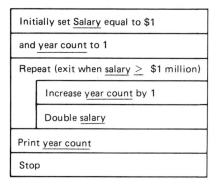

This is an example of a **structured flowchart.** It is a more-or-less formal description (depending on where we are in the development process) of the steps needed to solve the problem.

We discussed above how important it is to attempt to identify the control structure of the program as early as possible in the development process. That is, break it down into SEQUENTIAL, REPEAT, and IF blocks. Here is how they are represented in a structured flowchart:

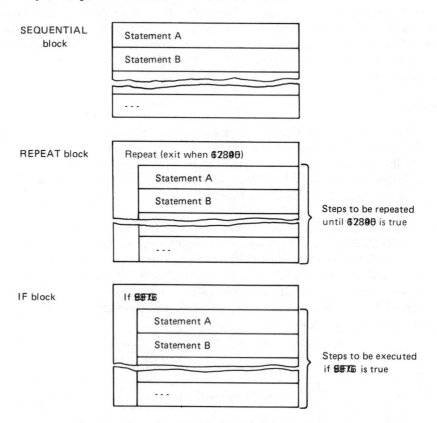

There is no IF block in this program, but we will see one in the next.

At this point we can begin to translate the description into BASIC, but first we must identify the variables we will need. I have underlined what appear to be the two variables in the program. Let's use:

$$S = \text{salary}$$
$$Y = \text{year count}$$

The variable Y is clearly a counter and "increase year count by 1" translates into LET Y = Y+1. To double the salary is the same as to multiply it by 2, so the next statement becomes LET S = S*2. We can now rewrite the structured flowchart to read as follows:

Step 3

```
LET Y = 1
LET S = 1
Repeat (exit when S >= 1000000)
        LET Y = Y+1
        LET S = S*2
PRINT Y
END
```

Everything is translated except for the "repeat" part. I have left it in lower-case to remind us of that. Chapter 4 gives us the mechanism for translating REPEAT blocks: use REPEAT and a GO TO statement to produce the loop and an IF statement to jump out of it when finished.

Step 4

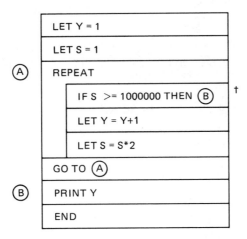

We are not ready for line numbers yet, so we will use letters to label the destinations of the GO TO and IF statements. Later, when we put in the line numbers, it will be easy to replace these labels with numbers.

---

†Another way of writing 1,000,000 is 1E6, that is, 1×10^6.

Before we move on, notice that there is only one step in the translation of the REPEAT loop that requires any thought, namely, where to put the IF statement. There are three possibilities:

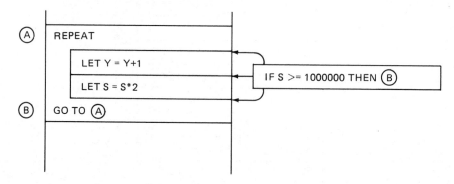

I'll leave it to you to determine why it is that the top position and the bottom one are both equally good, but that the middle position causes the loop to count one more year than it should. Every REPEAT loop has to be treated individually, but usually the correct decision is pretty clear if you analyze the process carefully.

The flowchart is now essentially a BASIC program, so that all that remains is to add line numbers and the documentation and put in the text that we plan to have it print out.

Step 5

```
100 REM TITLE: YEARS UNTIL SALARY REACHES $1 MILLION
110 REM PROGRAMMER: A. KITCHEN          DATE: 20-JUL-81
120 REM VARIABLES:
130 REM          Y = YEAR COUNT
140 REM          S = SALARY IN YEAR Y
150 REM
160 REM PROGRAM:
170          LET Y = 1
180          LET S = 1
190 REM REPEAT
200               IF S >= 1000000 THEN 240
210               LET Y = Y+1
220               LET S = S*2
230          GO TO 190
240          PRINT "IF MY SALARY IN THE FIRST YEAR IS $1"
250          PRINT "IT WILL TAKE";Y;"YEARS OF SUCCESSIVE"
260          PRINT "DOUBLING FOR IT TO REACH $1 MILLION."
9999         END
```

You can see that we have added quite a bit of window dressing (although very necessary; don't misunderstand me). I have underlined the meat of the program, that is, the statements from step 4. Oh, by the way, how long is it until my salary reaches $1,000,000? Run the program and find out.

6.5 ANOTHER PROJECT: INCOME ANALYSIS

Here is another illustration of program development, using structured flow-charts. This one is a little more involved and will give us a chance to test out all our procedures. By the way, I do hope that the subjects of this project and the last one don't lead you to the conclusion that all I think about is money!

The project is as follows. We are conducting a study of the incomes of a group of families and have decided to divide these families into three categories: poor, middle, and rich, according to the following guidelines. We define the "individual income" for a given family to be the total family income divided by the number of individuals in the family. If the individual income of a family is less than or equal to $4000, the family is described as "poor." If the individual income is greater than $16,000, the family is "rich"; otherwise, it is said to be "middle" income. We wish to write a program that will print a table showing each family's individual income and identifying which category it lies in. At the end, the program must cause the total number of families in each category to be printed, as well as the average individual income for each category. The data will be in the form of records consisting of the name of the head of each household, the total family income, and the number of individuals in the family:

```
DATA "AUER, M.", 14000, 5
DATA "BAYES, N.", 25500, 2
DATA "BERG, G.", 32000, 3
DATA "BOW, C.", 17000, 1
DATA "CHASE, C.", 28500, 2
DATA "FLYNN, E.", 90000, 5
        - - -
        - - -
DATA "ZUKOR, A.", 81000, 5
```

Resist the temptation to put dollar signs and commas in the data item describing income. The computer only recognizes pure numbers, that is, numbers consisting of an optional sign, digits, and a possible decimal point. Anything else will normally cause an error.

Example

The data statement

```
DATA "AUER, M.", $14000, 5
```

will cause an error message when the program is run. This one:

    DATA "AUER, M.", 14,000, 5

will not cause an immediate error. However, the computer will interpret each comma as a data separator, so that the AUER family will be recorded as having an income of $14 and the number of individuals in this family will be interpreted as 0. From then on, the data items will be out of phase with the variables as they are read in; for example,

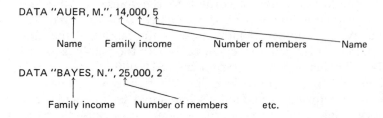

An error message will occur when the system attempts to interpret BAYES, N. as a number. By the way, the comma in the name (e.g., AUER, M.) does not cause the same problem because it is inside the quotes and therefore is treated as part of the character string and not as a data separator. ∎

Here is the plan for the output of the program:

RUN
TABLE SHOWING CATEGORIZATION OF FAMILIES BY INCOME,
WHERE:
   POOR --- INDIVIDUAL INCOME < = $4000
MIDDLE --- $4000 < INDIVIDUAL INCOME < = $16000
   RICH --- $16000 < INDIVIDUAL INCOME
INDIVIDUAL INCOME IS CALCULATED AS:
   FAMILY INCOME / NUMBER OF MEMBERS OF FAMILY
- -

NAME	INDIVIDUAL INCOME ($)	POOR	MIDDLE	RICH
AUER, M.	2800	X		
BAYES, N.	12750		X	
BERG, G.	10667		X	
BOW, C.	17000			X
CHASE, C.	14250		X	
- - -				
- - -				
ZUKOR, A.	16200			X
TOTALS:		???	???	???

- -

AVERAGE INDIVIDUAL INCOME FOR EACH CATEGORY:
POOR: $8389
MIDDLE: $9648
RICH: $86488
Ready

Before we plan the program, here are a few points that arise from the form decided on for the output. The heading INDIVIDUAL INCOME ($) is wider than the standard column field. There are various ways of handling this. We could, for instance, shorten the heading so that it fits into one column or we could construct a wider column (that requires a function that we haven't discussed yet). The solution we have chosen is to print INDIVID-UAL above INCOME($) so that the heading will fit in one column. The dollar values printed out are all rounded to the nearest dollar, so we must remember to do that in the program. The biggest question, however, arises in the calculation of the average individual incomes for the three categories. It is not clear what is intended here. Is the average for, say, the poor families equal to the total of all poor family incomes divided by the number of individuals who are members of poor families, or is it the total of all "individual incomes" which are $4000 or below divided by the number of poor families? Such a decision is one that must be made by the experimenter. It will depend on what the object of the study is, but in any case it is something that must be cleared up before the programming can continue. This is a very important point. Whether writing a program for yourself or to someone else's specifications, make sure that it is absolutely clear to you exactly what the goals of the program are before you continue with its development. In this case, assume that we intended the latter of the two interpretations, that is:

$$\text{Average individual income for a given category} = \frac{\text{sum of individual incomes (one for each family in that category)}}{\text{number of families in that category}}$$

Let's get on with the program. Here is an informal description.

Step 1

The following is to be repeated until the data have all been processed. Each family's record is read and the individual income for that family calculated. The family name and the individual income are printed; then a three-way decision must be made. If the individual income is ≤ $4000, an X is printed in the column headed POOR, the individual income is added to a variable that keeps a record of the total of all individual incomes for poor families, and a counter for the number of poor families is increased by 1. If the individual income is between $4000 and $16,000, similar steps are taken for the MIDDLE category and if it is above $16,000, the same is done for the RICH group. When all the records have been read, the averages for the three groups are calculated in turn (average = total/counter), and these and the totals for the three groups are printed.

Now let's formalize this as a structured flowchart. By the way, we didn't include the setting of totals and counters to zero in step 1. So we will add this to step 2.

Step 2

This program is not really very complicated (see the flowchart on the next page). It is broken by the IF blocks into three parts which are practically identical. We will, of course, see more complex and intricate programs later, but you will find that the structured approach has a taming effect on the nastiest procedure.

Notice that we have only two tools for logical control: the REPEAT and IF blocks. It can happen in some programs that limiting ourselves to these does not give the most efficient code. To combat this we could add more control structures built from other combinations of IF and GO TO statements. However, in general, the simplicity of our approach outweighs its occasional clumsiness.

Let's now identify variables and begin to translate into BASIC. As before, in the structured flowchart I have underlined those words that appear to refer to variables.

$T1$ = total for individual incomes in poor category
$T2$ = total for individual incomes in middle category
$T3$ = total for individual incomes in rich category
$C1$ = counter for poor families
$C2$ = counter for middle families
$C3$ = counter for rich families
$N\$$ = name of head of family
F = family income
M = number of family members
I = individual income for family
$A1$ = poor average income
$A2$ = middle average income
$A3$ = rich average income

Flowchart for Step 2

Set <u>poor</u>, <u>middle</u>, and <u>rich totals</u> to zero
Set <u>poor</u>, <u>middle</u>, and <u>rich counters</u> to zero
Print text and headings
Repeat (exit when all data has been processed)

Repeat (exit when all data has been processed):

Read a record (<u>name</u>, <u>family income</u>, <u>number of family members</u>)
Calculate <u>individual income</u> = <u>family income</u> / <u>number of fam. members</u> and round to nearest integer
Print <u>name</u>, <u>individual income</u> in first two columns
If <u>individual income</u> $\leq$ $4000

If individual income $\leq$ $4000:

Print "X" in POOR column
Add <u>individual income</u> to <u>poor total</u>
Add one to <u>poor counter</u>

If $4000 $<$ <u>individual income</u> $\leq$ $16000

If $4000 $<$ individual income $\leq$ $16000:

Print "X" in MIDDLE column
Add <u>individual income</u> to <u>middle total</u>
Add one to <u>middle counter</u>

If $16000 $<$ <u>individual income</u>

If $16000 $<$ individual income:

Print "X" in RICH column
Add <u>individual income</u> to <u>rich total</u>
Add one to <u>rich counter</u>

Print <u>totals</u> for three categories
Calculate <u>poor average income</u> = <u>poor total</u> / <u>poor counter</u>
Calculate <u>middle average income</u> = <u>middle total</u> / <u>middle counter</u>
Calculate <u>rich average income</u> = <u>rich total</u> / <u>rich counter</u>
Print text and <u>averages</u> for three categories
Data
Stop

As usual, we can indicate the end of the data by means of a flag. We'll add

DATA "****", 9999, 9999

to the end of the DATA statements. This, of course, determines the form of the IF statement in the REPEAT loop.

Step 3

LET T1 = 0
LET T2 = 0
LET T3 = 0
LET C1 = 0
LET C2 = 0
LET C3 = 0
PRINT text
PRINT" "," INDIVIDUAL"
PRINT "NAME", "INCOME ($)", "POOR", "MIDDLE", "RICH"

REPEAT (exit when N$ = "****")

READ N$, F, M
LET I = INT ((F/M) +0.5)
PRINT N$, I,[†]

If I $\leq$ 4000

PRINT "X"[†]
LET T1 = T1+I
LET C1 = C1+1

If 4000 $<$ I $\leq$ 16000

PRINT " "," "X"[†]
LET T2 = T2+I
LET C2 = C2 + 1

†Study carefully the way the comma is used to place items in the correct columns.

Step 3 continued

If 16000 < I
PRINT " ", " ", "X"[†]
LET T3 = T3+I
LET C3 = C3+1

PRINT "TOTALS:", " ",T1,T2,T3[†]
LET A1 = INT ((T1/C1)+0.5)
LET A2 = INT ((T2/C2)+0.5)
LET A3 = INT ((T3/C3)+0.5)
PRINT text
PRINT "POOR: $"; A1
PRINT "MIDDLE: $"; A2
PRINT "RICH: $"; A3
DATA statements
END

All that remains, apart from final polishing, is to translate the REPEAT and IF blocks. The REPEAT block is almost automatic: Make sure that you understand why, in this case, the IF-THEN statement follows immediately after the READ statement.

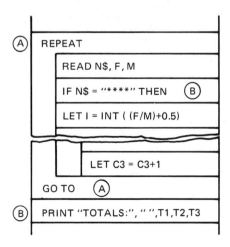

If you look back at the discussion in Chapter 5, you will see that the IF blocks are even easier to translate. For example,

IF I ≤ 4000	
	PRINT "X"
	LET T1 = T1+I
	LET C1 = C1+1

can be translated in either of the following ways:

IF I < = 4000 THEN PRINT "X"
IF I < = 4000 THEN LET T1 = T1+1
IF I < = 4000 THEN LET C1 = 1+1

or

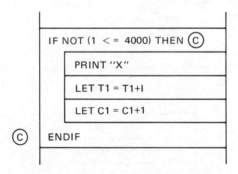

We will use the second form. Although the relation is a little clumsy looking, the format makes the program as a whole a little easier to read. Besides, many BASIC systems do not support the other. The relation

$$4000 < I \leq 16000$$

translates as

$$(4000 < I) \quad AND \quad (I <= 16000)$$

so that the second IF block can be written†

```
IF NOT ( (4000  < I) AND (I <= 16000)) THEN Ⓓ
          PRINT, "X"
          LET T2 = T2+I
          LET C2 = C2+1
Ⓓ   ENDIF
```

When all REPEAT and IF blocks are translated, the flowchart becomes

Step 4

```
LET T1 = 0
LET T2 = 0
LET T3 = 0
LET C1 = 0
LET C2 = 0
LET C3 = 0
PRINT text
PRINT " ", "INDIVIDUAL"
PRINT "NAME", "INCOME($)",  "POOR", "MIDDLE", "RICH"
Ⓐ  REPEAT
       READ N$, F, M
       IF N$ = "****" THEN   Ⓑ
       LET I = INT( (F/M)+0.5)
       PRINT N$, I,
```

†For another approach to this IF block, see Appendix V.

Step 4 continued

```
        IF NOT (I  < = 4000) THEN   Ⓒ
              PRINT "X"
              LET T1 = T1+I
              LET C1 = C1+1
  Ⓒ     ENDIF
        IF NOT ( (4000  <  I) AND (1  <=  16000) ) THEN   Ⓓ
              PRINT" ", "X"
              LET T2 = T2+I
              LET C2 = C2+1
  Ⓓ     ENDIF
        IF NOT (16000  <  I) THEN   Ⓔ
              PRINT" ", " ", "X"
              LET T3 = T3+I
              LET C3 = C3+1
  Ⓔ     ENDIF
     GO TO Ⓐ
  Ⓑ  PRINT "TOTALS:", " ", T1, T2, T3
     LET A1 = INT ( (T1/C1)+0.5)
     LET A2 = INT ( (T2/C2)+0.5)
     LET A3 = INT ( (T3/C3)+0.5)
     PRINT text
     PRINT "POOR: $"; A1
     PRINT "MIDDLE: $"; A2
     PRINT "RICH: $"; A3
     DATA statements
     END
```

The structured flowchart is now completely rewritten in BASIC. The last step is to add documentation, line numbers, and other finishing touches.

Step 5

```
100 REM TITLE: CLASSIFICATION OF FAMILIES BY INCOME
110 REM PROGRAMMER: A. KITCHEN          DATE: 20-JUN-81
120 REM VARIABLES:
130 REM          T1,T2,T3 = TOTALS FOR INDIVIDUAL INCOMES IN CATEGORIES:
140 REM                     POOR, MIDDLE, RICH
150 REM          C1,C2,C3 = COUNTERS FOR FAMILIES IN EACH CATEGORY
160 REM          N$ = NAME OF HEAD OF FAMILY
170 REM          F = FAMILY INCOME
180 REM          M = NUMBER OF FAMILY MEMBERS
190 REM          I = INDIVIDUAL INCOME FOR FAMILY
200 REM          A1,A2,A3 = AVERAGE INDIVIDUAL INCOMES FOR THE CATEGORIES
210 REM PROGRAM:
220      LET T1 = 0
230      LET T2 = 0
240      LET T3 = 0
250      LET C1 = 0
260      LET C2 = 0
270      LET C3 = 0
280      PRINT "TABLE SHOWING CATEGORIZATION OF FAMILIES BY INCOME"
290      PRINT "WHERE:"
300      PRINT "    POOR ----- INDIVIDUAL INCOME <= $4000"
310      PRINT "    MIDDLE --- $4000 < INDIVIDUAL INCOME <= $16000"
320      PRINT "    RICH ----- $16000 < INDIVIDUAL INCOME."
330      PRINT "INDIVIDUAL INCOME IS CALCULATED AS:"
340      PRINT "    FAMILY INCOME / NUMBER OF MEMBERS OF FAMILY."
350      PRINT "---------------------------------------------------"
360      PRINT ,"INDIVIDUAL"
370      PRINT "NAME","INCOME($)","POOR","MIDDLE","RICH"
380      PRINT "------","----------","----","------","----"
390 REM REPEAT
400          READ N$,F,M
410          IF N$ = "****" THEN 600
420          LET I = INT((F/M) + 0.5)
430          PRINT N$,I,
440          IF NOT(I <= 4000) THEN 480
450              PRINT "  X"
460              LET T1 = T1+I
470              LET C1 = C1+1
480 REM      ENDIF
490          IF NOT((4000 < I) AND (I <= 16000)) THEN 530
500              PRINT " ","  X"
510              LET T2 = T2+I
520              LET C2 = C2+1
530 REM      ENDIF
540          IF NOT(16000 < I) THEN 580
550              PRINT " "," ","  X"
560              LET T3 = T3+I
570              LET C3 = C3+1
580 REM      ENDIF
590      GO TO 390
600      PRINT "TOTALS:"," ",T1,T2,T3
610      PRINT "------------------------------------------------"
620      PRINT "AVERAGE INDIVIDUAL INCOME FOR EACH CATEGORY"
630      LET A1 = INT((T1/C1) + 0.5)
640      LET A2 = INT((T2/C2) + 0.5)
650      LET A3 = INT((T3/C3) + 0.5)
660      PRINT "POOR:   ";A1
670      PRINT "MIDDLE:";A2
680      PRINT "RICH:   ";A3
690 REM
```

Step 5 continued

```
1000 REM DATA: RECORD = NAME, FAM. INCOME, # OF MEMB. OF FAM.
1010     DATA "AUER, M.",14000,5
1020     DATA "BAYES, N.",25500,2
1030     DATA "BERG, G.",32000,3
1040     DATA "BOW, C.",17000,1
1050     DATA "CHASE, C.",28500,2
1060     DATA "FLYNN, E.",90000,5
3490     DATA "ZUKOR, A.",81000,5
4000     DATA "****",9999,9999
9999     END
```

6.6 AN OVERVIEW

Many of the difficulties of program development can be alleviated if one takes pains to proceed in a careful and systematic way. The major complications and sources of error arise within the logical structure of a program. If you are careful to identify those areas of the program that can be interpreted by REPEAT and IF blocks as early as possible in the development, you will find that the job will become relatively automatic. That is not to say that program development is an easy business. The invention of a general procedure, or **algorithm,** to solve a given problem can be a major undertaking. However, the use of structured flowcharts gives us a way of moving relatively painlessly from an informal description of the algorithm to the final program.

The translation of REPEAT and IF blocks can be summarized as follows:

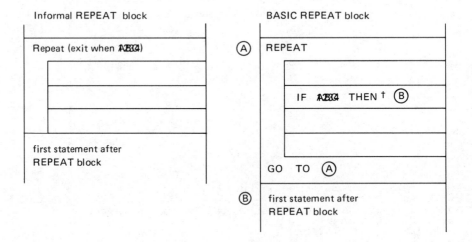

†The actual position of the IF statement may vary.

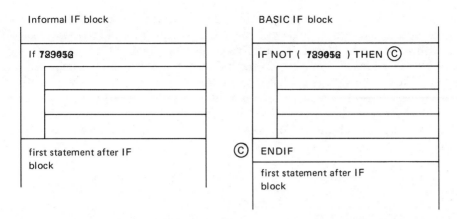

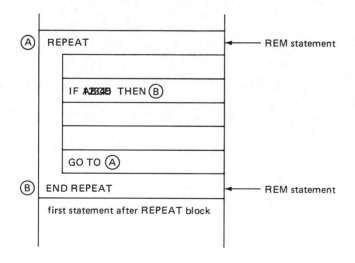

Notice that the label Ⓑ is the only one that is not attached to a REMARK statement. In fact, statement Ⓑ is the next statement to be executed after the REPEAT block. This can sometimes cause trouble when editing and correcting a program, because addition or deletion of statements just after the REPEAT block may require a change in the line number in the IF statement. It is easy to forget to make this adjustment and to end up with a faulty program. Here is another version of the BASIC REPEAT block. It's longer but it does make program editing a little easier.

Aside from this, the informal REPEAT block has one major weakness. It doesn't provide a way of indicating exactly where the IF-THEN statement should be placed when the loop is translated into BASIC. At an early stage in the development of a program this doesn't matter too much. In fact, it is better not to have to bother with details until the overall framework of the algorithm has been sketched out. However, there should be a way of indicating these details, if one needs to, before the description is translated into BASIC. Not to have this ability is to encourage sloppy programming habits— exactly what structured flowcharts are designed to combat!

The place in the loop where the relation in the "Repeat" statement is to be tested, and where the looping will finally stop, can be indicated by the word **Exit**.

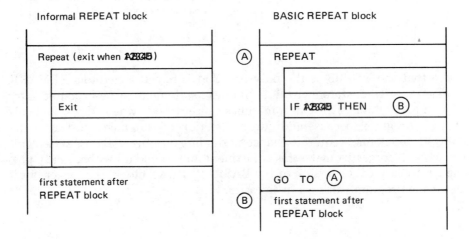

Example:

A REPEAT block, designed to sum a list of numbers, could be described informally like this:

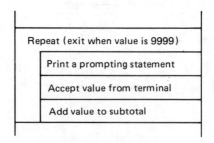

Once it has become clear that each value must be tested, to see if it is 9999, *before* it is added to the subtotal, the block could be rewritten:

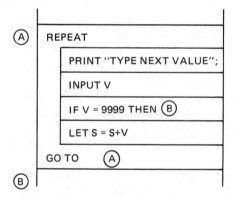

Its final translation into BASIC is, then, absolutely automatic.

6.7 DEBUGGING

Unfortunately, an occasional error does creep into even the best planned program. In fact, at first you may wonder if the day will ever come when all you have are occasional errors. However, with practice, bugs should become few and far between, particularly if you are careful about the way you develop your programs. In any case, it is important to realize that, just because one has finished writing the code for a program, one cannot assume that the whole process is over. Always act as if every program you write has errors.

Suppose that you have written a program and have **carefully proofread** the resulting code. The next step you should take, if possible, is to run the program with data for which you have already calculated the results. If the program processes a large quantity of data or prints out a long table, run it with a small amount of data to see if it handles all phases of the calculation correctly. For example, if the program proceeds in a number of different ways depending on the nature of the data, choose your test values so that they cover all the possibilities that could conceivably be encountered by the program during execution. Do, please, take to heart the words "small amount of data." It is more helpful and a lot less tedious to run a program five times, with a selection of 10 different data records each time, than to run it once, with 1000 records.

If the program produces invalid output, you have an error somewhere. First you should go back and double check that your algorithm (the general procedure you are using to solve the problem) is correct. This can be done by hand calculation; it is not cheating to use a calculator. If no errors are uncovered at this stage, the next step is to check your translation into BASIC. There are many different mistakes that can be made, but be on the lookout, in particular, for missing or misplaced statements. For example, watch for statements that have accidentally been included in a loop when they should have been outside it, or vice versa, and for incorrect exits from REPEAT loops. Also, double check your data. Sometimes, invalid output is the result of invalid data and not the fault of the program at all. "Garbage in, garbage out" is one of the aphorisms of the trade.

If, as often happens, you can still find nothing wrong, resist the temptation to blame the machine. Over ninety-nine and forty-four hundredths percent of the time it will be your fault.† Very rarely does the computer make an error. A computer error is a sign of a major problem with the machine or its software. In fact, when a machine is having problems, it is more likely to crash (i.e., to stop completely) than just to introduce errors into the programs it is executing. Debugging is like proofreading. It is amazing how often one can stare right past a glaring error. You must be persistent and patient.

In looking for an elusive bug, try to pinpoint where the error occurs. This can be done by adding PRINT statements, at various points in the program, to print out relevant variables. Put easily identifiable line numbers on these statements so that you can find them to delete them later. Then run the program with data for which you have done the calculations by hand. You can then identify where the error must be, by noting the point at which the machine's calculations are obviously incorrect or differ from yours.

Example:

```
10        LET Y = 1
20        LET S = 1
30        LET S = 2*S
40  REM   REPEAT
50            IF S > = 1000000 THEN 80
```

BAD PROGRAM

†I made up this statistic.

```
60          LET Y = Y+1
70          GO TO 40
80          PRINT Y
90          END
```

The machine appears to go dead after RUN is typed.

Assuming that the error has not been caught at an earlier stage, we can add PRINT statements at various points in the program to try to track down exactly when things start to go wrong.

```
10          LET Y = 1
20          LET S = 1
30          LET S = 2*S
31          PRINT 31, "Y="; Y, "S="; S
40   REM   REPEAT
50              IF S > = 1000000 THEN 80
60              LET Y = Y+1
61              PRINT 31, "Y="; Y, "S="; S
70          GO TO 40
71          PRINT 71, "S ="; S
80          PRINT Y
90          END
```

I have included the line numbers 31, 61, and 71 in the temporary PRINT statements so that we can tell which PRINT statement produced what output. Even though they are just for debugging, these temporary statements are quite elaborate. Don't skimp on the documentation, particularly when debugging a complicated program. If you don't identify each variable, you will be continually shuttling back and forth between the program and its RUN, trying to identify what number goes with what.

```
RUN
31      Y = 1      S = 2
61      Y = 2      S = 2
61      Y = 3      S = 2
61      Y = 4      S = 2
        - - -
        - - -
        forever
```

Notice that the machine never gets as far as statement 71. In fact, there is clearly something wrong before statement 61. The years, Y, are ticking away steadily, but the salary variable, S, is not increasing. As S will never reach 1,000,000 this way, looping continues forever. This alerts us to the fact that statement 30, which doubles S, is not performing properly. Clearly, it should be renumbered so as to lie inside the loop, not outside. ∎

Once all bugs have been identified, corrections can be made and the temporary PRINT statements deleted.

You may find that your initial attempts at debugging a program meet with failure. Don't give up. Success in this game comes only to the patient. Incidentally, many of your first errors will arise from incorrectly written statements. Your system will immediately print out an error message for each line incorrectly typed in. With that kind of feedback you should pass through this phase fairly quickly. In any case, you can avoid much pain and frustration by careful preparation before starting to type in your program at the terminal, and by proofreading the finished program before you run it.

Chapter 6: EXERCISES

Section 6.1

No exercises.

Section 6.2

    The following program segments suffer, in varying degrees, from the spaghetti syndrome. Starting with the first statement in each segment, draw in the lines of flow that the computer follows when processing them, just as was done with the example in the text. You do not have to understand what these segments are calculating. All you have to describe is the nature of the branching produced by the IF and GO TO statements.

1.
```
        - - - - -
100   INPUT A,B
110   IF A > 0 THEN 140
120   IF B > 0 THEN 140
130   GO TO 160
140   PRINT "AT LEAST ONE IS POSITIVE"
150   GO TO 100
160   PRINT "THEY ARE BOTH NEGATIVE"
170   GO TO 100
        - - -
```

2.
```
        - - -
140   INPUT A,B
150   PRINT A
160   GO TO 190
170   PRINT A*A
180   GO TO 220
190   PRINT B
200   PRINT B*B
210   IF A < B THEN 170
220   PRINT A*B
        - - -
```

3.
```
        - - - -
700   GO TO 730
710   IF X > 70 THEN 810
720   GO TO 780
730   LET X = X+1
740   LET E = E*(1+7/100)
```

```
750  LET C = C+E
760  LET D = D - 0.05*D
770  GO TO 710
780  IF X <> INT(X/10)*10 THEN 730
790  PRINT X,E,C,D
800  GO TO 700
810  PRINT
     - - - -
```

Section 6.3

1. Analyze the structure of the programs you have written to solve the exercises in Section 5.4 in terms of SEQUENTIAL, REPEAT, and IF blocks.

2. Analyze the block structure of the following segments. Don't confuse IF-THEN statements that control REPEAT loops with those that control IF blocks.

   (a)
   ```
   10            PRINT "TYPE IN TWO NUMBERS";
   20            INPUT A,B
   30            LET D = B
   40    REM   REPEAT
   50                LET Q = INT(A/D)
   60                LET R = A-Q*D
   70                IF R = 0 THEN 100
   80                LET D = R
   90            GO TO 40
   100           PRINT "THE G.C.D. OF";A;"AND";B;"IS";D
   9999          END
   ```

   (b)
   ```
   10            INPUT L,M,N
   20            IF L >= M THEN 80
   30                IF M >= N THEN 70
   40                    PRINT M - L
   50                    PRINT N - L
   60                    PRINT N - M
   70    REM      ENDIF
   80    REM   ENDIF
   9999          END
   ```

   (c)
   ```
   100           I = 2
   110           PRINT "UPPER LIMIT";
   120           INPUT N
   130   REM   REPEAT
   140               I = I+1
   150               IF I > N THEN 9999
   160               T = 0
   170               J = 1
   ```

```
180   REM      REPEAT
190              J = J +1
200              IF J > 1**0.5 THEN 250
210              LET Q = I/J
220              LET Q1 = INT Q
230              IF Q = Q1 THEN LET T = 1
240            GO TO 180
250            IF T = 1 THEN 270
260              PRINT "THE NUMBER";1;" IS A PRIME."
270   REM      ENDIF
280            GO TO 130
9999           END
```

Section 6.4

1. Translate these structured flowcharts into BASIC by translating the RE-
    PEAT and IF blocks and adding line numbers.

(a)

```
LET X = 1

Repeat (exit when E<0.001)

    LET X = (X + 2/X) /2

    LET E = X*X–2

PRINT "THE ANSWER IS";X

END
```

(b)

```
PRINT "WANNA HEAR A STORY";

INPUT R$

If R$ = "YES"

    Repeat (forever)

        PRINT "T'WAS A DARK AND STORMY NIGHT AND"

        PRINT "THE RAIN CAME DOWN IN TORRENTS."

        PRINT "THE FIRST MATE SAID TO THE CAPTAIN:"

        PRINT " 'CAPT'N, SPIN US A YARN.' "

        PRINT "SO THE CAPTAIN BEGAN:"

END
```

(c)

LET S = 0
LET N = 0
Repeat (exit when A = 9999)

> | PRINT "ENTER NUMBER"; |
> | --- |
> | INPUT A |
> | If A > 0 |

>> | LET S = S+A |
>> | --- |
>> | LET N = N+1 |

PRINT "AVERAGE OF POSITIVE NUMBERS:"; S/N
END

2. Neither of the program segments below performs the task described in its structured flowchart. Correct the programs by moving the IF statements.

(a)

Program to print the integers 1 through N
LET N = 0
Repeat (exit when N $\geq$ 10)

> | LET N = N + 1 |
> | --- |
> | PRINT N |

END

```
10          LET N = 0
20    REM   REPEAT
30            LET N = N + 1
40            IF N >= 10 THEN 9999
50            PRINT N
60          GO TO 20
9999        END
```

(b)

```
Program to print the integers 1 through N

LET N = 0

Repeat (exit when N > 10)

      LET N = N + 1

      PRINT N

END
```

```
10          LET N = 0
20    REM   REPEAT
30              IF N > 10 THEN 9999
40              LET N = N + 1
50              PRINT N
60          GO TO 20
9999        END
```

[*Hint: The descriptions of the REPEAT loops in these structured flow-charts are rather sloppy. For example, a strict interpretation of the phrase "exit when $N \geq 0$" would imply that we should stop the loop as soon as N reaches or exceeds 10. With this interpretation the translation in part (a) would appear to be correct. However, it doesn't do what it is supposed to. The correct way to interpret "exit when" as used in this book is to consider it as an informal description of the test that must be satisfied in order to exit from the loop, but <u>not where the test should be made</u>. That must be decided separately. See Section 6.6 for more on this.*]

3. If a sum of money is placed in a savings account that pays $I\%$ per annum, compounded quarterly, then each year that it remains in the account it increases (is multiplied) by a factor of $[1 + (I/400)]^4$. You deposit \$1 in an account paying 6¼%, compounded quarterly. How many years will you have to wait for this nest egg to reach or exceed \$1 million? Write a sequence of structured flowcharts for this problem which corresponds to steps 2 to 4 in the development of the salary program in the text; then write a fully documented program to solve the problem. [*Hint: The logical structure of this program is identical to that of the one discussed in the text.*]

4. (a) Imagine a strange store, which gives change only in quarters, dimes, and pennies. Write a fully documented program that will calculate the change due on a bill, given the bill and the amount tendered by the customer. Design your program from the following structured flowchart and sample run.

Input **bill** and **amount** tendered by customer
Calculate **change**
Convert **change** to pennies
Repeat (exit when **change** < 25¢)
Reduce **change** by 25¢
Increase **quarter count** by 1
Repeat (exit when **change** < 10¢)
Reduce **change** by 10¢
Increase **dime count** by 1
Penny count = **change**
Print **quarter**, **dime**, and **penny counts**
Stop

```
RUN
BILL?2.58
AMOUNT TENDERED?5.00
CHANGE DUE: 9 QUARTER(S), 1 DIME(S) AND 7 PENNY(IES)
Ready
```

(b) Here is a flowchart for a less peculiar change maker. It uses a RE-PEAT loop to handle the various denominations of change and reads them from DATA statements. Write a fully documented program for this change maker.

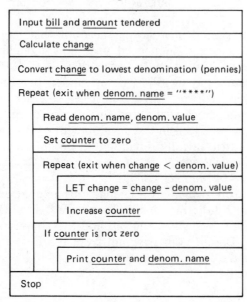

Use the following DATA for *denom. name, denom. value:*

```
"TWENTIES",2000
"TENS",1000
"FIVES",500
"ONES",100
"QUARTERS",25
"DIMES ",10
"NICKLES",5
"PENNIES",1
"****",9999
```

[*Hint: As most major currencies are now based on a decimal system (even English pounds, shillings, and pence have gone the way of the passenger pigeon, sadly!), this program can be used without modification almost anywhere in the world. Just change the DATA statements to represent the local denominations.*]

5. Develop a program, using structured flowcharts, to calculate the quotient and remainder when a positive integer *A* is divided by a positive integer *B*. Use the following technique: Repeatedly subtract *B* from *A* until what remains is less than *B*. This is the remainder. The quotient is the number of times *B* "goes into" *A*. How do you calculate it? [*Hint: This is another approach to Exercise 6 of Section 3.4. By the way, make sure that your program handles cases where $A < B$ correctly.*]

6. Develop a program to calculate the square root of a number, *A*, using the following approximation method. If one makes an estimate, *x*, of the value of the root of *A*, then a better approximation of the root is given by

$$\frac{1}{2}\left(x + \frac{A}{x}\right)$$

Take this as the new estimate, *x*, and repeat the calculation above to get an even better approximation. Continue this process until $|x^2 - A| < 0.0005$, that is, until x^2 is correct to three decimal places. [*Hint: There is no great loss in always taking the first estimate to be 1, no matter what the value of A. So all the user of the program should have to do is to enter the value of A. The BASIC function, ABS(X) = absolute value of X, will be useful in this program.*]

Section 6.5

1. (a) A doctor handles his office hours this way: each day his waiting room is full of patients, so he sees patients continuously until 5

p.m. For each patient, he takes a temperature reading if he can find a clean thermometer. Otherwise, he declares the patient fit. If the thermometer shows 102° F or above, he sends the patient to a hospital. If the patient's temperature is between 98.6 and 102° F, he sells the poor soul a bottle of Little Liver Pills. Otherwise, he sells the patient a hot water bottle. Construct a structured flowchart to describe a typical day in the life of this doctor.

(b) Crabcakes: Put 2 tbsp. butter and 2 tbsp. minced onion in pan and cook until onion is yellow. Remove from heat. Add 1 cup bread crumbs, 1 pound cooked crabmeat, 1 egg (well beaten), 1 tsp. mustard, and salt and pepper to taste. If mixture is too dry, add 2 tsp. milk. Shape into flat cakes. Sprinkle each one with flour. Brown cakes in butter. Reduce heat and cook slowly for 5 minutes. Construct a structured flowchart for this recipe.

In designing programs to solve the following exercises, use structured flowcharts to aid in the development and provide clear and concise documentation with remarks and printout.

2. (a) Here is a description of an algorithm for finding the largest of a list of numbers.

Accept first number
Temporarily set max = number
Repeat (exit when number = 99999)
Accept next number
If number accepted is larger than current max
Store this number as the new max
When all numbers have been checked, print the final value of max
Stop

Write a BASIC program that prints the largest of a list of numbers. The numbers can be typed in from the terminal or read from DATA statements. However, in the latter case, the full list should be printed as well as the maximum value. [*Hint: The flowchart does not handle an empty list properly, that is, one consisting of just the end-of-data flag, 99999.*]

(b) Write a program that will read the following data and print the name and dates of the justice of the U.S. Supreme Court who served the longest term.

Past Chief Justices, U.S. Supreme Court	Terms	
	Began	Ended
John Jay	1789	1795
Oliver Ellsworth	1796	1800
John Marshall	1801	1835
Roger Taney	1836	1864
Salmon Chase	1864	1873
Morrison Waite	1874	1888
Melville Fuller	1888	1910
Edward White	1910	1921
William Taft	1921	1930
Charles Hughes	1930	1941
Harlan Stone	1941	1946
Fred Vinson	1946	1953
Earl Warren	1953	1969

(c)   Modify the program in part (b) so that it will search for the Chief Justice with the shortest term as well.

3.   Use the following description to print a table showing the total winnings for each of the rodeo champions listed below.

```
Print table headings

Read year, name, winnings

Set total equal to winnings

Repeat (exit when all records have been read)

    Previous name = name

    Read year, name, winnings

    If previous name does not equal name

        Print previous name, total

        Set total to zero

    Add winnings to total

Stop
```

All-Around Champion Rodeo Cowboys

Year	Winner	Winnings ($1000)
1960	Harry Tompkins	32.5
1961	Benny Reynolds	31.3
1962	Tom Nesmith	32.6
1963	Dean Oliver	31.3
1964	Dean Oliver	31.2
1965	Dean Oliver	33.2
1966	Larry Mahan	40.4
1967	Larry Mahan	52.0
1968	Larry Mahan	49.1
1969	Larry Mahan	57.7
1970	Larry Mahan	41.5
1971	Phil Lyne	49.2
1972	Phil Lyne	60.9

[*Hint: This program cannot consolidate winnings unless each man's winning years are listed consecutively. For example, in 1975 Larry Mahan was All-Around Champion again. This would defeat the algorithm described here. More powerful techniques will be introduced in Chapter 8, which will enable us to solve this problem.*]

4.   (a)   Write a program to find the prime factors of any positive integer (e.g., 84 = 2 × 2 × 3 × 7). Here is the description of an algorithm to do this.

```
Accept number

Repeat (exit when number = 1)

    Find smallest factor of number

    Print smallest factor

    Let number = number/ smallest factor

Stop
```

The box "Find smallest factor of number" needs a little more expansion. Notice that, as every number is divisible by 1, "smallest factor" means smallest factor > 1. So this search proceeds as follows:

Let <u>integer</u> = 2
Repeat (exit when <u>quotient</u> is a whole number)
Quotient = <u>number</u>/ <u>integer</u>
Integer = <u>integer</u> + 1
Present value of <u>integer</u> is <u>smallest factor</u>

It is good programming practice to test individual segments of a program before incorporating them into the whole program. This enables one to find and correct errors before they are deeply embedded in program code and the problem of isolating them becomes monumental.

Write the segment "Find <u>smallest factor</u> of <u>number</u>" as a separate program first. Test it thoroughly: It should accept integers and print their smallest factors. When this program is working correctly, incorporate it into the main program. [*Hints: (1) To test whether Q is a whole number, compare Q with INT(Q). (2) It is crucial that the exit from "Repeat (exit when <u>number</u> = 1)" should occur at the correct point. A misplaced IF statement in this loop will have strange consequences. What does your program do when the number 1 is typed in?*]

(b)   Expand this program so that it will print a table of factorizations for the integers 2, 3, 4, . . . , 100.

5.   Write a program to calculate final letter grades for a class, given the class average (a) and standard deviation (d), as well as a list of the students' names and numerical grades. After printing the table of grades, the program should also print a tally showing total numbers of A's, B's, C's, D's, and F's.

The average and standard deviation can be calculated by a separate program if you wish; see Exercise 9 of Section 4.5. Given a student's numerical grade (g), the corresponding letter grade will be calculated according to the following scheme:

Range	Letter Grade
$g - a < -d$	F
$-d \leqslant g - a < -d/3$	D
$-d/3 \leqslant g - a < d/3$	C
$d/3 \leqslant g - a < d$	B
$d \leqslant g - a$	A

[*Hint: The range tests are a little simpler to calculate if you divide by d first [e.g., (g - a)/d < -1 gives F, etc.]. How could you design this program to calculate the average and standard deviation as well?*]

6. Write a program to calculate the greatest common divisor of two integers. Use the following approach: Given a pair of integers, construct a new pair consisting of the smaller one and the larger minus the smaller. For example, if the pair is (24, 15) the new pair will be (15, 9). Repeat this process until the two numbers are equal. This common value is the g.c.d. [*Hint: The greatest common divisor (g.c.d.) of A and B is the largest integer that divides both A and B exactly.*]

7. (a) Here is a simple version of the game of Nim. A pile of matches is laid on a table. Two players take turns removing matches from the pile. Each player may remove either 1, 2, or 3 matches at a time. The winner is the one who takes the last match. The strategy for winning this game is to take just the right number of matches each time so as to leave the other player with a pile that is a multiple of 4 (0, 4, 8, 16, . . .).

   Program the machine to play this game against a person sitting at the terminal. As this is the kind of game a child could play, the printout should be clear and lively. Of course, the machine must always win, and neither player should be allowed to cheat. To ensure this, here are some suggestions:

   (1) The machine lets the other player choose the number of matches for the game.

   (2) If this number is a multiple of 4, the machine lets the user go first; otherwise, it makes the first move.

   (3) If the user types in any move other than 1, 2, or 3, the machine rejects it.

   (4) The game ends when the number of matches remaining reaches zero, at which time the machine declares itself the winner.

   (b) Here is a more challenging version of this game. The setting is the same; the only difference is that this time the players may remove 1, 4, 7, or 9 matches. The winning strategy this time is to leave the other player with a pile that is either a multiple of 8 (0, 8, 16, etc.) or 2 plus a multiple of 8 (2, 10, 18, etc.) or 5 plus a multiple of 8 (5, 13, 21, etc.). If you want to give the other player a fighting chance, don't let the machine choose who starts. But remember, the machine's strategy for maximizing its chances of winning will have to be a little more complicated. [*Hint: For more information about games like this, see* The Master Book of Mathematical Recreations *by Fred Schuh, Dover Publications.*]

8. (a) Using the following table of data on the U.S. public school system,

write a program that will print out the (estimated) population, enrollment, and expenditure for any year between 1870 and 1976.

Year	U.S. Population (thousands)	Enrollment (thousands)	Expenditures (millions)
1870	39,818	6,872	$ 63
1900	75,995	15,503	214
1910	90,492	17,814	426
1920	104,512	21,578	1,036
1930	121,770	25,678	2,316
1940	130,880	25,434	2,344
1950	148,665	25,111	5,837
1960	179,323	36,087	15,613
1970	203,212	45,619	40,683
1976	213,051	44,791	70,629

The difficulty is that the values must be estimated, at least for the years that are missing from the table. One way to estimate these values is to use linear interpolation.

Here is how it is done. An estimate of the missing value (?) in this table:

Year	Quantity
Y1	Q1
Y	?
Y2	Q2

is given by

$$? = Q1 + \frac{Q2 - Q1}{Y2 - Y1} \times (Y - Y1)$$

[*Hint: For example:*

Population (1000s) in 1913 = pop. in 1910 + change between 1910 and 1913

$= pop. \ in \ 1910 + (change \ per \ year) \times (1913 - 1910)$

$= pop. \ in \ 1910 + \dfrac{pop. \ in \ 1920 - pop. \ in \ 1910}{1920 - 1910} \times (1913 - 1910)$

$= 90{,}492 + \dfrac{104{,}512 - 90{,}492}{1920 - 1910} \times (1913 - 1910)$

$= 94{,}698.$]

(b) Variations on this theme: Calculate expenditure per capita of total population and expenditure per pupil. Print a table of such data for all years in a given range, say 1940 to 1970.

Section 6.6

1. In the following structured flowcharts, AAAAAA, BBBBBB, and so on, represent BASIC statements.

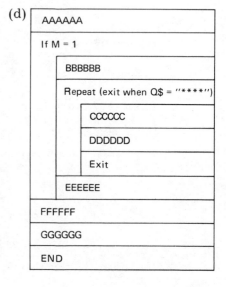

(a)
```
AAAAAA
BBBBBB
Repeat (exit when X = 9999)
    CCCCCC
    Exit
    DDDDDD
EEEEE
FFFFFF
GGGGGG
END
```

(b)
```
AAAAAA
BBBBBB
Repeat (exit when X = 0)
    Exit
    CCCCCC
    If Y ≥ X
        DDDDDD
        EEEEEE
    FFFFFF
GGGGGG
END
```

(c)
```
AAAAAA
BBBBBB
Repeat (exit when X ≥ 10)
    CCCCCC
    Repeat (exit when Y = 0)
        DDDDDD
        Exit
        EEEEEE
    Exit
FFFFFF
END
```

(d)
```
AAAAAA
If M = 1
    BBBBBB
    Repeat (exit when Q$ = "****")
        CCCCCC
        DDDDDD
        Exit
    EEEEEE
FFFFFF
GGGGGG
END
```

Translate the control statements in these flowcharts into BASIC.
[*Hint: Don't attempt to translate or replace AAAAAA, BBBBBB,
and so on. They are BASIC statements whose contents you do not
have to know in order to do the assignment.*]

Section 6.7

Identify and correct the errors in the following program segments.

1.

```
100     REM  SQUARES OF NUMBERS 1 THROUGH 100
110          LET N = 1
120     REM  REPEAT
130             PRINT "NUMBER", "SQUARE"
140            LET N = N + 1
150            IF N = 100 THEN 9999
160            PRINT N,N^N
170          GO TO 120
9999         END
```

2.

```
100     REM  THE AVERAGE OF A LIST OF NUMBERS
110          IF X=999 THEN 170
120     REM  REPEAT
130             INPUT X
140            LET S = S+X
150            LET A = S/N
160          GO TO 120
170          PRINT "AVERAGE=";A
9999         END
```

3.

```
100     REM  THE SQUARE ROOT OF A NUMBER
110          IF A > 0 THEN 150
120             PRINT "THIS NUMBER IS NEGATIVE"
130             PRINT "TYPE IN ANOTHER";
140              INPUT A
150     REM  ENDIF
160          PRINT "SQUARE ROOT OF";A;"IS";A ^ 0.5
9999         END
```

4.

```
100     REM  IF A,B,C ARE IN INCREASING ORDER
110     REM  "YES" IS PRINTED, OTHERWISE "NO"
120          INPUT A,B,C
130           IF A < B THEN 160
140           IF B < C THEN 160
150          GO TO 170
160          PRINT "YES"
170          PRINT "NO"
9999         END
```

5.
```
100   PRINT "ENTER THREE NUMBERS"
110   PRINT "SMALLEST FIRST, LARGEST LAST"
120   INPUT X,Y,Z
130   IF X = Z THEN PRINT "ALL ARE EQUAL"
140   IF X = Y OR Y = Z THEN PRINT "JUST TWO ARE EQUAL"
150   PRINT "NONE ARE EQUAL"
9999  END
```

[*Hint: Try to write more than one correct version of this program. Compare the efficiency and the readability of your solutions.*]

Chapter

7

More Loops

7.1 THE FOR/NEXT LOOP

In Chapter 4 I belabored the concept of a counter and, in fact, every major program that we have developed since has contained at least one of them. Although this is clearly due to the choice of problems, the point should not be lost on you that counters do appear in a great many programs.

Counters are often used to keep track of the occurrence of given events or to count certain quantities within a program (e.g., the counts of the numbers of poor, middle, and rich families in the last program in Chapter 5). However, they are most often used just to ensure that a certain segment of a program is repeated a given number of times. For example, here is a modification of the first program in Chapter 4:

```
10          LET N = 1
20    REM   REPEAT
30             IF N > 5 THEN 9999
40             PRINT "HUMPTY DUMPED HIS HAT ON THE WALL."
50             LET N = N+1
60          GO TO 20
9999        END
```

It causes the statement

```
PRINT "HUMPTY DUMPED HIS HAT ON THE WALL."
```

to be repeated five times, while the counter, N, increases from 1 to 5: that is,

```
RUN
HUMPTY DUMPED HIS HAT ON THE WALL.
HUMPTY DUMPED HIS HAT ON THE WALL.
HUMPTY DUMPED HIS HAT ON THE WALL.
HUMPTY DUMPED HIS HAT ON THE WALL.
HUMPTY DUMPED HIS HAT ON THE WALL.
Ready
```

And another example:

```
10          LET I = 1
20    REM   REPEAT
30             IF I > 10 THEN 9999
40             PRINT I
50             LET I = I+1
60          GO TO 20
9999        END
RUN
1
2
3
4
5
6
7
8
9
10
READY
```

In this case the statement PRINT I is repeated, while the variable I takes the values 1, 2, . . . , 10. Notice how similar the two programs are. This reflects their similar goals: to repeat a certain statement a given number of times. The HUMPTY program is, in a sense, the purest. There the counter, N, does nothing other than ensure that a silly sentence is repeated five times.

In the notation of structured flowcharts, a REPEAT loop to handle the repetition of a statement or block of statements 𝖹𝖪𝖦𝖱𝖹 times looks like this:

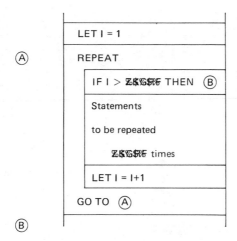

This is a little clumsy for such a commonly used operation. So to simplify
the notation, most computer languages introduce a special construction. In
BASIC this construction is known as the **FOR/NEXT loop.** Here are our
two little programs, rewritten using it:

```
10    FOR N = 1 TO 5
20        PRINT "HUMPTY DUMPED HIS HAT ON THE WALL.
30    NEXT N
9999  END
```

and

```
10    FOR I = 1 TO 10
20        PRINT I
30    NEXT I
9999  END
```

Notice how, as with the REPEAT loop, the body of the loop is indented.
We won't bother to look at runs of these programs, as they are the same as
before.

The idea is very simple. Whatever lies between the FOR and the NEXT
statements is repeated, while the counter increases, in steps of 1, from its
initial to its final value. These values are specified in the FOR statement. By
the way, it is important to realize that the FOR/NEXT loop does not really
add anything new. It is, however, a very convenient way of writing a common type of REPEAT loop. The convenience is only for us, though. The
computer has, in essence, to translate a FOR/NEXT loop into a REPEAT
loop in order to process it:

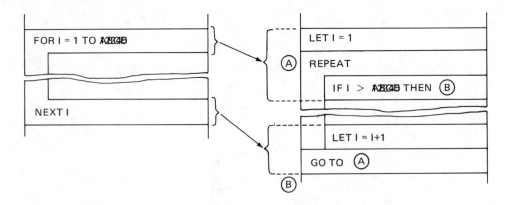

7.2 VARIATIONS ON A THEME

The counter in a FOR/NEXT loop doesn't have to start at 1.

Examples

1.
```
10    FOR I = 6 TO 13
20        PRINT I
30    NEXT I
9999  END
RUN
 6
 7
 8
 9
10
11
12
13
Ready
```

2. What does this one do?
```
10    FOR N = 68 TO 73
20        PRINT "HUMPTY DUMPED HIS HAT ON A WALL."
30    NEXT N
9999  END
```

Check your conclusion by running the program.   ∎

In fact, the initial and final values of the FOR statement can be specified by variables or even mathematical expressions.

Examples:

Valid FOR statements

1.   FOR I = 10 TO 25
2.   FOR J = 1 TO M
3.   FOR X = 0.5 TO 6
     (X takes the values 0.5, 1.5, 2.5, 3.5, 4.5, 5.5 successively; the next
     value, 6.5, exceeds 6 and so is not reached.)
4.   FOR G = L TO M*N   ∎

Here is an example of the use of a variable final value, perhaps the most common variation on the FOR/NEXT loop theme.

Example

```
10     PRINT "WHAT NUMBER SHALL I COUNT UP TO";
20     INPUT N
30     FOR I = 1 TO N
40         PRINT I
50     NEXT I
9999   END
```

When this program is run, a value for N is established by means of statement
20. Suppose, for example, that in response to

WHAT NUMBER SHALL I COUNT UP TO?

the user types 7; then the value 7 is stored in N, so that statement 30 can be
considered to read

FOR I = 1 TO 7

The corresponding run would look like this:

```
RUN
WHAT NUMBER SHALL I COUNT UP TO? 7
 1
 2
 3
 4
 5
 6
 7
Ready                                                                    ∎
```

Here are a couple of things to watch for when programming with FOR/ NEXT loops. It is most important that every FOR statement have a **matching** NEXT, somewhere later in the same program. By **matching,** I mean that the counter in the FOR and in the NEXT statements must be the same variable. Although the counter in a FOR/NEXT loop can be used in LET and PRINT statements, it is bad practice to do anything that might change the value of the counter inside the loop. That kind of construction will make your program harder to understand, and is always unnecessary.

Examples

1.
```
10     PRINT "WHAT NUMBER SHALL I COUNT UP TO";
20     INPUT N
30     FOR I = 1 TO N
40         PRINT I
50     NEXT N
9999 END
RUN

NEXT without FOR at line 50
FOR without NEXT at line 30

Ready
```

Such an error is easy to make but often hard to see afterward.

2.   Look carefully at this program segment, which is supposed to print a table of squares.

```
10     PRINT "NUMBER", "SQUARE"
20     FOR I = 1 TO 10
30         LET Q = I*I
40         PRINT I, Q
50         LET I = I+1
60     NEXT I
9999 END
RUN
NUMBER          SQUARE
  1               1
  3               9
  5               25
  7               49
  9               81
Ready
```

It is confusing. The numbers in the FOR statement lead one to expect a table of 10 rows. The problem is in line 50, which changes the value of the counter. For example, in the first pass through the loop, I starts out with the value 1. Statement 50 increases this to 2 and then the next line, 60 NEXT I, immediately increases it again, to 3, and returns control to the beginning of the loop. The following diagram shows the changing values of I in each pass through the FOR/NEXT loop:

		Pass					
Statement		1	2	3	4	5	6
10	PRINT "NUMBER, SQUARE"	–					
20	FOR I = 1 TO 10	1	3	5	7	9	11
30	LET Q = I*I	1	3	5	7	9	
40	PRINT I, Q	1	3	5	7	9	
50	LET I = I+1	2	4	6	8	10	
60	NEXT I	3	5	7	9	11	
9999	END						

If you find this explanation confusing, try translating the program into REPEAT loop form. It will be more complicated but every change will be spelled out in detail. ∎

In most versions of BASIC there is a modified FOR/NEXT loop that will count down as well as up, and will go either way in steps of any size. These examples show how it works.

Examples

1.
```
10    FOR K = 100 TO 150 STEP 10        RUN
20        PRINT K                       100
30    NEXT K                            110
9999  END                              120
                                        130
                                        140
                                        150
                                       Ready
```

2.

```
10    FOR I = 10 TO 1 STEP -1
20        PRINT I
30    NEXT I
40    PRINT "KABOOM!!!"
9999  END
```

<u>RUN</u>
```
10
9
8
7
6
5
4
3
2
1
KABOOM!!!
Ready
```

3.

```
10    FOR J = -0.2 TO 0.2 STEP 0.1
20        PRINT J,J*J
30    NEXT J
9999  END
```

<u>RUN</u>
```
-0.2      0.04
-0.1      0.01
 0        0
 0.1      0.01
 0.2      0.04
Ready
```

I won't say more. Experiment with FOR-STEP/NEXT on your system. It is a nice option to have available. However, most of the time you will find the simpler FOR/NEXT loop is all you need.

Finally, to summarize the syntax of these loops, the FOR and NEXT statements have the following general form:

> FOR *variable* = *expression1* TO *expression2*

or

> FOR *variable* = *expression1* TO *expression2* STEP *expression3*

and

> NEXT *variable*

where the variable in the FOR and its related NEXT statement must be the same. The quantities **expression1**, **expression2**, and **expression3** may be numbers, number variables, or mathematical expressions and represent, respectively, the initial value, the final value, and the optional step size for the loop. If STEP **expression3** is missing, the step size is taken to be 1. ∎

7.3 THE FOR/NEXT LOOP IN DATA PROCESSING

Flags were introduced in Chapter 4 and we used them in a number of programs as a way of signaling to the computer that the input of data was to be stopped. We can replace this flag approach by one involving a FOR/NEXT loop if we know ahead of time how many data records are to be processed.

Here are two program segments designed to add up a list of numbers. Segment 1 uses the flag approach and segment 2 handles the same problem with a FOR/NEXT loop.

1.

```
100      LET S = 0
110      PRINT "TYPE EACH NUMBER ON A"
120      PRINT "SEPARATE LINE AFTER THE"
130      PRINT "QUESTION MARK.  TO"
140      PRINT "TERMINATE INPUT TYPE 0."
150 REM REPEAT
160              PRINT "NUMBER";
170              INPUT A
180              IF A = 0 THEN 210
190              LET S = S+A
200      GO TO 150
210      PRINT "TOTAL IS";S
9999     END
```

```
RUN

TYPE EACH NUMBER ON A
SEPARATE LINE AFTER THE
QUESTION MARK.  TO
TERMINATE INPUT TYPE 0.
NUMBER? 385.9
NUMBER? 729.6
NUMBER? 94.4
NUMBER? 0
TOTAL IS 1209.9

Ready
```

2.

```
100      LET S = 0
110      PRINT "HOW MANY NUMBERS TO BE"
120      PRINT "SUMMED";
130      INPUT N
140      PRINT "TYPE EACH NUMBER ON A"
150      PRINT "SEPARATE LINE AFTER THE"
160      PRINT "QUESTION MARK."
170      FOR I=1 TO N
180          PRINT "NUMBER";I;
190          INPUT A
200          LET S = S+A
210      NEXT I
220      PRINT "TOTAL IS";S
9999     END
```

```
RUN

HOW MANY NUMBERS TO BE
SUMMED? 3
TYPE EACH NUMBER ON A
SEPARATE LINE AFTER THE
QUESTION MARK.
NUMBER 1 ? 385.9
NUMBER 2 ? 729.6
NUMBER 3 ? 94.4
TOTAL IS 1209.9

Ready
```

We can handle data stored in DATA statements in a similar way. Here are two segments that do the same rather silly thing:

1.

```
100 REM REPEAT
110              READ N$
120              IF N$ = "***" THEN 150
130              PRINT N$;" AND ";
140      GO TO 100
150      PRINT "..."
160 REM DATA:
170      DATA "LIEDERKRANZ","REBLOCHON","CAERPHILLY"
180      DATA "PORT DU SALUD","DOLCELATTE","WENSLEYDALE"
190      DATA "BRIE","DOUBLE GLOUCESTER"
200      DATA "***"
9999     END
```

```
2.    100       READ Q
      110       FOR J=1 TO Q
      120           READ N$
      130           PRINT N$;" AND ";
      140       NEXT J
      150       PRINT "..."
      160 REM NUMBER OF RECORDS
      170       DATA 8
      180 REM DATA:
      190       DATA "LIEDERKRANZ","REBLOCHON","CAERPHILLY"
      200       DATA "PORT DU SALUD","DOLCELATTE","WENSLEYDALE"
      210       DATA "BRIE","DOUBLE GLOUCESTER"
      9999      END
```

In program 1 a flag *** is used by statement 120 to terminate the REPEAT loop. In program 2 statement 100 causes the first data item, the number 8, to be read into Q. The statement in line 110 is then interpreted as

```
FOR J = 1 TO 8
```

so that eight data records are read and printed in turn. By the way, notice that these programs appear to break the rule of "one record per DATA statement." In this case each record in the list consists of just one name, so there is, really, no record structure to preserve. The data comprise a simple list of names and would not be greatly clarified by giving each item a separate DATA statement. However, beware! If there is a chance that you might, at a later time, have to change some of the items, write them one to a DATA statement. You will be glad you did.

To summarize, there are two ways of controlling the input of data: (1) by means of a REPEAT loop and a flag at the end of the data list; and (2) by means of a FOR/NEXT loop and a data record count at the beginning of the data list.

7.4 DRAWING PICTURES: THE TAB FUNCTION

The computer is not just a brute calculator. Among its many gifts is an ability to draw. In fact, much architectural and technical drawing is now computer controlled and, recently, computers have even invaded the art world. Of course, one must connect the computer to sophisticated equipment, high-resolution video screens and plotters, to produce high-quality graphics. However, even on an ordinary terminal, we can do some interesting things.

Suppose that we want to program the computer to draw a diagram like this:

```
      *
     ***
    *****
   *******
    *****
     ***
      *
```

In order to tackle this problem, it is helpful to number the rows and columns of the diagram.

	1	2	3	4	5	6	7
1				*			
2			*	*	*		
3		*	*	*	*	*	
4	*	*	*	*	*	*	*
5		*	*	*	*	*	
6			*	*	*		
7				*			

Most terminals can print only one line at a time. So this forces a direction on our solution. If we can solve the problem of printing each individual line of stars, we can put all this together to print the whole picture. In terms of structured flowcharts, the problem can be handled as follows. To draw a picture using stars:

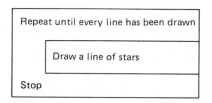

Put this way, the development so far may sound a little silly. But don't laugh at it. A divide-and-conquer strategy, in which a difficult problem is solved by dividing it into a succession of simpler and more accessible ones, can be very helpful when one is faced with an intractable programming project.

A typical line of the diagram looks like this:

	1	2	3	4	5	6	7
2			*	*	*		

To print such a line we must tell the machine where to start and where to stop printing stars. Now, wherever there are no stars there are blanks. So we could handle this by a process that decides, at each position, whether to print a blank or a star. However, instead of doing this we will introduce a new function that will make the job easier.

The TAB function allows us to move the print head of the terminal to any position on the line, just like a typewriter tab setting. Please don't confuse this function with the TAB key which is to be found on some terminals.

Here is an example of the use of the TAB function.

```
10      PRINT TAB(5);"*"
9999 END
RUN
12345678†
        *
Ready
```

Before you start wondering whether there is an error in this output, let me explain. The occurrence of TAB(5) in the PRINT statement causes the print head to move to position 5; then the semicolon causes the next item, a star, to be printed right after this (i.e., in the sixth position). Incidentally, in many versions of BASIC, TAB(5) generates four blank spaces so that the star is actually placed in the fifth column.

TAB can be used more than once in the same line. Each successive tab position is measured from the beginning of the line, not from the previous tab position.

Example

```
10      PRINT TAB(3);"A";TAB(7);"BC";TAB(15);"DEF"
9999 END
RUN
12345678901234567890
   A    BC        DEF
Ready
```

It is a useful tool for printing narrow and wide columns where the standard columns, produced by the comma, are not suitable. We could have put this function to good use earlier when we were trying to print tables that included very long names.

Example

```
10      PRINT "NAME";TAB(22);"NUMBER OF WIVES"
20      FOR I=1 TO 4
30          READ N$,W
40          PRINT N$;TAB(26);W
50      NEXT I
```

†These numbers are not actually printed. They are included to show exactly where the printing does take place.

```
60    DATA "SOLOMON",700
70    DATA "AUGUSTUS THE STRONG",365
80    DATA "JOSEPH SMITH",49
90    DATA "IKE WARD",16
9999 END
```

RUN

```
NAME                       NUMBER OF WIVES
SOLOMON                        700
AUGUSTUS THE STRONG            365
JOSEPH SMITH                    49
IKE WARD                        16
```

Ready   ■

Variables and mathematical expressions can be used in TAB.

Example

These two programs produce the same output:

```
10    FOR I = 0 TO 4          10    FOR I = 1 TO 5
20        PRINT TAB(I);"$"     20        PRINT TAB(I-1);"$"
30    NEXT I                   30    NEXT I
9999  END                     9999  END
```

Either one, when run, will produce this (the numbers are to show position only and are not printed):

```
RUN
123456789
$
 $
  $
   $
    $
Ready
```

Note: TAB(0) is just to the left of the print zone so that the first dollar sign appears in position 1. The second form of the program has the advantage that the end points of the FOR/NEXT loop correspond to the actual initial and final positions of the stars.   ■

The TAB function can be used only in PRINT statements and it can be used only to move the print head to the right.

Examples

Illegal and dangerous uses of TAB:

1.   LET A$ = TAB(3)
2.   LET X = TAB(3)
3.   PRINT TAB(20);"*";TAB(10);"*"
   (This asks the print head to move left to print the second star, after having printed the first one. Try this on your system and see what happens.)
4.   PRINT TAB(200);"OOPS"
   (In this case the tab position is well beyond the edge of the paper for most systems. What happens?)   ■

Investigate the use of TAB when printing numbers or numerical variables. The effect is not too different. Just remember that numbers, when printed, are usually preceded by a blank. Run this program to see the difference.

```
10    FOR I = 0 TO 9
20        PRINT TAB(I);"*"
30        PRINT TAB(I);I
40    NEXT I
9999  END
```

7.5 BACK TO THE DRAWING BOARD

Let's return to printing the diamond pattern. The line

1	2	3	4	5	6	7
		*	*	*		

could be printed by the statement

```
PRINT TAB(2);"***"
```

This is nice and compact and, in fact, we could polish off the whole program using this idea. Here is a program to print the diamond:

```
10    PRINT TAB(3);"*"
20    PRINT TAB(2);"***"
30    PRINT TAB(1);"*****"
40    PRINT TAB(0);"*******"
```

```
50    PRINT TAB(1);"*****"
60    PRINT TAB(2);"***"
70    PRINT TAB(3);"*"
9999  END
```

However, this shouldn't really satisfy you. When designing a program for a given task, always try to design it to be as flexible and powerful as possible, within reason. If you don't, I can guarantee that you'll wish later that you had done so. For example, this program clearly cannot draw any of these patterns:

and although we now see how they could be tackled, the situation isn't very satisfactory. As the mathematicians love to say, this solution isn't particularly elegant, and from a more practical point of view, it isn't very useful.

A more fruitful way to look at the problem of printing a line of stars is to notice that they have to be printed in given positions, starting at one place on the line and ending at a later one. For instance,

1	2	3	4	5	6	7
		*	*	*		

could be handled by

    PRINT TAB(2);"*";TAB(3);"*";TAB(4);"*"

How about using a FOR/NEXT loop for this:

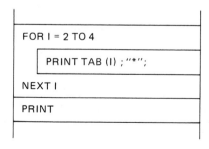

(Why is the last PRINT statement there?) Perhaps even better, we can make the end points of the loop coincide with the beginning and end positions of the line of stars.

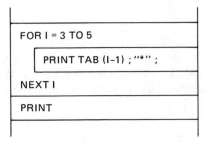

```
FOR I = 3 TO 5
    PRINT TAB (I-1) ; "*" ;
NEXT I
PRINT
```

Similarly,

1	2	3	4	5	6	7
	*	*	*	*	*	

is printed by

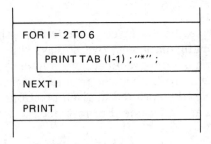

```
FOR I = 2 TO 6
    PRINT TAB (I-1) ; "*" ;
NEXT I
PRINT
```

In each case the only differences are in the values of the end points. That is, they are all special cases of

```
FOR I = B TO E
    PRINT TAB (I-1) ; "*" ;
NEXT I
PRINT
```

All we have to do for each line is assign values to B and E. This can be done by means of the statement READ B,E from the following DATA statements:

```
DATA 4,4
DATA 3,5
DATA 2,6
DATA 1,7
DATA 2,6
DATA 3,5
DATA 4,4
```

The flowchart for this project can be rewritten, thus:

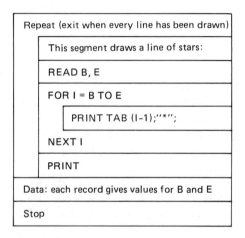

```
Repeat (exit when every line has been drawn)
    This segment draws a line of stars:
        READ B, E
        FOR I = B TO E
            PRINT TAB (I-1);"*";
        NEXT I
        PRINT
    Data: each record gives values for B and E
Stop
```

The rest is easy. The REPEAT block causes as many repetitions as there are lines of stars in the diagram. So it can be interpreted as a FOR/NEXT loop. Our diagram has seven lines, so

```
FOR J = 1 TO 7
```

will suffice. However, in line with our goal of keeping the program as general as possible, we will replace the 7 by a variable, L, and read the actual value into L before the loop starts. Skipping the final flowchart step, here is the program.

```
100 REM TITLE: SIMPLE PICTURE PRINTING
110 REM PROGRAMMER: A. KITCHEN          DATE: 25-AUG-81
120 REM DESCRIPTION: THIS PROGRAM PRINTS SIMPLE DIAGRAMS
130 REM           USING STARS (*).  THE NUMBER OF LINES IN
140 REM           THE DIAGRAM AND THE BEGINNING & ENDING
150 REM           POSITIONS FOR THE STARS IN EACH LINE ARE
160 REM           PROVIDED IN DATA STATEMENTS.
170 REM VARIABLES:
180 REM           L = NUMBER OF LINES
190 REM           J = LINE COUNTER
200 REM           B = BEGINNING POSITION FOR LINE OF STARS
210 REM           E = ENDING POSITION FOR LINE OF STARS
220 REM           I = STAR POSITION ON EACH LINE
```

```
230 REM PROGRAM:
240       READ L
250       FOR J=1 TO L
260 REM           DRAW A LINE OF STARS
270               READ B,E
280               FOR I=B TO E
290                   PRINT TAB(I-1);"*";
300               NEXT I
310               PRINT
320       NEXT J
330 REM DATA:
340 REM           NUMBER OF LINES
350       DATA 7
360 REM           RECORD = BEGIN, END (FOR EACH LINE)
370       DATA 4,4
380       DATA 3,5
390       DATA 2,6
400       DATA 1,7
410       DATA 2,6
420       DATA 3,5
430       DATA 4,4
9999      END
```

This program is quite general. By changing the DATA statements, we can change the number of lines printed as well as the beginning and ending points on each line. In this way we can produce quite a range of different patterns from this program alone.

The program is still rather limited. How can it be modified to print diagrams using characters other than the star, even to print each line using a different character? In what other ways is it limited? What kinds of diagrams can it, or can't it, print?

One last comment, before we leave this topic: Notice that, in the program we have just completed, there are two FOR/NEXT loops **nested** one within the other. The inside one handles the printing of characters for an individual line; the outside one controls the number of lines.

When you write programs involving FOR/NEXT loops that overlap in this way, use a different variable for the counter in each loop. All kinds of weird things will happen if you don't. Also, make sure that one loop lies completely within the other. Here are examples of legal and illegal patterns:

| | Legal | |
Illegal: Overlapping, Not Nested	Overlapping and Nested	Not Overlapping
10 FOR J = C TO D	10 FOR J = C TO D	10 FOR J = C TO D
- - -	- - -	- - -
50 FOR I = A TO B	50 FOR I = A TO B	50 NEXT J
- - -	- - -	- - -
100 NEXT J	100 NEXT I	100 FOR I = A TO B
- - -	- - -	- - -
170 NEXT I	170 NEXT J	170 NEXT I

Remember, the criterion for legality is: If two loops overlap, one should lie entirely inside the other.

Chapter 7: EXERCISES

Section 7.1

1. For each of (a) to (k) below, substitute an appropriate expression into
    the blank space in this program segment, so that it will print the given
    list. [*Hint: The answer to part (a) is I.*]

    ```
    10    FOR I = 1 TO 10
    20       PRINT [          ]  ;
    30    NEXT I
    9999  END
    ```

    (a) 1 2 3 4 5 6 7 8 9 10
    (b) 10 20 30 40 50 60 70 80 90 100
    (c) 0.5 1 1.5 2 2.5 3 3.5 4 4.5 5
    (d) 2 3 4 5 6 7 8 9 10 11
    (e) 3 5 7 9 11 13 15 17 19 21
    (f) 27 26 25 24 23 22 21 20 19 18
    (g) 1 8 27 64 125 216 343 512 729 1000
    (h) 2 4 8 16 32 64 128 256 512 1024
    (i) 1 4 12 32 80 192 448 1024 2304 5120
    (j) **********
    (k) ** ** ** ** ** ** ** ** ** **
    [*Hint: Part (i) is a little nasty.*]

Section 7.2

1. Fill in the blanks so that these produce the same output.

    ```
    10         LET I = 0                10    FOR J = ____ TO ____
    20    REM  REPEAT                   20       PRINT J
    30          IF I >= 10 THEN ____    30    NEXT J
    40          PRINT I                 9999  END
    50          LET I = ____
    60         GO TO 20
    9999       END
    ```

2. Show the output from this segment:

    ```
    10    INPUT B,E,S
    20    FOR I = B TO E STEP S
    ```

```
30      PRINT I
40    NEXT I
50    PRINT I
9999  END
```

corresponding to the following input:

(a) 1, 10, –1   (b) 10, 1, –1
(c) 1, 10, 2   (d) 10, 1, –2
(e) 1, 2, 0.3   (f) 1, 2, 0
(g) 0.6, 9.4, 1

[*Hint: Check your answers on the computer. There is some variation from one system to another in the handling of FOR/NEXT loops.*]

3. Rewrite the following without using FOR/NEXT loops.

(a)
```
10    FOR I = 1 TO 10
20       PRINT I
30       LET I = I+1
40    NEXT I
9999  END
```

(b)
```
10    FOR I = 1 TO 10 STEP 3
20       PRINT I
30    NEXT I
9999  END
```

(c)
```
10    INPUT B,E
20    FOR I = B TO E
30       PRINT I
40    NEXT I
9999  END
```

(d)
```
10    INPUT B,E,S
20    FOR I = B TO E STEP S
30       PRINT I
40    NEXT I
9999  END
```

[*Hint: Your translations will not work predictably if you terminate the loop when I = E. Because of truncation errors in the internal storage of the values of I, B, E, and S, the relation I = E may never be satisfied exactly. It is better to test for I $\geqslant$ E or I $>$ E. But beware of part (d). If the step size is negative, a different test will be required.*]

4. The following are examples of poor or invalid program logic. Describe what happens when these segments are run. The performance of some may vary from system to system, so experiment on the computer.

(a)
```
10  FOR J = 10 TO 1
20     PRINT J
30  NEXT J
```

(b)
```
10  FOR K = 1 TO 10
20     PRINT K
30     GO TO 10
40  NEXT K
```

(c)
```
10  FOR I = 1 TO 5
20     PRINT I
30     LET I = 2
40  NEXT I
```

(d)
```
10  LET L = 4
20  GO TO 40
30  FOR L = 1 TO 10
40     PRINT L
50  NEXT L
```

(e)
```
10  FOR J = 1 TO 5
20     PRINT J
30     LET J = J–1
40  NEXT J
```

(f)
```
10  FOR I = 1 TO N
20     INPUT N
30     PRINT I
40  NEXT I
```

(g)
```
10  FOR I = 1 TO 50
20     PRINT "IF AYATOLLAH ONCE,"
```

```
30      PRINT "AYATOLLAH 50 TIMES ALREADY!"
40      LET K = I
50   NEXT K
```

[*Hint: Trace these segments by hand. You will find this helpful in understanding exactly why they behave as they do.*]

Section 7.3

1. Explain why these segments are poorly designed.

    (a)
    ```
    10      PRINT "NUMBER","SQUARE"
    20      INPUT Q
    30      FOR I = 1 TO Q
    40         READ N
    50         PRINT N, N*N
    60      NEXT I
    70      DATA 2,3,5,7,11
    80      DATA 13,17,19,23,29
    9999 END
    ```

    (b)
    ```
    10      FOR J = 1 TO 20
    20         PRINT "NUMBER";
    30         INPUT A
    40         LET S = S+A
    50      NEXT J
    60      PRINT "SUM =";S
    9999 END
    ```

2. Many of the programs in the earlier chapters can be handled by a FOR/NEXT loop in one of these two forms:

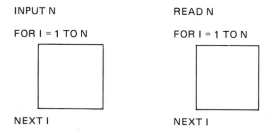

```
INPUT N

FOR I = 1 TO N

    ┌──────────┐
    │          │
    │          │
    │          │
    └──────────┘

NEXT I
```

```
READ N

FOR I = 1 TO N

    ┌──────────┐
    │          │
    │          │
    │          │
    └──────────┘

NEXT I
```

Choose a couple of programs from the following list and rewrite them using FOR/NEXT loops.

Section 4.5
   4 (Average of a list)
   5 (Squares and triangular numbers)
   6 (Factorials)
   7 ("Roll-over" song)
   8 (Amortization table)
   9 (Average and standard deviation)
Section 5.4
   1 (Salesmen's salaries)
   2 (Vermont towns)

3 (Harpsichords)
4 (Math quiz: Ask student "How many questions?" first)
Section 6.5
1 (Maximum of a list, Chief Justices)
2 (Rodeo champions)

3. (a) Write a program that accepts a name from the terminal and then checks it against a list of names stored in DATA statements. The program must print the position of every occurrence of the name in the list. [*Hint: For example, if this list is the one stored:*

MAY
ABE
LIZ
SAM
TOM
LIZ
LIZ
ABE

a typical run of the program should look like this:

RUN
NAME? LIZ
POSITIONS ARE: 3 6 7
Ready]

(b) Rewrite program (a) so that it only prints the position of the first occurrence of the name in the list. Furthermore, design it so that if the name is not in the list, the message "NOT FOUND" is printed. [*Hint: You may find that your solution leads you to a structure something like this:*

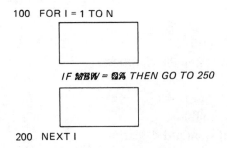

100 FOR I = 1 TO N

IF *M$W* = *Q$* THEN GO TO 250

200 NEXT I

Some programmers frown on such things. It is, after all, a REPEAT loop with two exits (one if I = N and the other if M$W = Q$) and

such things can be confusing. However, this construction is per-
fectly acceptable if it leads to a clear and simple program. Look
upon it as another variation on the REPEAT or FOR/NEXT
construction.]

Section 7.4

1. What is printed by the following statements?
    (a) PRINT TAB(7);"*"
    (b) PRINT TAB(7);7
    (c) PRINT TAB(10);"*";TAB(20);"HERE"
    (d) PRINT TAB(20);"*";TAB(10);"NOT HERE"
    (e) PRINT TAB(10),"*"
    (f) PRINT TAB(20.3);"*"
    (g) PRINT TAB(20.7);"*"
    (h) PRINT TAB(INT(20.7));"*"
    (i) PRINT TAB(INT(20.7 + 0.5));"*"
    [*Hint: Although TAB is normally followed by a semicolon, some sys-*
    tems require a comma; if yours is such a system, replace ';' by ','.]

2. Show exactly what is printed by these segments.
    (a) ```
         10   FOR I = 1 TO 7
         20   PRINT "*";TAB(I);"*";TAB(8);"*"
         30   NEXT I
         9999 END
         ```
    (b)  ```
         10    FOR X = -8 TO 8
         20        LET Y = X*X
         30        PRINT TAB(Y);"*"
         40    NEXT X
         9999  END
         ```

3. Fill in the blanks so that this

    ```
    10    PRINT TAB (____);"*"
    20    PRINT TAB (____);"* *"
    30    PRINT TAB (____);"* * *"
    40    PRINT TAB (____);"* * * *"
    9999  END
    ```

    produces

[*Hint: There is more than one answer in each case, as the pattern can appear anywhere on the page.*]

4.   Write programs that use FOR/NEXT loops and the TAB function to produce the letters T, L, N, V, M, Z. [*Hint: See Exercise 2(a) for a prototype. There is no limit on the size of the letters.*]

5.   Design a program to print a table of roots. The table should have 11 columns, the first consisting of the integers 1, 2, 3, . . . , 50, the second containing the square roots of these, with the 4th, 6th, 8th, . . . , 20th roots in subsequent columns.

Use the TAB function to produce the nonstandard column widths for this table. Also, round all answers to three decimal places to allow room to print all these columns. [*Hint: If your terminal prints no more than 80 characters per line, space will be tight. So plan carefully. Make sure that the table is well documented. Notice how little the entries in the last column vary. This illustrates the fact that for any number x, $\sqrt[n]{x} \approx 1$ when n is sufficiently large.*]

6.   The TAB function can be used to produce a reasonable plot of a function $y = f(x)$. The simplest way to do this is to plot the graph on its side (x direction down the page, y direction from left to right). A simple example is given in Exercise 2(b).

In general, the values of $y = f(x)$ must be scaled so that they produce legal TAB positions. Here is a systematic way of designing such programs. Suppose that $y = f(x)$ is to be plotted over the interval $A \leqslant x \leqslant B$ and that the values of $f(x)$ lie in the range $M \leqslant y \leqslant N$. Then, in order to plot a graph using the print positions 10 through 70, each value of $y = f(x)$ must be scaled by

$$Y1 = 9 + 60\left(\frac{y - M}{N - M}\right)$$

before being used in the TAB function.

For example: To plot $y = x^3$, for $-2 \leqslant x \leqslant 2$ in steps of 0.1, notice first that $-8 \leqslant y \leqslant 8$ in this interval. Thus

```
- - -           - - -
200            FOR X = -2 TO 2 STEP 0.1
210  REM         CALCULATE Y VALUE
220               LET Y = X ^3
230  REM         SCALE THIS VALUE
240               LET Y1 = 9 + 60*(Y + 8)/16
250  REM         ROUND VALUE
260               LET Y1 = INT(Y1 + 0.5)
270  REM         PLOT POINT
280               PRINT TAB(Y1);"*"
290            NEXT X
- - -           - - -
```

Write programs to plot these functions over the given x intervals (y ranges given).

(a) $y = x^2$ for $-7 \leqslant x \leqslant 7$ in steps of 0.5 ($0 \leqslant y \leqslant 49$)

(b) $y = \dfrac{1}{x^2 + 1}$ for $-3 \leqslant x \leqslant 3$ in steps of 0.25 ($0 \leqslant y \leqslant 1$)

(c) $y = 2^x$ for $-4 \leqslant x \leqslant 2$ in steps of 0.25 ($0 \leqslant y \leqslant 4$)

(d) $y = \sin(x)$ for $0 \leqslant x \leqslant 10$ in steps of 0.2 ($-1 \leqslant y \leqslant 1$)
[*Hint: BASIC provides the function SIN(X). To change the length of the graph (x direction), change the step size or the limits of the loop. To change the width (y direction) or position of the graph, change the constants 9 and 60. Experiment!*]

Here is a sampling of other functions for plotting. You must choose the x intervals and estimate the y ranges:

$$y = x^3 - x, \quad y = x^{2/3}, \quad y = \frac{x}{x^2 + 1}, \quad y = \sin x + \sin 2x, \quad y = \sin x + \sin 2x + \sin 3x$$

Some functions are not defined for every value of x (e.g., $y = 1/x^2$ is not defined for $x = 0$). One way to handle such points is to print a blank line (i.e., do not print a star) at each x value for which y is not defined.

Plot $y = 1/x^2$ for $-4 \leqslant x \leqslant 4$ in steps of 0.25 ($0 \leqslant y \leqslant 16$).

Section 7.5

1. Determine whether the program developed in this section is capable of printing each of the following patterns. If it is, construct the necessary DATA statements.

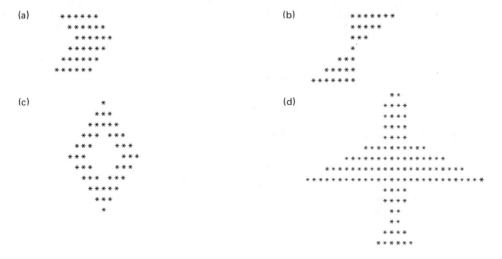

(e)

```
            ****
          *******
          *******
           *****
            **
            ****
    *******************
    *******************
           ****
          ******
         *******
        *********
       **********
      *************
     *************
```

2. Write a program that will repeat any of the patterns above endlessly down the page. [*Hint: All one has to do is to repeat the pattern program over and over. The only problem with this is that the program runs through all the DATA statements on the first cycle. Remember the RESTORE statement!*]

3. A convenient way to represent numerical data is by means of a bar chart. Bar charts are often used in statistics and economics because of their visual impact. Trends tend to stand out more clearly in diagrams than in raw numerical data. Here is a bar chart for the data 4, 2, 9, 18, 19, 12, 13, 7.

```
 4      ****
        ****

 2      **
        **

 9      ********
        ********

18      *****************
        *****************

19      ******************
        ******************

12      ***********
        ***********

13      ************
        ************

 7      *******
        *******
```

(a) Write a program that will read a list of values from DATA statements and print out a bar chart for these values.

(b) Can the program you wrote for part (a) handle these values: 417, 279, 950, 1824, 1991, 1237, 1303, 745? If it can't, modify it so that it can print (approximate) bar charts for data values in, say, the range 1 to 2000. [*Hint: You will have to scale the values down before plotting them.*]

4. Rewrite the graph plotting programs in Exercise 6 of Section 7.4 so
    that they produce bar charts.

    [*Hint:* For example

    ```
    ********                          instead of          *
    ****                                               *
    **                                              *
    *                                               *
    *                                               *
    *                                               *
    **                                              *
    ****                                               *
    ********                                          *  ]
    ```

5. (a) This pattern: `1 2 3 4 5 6 7 8 9 0 1`

    ```
                    *                    1
                  * * *                  2
                * * * * *                3
              * * * 0 * * *              4
            * * * 0 0 0 * * *            5
          * * * 0 0 0 0 0 * * *          6
                0 0 0                    7
                  0                      8
    ```

    cannot be produced by the program discussed in this section.
    Write a program that will print this pattern given the following
    DATA statements.

    ```
    DATA 8
    DATA 1,"*",6,6
    DATA 1,"*",5,7
    DATA 1,"*",4,8
    DATA 3,"*",3,5,"0",6,6,"*",7,9
    DATA 3,"*",2,4,"0",5,7,"*",8,10
    DATA 3,"*",1,3,"0",4,8,"*",9,11
    DATA 1,"0",5,7
    DATA 1,"0",6,6
    ```

    [*Hint: Each DATA statement, apart from the first, contains the
    information for one line of the diagram. For example, the DATA
    statement for the line*

    `1 2 3 4 5 6 7 8 9 0 1`

    `* * * 0 0 0 * * *`

    is

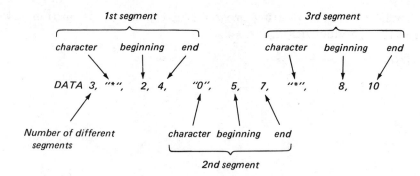

The simple flowchart in Section 7.4 should be augmented to read

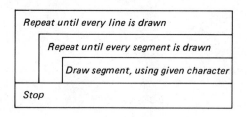

(b) Construct DATA statements to produce other diagrams. For example:

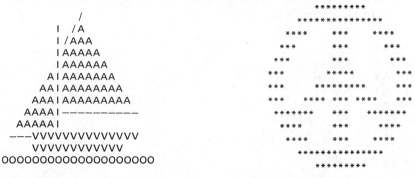

6. Describe what is printed when each of these program segments is executed.

(a)
```
10  FOR J = 1 TO 3
20      FOR I = 5 TO 1 STEP –1
30          PRINT J;
40      NEXT I
50  NEXT J
```

(b)
```
10  FOR J = 1 TO 3
20      FOR I = 5 TO 1 STEP –1
30          PRINT I;
```

```
       40      NEXT I
       50      PRINT
       60  NEXT J
```

(c)
```
   10  FOR J = 1 TO 3
   20      FOR I = 5 TO 1 STEP –1
   30          PRINT J;
   40      NEXT I
   50  NEXT J
```

(d)
```
   10  FOR I = 5 TO 1 STEP –1
   20      FOR J = 1 TO 3
   30          PRINT I;
   40      NEXT J
   50  NEXT I
```

(e)
```
   10  FOR J = 1 TO 3
   20      FOR I = J TO 5
   30          PRINT I
   40      NEXT I
   50  NEXT J
```

7. Fill in the blanks:

```
10  FOR I = 1 TO ____
20      FOR J = ____ TO ____
30          PRINT TAB(J);"*";
40      NEXT J
50      PRINT
60  NEXT I
```

so that this segment produces

(a)
```
* * * * * *
 * * * * *
  * * * *
   * * *
    * *
     *
```

(b)
```
* * * * * *
 * * * * *
  * * * *
   * * *
    * *
     *
```

(c)
```
* * * * * * *
 * * * * *
  * * *
   *
```

[*Hint: The position of these patterns on the page is not critical.*]

Chapter

8

Lists and Arrays

8.1 DATA PROCESSING AND LISTS

Almost all business data processing and much scientific calculation, particularly in the social sciences, concerns the processing of large quantities of data. These data usually take the form of long lists of numbers or names, or of records, where each record may consist of a number of different data items.

Examples

1. Simple list of numerical data:

    104.30
    29.00
    18.03
    1537.50
    5.54
    47.49
    17.00
    93.25
    101.25
    6.00

2. A list of records, where each record consists of two items (or fields):[†]

    Pillow, 332
    Broad Axe, 500
    Economy, 7176
    Primos, 1000
    Plum, 24700
    Uledi, 500
    Roulette, 700
    Yoe, 790
    Grindstone, 950
    Moon, 600

[†]In case you are wondering, these are small towns and villages in Pennsylvania with their populations.

24.10   Dry Tavern, 400
                                    Forty Fort, 6114
                                    Scotland, 500
                                    Library, 4600
                                    Fairchance, 1906   ■

To understand some of the tasks performed in data processing, consider
the following example. A company that provides charge account services to
its customers must keep complete records on all these accounts. The data on
an individual account form a record consisting of, at the very least:

> account number, customer name, address, line of credit, current bal-
> ance, expiration date of charge card

Every month the billing department must go through all the accounts in
order to print and mail statements to the customers. This is straightforward.
However, there are other tasks that have to be done. If an individual customer has a question about his account or makes a charge or a payment, the
company has to be able to search quickly through all its records in order to
retrieve that one account. The accounts may be searched for by name or by
account number. In either case, it will increase the efficiency of the search if
the accounts are listed in some definite order, say, alphabetical or numerical.
This leads to another task. When new accounts are added, they will have to
be placed in appropriate positions in the list. A related task is that of sorting
(e.g., sorting a list of names into alphabetical order). All these procedures
are, in principle, relatively simple but time consuming. They are admirable
jobs to assign to a computer.

8.2 ARRAYS

There is one ability which is required of the computer in order that it can
handle the kinds of jobs discussed above. It must, given a list of data values,
be able to retrieve the item which is stored at any particular position in that
list. To show you what I mean, consider the following simple case. A very
small store has a very small number of charge account customers. Here is a
table showing the current balances owed by these customers:

Customer Number	Balance Owed ($)
1	17.35
2	5.99
3	9.85
4	23.10
5	36.04

How can we write a program that will print out the balance owed by a given customer when that person's number is typed in? That is, something like this:

```
RUN
TYPE CUSTOMER NUMBER? 3
CUSTOMER 3 HAS A BALANCE OF $ 9.85
Ready
```

Suppose that we attempt to write such a program. First the list of balances must be stored in variables:

```
100  LET A = 17.35
110  LET B = 5.99
120  LET C = 9.85
130  LET D = 23.10
140  LET E = 36.04
```

Then the customer number must be requested:

```
150  PRINT "TYPE CUSTOMER NUMBER";
160  INPUT N
```

What do we do next? How can we use the customer number to pick out one of the five values? For example, if we type in 3, how do we get the machine to return the value of the third variable, C? Here is a crude solution:

```
170       PRINT "CUSTOMER";N;"HAS A BALANCE OF $";
180       IF NOT (N = 1) THEN 200
190            PRINT A
200 REM ENDIF
210       IF NOT (N = 2) THEN 230
220            PRINT B
230 REM ENDIF
240       IF NOT (N = 3) THEN 260
250            PRINT C
260 REM ENDIF
270       IF NOT (N = 4) THEN 290
280            PRINT D
290 REM ENDIF
300       IF NOT (N = 5) THEN 320
310            PRINT E
320 REM ENDIF
9999      END
```

This is not particularly satisfactory. It is a little better if we can use the nonjumping IF:

```
170       PRINT "CUSTOMER";N;"HAS A BALANCE OF $";
180       IF N = 1 THEN PRINT A
190       IF N = 2 THEN PRINT B
```

```
200      IF N = 3 THEN PRINT C
210      IF N = 4 THEN PRINT D
220      IF N = 5 THEN PRINT E
9999     END
```

However, for any reasonably large accounting system, the number of IF statements would be huge. The BASIC language comes to our rescue with a special type of variable designed for the storage and retrieval of lists. Here is an improved version of our program:

```
100      LET B(1) = 17.35
110      LET B(2) = 5.99
120      LET B(3) = 9.85
130      LET B(4) = 23.10
140      LET B(5) = 36.04
150      PRINT "TYPE CUSTOMER NUMBER";
160      INPUT N
170      PRINT "CUSTOMER";N;"HAS A BALANCE OF $";B(N)
9999     END
```

This list of variables, B(1), B(2), B(3), B(4), and B(5), is called an **array**, the array B. In this case, the array consists of five simple variables, the **components** of B, each of which is capable of storing a number. These components, B(1), B(2), and so on, are often referred to as **subscripted variables**.

Earlier we used the analogy of the mailbox to illustrate the concept of a variable. An array can be thought of as a group of numbered mailboxes or post office boxes.

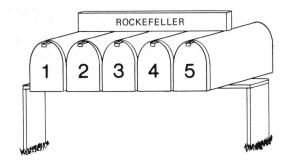

Let's look at what happens when this program is executed. Statements 100 to 140 cause the balances to be stored in the array. Suppose that the value 3 is typed in response to the INPUT statement. This is stored in N so that the term B(N) (in statement 170) is interpreted by the system as B(3). The following diagram indicates the situation:

After line 160

```
100     LET B(1) = 17.35   N  [ 3 ]   B(1)   [ 17.35 ]
                                       B(2)   [  5.99 ]
---                                    B(3)   [  9.85 ]
---                                    B(4)   [ 23.10 ]
160     INPUT N                        B(5)   [ 36.04 ]
170     PRINT "CUSTOMER";N;...
9999    END
```

After line 170

```
N  [ 3 ]   B(1)   [ 17.35 ]
           B(2)   [  5.99 ]
        →  B(3)   [  9.85 ]
           B(4)   [ 23.10 ]
           B(5)   [ 36.04 ]

9999    END
```

B(N) is interpreted as B(3)

Of course, from the point of view of the person running the program, this run looks identical to that of the previous version:

```
RUN
TYPE CUSTOMER NUMBER? 3
CUSTOMER 3 HAS A BALANCE OF $ 9.85
Ready
```

The array B(1), B(2), B(3), B(4), B(5) must not be confused with the variables B1, B2, B3, B4, B5. In the latter, the digits 1, 2, 3, 4, 5 cannot be interpreted as numbers. They are just symbols that form part of the names of these variables. Replace B(N) by BN in the program above and see if it will run. The quantity inside the parentheses, the **subscript,** is a pointer that indicates the position of a given component of the array.

Example

B(4) indicates the fourth element in the list stored in the array B. ∎

The real power of the concept of an array arises from the fact that the subscript can be a variable or even a mathematical expression.

Examples

Study these segments of BASIC code, where the array B contains the same values as before but the code from line 150 on has been changed as shown.

1.

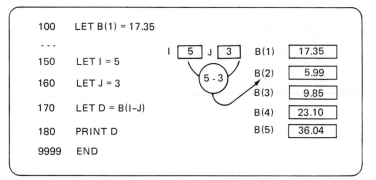

```
100     LET B(1) = 17.35
- - -
150     LET I = 5
160     LET J = 3
170     LET D = B(I–J)
180     PRINT D
9999    END
```

RUN

5.99

Ready

2.

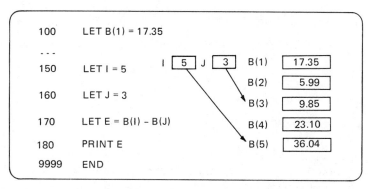

```
100     LET B(1) = 17.35
- - -
150     LET I = 5
160     LET J = 3
170     LET E = B(I) – B(J)
180     PRINT E
9999    END
```

RUN

26.19

Ready

3.

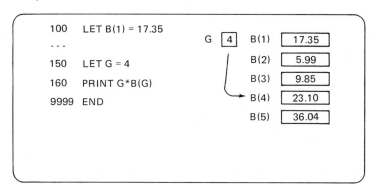

```
100     LET B(1) = 17.35
- - -
150     LET G = 4
160     PRINT G*B(G)
9999    END
```

RUN

92.4

Ready

4.

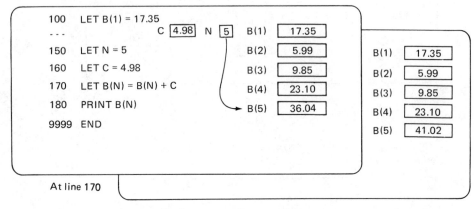

```
100   LET B(1) = 17.35
- - -
150   LET N = 5
160   LET C = 4.98
170   LET B(N) = B(N) + C
180   PRINT B(N)
9999  END
```

C 4.98   N 5

B(1)	17.35
B(2)	5.99
B(3)	9.85
B(4)	23.10
B(5)	36.04

B(1)	17.35
B(2)	5.99
B(3)	9.85
B(4)	23.10
B(5)	41.02

At line 170

After line 170

RUN

41.02

Ready   ■

From the examples above, it should also be clear that the components of the array behave like any other variable and can be used anywhere that simple variables can be used.

An array name consists of a single letter.[†] There is no confusion with ordinary numerical variables because an array name is always followed by a quantity in parentheses. The general pattern is

array name (subscript)

Example

These are typical arrays:

       Array A: A(1), A(2), A(3), . . . , A(9)
       Array K: K(1), K(2), K(3), . . . , K(50)   ■

[†]Many systems allow array names consisting of a letter followed by a digit [e.g., A3(1), A3(2), etc.]

Although it is legal on many systems to use, say, the simple variable A in the same program as the array A, this can be confusing to someone reading the program and should be avoided if possible.

Now, as the subscript of an array can be a variable, it may have occurred to you that a FOR/NEXT loop could be used to store data in the array, B, of the customer balance program:

```
100        FOR I=1 TO 5
110              READ B(I)
120        NEXT I
130        PRINT "CUSTOMER NUMBER";
140        INPUT N
150        PRINT "CUSTOMER";N;"HAS A BALANCE OF $";B(N)
160 REM DATA: RECORD = CUSTOMER BALANCE
170        DATA 17.35
180        DATA 5.99
190        DATA 9.85
200        DATA 23.1
210        DATA 36.04
9999       END
```

This program is not any shorter, but it is more amenable to generalization. We can increase its flexibility by reading in the value of the upper limit of the FOR/NEXT loop. Here is a version involving 15 customers:

```
100 REM TITLE: CUSTOMER BALANCES
110 REM PROGRAMMER: A. KITCHEN            DATE: 6-AUG-81
120 REM
130 REM VARIABLES:
140 REM          K = TOTAL # OF CUSTOMER RECORDS
150 REM          I = COUNTER
160 REM          B(I) = BALANCE FOR CUSTOMER I
170 REM          N = CUSTOMER NUMBER
180 REM
190 REM PROGRAM:
200 REM READ NUMBER OF RECORDS:
210        READ K
220 REM READ RECORDS INTO ARRAY:
230        FOR I=1 TO K
240              READ B(I)
250        NEXT I
260 REM SEARCH FOR NTH RECORD
270        PRINT "CUSTOMER NUMBER";
280        INPUT N
290        PRINT "CUSTOMER";N;"HAS A BALANCE OF $";B(N)
300 REM DATA:
310 REM          NUMBER OF RECORDS
320        DATA 15
330 REM          RECORD = CUSTOMER BALANCE
340        DATA 17.35
350        DATA 5.99
360        DATA 9.85
370        DATA 23.10
380        DATA 36.04
390        DATA 21.50
400        DATA 7.89
410        DATA 50.40
420        DATA 23.15
430        DATA 98.03
```

```
440     DATA 15.97
450     DATA 47.50
460     DATA 46.28
470     DATA 75.00
480     DATA 9.35
9999    END
```

Suppose that we run this:

```
RUN
subscript out of range in line 240
Ready
```

What's the problem? There can't be anything really wrong with the logic of the program, as an almost identical program worked before. There is, however, an important statement missing. Although we have not discussed any restrictions on the number of components in an array, an absolute limit is always imposed, at least by the size of the computer's memory. In practice, one must reserve a specific number of locations for an array before using it. The reason we had no trouble before is that if nothing else is said, the system will automatically set aside 10 locations for each array used in a program.[†] If more are needed, they must be assigned as follows:

```
195       DIM B(50)
200  REM  READ NUMBER OF RECORDS:
210       READ K
220  REM  READ RECORDS INTO ARRAY:
```

The statement DIM B(50), referred to as a **dimension statement**, allocates 50 storage locations B(1), B(2), . . . , B(49), B(50). In fact we only need room for 15 customer balances, but if we reserve more, we won't have to change this statement when we add more customers later. The diagram on the next page shows the storage picture after the data have been read into the array. On some computer systems, the values of B(16), . . . , B(50) will be automatically set to zero. On others, their contents will be unpredictable, depending on what was previously stored in that area of memory. **Never** retrieve a value from a variable if you have not already assigned one to it at an earlier stage in the program.

The dimension statement for an array should appear at the beginning of the program, before the first statement in which the array is used. In most recent versions of BASIC, arrays of character string variables can be formed,

---

[†]In fact, the ANSI standard for minimal BASIC requires that 11 locations be reserved to hold components numbered 0, 1, 2, . . . , 10. Thus the array B actually includes a component B(0) as well as B(1), B(2), . . . , B(10).

```
        K [    15    ]                    B(1)   [  17.35  ]
                                          B(2)   [  5.99   ]
                                                   - - -
                                          B(15)  [  9.35   ]
                                          B(16)  [         ]
                    No values have been {
                    assigned to these         - - -
                    locations             B(50)  [         ]
```

too, and their dimensions must be specified in the same way. Always **dimension** every array used in a program, even if it requires fewer than 10 locations. This alerts anyone reading the program to the fact that arrays are being used and helps protect the array from invalid access; see Example 3 below.

Examples

1. DIM N(1000)

   This establishes 1000 locations, N(1), N(2), . . . , N(999), N(1000), each of which can be used to store a number.

2. DIM A(1500),N(1500),C(2),E(2),G(2)
   DIM Q(100)

   Any number of different arrays can be dimensioned in one statement and any number of dimension statements may appear in one program.

3. Character string arrays behave similarly to numerical arrays. However, not all systems provide them, so check your manuals.

```
100    DIM G$(3)
110    FOR I = 1 TO 3
120       READ G$(I)
130    NEXT I
140    PRINT "ENTER 1, 2, OR 3";
150    INPUT L
160    PRINT G$(L)
170    DATA "GOOD","BETTER","BEST"
9999   END
RUN
ENTER 1, 2, OR 3? 5
Subscript out of range in line 160
Ready
```

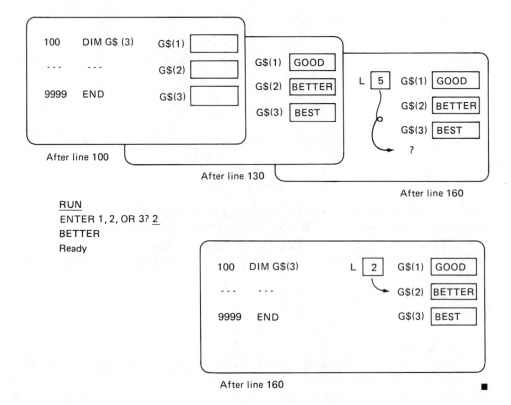

After line 100

After line 130

After line 160

RUN
ENTER 1, 2, OR 3? 2
BETTER
Ready

After line 160

8.3   AN EXAMPLE: LOADED DICE?

In this section we discuss an elegant use of arrays to solve a fairly common type of problem in computer science: keeping simultaneous counts of a number of different items or events.

You are shooting craps on the street corner with a group of friends. After a while you begin to suspect that the dice are loaded, so at the end of the game, you surreptitiously pocket them and take them home. You decide to test each one by throwing it 600 times and keeping track of the number of times that each number comes up.

Of course, you can keep the tallies by hand:

1	2	3	4	5	6
ⵌⵌⵌ ⵌⵌⵌ ‖	ⵌⵌⵌ ‖‖‖‖	ⵌⵌⵌ ⵌⵌⵌ ‖	ⵌⵌⵌ ‖‖	ⵌⵌⵌ ⵌⵌⵌ ‖‖	ⵌⵌⵌ

but this is tedious work and the counts have to be totalled afterward. Instead, you decide to pull out your computer and write a program. Here is a plan of the output you want:

```
RUN
THIS PROGRAM WILL ACCEPT 600
THROWS OF A DIE. AFTER EACH
QUESTION MARK, ENTER 1,2,3,4,5, OR 6.
? 5
? 5
? 1
? 4
? 3
? 2
? 4
etc.
TOTALS
NUMBER OF 1'S: 94
NUMBER OF 2'S: 113
NUMBER OF 3'S: 106
- - -
NUMBER OF 6'S: 88
Ready
```

and here is a flowchart for the program:

```
┌──────────────────────────────────────────────────────┐
│ Set up six counters to tally throws                    │
│                                                        │
│ Print instructions                                     │
├──────────────────────────────────────────────────────┤
│ FOR I = 1 TO 600                                       │
│   ┌──────────────────────────────────────────────┐    │
│   │ Accept Score                                   │    │
│   │ If throw is 1, increase 1st counter by 1       │    │
│   │ If throw is 2, increase 2nd counter by 1       │    │
│   │ - - -                                          │    │
│   │ If throw is 6, increase 6th counter by 1       │    │
│   └──────────────────────────────────────────────┘    │
├──────────────────────────────────────────────────────┤
│ NEXT I                                                 │
├──────────────────────────────────────────────────────┤
│ FOR J = 1 TO 6                                         │
│   ┌──────────────────────────────────────────────┐    │
│   │ Print value stored in Jth counter             │    │
│   └──────────────────────────────────────────────┘    │
├──────────────────────────────────────────────────────┤
│ NEXT J                                                 │
├──────────────────────────────────────────────────────┤
│ STOP                                                   │
└──────────────────────────────────────────────────────┘
```

An array seems a natural candidate for storing the six counts. Let's suppose you use D(1), D(2), . . . , D(6): D(1) to store the count of 1's; D(2) the count of 2's; and so on. To set up the counters you must dimension the array, D, and set all its components equal to zero. Here is a partial translation of the first block of the flowchart.

```
DIM D(6)

FOR J = 1 TO 6

    LET D(J) = 0

NEXT J

Print instructions
```

The final FOR/NEXT loop is easy, too:

```
FOR J = 1 TO 6

    PRINT "NUMBER OF";J;" 'S:";D(J)

NEXT J
```

All that remains is to tackle the body of the loop that performs the counting. If your system allows you to use the nonjumping IF, the following direct translation can be made:

```
INPUT S

IF S = 1 THEN LET D(1) = D(1) + 1
IF S = 2 THEN LET D(2) = D(2) + 1
IF S = 3 THEN LET D(3) = D(3) + 1
IF S = 4 THEN LET D(4) = D(4) + 1
IF S = 5 THEN LET D(5) = D(5) + 1
IF S = 6 THEN LET D(6) = D(6) + 1
```

However, if this approach is not available to you, you have to translate each of these IF statements as follows:

```
        IF NOT (S = 1) THEN    Ⓐ
            LET D(1) = D(1) + 1
 Ⓐ     ENDIF

        IF NOT (S = 2) THEN    Ⓑ
            LET D(2) = D(2) + 1
 Ⓑ     ENDIF

        etc.
```

and your workman-like solution begins to look a little clumsy.

Now, you may already have seen ways around this problem, but if your solution involves an additional FOR/NEXT loop, look again. Look at the original set of IF statements. Together they say:

"Whatever the score (1, 2, etc.), increase the corresponding component of D (D(1), D(2), etc.) by 1."

Put another way, this is

"whatever the value of S, increase D(S) by 1."

Writing this in BASIC, we put, simply:

LET D(S) = D(S) + 1

This trick knocks the stuffing out of the problem. The six IF blocks are replaced by just one statement. Here is the complete program:

```
100 REM TITLE: DIE TALLY
110 REM PROGRAMMER: A. KITCHEN            DATE: 16-AUG-81
120 REM
130 REM VARIABLES:
140 REM         D(1),D(2),... = COUNTS FOR SCORES 1,2,...
150 REM         J = SUBSCRIPT OF ARRAY D
160 REM         I = COUNTER FOR NUMBER OF THROWS
170 REM         S = SCORE ON CURRENT THROW
180 REM
190 REM PROGRAM:
200     DIM D(6)
210     FOR J=1 TO 6
220         LET D(J) = 0
230     NEXT J
240     PRINT "THIS PROGRAM WILL ACCEPT 600 THROWS OF A"
250     PRINT "DIE.  AFTER EACH QUESTION MARK, ENTER A"
260     PRINT "NUMBER IN THE RANGE 1,2,3,4,5,6."
270     FOR I=1 TO 600
280         INPUT S
290         LET D(S) = D(S)+1
300     NEXT I
310     FOR J=1 TO 6
320         PRINT "NUMBER OF";J;"'S:";D(J)
330     NEXT J
9999    END
```

The trick we used is very simple, so simple in fact that, as with a tongue twister, you may find that you have trouble getting your mind around it. This example traces a couple of passes through the counting loop of the program.

Example

RUN
THIS PROGRAM WILL ACCEPT 600
THROWS OF A DIE. AFTER EACH
QUESTION MARK, ENTER 1,2,3,4,5, OR 6 .

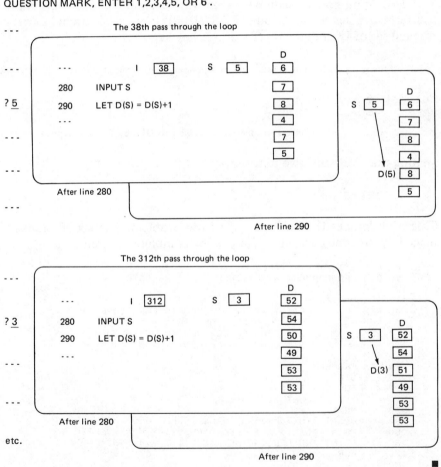

By the way, after all this testing, you decide that the dice were fair. It was just a run of bad luck!

8.4 SEARCHING: THE BEER CAN FILE

The customer accounts program discussed earlier in the chapter is a little too simple to be realistic. In practice, most lists involve individual records with more complex structure. For example, as described above, a typical charge account record might consist of

Account number, name, address, line of credit, current balance, etc.

The process of searching for an individual record usually consists of having the computer accept a name or account number, after which it checks each record in turn until it finds the record with the given name or account number. The individual items, such as account number, name, and so on, which make up a record, are referred to as **record fields** and that field which is used as a basis for the search is called a **key**. For example, to search for an account belonging to Phoebe P. B. Beebie, the name field would be used as the key.

Here is a project that requires this type of searching procedure. My elder son is an avid collector and trader of old (empty!) beer cans. He keeps records on each brand in his collection of about 2000 cans. Each record includes the name, place of manufacture, size, color, type of can, and other information important only to beer can collectors. Here is a simplified and slightly fictionalized excerpt from his records:

Name	Beverage Type	Can Type	Place of Origin	Quantity
Ace	Beer	Tab	Australia	1
Alpine	Beer	Punch	Canada	3
Badger	Beer	Tab	England	1
Beverwyck	Ale	Cone	New York	1
Brahma Chopp	Beer	Tab	Brazil	2
Budweiser	Beer	Flat	Missouri	2
Cardinal	Beer	Tab	Switzerland	2
Cinci	Beer	Punch	Canada	3
Corona	Beer	Tab	Puerto Rico	1
Dawson's	Ale	Cone	Massachusetts	1
Falstaff	Beer	Tab	Rhode Island	5
Grolsch	Beer	Tab	Holland	1
Holsten	Beer	Tab	Germany	1
Marston's	Beer	Party	England	1
Newcastle Brown	Ale	Tab	England	3
Old Frothingslosh	Ale	Tab	Pennsylvania	7
Pabst	Beer	Flat	Wisconsin	2
Reschs	Beer	Tab	Australia	2
Ruddles	Ale	Party	England	1
Sapporo	Beer	Tab	Japan	1
Stegmaier	Beer	Flat	Pennsylvania	2
Tecate	Beer	Tab	Mexico	4
XXX	Light	Tab	Mexico	2

He has this information on index cards. However, let's suppose that he wants to store these records in the computer in such a way that he can easily make changes to them. This will require writing a program that is capable of searching through the data (using, say, the brand name as a key). It should provide facilities for the printing of information on individual cans, as well as for the updating of the records as cans are acquired and traded.

Before we start this project, I want to reiterate that we should start at the end. That is, we should start by planning what output we want the program to produce and what a typical run should look like. If one is writing the program to someone else's specifications, it is particularly important to spell this part out in detail and to discuss it with him before continuing with the planning of the program. This way misunderstandings can be ironed out before a large amount of time has been committed to a false start.

To keep the program simple, let's assume that the only modification which is allowed is a change in the quantity field of any given record. Here is how it might be handled:

```
RUN
CAN COLLECTION UPDATE PROGRAM
TO REVIEW THE INFORMATION ON A CAN: TYPE CAN NAME, WHEN PROMPTED
TO UPDATE THE QUANTITY FOR THIS BRAND: TYPE THE CHANGE (IN RESPONSE
TO "UPDATE?") (+) FOR CANS RECEIVED, (-) FOR THOSE TRADED AWAY. IF THERE
IS NO CHANGE, TYPE 0 (ZERO).
THIS PROGRAM MAY BE STOPPED AT ANY TIME BY PRESSING THE BREAK KEY.
NAME? OLD FROTHINGSLOSH
BEV: ALE          CAN: TAB          ORIGIN: PENNSYLVANIA          QTY: 7
UPDATE? -2
NAME? MARSTON'S
BEV: BEER         CAN: PARTY        ORIGIN: ENGLAND              QTY: 1
UPDATE? 0
NAME? OLD FROTHINGSLOSH
BEV: ALE          CAN: TAB          ORIGIN: PENNSYLVANIA          QTY: 5
UPDATE? ^C     (BREAK key was pressed)
Ready
```

We can start by storing all the data in arrays. For example:

$$N\$(1), \ldots, N\$(50) = \text{can name}$$
$$B\$(1), \ldots, B\$(50) = \text{beverage type}$$
$$C\$(1), \ldots, C\$(50) = \text{can type}$$
$$P\$(1), \ldots, P\$(50) = \text{place of origin}$$
$$Q(1), \ldots, Q(50) = \text{quantity}$$

We will set aside room for 50 records even though we have only 23 different brands at the moment. Getting data into the arrays is straightforward.

```
200       DIM N$(50),B$(50),C$(50),P$(50),Q(50)
210 REM READ NUMBER OF RECORDS:
220       READ K
230 REM READ RECORDS INTO ARRAYS:
240       FOR I=1 TO K
250               READ N$(I),B$(I),C$(I),P$(I),Q(I)
260       NEXT I

1000 REM DATA:
1010 REM          NUMBER OF RECORDS
1020      DATA 23
1030 REM          RECORD = NAME,BEVERAGE,CAN,PLACE OF ORIGIN,QUANTITY
1040      DATA "ACE","BEER","TAB","AUSTRALIA",1
1050      DATA "ALPINE","BEER","PUNCH","CANADA",3
1060      DATA "BADGER","BEER","TAB","ENGLAND",1
1070      DATA "BEVERWYCK","ALE","CONE","NEW YORK",1
1080      DATA "BRAHMA CHOPP","BEER","TAB","BRAZIL",2
1090      DATA "BUDWEISER","BEER","FLAT","MISSOURI",2
1100      DATA "CARDINAL","BEER","TAB","SWITZERLAND",2
1110      DATA "CINCI","BEER","PUNCH","CANADA",3
1120      DATA "CORONA","BEER","TAB","PUERTO RICO",1
1130      DATA "DAWSON'S","ALE","CONE","MASSACHUSETTS",1
1140      DATA "FALSTAFF","BEER","TAB","RHODE ISLAND",5
1150      DATA "GROLSCH","BEER","TAB","HOLLAND",1
1160      DATA "HOLSTEN","BEER","TAB","GERMANY",1
1170      DATA "MARSTON'S","BEER","PARTY","ENGLAND",1
1180      DATA "NEWCASTLE BROWN","ALE","TAB","ENGLAND",3
1190      DATA "OLD FROTHINGSLOSH","ALE","TAB","PENNSYLVANIA",7
1200      DATA "PABST","BEER","FLAT","WISCONSIN",2
1210      DATA "RESCHS","BEER","TAB","AUSTRALIA",2
1220      DATA "RUDDLES","ALE","PARTY","ENGLAND",1
1230      DATA "SAPORO","BEER","TAB","JAPAN",1
1240      DATA "STEGMAIER","BEER","FLAT","PENNSYLVANIA",2
1250      DATA "TECATE","BEER","TAB","MEXICO",4
1260      DATA "XXX","LIGHT","TAB","MEXICO",2
9999      END
```

The FOR/NEXT loop reads one record at a time, the five fields of the Ith record being stored in N$(I), B$(I), C$(I), P$(I), Q(I). Here is the storage picture after the execution of statements 200 through 260.

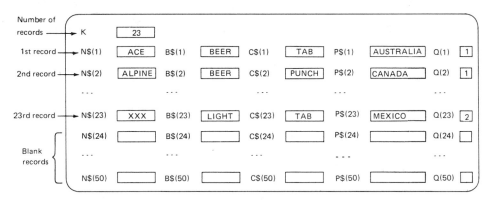

Check to see if your system requires quotes around character strings in DATA statements. Many systems don't, and this can save a lot of time when typing large numbers of DATA statements. However, the strings themselves should not include commas, as, without quotes, these will be interpreted as data separators. Beware of other idiosyncracies: My system suppresses embedded blank spaces if the string is not enclosed in quotes (e.g., OLD FROTHINGSLOSH becomes OLDFROTHINGSLOSH).

Before attempting to finish this program, we must write out a structured flowchart to help focus on the main problem—the searching process. In the previous project the array subscript played the role of a key. Here the search is based on the brand name of the can, so the simple approach used in that program will not work.

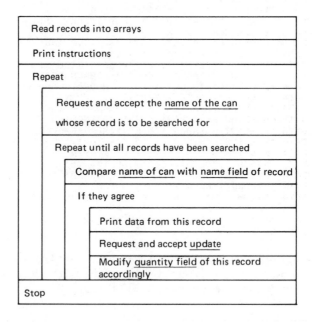

The first box of the chart has already been translated by statements 200 through 260. The next box can be handled by a sequence of PRINT statements. The outer REPEAT block is of the simplest kind:

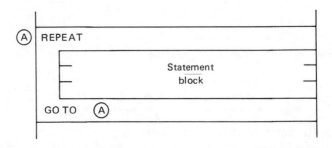

There is no terminating condition, because we decided to use the BREAK key (or CTRL/C) to stop this loop.

The translation of the first box in this REPEAT block is straightforward. The can name requested by the user should be stored in a special variable, say, R$, so that it is available to be compared with the name fields N$(1), N$(2), . . . , N$(23) of the records. The inner REPEAT block can be handled by a FOR/NEXT loop, so that the body of the procedure becomes

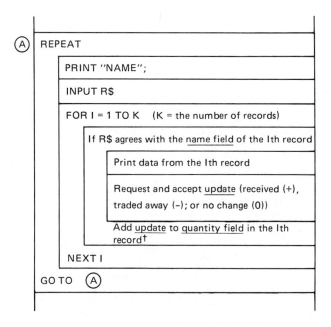

The box

Compare name of can with name field of record

has disappeared; this was a phoney. It was really a description of the relation that controls the IF block and not a separate segment of the program. Be on guard for such glitches. One must constantly massage the description of a procedure as one refines it. Don't worry if your initial flowchart does not follow the strict SEQUENTIAL/REPEAT/IF block form. Your goal should be to get it into this form as it develops.

Back to the program! The Ith record is stored in

N$(I), B$(I), C$(I), P$(I), Q(I)

---

†When the value of update represents cans traded away, the negative sign will ensure that it is subtracted from the quantity field [e.g., 7+(-2) = 5] .

We need to introduce a variable, U, to store the value of <u>update</u>. Beyond that, the development of the IF block is straightforward:

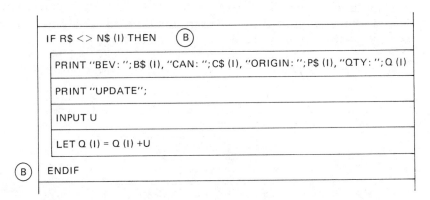

```
IF R$ <> N$ (I) THEN        B

   PRINT "BEV: ";B$ (I), "CAN: ";C$ (I), "ORIGIN: ";P$ (I), "QTY: ";Q (I)

   PRINT "UPDATE";

   INPUT U

   LET Q (I) = Q (I) +U

B │ ENDIF
```

Gathering all the threads together, we have the following program:

```
100 REM TITLE: BEER CAN FILE MANAGEMENT
105 REM PROGRAMMER: A. KITCHEN            DATE: 17-SEP-81
110 REM DESCRIPTION: THIS PROGRAM MAINTAINS A FILE OF
115 REM             INFORMATION ON A COLLECTION OF EMPTY
120 REM             BEER CANS.  RECORDS FOR INDIVIDUAL
125 REM             CANS MAY BE REVIEWED AND, TO A LIMITED
130 REM             EXTENT, UPDATED.
135 REM VARIABLES:
140 REM          K = NUMBER OF RECORDS
145 REM          I = RECORD POINTER
150 REM          N$(I) = NAME FIELD OF ITH RECORD
155 REM          B$(I) = BEVERAGE FIELD OF ITH RECORD
160 REM          C$(I) = CAN-TYPE FIELD OF ITH RECORD
165 REM          P$(I) = PLACE/ORIGIN FIELD OF ITH RECORD
170 REM          Q(I) = QUANTITY FIELD OF ITH RECORD
175 REM          R$ = NAME REQUESTED BY USER
180 REM          U = (UPDATE) NUMBER OF CANS RECEIVED OR TRADED
190 REM PROGRAM:
200     DIM N$(50),B$(50),C$(50),P$(50),Q(50)
210 REM READ NUMBER OF RECORDS:
220     READ K
230 REM READ RECORDS INTO ARRAYS:
240     FOR I=1 TO K
250         READ N$(I),B$(I),C$(I),P$(I),Q(I)
260     NEXT I
270     PRINT "CAN COLLECTION UPDATE :"
280     PRINT "TO REVIEW THE INFORMATION ON A CAN: TYPE CAN NAME,"
290     PRINT "WHEN PROMPTED.
300     PRINT "TO UPDATE THE QUANTITY FOR THIS BRAND: TYPE THE CHANGE"
310     PRINT "IN RESPONSE TO 'UPDATE?',(+) FOR CANS RECEIVED,(-) FOR"
320     PRINT "THOSE TRADED AWAY. IF THERE IS NO CHANGE, TYPE 0 (ZERO)."
330     PRINT "THIS PROGRAM MAY BE STOPPED AT ANY TIME BY PRESSING"
340     PRINT "THE BREAK KEY."
350 REM REPEAT
360         PRINT "NAME";
370         INPUT R$
380 REM     SEARCH FOR RECORD:
390         FOR I=1 TO K
400             IF R$ <> N$(I) THEN 480
```

```
410 REM                                 PRINT RECORD:
420                                      PRINT "BEV: ";B$(I),"CAN: ";C$(I),
430                                      PRINT "ORIG: ";P$(I);TAB(55);"QTY: ";Q(I)
440 REM                                  UPDATE RECORD:
450                                      PRINT "UPDATE";
460                                      INPUT U
470                                      LET Q(I) = Q(I)+U
480 REM                    ENDIF
490              NEXT I
500        GO TO 350
1000 REM DATA:
1010 REM           NUMBER OF RECORDS
1020      DATA 23
1030 REM           RECORD = NAME,BEVERAGE,CAN,PLACE OF ORIGIN,QUANTITY
1040      DATA "ACE","BEER","TAB","AUSTRALIA",1
1050      DATA "ALPINE","BEER","PUNCH","CANADA",3
1060      DATA "BADGER","BEER","TAB","ENGLAND",1
1070      DATA "BEVERWYCK","ALE","CONE","NEW YORK",1
1080      DATA "BRAHMA CHOPP","BEER","TAB","BRAZIL",2
1090      DATA "BUDWEISER","BEER","FLAT","MISSOURI",2
1100      DATA "CARDINAL","BEER","TAB","SWITZERLAND",2
1110      DATA "CINCI","BEER","PUNCH","CANADA",3
1120      DATA "CORONA","BEER","TAB","PUERTO RICO",1
1130      DATA "DAWSON'S","ALE","CONE","MASSACHUSETTS",1
1140      DATA "FALSTAFF","BEER","TAB","RHODE ISLAND",5
1150      DATA "GROLSCH","BEER","TAB","HOLLAND",1
1160      DATA "HOLSTEN","BEER","TAB","GERMANY",1
1170      DATA "MARSTON'S","BEER","PARTY","ENGLAND",1
1180      DATA "NEWCASTLE BROWN","ALE","TAB","ENGLAND",3
1190      DATA "OLD FROTHINGSLOSH","ALE","TAB","PENNSYLVANIA",7
1200      DATA "PABST","BEER","FLAT","WISCONSIN",2
1210      DATA "RESCHS","BEER","TAB","AUSTRALIA",2
1220      DATA "RUDDLES","ALE","PARTY","ENGLAND",1
1230      DATA "SAPORO","BEER","TAB","JAPAN",1
1240      DATA "STEGMAIER","BEER","FLAT","PENNSYLVANIA",2
1250      DATA "TECATE","BEER","TAB","MEXICO",4
1260      DATA "XXX","LIGHT","TAB","MEXICO",2
9999      END
```

If you analyze this program carefully you will find that it is rather inefficient. For instance, if the user types the name ACE, the second FOR/NEXT loop (between lines 390 and 490) tests all the records, even though the record requested is the first one in the list. It would be more efficient if control branched out of the FOR/NEXT loop as soon as the correct record was found. Another obvious limitation of the program is its inability to add new records or to remove outdated ones. Solutions to some of these problems are discussed in the exercises.

A more subtle problem involves the strategy of searching. The technique used in this program, even when modified in the way I just suggested, is intolerably slow when the number of records is large. (See Exercise 5 of Section 8.4 for a faster searching technique.)

There is another weakness in this program, which renders it practically useless except as a programming exercise. Try running the program and updating one of the records. Review the record to ensure that the modification has been made; then exit from the program by pressing the BREAK key (or

CTRL/C). Now run the program again and check the same record. Does the quantity printed out still reflect the changes you made? Can you explain what happened?

The only way to make this program useful would be to have it running continually. The weakness of DATA statements is that although they provide for permanent storage of data, the values stored in them cannot be changed by the program that contains them. On the other hand, the contents of a variable are easily changed under program control but are lost when the program stops execution. In Chapter 11 we will study data files and discover how they provide the solution to this problem.

8.5 RECTANGULAR ARRAYS

Suppose that we want to solve this pair of equations. Here is one way of doing it:

$$x + 2y = 3 \qquad \boxed{\begin{array}{ccc} 1 & 2 & 3 \\ 4 & 3 & 5 \end{array}}$$
$$4x + 3y = 5$$

We can subtract four times the first from the second:

$$x + 2y = 3 \qquad \boxed{\begin{array}{ccc} 1 & 2 & 3 \\ 0 & -5 & -7 \end{array}}$$
$$-5y = -7$$

divide the second by –5:

$$x + 2y = 3 \qquad \boxed{\begin{array}{ccc} 1 & 2 & 3 \\ 0 & 1 & 1.4 \end{array}}$$
$$y = 1.4$$

subtract twice the second from the first:

$$x \quad = 0.2 \qquad \boxed{\begin{array}{ccc} 1 & 0 & 0.2 \\ 0 & 1 & 1.4 \end{array}}$$
$$y = 1.4$$

and we have the answer: $x = 0.2$, $y = 1.4$.

To the right of the calculations are written the coefficients and constants of the equations alone, without the variables and mathematical operators. Notice that in the last rectangle of numbers, the answers are in the third column. In fact, one can solve this set of equations just as easily by manipulating the rectangular pattern of coefficients and constants as by working with the equations themselves. This fact is well known to mathematicians and has led to an extensive theory of these rectangular patterns, or **matrices**, as they are called. Applications of matrices now reach into all branches of science, as well as finding a place in economics and certain areas of business.

In a sense, a matrix is an extension of the idea of a list. Whereas a list is a one-dimensional thing, its values can be listed in a column down the page. A matrix is two-dimensional; its values are written across in rows as well as down in columns.

List	Matrix				
2	4	13	2	17	5
7	9	3	21	0	1
4	18	4	1	2	6
3	7	8	16	5	3
9					

Most computing languages provide variables for storing matrices. They are called **rectangular arrays** (or **doubly subscripted arrays**). These are an extension of the array concept, which should, by now, be an acquaintance if not an old friend. For example, the matrix

$$1 \quad 2 \quad 3$$

$$4 \quad 3 \quad 5$$

can be stored in the rectangular array, A:

A(1,1) [   ]   A(1,2) [   ]   A(1,3) [   ]
A(2,1) [   ]   A(2,2) [   ]   A(2,3) [   ]

Just as a simple array keeps track of the position of an item in a list, so a rectangular array keeps track of the row and column positions of an item in a matrix.

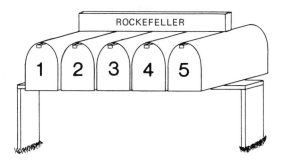

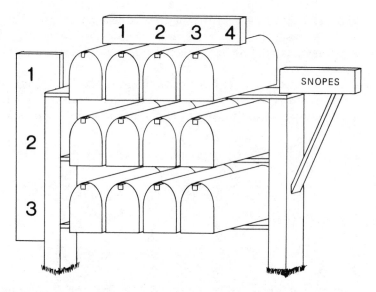

The individual parts of a rectangular array are called **elements** (or **doubly subscripted variables**). Each element is a variable capable of storing a number.

Example

A(1,1)	1	A(1,2)	2	A(1,3)	3
A(2,1)	4	A(2,2)	3	A(2,3)	5

In this array, A(2,3) is the element in the second row and third column of the array. It contains the value 5. ∎

The general pattern is

array name (row subscript, column subscript)

where the **array name** is a single letter. The **row subscript** gives the row in which the element lies and the **column subscript** gives the column. The subscripts can be integers, numerical variables, or mathematical expressions as in the case of ordinary arrays.

Examples

Suppose that the variables X, Y, Z have these values:

X	4	Y	2	Z	1

and the rectangular array, M, the following:

M(1,1)	7.1	M(1,2)	1.5	M(1,3)	9.4
M(2,1)	4.4	M(2,2)	6.0	M(2,3)	3.9
M(3,1)	5.7	M(3,2)	2.3	M(3,3)	8.7

Study the output from the following print statements:

1.

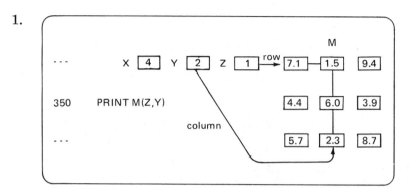

RUN
- - -
1.5
- - -
Ready

2.

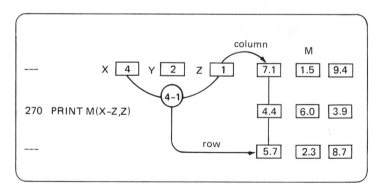

RUN
- - -
5.7
- - -
Ready

3.

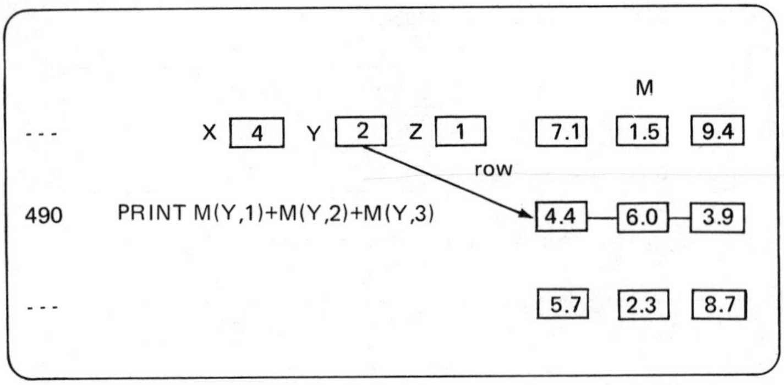

M

X [4] Y [2] Z [1] [7.1] [1.5] [9.4]

row

490 PRINT M(Y,1)+M(Y,2)+M(Y,3) ➜ [4.4]—[6.0]—[3.9]

[5.7] [2.3] [8.7]

RUN

- - -

14.3

- - -

Ready

Another way of calculating this sum is

```
450  LET S = 0
460  FOR J = 1 TO 3
470      LET S = S + M(Y,J)
480  NEXT J
490  PRINT S
```

See Section 4.5 for this technique. This is, of course, more complicated than statement 490 above. However, if the array were large, this would be the only way to do it.

4. The following segment sums all the elements of the rectangular array M, row by row. Trace it carefully.

```
- - -
300  LET S = 0
310  FOR I = 1 TO 3
320      FOR J = 1 TO 3
330          LET S = S + M(I,J)
340      NEXT J
350  NEXT I
360  PRINT S
- - -
```

Rectangular arrays must be "dimensioned" just as simple arrays are. The method is similar, but two values must be specified instead of one: the row dimension and the column dimension.

Example

1. The array A for storing the matrix

    $$\begin{matrix} 1 & 2 & 3 \\ 4 & 3 & 5 \end{matrix}$$

    is dimensioned as follows:

    DIM A(2,3)

2. DIM K(3,5) establishes a rectangular array of 15 elements arranged in three rows and five columns:

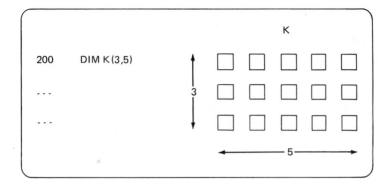

The applications of matrices mentioned at the beginning of this section tend to be highly technical and specialized. However, there are many applications of rectangular arrays in computer programming which are of more general interest. For example, in many computer games they provide a convenient way of storing the current state of play (the game board patterns in chess and checkers). They also provide a powerful tool for handling tables of numbers that must be processed up and down columns as well as across rows. We'll finish this section with an example that illustrates these techniques.

Here is a table of U.S. nut production (no peanuts, sorry) for the years 1974 to 1979, given to the nearest 1000 tons.

| Year | U.S. Nut Production (1000 tons) | | |
	Pecans	Almonds	Walnuts
1974	69	189	157
1975	124	160	199
1976	52	142	184
1977	118	157	193
1978	125	91	160
1979	111	185	205

We have been asked to write a program that will print out this table augmented with the following information:

1.   The total nut production for each year
2.   The average production per year, over the six years given, for each category of nut

In other words, the program must fill out this table:

YEAR	PECANS	ALMONDS	WALNUTS	TOTAL
1974	- - -	- - -	- - -	- - -
- - -	- - -	- - -	- - -	- - -
- - -	- - -	- - -	- - -	- - -
1979	- - -	- - -	- - -	- - -
AVE.	- - -	- - -	- - -	

So we have to sum the rows and average the columns of the original table. Here is a flowchart:

```
┌──────────────────────────────────────────────────────┐
│ Read the table from DATA statements                  │
├──────────────────────────────────────────────────────┤
│ Repeat for each year (each row)                      │
│   ┌──────────────────────────────────────────────┐   │
│   │ Sum numbers in row                            │   │
│   │ to get total for that year                    │   │
│   └──────────────────────────────────────────────┘   │
├──────────────────────────────────────────────────────┤
│ Repeat for each type of nut (each column)            │
│   ┌──────────────────────────────────────────────┐   │
│   │ Sum numbers in column                         │   │
│   │ Divide sum by 6                               │   │
│   │ to get average for that type of nut           │   │
│   └──────────────────────────────────────────────┘   │
├──────────────────────────────────────────────────────┤
│ Print the augmented table                            │
│ Stop                                                 │
└──────────────────────────────────────────────────────┘
```

We will need an array, $S(1), \ldots, S(6)$, to store the row sums and one, $A(1)$, $A(2)$, $A(3)$, for the column averages. If we do this, the two REPEAT blocks can be written as FOR/NEXT loops.

```
Read the table from DATA statements

FOR I = 1 TO 6

    Sum numbers in the Ith row
    and store sum in S(I)

NEXT I

FOR J = 1 TO 3

    Sum numbers in the Jth column
    and store sum in A(J)
    Divide A(J) by 6

NEXT J

Print the augmented table
Stop
```

Suppose that we use a rectangular array, N, of six rows and three columns, to store the data:

N(1,1) [69]   N(1,2) [189]   N(1,3) [157]

N(2,1) [124]   N(2,2) [160]   N(2,3) [199]

- - -   - - -   - - -

N(6,1) [111]   N(6,2) [185]   N(6,3) [205]

Then

```
Sum numbers in the Ith row

and store sum in S(I)
```

can be translated as

```
LET S(I) = N(I,1) + N(I,2) + N(I,3)
```

However, we'll write the segment like this instead:

```
LET S(I) = 0
FOR J = 1 TO 3
      LET S(I) = S(I) + N(I,J)
NEXT J
```

(See Example 3 from the beginning of this section.)
This is not shorter by any means, but it has the advantage that it will always work. For example, if we want to tackle an array with 100 columns, all we have to do is change 3 to 100.

The averaging of the columns can be handled in the same way.

```
LET A (J) = 0
FOR I = 1 TO 6
      LET A (I) = A (J) + N (I,J)
NEXT I
LET A (J) = A (J)/6
```

Notice how, in this one, we sum down the Jth column; that is, the row subscript, I, goes from 1 to 6. For example, in the case of J = 2:

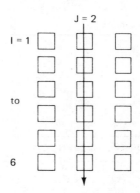

In the previous block, on the other hand, summation was across the Ith row as the column subscript, J, went from 1 to 3.

If we plug these blocks into the flowchart, we have:

```
Read the table from DATA statements

FOR I = 1 TO 6

  LET S (I) = 0

  FOR J = 1 TO 3

    LET S (I) = S (I) + N (I,J)

  NEXT J

NEXT I

FOR J = 1 TO 3

  LET A (J) = 0

  FOR I = 1 TO 6

    LET A (J) = A (J) + N (I,J)

  NEXT I

  LET A (J) = A (J) /6

NEXT J

Print the augmented table

Stop
```

Both the initial "Read" block and the final "Print" block have a structure similar to the "Summing" and "Averaging" blocks. It is standard convention to read data into rectangular arrays row by row, so that reading the table is handled as follows:

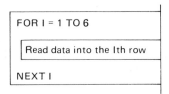

```
FOR I = 1 TO 6

  Read data into the Ith row

NEXT I
```

which becomes

```
FOR I = 1 TO 6

    FOR J = 1 TO 3

        READ N (I,J)

    NEXT J

NEXT I
```

The task of printing the table is complicated by the fact that we have to print the sums and averages as well. In spite of this, the "print" block has the same style as the other three and offers no real difficulty. Here is the complete program:

```
100 REM TITLE: ANALYSIS OF U.S. NUT PRODUCTION, 1974-79
110 REM PROGRAMMER: A. KITCHEN          DATE: 8-AUG-80
120 REM
130 REM VARIABLES:
140 REM         I = ROW SUBSCRIPT
150 REM         J = COLUMN SUBSCRIPT
160 REM         N(I,J) = PRODUCTION (1000 TONS), ITH YR, JTH NUT TYPE
170 REM         S(I) = TOTAL PRODUCTION, ITH YEAR
180 REM         A(J) = AVE. PRODUCTION/YR., JTH NUT TYPE
190 REM
200 REM PROGRAM:
210     DIM N(6,3),S(6),A(3)
220 REM READ DATA FOR TABLE:
230     FOR I=1 TO 6
240         FOR J=1 TO 3
250             READ N(I,J)
260         NEXT J
270     NEXT I
280 REM TOTALS FOR EACH YEAR:
290     FOR I=1 TO 6
300         LET S(I) = 0
310         FOR J=1 TO 3
320             LET S(I) = S(I)+N(I,J)
330         NEXT J
340     NEXT I
350 REM AVERAGE FOR EACH TYPE OF NUT
360     FOR J=1 TO 3
370         LET A(J) = 0
380         FOR I=1 TO 6
390             LET A(J) = A(J)+N(I,J)
400         NEXT I
410         LET A(J) = A(J)/6
420     NEXT J
430 REM PRINT THE TABLE
440     PRINT " ","U.S. NUT PRODUCTION (1000 TONS)"
450     PRINT "YEAR","PECANS","ALMONDS","WALNUTS","TOTAL"
460     PRINT
470     FOR I=1 TO 6
480         PRINT 1973+I,
```

```
490                FOR J=1 TO 3
500                    PRINT N(I,J),
510                NEXT J
520                PRINT S(I)
530     NEXT I
535     PRINT
540     PRINT "AVE.",
550     FOR J=1 TO 3
560         PRINT A(J),
570     NEXT J
580     PRINT
590 REM DATA: RECORD = PECANS,ALMONDS,WALNUTS IN GIVEN YR.
600     DATA 69,189,157
610     DATA 124,160,199
620     DATA 52,142,184
630     DATA 118,157,193
640     DATA 125,91,160
650     DATA 111,185,205
9999    END
```

This program illustrates a phenomenon that attends almost every use of rectangular arrays: namely, the proliferation of nested FOR/NEXT loops. This arises because so much of the processing takes the following form, or something like it:

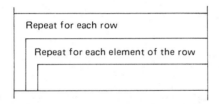

which translates into

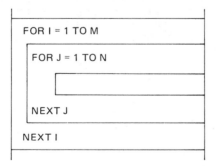

where M is the number of rows and N the number of elements in each row (which is the same as the number of columns).

On many systems, special statements called MAT (matrix) statements are provided for handling some of these problems.

Example

```
---
230  FOR I = 1 TO 6
240     FOR J = 1 TO 3
250        READ N(I,J)
260     NEXT J
270  NEXT I
---
```

can be rewritten as

```
---
230  MAT READ N
---
```

 ■

If you are interested in investigating this further, consult the BASIC manual for your system. However, I should warn you that there is only one place in the Nut program where a MAT statement could be used, and that is the one given as an example here. As this is the simplest of the nested FOR/NEXT loops in the program, the gain is not very impressive.

8.6 USAGE AND ABUSAGE[†]

Once one has discovered arrays it is easy to fall into the trap of using them indiscriminately for all processing that involves a large amount of data. Before you do use an array in a program, ask yourself whether it is possible to do the same thing without arrays. They take up a lot of space and should be used only if they are absolutely necessary or if they add to the flexibility and clarity of the program. Here is a typical example:

```
100       DIM A(20)
110       LET S = 0
120       PRINT "HOW MANY NUMBERS";
130       INPUT N
140       PRINT "TYPE EACH NUMBER ON A"
150       PRINT "SEPARATE LINE, AFTER"
160       PRINT "THE QUESTION MARK."
170       FOR I=1 TO N
180            PRINT "NUMBER";I;
190            INPUT A(I)
200            LET S = S+A(I)
210       NEXT I
220       PRINT "TOTAL IS";S
9999      END
```

[†]With apologies to Eric Partridge.

The program above uses up to 23 storage locations, A(1), A(2), A(3), . . . , A(20), S, I, N. On the other hand, the following program uses only four variables, A, S, I, N:

```
100       LET S = 0
110       PRINT "HOW MANY NUMBERS";
120       INPUT N
130       PRINT "TYPE EACH NUMBER ON A"
140       PRINT "SEPARATE LINE AFTER"
150       PRINT "THE QUESTION MARK."
160       FOR I=1 TO N
170             PRINT "NUMBER";I;
180             INPUT A
190             LET S = S+A
200       NEXT I
210       PRINT "TOTAL IS";S
9999      END
```

The second is not only simpler, but also more general. The first would have to be modified if we wanted to sum more than 20 numbers.

The conservation of storage space is not a critical consideration for a program of this size, but can be of great importance in a large one or in one that processes large amounts of data. On the other hand, there are many situations where arrays are needed and where their use genuinely simplifies a program.

Your goal should be to design clear and flexible programs. It is good to try to keep them short, but it is counterproductive to indulge in complicated tricks to shorten programs or conserve space, unless your programs are really stretching memory to the limit. The popular computing press is littered with poorly designed and ill-documented programs, whose only excuse for their shocking state of undress is the necessity of saving space. One solution to the problem of limited memory is to keep two copies of each long program: a fully documented one that is only listed and never run, this is for reference when problems arise or modifications are to be made, and a streamlined version, which is the one executed.

Chapter 8: EXERCISES

Section 8.1

No exercises.

Section 8.2

1. If these variables have the values $X = 3$, $Y = 1$, $A(1) = 7$, $A(2) = 35$, $A(3) = 5$, $A(4) = 1$, what is printed by each of the following statements?
   (a) PRINT A(2)   (b) PRINT A(X)   (c) PRINT A(X-Y)
   (d) PRINT A(X) - A(Y)   (e) PRINT A(A(4))

2. If these variables have the values $A = 2$, $B = 3$, $L(1) = 9$, $L(2) = 4$, $L(3) = 1$, $L(4) = 6$, $L(5) = 7$, what is printed by each of the following statements?
   (a) PRINT L(A)   (b) PRINT L(B+1)   (c) PRINT L(A)*A
   (d) PRINT L(A*A)   (e) PRINT L(L(B))   (f) PRINT
                                                 L(L(B-A)-L(A+B))

3. Show what is printed when these program segments are run.

   (a)
   ```
   100   DIM X(5)
   110   LET X(1) = 19
   120   LET X(2) = 27
   130   LET X(3) = 35
   140   LET X(4) = 43
   150   LET X(5) = 51
   160   FOR I = 1 TO 5
   170      PRINT X(6-I)
   180   NEXT I
   9999  END
   ```

   (b)
   ```
   100   DIM M(7)
   110   FOR J = 1 TO 7
   120      READ M(J)
   130   NEXT J
   140   FOR I = 1 TO 3
   150      PRINT M(2*I)
   160   NEXT I
   170   DATA 9,4,3,7,2,5,8
   9999  END
   ```

   (c)
   ```
   100          DIM V(2)
   110   REM  REPEAT
   120          INPUT A
   130          LET A = 0 THEN 160
   140          LET V(A) = V(A) + 1
   150       GO TO 110
   160       PRINT V(1), V(2)
   9999      END
   RUN
   ? 1
   ? 2
   ? 1
   ? 1
   ```

```
? 2
? 1
? 0
```
Complete this run.

4. Show what is printed when these program segments are run.

(a)
```
100   LET A(1) = 3
110   LET A(2) = 1
120   LET A(3) = 2
130   FOR I = 1 TO 3
140      LET J = A(I)
150      PRINT A(J)
160   NEXT I
9999  END
```

(b)
```
100   LET A(1) = 3
110   LET A(2) = 1
120   LET A(3) = 2
130   LET J = 1
140   FOR I = 1 TO 3
150      LET J = A(J)
160      PRINT A(J)
170   NEXT I
9999  END
```

5. Show what is printed when this program segment is run.

```
100        DIM A$(9)
110        FOR I = 1 TO 9
120           READ A$(I)
130        NEXT I
140   REM  REPEAT
150           READ N
160           IF N = 1 THEN 190
170           PRINT A$(N);
180        GO TO 140
190   REM
200        DATA "!","A","E","H","I","S","T","Y"," "
210        DATA 8,3,6,9,7,4,2,7,9,5,6,9,5,7,1
9999       END
```

6. Trace this program carefully, showing the contents of the array L and the variable T after each pass through the second FOR–NEXT loop.

```
100        DIM L(6)
110        FOR I = 1 TO 6
120           READ L(I)
130        NEXT I
140        FOR I = 1 TO 5
150           IF L(I) < = L(I+1) THEN 190
160              LET T = L(I)
170              LET L(I) = L(I+1)
180              LET L(I+1) = T
190   REM     END IF
200        NEXT I
210        FOR I = 1 TO 6
220           PRINT L(I)
230        NEXT I
240        DATA 4,7,5,3,8,6
9999  END
```

7. Identify which of these statements contain errors. Describe the errors.
    (a)   LET DIM A = 10
    (b)   LET A(I$) = "HOHO"
    (c)   DIMENSION A(N)
    (d)   FOR N$ = 1 TO 10
    (e)   IF B > A AND < C PRINT "B IS IN THE MIDDLE"
    (f)   LET X = 3(A+B)
    (g)   LET X = B(A+3)
    (h)   PRINT X < 5 >
    (i)   DIM, M(I), N(I)
    (j)   DATA A(1), A(2), A(3)

8. (a)   Write a program to accept a list of numbers and then print the list in reverse order.
    (b)   Write a program to read a list of numbers and then print two columns side by side, one consisting of the list in the order in which it was entered and the other in reverse order.

9. Modify the customer balance program of this section (the final version) so that it will accept two numbers M and N (with M ≤ N) and print the balances for all customer numbers in the range M to N.

10. (a)   Write a program to accept any list of numbers and then print two lists, one consisting of the negative numbers from the original list and the other the remaining numbers from the list. [*Hint: As each number is entered, place it in one of two arrays, N for the negative ones and P for the rest. Give N and P adequate dimensions [e.g., DIM N (50), P(50)], but don't pad the lists with extra zeros when they are printed out.*]
    (b)   Rewrite the program in part (a) so that the two lists are printed side by side down the page. [*Hint: This is more challenging. The lists may be of different lengths. Don't pad the shorter one with extra zeros.*]
    (c)   Rewrite part (b) so that the program first calculates the mean (average) of the list and then produces two lists: the first consisting of those values that are less than the mean and the second those that are greater than or equal to the mean.

11. (a)   Many techniques in data processing depend on the fact that the data being used are in a systematic order. For example, it is easier to search for a name in a list if the list is in alphabetical order (imagine using a telephone directory in which the order of the entries was completely random). Similarly, it is often helpful to put numbers in increasing (e.g., 4, 7, 13, 25, 51, 60) or decreasing (e.g., 60, 51, 25, 13, 7, 4) order. Putting a jumbled list of data values into a standard order is referred to as **sorting**.
          Here is a simple, although not very fast, sorting technique

called **bubble sort.** It will sort a list of numbers stored in an array L(1), . . ., L(N) into increasing order:

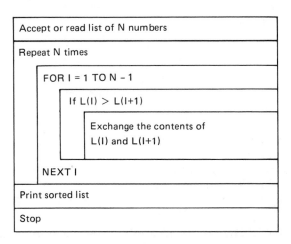

The FOR–NEXT loop causes the list to be scanned once. Adjacent numbers are interchanged if they are out of order. By the time this process has been repeated often enough (N times are certainly sufficient—can you explain why?) all inverted orderings have been eliminated and the list is sorted.

(b) Write a program to find the median of a list of numbers. The median is defined to be a value for which half the values in the list are above it and half below. It can be found by sorting the list into increasing order and then choosing the middle element of the sorted list, if the length of the list is odd, or the average of the two middle values, if the length of the list is even. The median is used, like the mean (average), as a measure of the "middle" of a range of data values.

12. (a) Write a program to print the song "Old MacDonald's Farm." Here is a typical verse:

```
Old MacDonald had a farm
E-I-E-I-O!
And on that farm he had a dog.
E-I-E-I-O!
With a bow-wow here and a bow-wow there,
Here a bow,
There a wow
```

Everywhere a bow-wow.
With a moo-moo here and a moo-moo there,
Here a moo,
There a moo,
Everywhere a moo-moo.
etc.

Remember that the "with-a" part has to be repeated for every animal mentioned so far. One approach is to store data of the following form:

DATA "DUCK", "QUACK", "QUACK"
DATA "COW", "MOO", "MOO"
DATA "DOG", "BOW", "WOW"
DATA "DONKEY", "HEE", "HAW"
etc.

in three character string arrays, then to print more of the data with each successive verse. Take care though; the animals appear in each verse in the reverse of the order in which they are introduced. [*Hint: By the way, if your BASIC does not provide character string arrays, this song can be handled by reading directly from the DATA statements. For that, you will need the RESTORE statement and a few cute tricks up your sleeve.*]

   (b)   Use the same approach to print "The Twelve Days of Christmas."

13. Write a program that reads a list of numbers (or names) into an array and then allows the user to insert or delete items. When an item at a given position is deleted, the rest of the list should move up to close the gap. When an item is inserted at a given position, the item already there, as well as its successors, should be moved down to make room. For example:

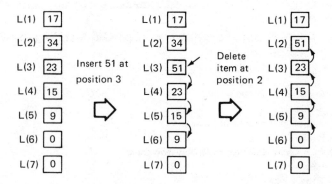

At the end of the run the final version of the list should be printed.

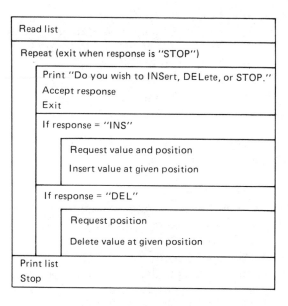

Section 8.3

1. Rewrite the program discussed in this section so that it keeps tallies of the combined scores produced by throwing a pair of dice together. [*Hint: The range of possible scores is 2, 3, . . . , 12.*]

2. (a) Write a program to accept a list of any length, terminated by the flag 9999, where the individual entries are integers in the range 1 to 10, and to count the number of 1's, 2's, . . . , 10's in the list.

    (b) Modify the program in part (a) so that it prints the results in the form of a bar chart. [*Hint: Exercise 3 of Section 7.5 discusses bar charts.*]

3. Write a program to accept a list of exam grades in the range 0 to 100 and keep counts of the number of grades that fall in these ranges:

    0 to 9
    10 to 19
    20 to 29
    - - -
    90 to 100

The program should print a bar chart showing the distribution of grades into the 10 ranges. [*Hint: If X is in the range 0 to 99, then INT(X/10) is an integer in the range 0 to 9. A perfect score, 100, will have to be treated separately.*]

Section 8.4

1. (a) Rewrite the beer can file management program so that the search stops as soon as the can requested is found. Also, include in the program the ability to print THIS CAN IS NOT ON FILE, if the can is not on the list. [*Hint: See Exercise 3(b) of Section 7.3.*]

   (b) Modify the beer can program so that if the can requested is not on the list, the program responds with a message like this:

   THIS CAN IS NOT ON FILE. DO YOU WISH TO ADD IT
   TO THE LIST?

   and then allows the user to add the complete record (beverage type, can type, place of origin, quantity) to the end of the list. [*Hint: Store the new record in the (K + 1)st locations of the arrays and increase the record count, K, by 1.*]

2. (a) Using the beer can records in the chapter, write a program to print all the records corresponding to a can type specified by the user. That is, if the user types TAB, it will list all records for TAB top cans.

   (b) Augment the program in part (a) to allow the user to specify the place of origin and/or the can type. [*Hint: For example: all TAB top cans, or all ENGLISH cans, or even all ENGLISH TAB tops.*]

3. a) Given the following catalog, write a program that will accept an item name and a quantity, and then will search the catalog and print the total cost for the quantity ordered. It should do this repeatedly for as long as required.

Item	Cost ($)
Fulton Washer	4.44
Chicago Washer	2.75
Desplaines Washer	2.72
Sears Washer	5.66
Acme Washer	4.25
Ball-bearing Washer	4.90
Large Washer	5.00
Western Washer	3.10
Seroco Wringer	2.24
Curtis Wringer	3.25
Hotel Wringer	5.94
Alpine Wringer	2.65
Acme Sweeper	1.65
Imperial Sweeper	1.98
Elite Sweeper	2.35

(b) Modify the program to allow the user to type in a number of different item names and a quantity for each name. The program should calculate the cost of the total order.

4. Write a program that will read the following list and, for each golfer mentioned, print his total winnings for the years that he was the leading money maker. This is, of course, the same problem as Exercise 3 of Section 6.5, except that the winning years for each golfer are not necessarily consecutive.

PGA Leading Money Makers, 1958–1978

Year	Name	Winnings ($1000)
58	Palmer	42
59	Wall	53
60	Palmer	57
61	Player	66
62	Palmer	81
63	Palmer	128
64	Nicklaus	113
65	Nicklaus	141
66	Casper	122
67	Nicklaus	189
68	Casper	205
69	Beard	175
70	Trevino	157
71	Nicklaus	244
72	Nicklaus	321
73	Nicklaus	308
74	Miller	353
75	Nicklaus	323
76	Nicklaus	266
77	Watson	311
78	Watson	362

[*Hint: Don't store the data in arrays. You will, however, need arrays to store a record of each golfer's name and his subtotal. As each name is read, it will have to be searched for among the existing records and the appropriate one updated or a new one established. At the end, all records will be printed.*]

5. In the beer can program, when the name of a can is entered, each record is checked in turn, starting with the first, until the required record is found. This means that for a can near the end of the list, practically the whole list must be searched. If the list is in alphabetical order, this approach is clearly rather silly. Imagine looking for the telephone number of Julius C. Wyzykowsky by starting in the A's.

Here is a much faster way to search a list given in some standard order (alphabetical or numerical). To illustrate, imagine that you have a telephone directory with just one name listed per page. You are looking for the number of, say, Charles H. Maibauer. Open the book at the middle and read the name you find there. Suppose that it is James Keagle. You now know that Mr. Maibauer is in the second half of the directory, so tear off the first half and throw it away. In one step you have eliminated half the names in the list from consideration. Repeat this whole process with the remaining half of the directory, that is, open it at the middle and read the name. This time you find Joe Phimprachahn, which means that Maibauer is listed in the first half of what is left. Repeat this process until you find the number.

(a) Suppose that your directory contains 32 pages. What is the maximum number of times that you will ever have to repeat the cycle just described in order to reach a name? What is the maximum number of names you will ever have to read if you insist on checking the names in order from the beginning?

(b) The technique described above is a powerful one for searching lists that have been sorted. It goes by the name of **interval halving** or **binary search.** From the informal description just given, write a structured flowchart to search for an item in a list that is stored in an array. [*Hint: As we haven't discussed how to handle alphabetical ordering yet, assume that the items in the list are numbers.*]

(c) Write a program using the flowchart developed in part (b) and test it. To check your algorithm, have the program print the position of the item in the list.

(d) What does your program do when presented with a number that is not in the list? Modify it so that it handles this situation by printing NOT IN LIST. [*Hint: You may have to go back and redesign your algorithm.*]

Section 8.5

1. Suppose that these variables have the values $L = 3$, $M = 5$, $N = 1$, $T(1,1) = 4.9$, $T(1,2) = 7.3$, $T(2,1) = 5.1$, $T(2,2) = 3.5$, $T(3,1) = 1.1$, $T(3,2) = 6.3$, $T(4,1) = 7.6$, $T(4,2) = 8.2$. What is printed by each of the following statements?

(a) PRINT T(4,1) (b) PRINT T(L,N)

(c) PRINT T(M-N,M-L) (d) PRINT 2*T(2*N,2*L-M)

(e) PRINT T(L,N) + T(L,N+1)

2. If the rectangular array S contains this matrix:

$$2 \quad 4 \quad 8$$

$$3 \quad 9 \quad 27$$

$$4 \quad 16 \quad 64$$

what is printed by these segments?

(a)
```
200  FOR I = 1 TO 3
210      FOR J = 1 TO 3
220          PRINT S(I,J),
230      NEXT J
240      PRINT
250  NEXT I
```

(b)
```
200  FOR I = 1 TO 3
210      FOR J = 1 TO 3
220          PRINT S(J,I),
230      NEXT J
240      PRINT
250  NEXT I
```

(c)
```
200  FOR J = 1 TO 3
210      FOR I = 1 TO 3
220          PRINT S(J,I),
230      NEXT I
240      PRINT
250  NEXT J
```

(d)
```
200  FOR I = 1 TO 3
210      PRINT S(I,I)
220  NEXT I
```

(e)
```
200  FOR J = 1 TO 3
210      PRINT S(4-J,J)
220  NEXT J
```

3. What is stored in the rectangular array, W, by each of these segments?

(a)
```
200      DIM W(4,4)
210      FOR I = 1 TO 4
220          FOR J = 1 TO 4
230              LET W(I,J) = I
240              IF J < I THEN 260
250                  LET W(I,J) = J
260  REM          ENDIF
270          NEXT J
280      NEXT I
```

(b)
```
140      DIM W(4,4)
150      FOR I = 1 TO 4
160          FOR J = 1 TO 4
170              LET W(I,J) = (I – 1)*4 + J
180          NEXT J
190      NEXT I
```

(c)
```
200      DIM W(4,4)
210      FOR I = 1 TO 4
220          FOR J = 1 TO 4
230              READ W(I,J)
240          NEXT J
250      NEXT I
260      FOR I = 1 TO 4
270          FOR J = 1 TO 4
280              LET M = (W(I,J) + W(J,I))/2
290              LET W(I,J) = M
300              LET W(J,I) = M
310          NEXT J
320      NEXT I
500      DATA 1,9,4,7
510      DATA 3,5,2,8
520      DATA 4,6,5,2
530      DATA 4,6,5,2
```

4. Suppose that the rectangular array, A, contains this matrix before each of the following segments is executed:

$$
\begin{matrix}
1 & 1 & 1 & 1 & 1 \\
2 & 2 & 2 & 2 & 2 \\
3 & 3 & 3 & 3 & 3 \\
4 & 4 & 4 & 4 & 4 \\
5 & 5 & 5 & 5 & 5
\end{matrix}
$$

What does A contain afterward?

(a)
```
320  FOR I = 1 TO 5
330     FOR J = 1 TO I
340        LET T = A(I,J)
350        LET A(I,J) = A(J,I)
360        LET A(J,I) = T
370     NEXT J
380  NEXT I
```

(b)
```
320  FOR I = 1 TO 5
330     FOR J = 1 TO 5
340        LET T = A(I,J)
350        LET A(I,J) = A(J,I)
360        LET A(J,I) = T
370     NEXT J
380  NEXT I
```

5. Write a program to read a matrix of any dimensions, up to 15 rows and 15 columns, and print it organized into rows and columns. [*Hint: The DATA statements must contain information on the number of rows and columns. Using the TAB function, you will have to arrange the print out so that each column is no more than five characters wide. This will limit the size of the numbers that can be printed.*]

6. Cramer's rule gives the solution of a pair of simultaneous equations:

$$
\begin{cases}
ax + by = h \\
cx + dy = k
\end{cases}
$$

as

$$
x = \frac{hd - bk}{ad - bc} \quad \text{and} \quad y = \frac{ak - hc}{ad - bc}
$$

if $ad - bc \neq 0$.

Write a program that accepts the matrix of coefficients

$$
\begin{matrix}
a & b & h \\
c & d & k
\end{matrix}
$$

of any such pair of equations, stores it in a rectangular array, and then prints the solution if $ad - bc \neq 0$, and the message "NO UNIQUE SOLUTION" otherwise.

7. Suppose that A is a rectangular array of three rows and four columns. Write a program to store 1 in A(1,1), 2 in A(1,2), 4 in A(1,3), and so on, storing double the previous entry in the next location. Fill the array row by row, from left to right. Finally, print A. [*Hint: Calculate each value to be stored rather than reading it from DATA statements.*]

8. (a) Write a program that will read a matrix of any size from DATA statements and then sum any row specified by the user. The program should repeat this as often as the user desires.

   (b) Modify the program in part (a) so that the user may select any column or row to be summed.

9. These are the 1980 election returns from Hawaii, tabulated by island:

Island	Carter	Reagan	Anderson
Hawaii	15,366	17,630	14,247
Oahu	96,494	99,623	25,341
Kuai	9,081	5,883	1,352
Maui	12,674	10,359	2,237

   Write a program that prints a table showing the percentage of the vote on each island received by each candidate, as well as the percentage of the vote from all the islands going to each candidate.

10. The following is a table of air distances between selected U.S. cities:

	Boston	Miami	New Orleans	New York	Phila- delphia	Wash- ington
Boston	0	1255	1359	188	271	393
Miami	1255	0	669	1092	1019	923
New Orleans	1359	669	0	1171	1089	966
New York	188	1092	1171	0	83	205
Philadelphia	271	1019	1089	83	0	123
Washington	393	923	966	205	123	0

   Write a program that will accept any two of these cities and return the distance between them. It should repeat this as often as required. [*Hint: Store the distances in a rectangular array. The two cities entered by the user will specify the row and column of the table. Unfortunately, the city names are not numbers. You will have to store all the names in an array, say C$(1), . . . , C$(6), and then search for each city entered to find its position in this list. If your system does not support character string arrays, this can be handled by a sequence of IF statements.*]

11. Graphing: In Exercise 6 of Section 7.4 we discussed the graphing of functions. However, because of the limitations of the terminal, we were forced to graph the functions on their sides (up and down the page,

rather than across it). Rectangular arrays give us much more freedom. We can store the diagram in an array and then print it out in any orientation we want, just by the way we print the array.

The simplest way to store the diagram is to set all locations of the array equal to zero, first, and then store 1's in those elements which correspond to points in the final diagram. For example,

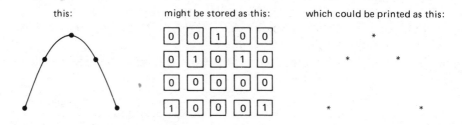

this: might be stored as this: which could be printed as this:

For this exercise we'll print the graphs in an area 60 characters across and 40 lines up and down, so we will require an array with 40 rows and 60 columns.

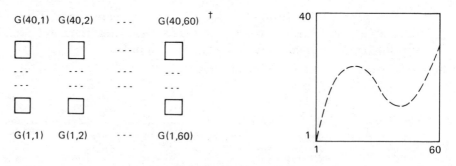

Now, suppose that we want to graph a function $y = f(x)$ over the interval $A \leqslant x \leqslant B$ and that the values of $f(x)$ lie in the range $M \leqslant y \leqslant N$; then we must scale the x-values to lie in the range 1 to 60 and the y-values to lie in the range 1 to 40:

$$X1 = 1 + 59\left(\frac{x - A}{B - A}\right)$$

$$Y1 = 1 + 39\left(\frac{y - M}{N - M}\right)$$

For example: To plot $y = x^3$ for $-2 \leqslant x \leqslant 2$ in steps of 0.05, we notice that for x in this range y lies in the range $-8 \leqslant y \leqslant 8$. The following

---

†Note that the array will be used upside down.

segment will store the plot in a rectangular array, G:

```
200         DIM G(40,60)
210         FOR I = 1 TO 40
220            FOR J = 1 TO 60
230               LET G(1,J) = 0
240            NEXT J
250         NEXT I
260         FOR X = -2 TO 2 STEP 0.05
270 REM        CALCULATE Y VALUE:
280            LET Y = X^3
290 REM        SCALE X AND Y:
300            LET X1 = 1 + 59*(X + 2)/4
310            LET Y1 = 1 + 39*(Y + 8)/16
320 REM        ROUND THEM:
330            LET X1 = INT(X1 + 0.5)
340            LET Y1 = INT(Y1 + 0.5)
350 REM        STORE POINT (X1,Y1) IN ARRAY:
360            LET G(Y1,X1) = 1†
370         NEXT X
```

(a) Complete the program to plot $y = x^3$: Check the array G row by row, printing "*" if the corresponding element of G is 1, and a blank space if the element is 0. You must read the stored graph from G beginning with the fortieth row and working back to the first. Why? What happens if you start with the first row?

Write programs to plot these functions over the given intervals. Experiment with different step sizes.

(b) $y = x^2$ for $-7 \leqslant x \leqslant 7$ $(0 \leqslant y \leqslant 49)$

(c) $y = \dfrac{1}{x^2 + 1}$ for $-3 \leqslant x \leqslant 3$ $(0 \leqslant y \leqslant 1)$

(d) $y = 2^x$ for $-4 \leqslant x \leqslant 2$ $(0 \leqslant y \leqslant 4)$

(e) $y = \sin x$ for $0 \leqslant x \leqslant 10$ $(-1 \leqslant y \leqslant 1)$

[Hint: For smaller or larger graphs or ones of different proportions, all you have to do is change the values 40 and 60.]

12. Write a program to plot curves given by a pair of equations of the form

$$x = \sin 2H\pi t$$

$$y = \sin 2K\pi t$$

---

†Notice that $X1$ and $Y1$ seem to be in the wrong order. This is, in fact, the correct way. The row subscript indicates the position in the up-and-down direction, the y-direction. The column subscript indicates the x-direction.

for $0 \leqslant t \leqslant 1$ ($\pi = 3.14159$). The ranges of x and y both lie between -1 and 1. Different integer values for H and K produce different members of a family of fascinating curves called Lissajous figures (or Bowditch curves). Your program should allow the user to specify values for H and K before plotting the curve.

Section 8.6

No exercises.

Chapter
9

Character Strings[†]

9.1 CHARACTER MANIPULATION

In the early days, the computer was conceived of as a high-speed automatic calculator, a big number cruncher that could be left for hours to tackle nasty numerical calculations. For example, the jobs tackled by the first modern computers, in the 1940s, included the calculation of ballistics tables as well as some of the computations involved in the development of the first atomic bomb.[‡]

Over the last 30 years the computer's field of influence has steadily widened. A large and growing number of current applications involve more in the way of manipulation and processing of text and alphabetic data than of numerical calculations.

Particularly rapid growth has occurred in the development of word-processing systems, what might be called intelligent typewriters. These systems allow letters and reports, in fact any kind of text, to be written and edited on a screen before the final copy is printed. They are, in fact, becoming indispensable tools in the publishing and newspaper business.[§] You have

---

[†]There is a wide variation in the extent to which different versions of BASIC support character strings and string manipulation. This chapter describes a typical system. See Appendix III for information on other systems.

[‡]Very nasty calculations indeed!

[§]A number of these systems can be seen on the newsroom set of the recent television series "Lou Grant."

already had some experience with a limited version of such a system, while writing and running BASIC programs. All computer systems provide the means to correct and modify programs. Word processors provide similar facilities, but in much more flexible and powerful form (insertion, correction, and deletion of sections of text, centering, right justification—that is, rearranging the text so that the right margin is straight, paragraphing, paging, and many other marvelous conveniences). Such systems usually include a disk storage system as well. This is very useful for keeping records of correspondence as well as for the printing of form letters. In fact, these systems are particularly adept at producing that boon (bane?) of modern business, the individualized form letter. I'm sure you have, at some point, received a promotional letter in which you are referred to by name throughout, a letter that appears to have been written specifically to you. It is easy to be caught off guard by such things and to believe for a moment that you really are, as the letter claims, a preferred customer. Ah, the power of the computer!

Most information retrieval systems have the ability to search for records by name. The beer can program in Chapter 8 showed how simple this process can be. Even in the sciences, the application of the computer is being stretched beyond the traditional numerical and statistical calculations to include the symbolic manipulation of relations and formulas. This development, too, requires the computer to be able to handle strings of characters, although they are not text in the normal sense of the word.

To be able to do sophisticated things with character data, we require more powerful tools. For example, to make changes in a line of text requires that there be a way of chopping strings of characters into pieces and then a way of glueing them back together again. Furthermore, for efficient processing of lists consisting of, say, names, the computer must have the ability to put strings of characters in alphabetical order. This involves being able to compare character strings to determine which of them comes first in the normal dictionary ordering of words. In this chapter we discuss how these things are done in BASIC.

9.2   A REVIEW AND A WARNING

So far we have manipulated text in a relatively undemanding way. We have learned that character strings can be printed:

```
PRINT "THINGS HAVE COME TO A TERRIBLE PASS"
PRINT "WHEN A MAN CAN'T CUDGEL HIS OWN JACKASS."
```

can be accepted from the terminal (or from DATA statements):

```
PRINT "WHEN DID YOU LAST SEE YOUR FATHER";
INPUT R$
```

or assigned to variables:

```
LET D$ = "YESTERDAY"
```

and can be tested:

```
IF R$ = D$ THEN 150
```

A couple of programs have even used arrays to store character strings. However, before we get any deeper into this, I must issue a warning.

I have emphasized a number of times that there are many dialects of BASIC. The variations are particularly wide when it comes to character string manipulation. They start right in the definition of a string variable. On some systems, the number of characters that can be stored in a single string variable is limited only by the available space in memory. On others a definite limit is set, say 255 or 72 (approximately one line of characters) or even as few as 18. On top of this, some versions require that the maximum number of characters that a string variable can hold be specified at the beginning of a program.

Example

In most dialects of BASIC, the statement

```
DIM A$(20)
```

indicates that A$ is an array capable of storing 20 separate strings of characters (whose lengths may or may not be limited by the system). However, on a few systems it means that A$ is a simple string variable that can hold up to 20 characters. ∎

From the example above, it should be obvious that a system which specifies the size of its string variables in this way is less likely to be able to support arrays of string variables. If yours is such a system, you are entitled to feel disadvantaged.

Returning to our review of character strings, note that BASIC allows strings to be INPUT[†] with or without quotation marks.

[†]My wife takes great exception to this use of a noun as a very. "Just another example of the impact of jargon on the English language" or, in current journalese, "of jargon impacting the language." There, that's another one!

Example

```
10    PRINT "WHAT IS YOUR NAME";
20    INPUT N$
30    PRINT "HI ";N$;"! HOW ARE YAH?"
9999  END
RUN
WHAT IS YOUR NAME? HARRY
HI HARRY! HOW ARE YAH?
Ready
RUN
WHAT IS YOUR NAME? "HARRY"
HI HARRY! HOW ARE YAH?
Ready
```

■

However, the comma is still used as a data separator, so that if a comma appears naturally as part of a text that is to be entered, the text must be enclosed in quotes.

Example

```
RUN
WHAT IS YOUR NAME? ORWELL, HARRY
HI ORWELL! HOW ARE YAH?
Ready
```

The INPUT statement only reads up to the comma, so that ORWELL is stored in N$ and HARRY is ignored.

```
RUN
WHAT IS YOUR NAME? "ORWELL, HARRY"
HI ORWELL, HARRY! HOW ARE YAH?
Ready
```

In this final example, the comma is inside the quotes and so is considered part of the string.   ■

Many BASIC dialects provide a special INPUT statement, INPUT LINE (or LINE INPUT on some systems), which accepts a whole line of text, commas and all, without requiring quotes.

Example

```
10    PRINT "WHAT IS YOUR NAME";
20    INPUT LINE N$
```

```
30    PRINT "GOOD DAY ";N$;" HOW ARE YOU, SIR?"
9999  END
RUN
WHAT IS YOUR NAME? GEORGE BERKELEY, BISHOP OF CLOYNE.
GOOD DAY GEORGE BERKELEY, BISHOP OF CLOYNE.
HOW ARE YOU, SIR?
Ready
```

So eager is INPUT LINE to accept everything that it even accepts the non-printing characters, carriage return (CR) and line feed (LF), produced when the RETURN key is pressed to enter the name. It stores the whole thing in N$:

N$	G	E	O	R	G	E		B	E	R	K	E	L	E	Y	,		B	I	S	H	O	P		O	F	

																			C	L	O	Y	N	E	.	CR	LF	

and this is what forces HOW ARE YOU, SIR? onto the next line when N$ is printed out. ■

9.3 LEXICOGRAPHICAL ORDERING

In a dictionary (or lexicon, whence lexicographical) words are placed in what we informally refer to as alphabetical order: that is, all the words beginning with A first, then those beginning with B, and so on. Within the A's, the first words to appear are those whose second letter is A, then those with second letter B, and so on.

Example

Here is the beginning of Webster's Third International Dictionary:

a (13 entries)	aardvark
aa	aardwolf
AA (2 entries)	aarhus
AAA	aaronic
AAC	aaronite
aachen	aaron's beard
aalii	aaron's rod
A and M	aasvogel
AAR	AAUP

(By the way, aa could come in handy some time if you are a Scrabble player. It is a type of lava.) ∎

In order to determine the order in which two words appear, one compares their letters in pairs, starting from the first, until a mismatch occurs. The relative order of the words is then determined by the order of these two letters in the alphabet.

Example

The first four letters agree, but L is before O in the alphabet; thus COUPLING appears before COUPON in the dictionary. ∎

Essentially the same rule is followed by the computer in determining the ordering of character strings. The symbols =, <, >, <=, >=, and <> can thus be used to test relations between character strings in the way that we have already used them with numbers. However, another of our recurrent warnings: Some systems allow comparison of strings only for equality and inequality. That is, only the operators = and <> are allowed in string relations. So check your manuals.

Examples

1. "COUPLING" < "COUPON" is true.
    Read "COUPLING" < "COUPON" as COUPLING lies before COUPON in the dictionary ordering.
2. "HOPHEAD" >= "SQUAMULOSE" is false. ∎

The characters that may be used in a string are not, of course, restricted to uppercase letters. The digits and all the mathematical and punctuation symbols may be used and on many systems the lowercase letters are also available. The alphabet has to be extended to handle this. The way in which this is done varies from one system to another. Here is one fairly standard ordering† for digits and upper- and lowercase letters:

space0123456789ABCDEFGHIJKLMNOPQRSTUVWXYZabcdefghijklmnopqrstuvwxyz

†See Appendix III.

Examples

1. "28" > "2174" is true, whereas 28 > 2174 is false.
    The first compares them as character strings, the second as numbers.
2. "BUG" < "apple" is true.
    This is a departure from the convention of the dictionary. It occurs be-
    cause all uppercase letters are listed before the lowercase alphabet, in
    the ordering used by the computer. On the other hand, the following
    ordering of letters is normally assumed in a dictionary:

    aAbBcCdDeEfFgGhHiIjJkKlLmMnNoOpPqQrRsStTuUvVwWxXyYzZ   ∎

Character string relations are used in IF statements in a similar way to
mathematical relations. For example, what responses will stop this program?

```
10    REM  REPEAT
20              PRINT "WANNA COME UP AND SEE MY ETCHINGS";
30              INPUT R$
40              IF R$ >= "YES" THEN 60
50         GO TO 10
60         PRINT "WOWEE!"
9999       END
```

For many purposes the equality, =, and inequality, <>, are the only relations
one really needs. However, sorting and searching techniques require the
others as well. Experiment with the following program to become familiar
with the ordering of character strings:

```
10    REM  REPEAT
20              INPUT A$,B$
30              IF A$ < B$ THEN PRINT A$;" PRECEDES ";B$
40              IF A$ = B$ THEN PRINT A$;" EQUALS "; B$
50              IF A$ > B$ THEN PRINT A$;" FOLLOWS ";B$
60         GO TO 10
9999       END
```

For example, try HOTEL and HOT POTATO then HOTEL and HOTPOTATO
or ONE FOR THE ROAD and 1 FOR THE ROAD.

9.4 CUTTING AND PASTING

Computer processing of character data often involves a search for groups of
characters, as well as the ability to perform various types of surgery on text.
For example, typical applications involve the counting of the number of

appearances of a given word in a text, or the deletion or replacement of a word or phrase.

A celebrated application of such techniques involved the analysis of a series of political essays, known as the Federalist Papers, which appeared in New York newspapers during the years 1787–1788. Although they were written under the pseudonym "Publius," the majority are known to have been written by Alexander Hamilton, while a smaller number were contributed by James Madison and a handful by John Jay. However, the authorship of 15 of them has long been in question. From an elaborate computer analysis of the known writings of these men (principally by frequency counts of certain phrases that were part of each man's style) it is now believed that Madison was the sole author of the disputed essays.

A more mundane application of the computer's ability to dissect and compare character strings is in the design of word processors, as discussed at the beginning of this chapter.

To perform such tasks, a computer language must:

1.   Have the ability to select "pieces" from a character string
2.   Provide the means to "glue" strings together to produce larger ones
3.   Be able to count the number of characters in a string

Unfortunately, not every version of BASIC is able to do these things and, among the versions that can, the notation for doing them varies widely. As usual, we will adopt the coward's way out, by describing just one typical system.†

In DEC BASIC-PLUS, a function, called the MID function, provides the scalpel we require for string surgery:

MID(X\$,I,J) is that piece, or substring, of the character string stored in X\$, which starts at the Ith character and is J characters long.

Examples

1.   MID("COPACETIC",3,4) is the substring "PACE".

$$\begin{array}{ccccccccc} 1 & 2 & 3 & 4 & 5 & 6 & 7 & 8 & 9 \\ C & O & \boxed{P\ A\ C\ E} & T & I & C \end{array}$$

Read it as follows:

In this string, start at character 3 and take 4 characters.

MID ("COPACETIC", 3, 4)

---

†For a comparison of string manipulation on various systems, see Appendix III.

2. If E$ = "LHUDE SING GODDAM", L=9, P=5 then MID(E$,L,P) is the substring "NG GO". Note that the blank spaces also count as characters:

```
1  2  3  4  5  6  7  8  9  0  1  2  3  4  5  6  7
L  H  U  D  E     S  I [N  G     G  O] D  D  A  M
```

3. MID(N$,1,1) is the first character in N$.
4. How would you describe MID(N$,I,1)?   ■

The MID function is a rather forbidding beast. However, with time, you should grow to appreciate its power and, perhaps, even its ugly face. Remember the pattern:

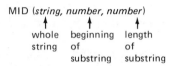

```
MID (string, number, number)
      ↑        ↑        ↑
    whole  beginning  length
    string  of         of
            substring  substring
```

Here is a short program that you can use to get familiar with MID:

```
10     PRINT "TYPE A STRING OF CHARACTERS";
20     INPUT X$
30     PRINT "TYPE TWO POSITIVE INTEGERS";
40     INPUT I,J
50     PRINT "MID(";X$;",";I;",";J;") IS ";MID(X$,I,J)
9999   END
```

Many versions of BASIC provide essentially the same function, although its name may vary [e.g., MID$(X$,I,J) or STR(X$,I,J); see Appendix III]. If your system supports such a function, the programs we discuss in this chapter will run correctly for you, after a simple name change.

The operation of glueing two strings together to produce a larger one is referred to as **concatenation**. Concatenation can be thought of as a kind of addition, so the symbol **+** is used to denote it.

Examples

1.
```
10     LET P$ = "APPLE PIE"
20     LET M$ = "MOM"
30     LET C$ = "CHEVROLET"
40     LET A$ = P$+M$+C$
50     PRINT A$
9999   END
RUN
APPLE PIEMOMCHEVROLET
Ready
```

The + sign joins strings together, end to end. If spaces are required, they must be included.

2.  ```
    10    LET L$ = "HI"
    20    LET R$ = "HO"
    30    LET S$ = L$+" "+R$
    40    PRINT S$
    9999  END
    RUN
    HI HO
    Ready
    ```
    ∎

By the way, the other mathematical operators have no meaning when used with strings. Expressions such as A$-B$ and A$*B$ will just produce error messages.

The third tool required for string manipulation, a means to count the number of characters in a string, is provided by the function LEN(X$).

Examples

1.  ```
    10    LET A$ = "ANTIDISESTABLISHMENTARIANISM"
    20    PRINT "THERE ARE";LEN(A$);"CHARACTERS IN ";A$;"."
    9999  END
    RUN
    THERE ARE 28 CHARACTERS IN ANTIDISESTABLISHMENTARIANISM.
    Ready
    ```

2. Spaces are counted, too:

    ```
    10    LET X$ = "HONI SOIT QUE MAL Y PENSE"
    20    LET Y$ = " WHAT? "
    30    PRINT LEN(X$);LEN(Y$)
    9999  END
    RUN
     25  7
    Ready
    ```

3. The LEN function is useful for controlling FOR/NEXT loops. What does this program do? First, describe what MID(P$,I,1) does.

    ```
    10    LET P$ = "STOP NO EVIL STAR WAS EVE"
    20    FOR I = LEN(P$) TO 1 STEP -1
    30       PRINT MID(P$,I,1);
    40    NEXT I
    9999  END
    ```
    ∎

While MID(X\$,I,J) returns a string, the function LEN(X\$) produces a number. Be careful to distinguish the situations where character strings or numbers can be used from those where they cannot. For example,

```
LET L = LEN(N$)
FOR I = 1 TO LEN(N$)
```

and

```
LET A$ = MID(X$,I,2)
```

are legal statements, but

```
LET L$ = LEN(N$)
FOR I = 1 TO N$
FOR X$ = 'A' TO 'Z'
LET A = MID(X$,I,2)
```

and

```
LET B$ = MID(X$,'A',2)
```

are nonsense.

9.5   IDENTIFICATION CODES: A SIMPLE EXAMPLE

Typically, computerized record-keeping systems use account numbers or names as keys for identifying records. However, another approach involves the use of a compact key code derived from the name or other vital statistics of the record. For example, I am a member of the Mathematical Association of America. For billing purposes I have been assigned an identification code which starts with the symbols KTANT. This is derived from my name as follows:

KITCHEN, ANDREW T.

That is, the first letter and next consonant of my first and family names, plus my middle initial. Of course, there is a distinct possibility that two individuals could have the same code, so it has to be augmented with, say, a sequence of digits.

Computer generation of this type of code can be handled by means of the MID function. Let's look at a simple version of this problem. We will write a program that will accept people's names and then print out their initials. A typical run will look like this:

```
RUN
ENTER YOUR FULL NAME, PROPERLY SPACED:
? FRANCOIS MARIE AROUET VOLTAIRE
YOUR INITIALS ARE F. M. A. V.
Ready
```

A first description of the process might look like this:

Print message and accept the full name
Search for initials
Print initials
Stop

This is pretty crude, but it does isolate the problem. Finding the first initial is straightforward. Suppose that we use the variable N$ to store the full name; then MID(N$,1,1) is the first character in N$. The remaining ones are a little harder to isolate. However, they are distinguished from all other letters by the fact that they are each preceded by a space. As we find the initials we will store them in a variable, I$. Here is a refinement of the program description:

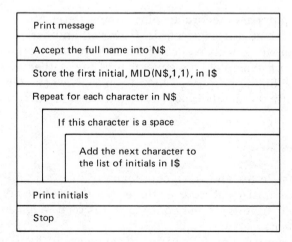

The first three blocks of this chart present no problems. In the REPEAT block the computer must check each character from N$ in turn, from the first to the last. This can be handled by a FOR/NEXT loop:

```
PRINT "ENTER YOUR FULL NAME, PROPERLY SPACED:"

INPUT N$

LET I$ = MID(N$,1,1)+". "

FOR J = 1 TO LEN(N$)

    If the Jth character is a blank

        Add the (J+1)st character to I$

NEXT J

PRINT "YOUR INITIALS ARE ";I$

END
```

This leaves the IF block to be tackled. The MID function can be used to isolate the appropriate character in N$. The Jth character is given by MID (N$,J,1), so that the IF block becomes

```
If MID(N$,J,1) = " "

    LET I$ = I$+MID(N$,J+1,1)+". "
```

Notice the technique for adding characters to the end of a character string:

```
LET I$ = I$+MID(N$,J+1,1)+". "
```

This is similar to the technique used in Chapter 4 for adding numbers to a sum, namely:

```
LET S = S + A
```

The translation is now done:

```
PRINT "ENTER YOUR FULL NAME, PROPERLY SPACED:"

INPUT N$

LET I$ = MID(N$,1,1) + ". "

FOR J = 1 TO LEN(N$)

    IF MID(N$,J,1)<>" " THEN     (A)

        LET I$ = I$ + MID(N$,J,1) + ". "

(A)     ENDIF

NEXT J

PRINT "YOUR INITIALS ARE ";I$

END
```

and here is the completed program:

```
100 REM TITLE: PRINT INITIALS
110 REM PROGRAMMER: A. KITCHEN           DATE: 10-AUG-80
120 REM
130 REM VARIABLES:
140 REM        N$ = NAME ENTERED
150 REM        I$ = STRING OF INITIALS FROM N$
160 REM        J = COUNTER FOR CHARACTERS OF N$
170 REM PROGRAM:
180     PRINT "ENTER YOUR FULL NAME, PROPERLY SPACED:"
190     INPUT N$
200     LET I$ = MID(N$,1,1)+"."
210     FOR J=1 TO LEN(N$)
220         IF MID(N$,J,1) <> " " THEN 240
230             LET I$ = I$+MID(N$,J+1,1)+"."
240 REM         ENDIF
250     NEXT J
260     PRINT "YOUR INITIALS ARE ";I$
9999    END
```

9.6 WORD PROCESSING: A MORE CHALLENGING PROJECT

We discussed the term "word processing" at the beginning of this chapter. The concept covers a multitude of separate techniques. However, one that is basic to the whole process is the deletion or replacement of groups of characters within a text. Take, for example, this "personalized" form letter:

Dear Mr. Kitchen:

All of us at the Green Island Mesa Investment Corporation want to congratulate the Kitchen family on winning a fabulous free gift. All you have to do, Mr. Kitchen, to receive this gift, is to bring Mrs. Kitchen and the kids to the Top-o-the-Town Motel, between 4 p.m. and 6 p.m. on Friday, September 15. There you and the whole Kitchen family will see a free movie on real estate investment in Arizona, the fastest growing state in the Union.

Sincerely,

Your friends at GIMIC

Thousands of such letters can be produced by computer. All that is required is a mailing list and a master copy of the letter. The master copy would be stored in computer memory, with a special character or string of characters replacing every occurrence of the family name. For example, a row of stars, ****, could be used:

*Dear Mr. ****:*

*All of us at the Green Island Mesa Investment Corporation want to congratulate the **** family on winning a fabulous . . . .*

The computer could then read each record from the mailing list, replace the markers in the master copy of the letter with the family name, type the letter, and address it. With a little extra effort, the machine could be programmed to change the title, Mr. Ms., Mrs., and so on, and to add other homey touches.

Let's tackle a variation on this theme. We will write a program that will accept a text and will allow every occurrence of a specified sequence of characters to be replaced by a string that has been typed in at the terminal. A sample run will make the goal clear:

```
RUN
ENTER TEXT. (ENCLOSE EACH LINE IN QUOTES. TO
STOP INPUT OF TEXT, TYPE *END* ON A SEPARATE LINE)
? "ROSE-PROSE, SELECTED BY A. KITCHEN."[†]
? "A ROSE IS A ROSE IS A ROSE."
? "OH, MY LOVE IS LIKE A RED, RED ROSE.
? "GATHER YE ROSEBUDS WHILE YE MAY."
? "HARD-BOILED, UNBROKEN EGG, WHAT CAN YOU CARE"
? "FOR THE ENFOLDED PASSION OF THE ROSE?"
```

[†]With apologies to Gertrude Stein, Robert Burns, Robert Herrick, H. Phelps Putnam, and Thomas Paine. Notice that lines which include commas or spaces must be enclosed in quotes.

```
? "AS HE ROSE LIKE A ROCKET, HE FELL LIKE THE STICK."
? *END*
YOU MAY EDIT THIS TEXT, OR PRINT IT, OR STOP THE PROGRAM.
TYPE EDIT, PRINT, OR STOP? EDIT
STRING TO BE REPLACED? ROSE
STRING TO REPLACE 'ROSE'? RUTABAGA
TYPE EDIT, PRINT, OR STOP? PRINT
RUTABAGA-PRUTABAGA, SELECTED BY A. KITCHEN.
A RUTABAGA IS A RUTABAGA IS A RUTABAGA.
OH MY LOVE IS LIKE A RED, RED RUTABAGA.
GATHER YE RUTABAGABUDS WHILE YE MAY.
HARD-BOILED, UNBROKEN EGG, WHAT CAN YOU CARE
FOR THE ENFOLDED PASSION OF THE RUTABAGA?
AS HE RUTABAGA LIKE A ROCKET, HE FELL LIKE THE STICK.
TYPE EDIT, PRINT, OR STOP? STOP
Ready
```

Once the text has been typed in, the program allows the user to choose various options. This means that the logic will be fairly complicated. Of the three options, EDIT, PRINT, and STOP, STOP plays a different role from the others. The second part of the program is really a REPEAT loop, which allows the user to edit or print the text. The response STOP terminates this looping.

Print message
Accept text
Print message
Repeat (exit when the response is STOP)
Request response
Accept response
Exit
If response is EDIT
Edit text
If response is PRINT
Print text
Stop

The block "Accept text" is itself a repeat loop, as is "Print text." The block "Edit text" can also be developed further. Here is an expanded version of the flow chart:

Print message describing how to type in the text
Repeat (exit when line typed in is *END*)
INPUT a line of the text
Add it to the stored text
Print message describing the available commands
Repeat (exit when the response is STOP)
Request a response (EDIT, PRINT, or STOP)
INPUT a response
Exit
If response is EDIT
Print message requesting string to be replaced
INPUT string to be replaced (old string)
Print message requesting replacement string
INPUT new string
Repeat until whole text has been processed
Find next occurrence of old string
Replace it with new string
If response is PRINT
Repeat until whole text has been processed
Print a line of text
Stop

There is one problem that will cause us grief unless we tackle it before we get much further. We must be sure that when the program stores the original text, it does not lose track of the line breaks. If we are not careful, the text will be returned to us as one long line when we type PRINT. One solution to this is to use an array, T$(1), T$(2), T$(3), . . . , to store the text. The first line would then go into T$(1), the second into T$(2), and so on (see Exercise 3 of Section 9.6). This is a good solution but it will make the EDIT block more complicated, so we will store the whole text in one variable T$.† However, another way must be found to separate the lines. Here is a translation of the first REPEAT block. It accepts the text and stores it in a single variable, T$, placing a special marker, #, at the end of each line:

```
LET T$ = " "

Repeat (exit when L$ = "*END*")

    INPUT L$

    Exit

    Add line to text:
    LET T$ = T$+L$+"#"
```

The basic pattern of this segment is very close to that of the routine which we developed in the previous section and to that used in Chapter 4 to sum a list of numbers. T$ is cleared initially by storing "nothing" in it. Then each new line, L$, and an end-of-line marker, #, is tacked onto the end of the text, T$.

More sticky points appear in the "If response is EDIT" and the "If response is PRINT" blocks. The EDIT block, partially translated, becomes

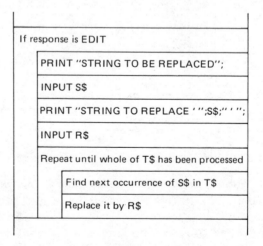

```
If response is EDIT

    PRINT "STRING TO BE REPLACED";

    INPUT S$

    PRINT "STRING TO REPLACE ' ";S$;" ' ";

    INPUT R$

    Repeat until whole of T$ has been processed

        Find next occurrence of S$ in T$

        Replace it by R$
```

†For some systems, with restrictions on the size of string variables, this is a severe restriction on the length of the text. On such a system the array approach will be necessary. If your system has string variables of limited size and does not support string arrays, then cry!

To understand what is necessary, envision yourself doing the process described in the Repeat loop, that is, searching for a given string of characters in a text (remember, they may be rather well hidden, so your search has to be thorough). For example, suppose that S$ contains "ROSE" and T$ contains lines which start:

```
I SAT, MOROSELY, WATCHING THE . . . .
```

The word "ROSE" contains four characters, so every sequence of four characters in T$ must be compared with "ROSE." These substrings of T$, listed in order of appearance, are

```
I▲SA  ▲SAT  SAT,  AT,▲  T,▲M  ,▲MO  ▲MOR  MORO  OROS  ROSE  OSEL  etc.
```

where the symbol ▲ indicates a blank space. They can be selected in turn by the MID function, so that the comparisons can be described as follows:

```
MID(T$,1,4) = S$?  MID(T$,2,4) = S$?  MID(T$,3,4) = S$?  etc.
```

At first glance it appears that a FOR/NEXT loop could handle this. The loop must stop at the last four-character substring in the text; in other words, three characters before the last one in T$, and so could be written like this:

```
FOR I = 1 TO LEN(T$)-3
    If MID(T$,I,4) = S$
        Replace this piece of T$ by R$
NEXT I
```

We shall see that this approach does not, in fact, lead to a correct solution. However, it will be helpful to pursue it further before discussing why it is inadequate.

The string S$ will not always have four characters. Once again, however, the LEN function comes to our rescue. We can replace 4 by LEN(S$) in the MID function:

```
MID(T$,I,LEN(S$))
```

and 3 by LEN(S$)–1 in the FOR statement:

```
FOR I = 1 TO LEN(T$)-LEN(S$)+1
```

Actually, as these expressions tend to make the formulas rather difficult to read, it is better to calculate them ahead of time:

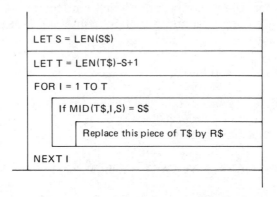

LET S = LEN(S$)

LET T = LEN(T$)–S+1

FOR I = 1 TO T

    If MID(T$,I,S) = S$

        Replace this piece of T$ by R$

NEXT I

This has the added advantage that it speeds up processing, because S and T do not have to be recalculated each time through the loop.

It remains to tackle the IF block. The simplest way to replace MID(TS,I,S) with the new string, R$, might appear to be like this:

    LET MID(T$,I,S) = R$ BAD

However, there are two problems with this idea: (1) it is illegal to have anything other than a variable on the left-hand side of a LET statement; and (2) even if it were possible, the length of R$ will not always be the same as that of the string it is replacing (e.g., "RUTABAGA" and "ROSE"). We have to perform surgery on T$ to remove one string and insert the other.

Example

Assuming the following assignments:

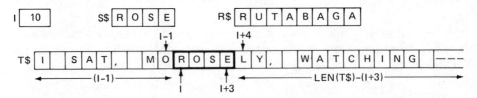

the copy, MID(T$,I,4), of ROSE is to be replaced with RUTABAGA. This can be done by cutting off the beginning and end of T$:

B$ = MID(T$,1,I–1) | I | | S | A | T | , | | M | O |

E$ = MID(T$,I+4,LEN(T$)-(I+3)) | L | Y | , | | W | A | T | C | H | I | N | G | | --- |

and then inserting R$ between them:

B$+R$+E$ | I | | S | A | T | , | | M | O | R | U | T | A | B | A | G | A | L | Y | , | | W | A | T | C | H | | --- |

In the general case, 4 must be replaced by S = LEN(S$), so that I+4 becomes I+S and

$$LEN(T\$) - (I+3) = LEN(T\$) - 3 - I$$

becomes

$$LEN(T\$) - (S-1) - I = (LEN(T\$) - S + 1) - I = T - I$$

Thus "replace this piece of T$ by R$" is translated as

LET B$ = MID(TR,1,I-1)[†]
LET E$ = MID(T$,I+S,T-I)
LET T$ = B$ + R$ + E$

and so the Repeat loop now reads:

FOR I = 1 TO T

   IF MID(T$,I,S) = S$

      Remove this segment:
      LET B$ = MID(T$,1,I-1)
      LET E$ = MID(T$,I+S,T-I)

      Replace it with R$:
      LET T$ = B$ + R$ + E$

NEXT I

[†]Most systems that provide the MID function also support two other functions, LEFT and RIGHT, which select the left- and right-hand ends of a string. Using these functions, B$ = LEFT(T$, I-1) and E$ = RIGHT(T$,I+S), which are a little simpler than the MID versions.

Before we grow too attached to this solution, we should return to the question we sidestepped earlier, namely: why is this approach unsatisfactory?

Our solution contains two serious flaws. What, for instance, would happen if we were to use a program based on this flowchart to replace the string "ROSE" by "AROSE"? Unless we skip over the new string, the substring "ROSE" of "AROSE" will be the next one to be changed. Can you see what effect this would have?

Whenever a substitution is made, the counter, I, must be increased by R, where R = LEN(R$):

    LET I = I + R

while at other times the increment should be 1:

    LET I = I + 1

The fixed step size provided by the FOR/NEXT loop is not flexible enough to handle this.

The second problem arises from the fact that the length of the text is constantly changing as substitutions are made, except in the case where the new string R$ has the same length as S$. For example, each substitution of RUTABAGA for ROSE increases the length of T$ by four characters (the difference in length between the new and the old strings). Thus the upper limit, T, of the FOR/NEXT loop may bear no relation at all to the actual length of the final text stored in T$. In what way does this affect the performance of the program?

Both of these problems force us to discard the FOR/NEXT loop and replace it with a more general Repeat loop. The following flowchart for the EDIT block describes the solution:

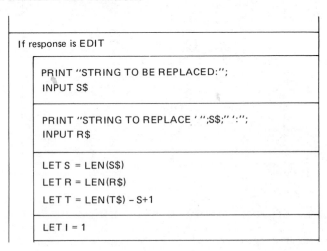

```
If response is EDIT

    PRINT "STRING TO BE REPLACED:";
    INPUT S$

    PRINT "STRING TO REPLACE ' ";S$;" ':";
    INPUT R$

    LET S = LEN(S$)
    LET R = LEN(R$)
    LET T = LEN(T$) - S+1

    LET I = 1
```

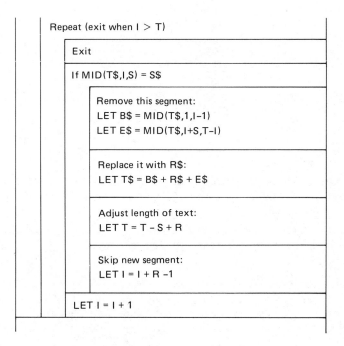

The last major step is to fill in the details in the "If response is PRINT" block. It is not enough to give the instruction:

PRINT T$

In the example originally given, this would just produce

RUTABAGA-PRUTABAGA, SELECTED BY A. KITCHEN#A RUTABAGA IS A . . .

Remember that each line is followed by an end-of-line marker (#). The characters in T$ must be printed one by one, at the same time checking for these markers. When a # is found, it should not be printed. Instead, the printhead of the terminal should be moved to the beginning of the next line.

If response is PRINT
FOR I = 1 TO LEN(T$)
Get the Ith character: LET C$ = MID(T$,I,1)

```
            If C$ is not "#"
                PRINT C$;
            If C$ is "#"
                PRINT
        NEXT I
```

The semicolon in PRINT C$ causes each character to be printed right after the preceding one and the statement PRINT causes the print head to move to the beginning of the next line.

   To finish, here is a structured description of the whole program. There are still details to fill in, but they are all straightforward.

```
PRINT "ENTER TEXT. (ENCLOSE EACH LINE IN QUOTES. TO"
PRINT "STOP INPUT OF TEXT, TYPE *END* ON A SEPARATE LINE)"
LET T$ = ""

Repeat (exit when L$ = "*END*")
    INPUT L$
    Exit
    Add line to text:
    LET T$ = T$ + L$+"#"
PRINT "YOU MAY EDIT THIS TEXT, OR PRINT IT, OR STOP THE PROGRAM."

Repeat (exit when A$ = "STOP")
    PRINT "TYPE EDIT, PRINT, OR STOP";
    INPUT A$
    Exit
    PRINT

    If A$ = "EDIT"
        PRINT "STRING TO BE REPLACED:";
        INPUT S$

        PRINT "STRING TO REPLACE ' ";S$;" ':";
        INPUT R$
```

```
LET S = LEN(S$)
LET R = LEN(R$)
LET T = LEN(T$) – S + 1

LET I = 1

Repeat (exit when I > T)

    Exit

    If MID(T$,I,S) = S$)

        Remove this segment:
        LET B$ = MID(T$,1,I–1)
        LET E$ = MID(T$,I+S,T–I)

        Replace it with R$:
        LET T$ = B$ + R$ + E$

        Adjust length of text:
        LET T = T – S + R

        Skip new segment:
        LET I = I + R – 1

    LET I = I + 1

IF A$ = "PRINT"

    FOR I = 1 TO LEN(T$)

        Get the Ith character:
        LET C$ = MID(T$,I,1)

        If C$ <> "#"

            PRINT C$;

        If C$ = "#"

            PRINT

    NEXT I

PRINT

END
```

The program we have written is a very limited text editor. More functions could be included quite easily, by adding an extra IF block to handle each new command, in exactly the same way that the commands EDIT and PRINT are handled.

This program should give you an idea of how challenging non-numerical programming can be. The programming required may be quite difficult, but the problems involved are invariably interesting.

Chapter 9: EXERCISES

Section 9.1

No exercises.

Section 9.2

1. Show what is printed by each of the following statements:
    (a) PRINT "1";"2";"3";"4"   (b) PRINT 1;2;3;4
    (c) PRINT "1","2","3","4"   (d) PRINT 1,2,3,4
    (e) PRINT "#";"1234"   (f) PRINT "#";1234

2. What must you type in order to stop this program?

```
100    REM  REPEAT
110           PRINT "SHOULD I STOP";
120           INPUT R$
130            IF R$ = " YES " THEN 9999
140           GO TO 100
9999          END
```

3. When the following program is executed:

```
100    PRINT "YOUR NAME";
110    INPUT N$
120    PRINT N$; " IS A PRETTY NAME."
9999   END
```

What is the computer's response to each of these names typed by the user?

    (a) FLOYD SKLOOT   (b) F. SKLOOT   (c) SKLOOT, FLOYD
    (d) "SKLOOT, FLOYD"   (e) 'SKLOOT, FLOYD'   (f) SKLOOT; FLOYD

4. What is printed when this program is run?

```
100    REM  REPEAT
110           READ F$
120           IF F$ = "SICK" THEN 150
130           PRINT F$
140           GO TO 100
150    REM
160           DATA "HOT DOG"
170           DATA 'FLUFFER NUTTER'
```

```
180         DATA JELLY BEANS
190         DATA "SICK"
9999        END
```

5. Describe the printout produced when the following program is run.

```
100   DIM L$(10)
110   FOR I = 1 TO 2
120      READ N
130      FOR J = 1 TO N
140            READ L$(J)
150      NEXT J
160      READ M
170      FOR J = 1 TO M
180            READ K
190            PRINT L$(K);
200      NEXT J
210      PRINT
220   NEXT I
230   DATA 10,"S","C","R","I","B","B","L","E","A","N"
240   DATA 5,6,9,1,4,2
250   DATA 9,"E","V","I","L","S","O","N","G","!"
260   DATA 6,4,3,2,1,5,9
9999  END
```

6. (a) Write a program that accepts four letters and then prints all the
         four-character strings that can be produced using any of these let-
         ters. [*Hint: Repetitions of letters are allowed; for example, if the
         letters are F, O, R, T, then TOOT and FFFF will be in the list.*]

    (b) Write a program that accepts four letters and then prints all four-
         character strings which are rearrangements of these letters. [*Hint:
         No repetitions of letters are allowed; for example, TOOT and
         FFFF will not be in the list.*]

    (c) Write a program that accepts four letters and then prints all the
         one, two, three, and four-character strings which are rearrange-
         ments of these letters. [*Hint: Repetitions of letters not allowed.*]

Section 9.3

1. Experiment with the last program in this section to familiarize yourself
    with alphabetical (lexicographical) ordering. Try including characters
    other than uppercase letters (lowercase letters, digits, punctuation char-
    acters, the space character, etc.)

2. Describe the three-character strings that will stop this program:

```
100    REM  REPEAT
110          PRINT "WANNA STOP";
120          INPUT R$
130          IF ("YES" < = R$) AND (R$ < = "YG") THEN 9999
140          GO TO 100
9999         END
```

3. What is printed when this program is run?

```
100          DIM A$(5),B$(5)
110          FOR I = 1 TO 5
120              READ A$(I)
130          NEXT I
140          FOR I = 1 TO 5
150              READ B$(I)
160          NEXT I
170          FOR I = 1 TO 5
180              IF NOT (A$(I) < = B$(I)) THEN 200
190                      PRINT A$(I);
200    REM      ENDIF
210              IF NOT (A$(I) > B$(I)) THEN 230
220                      PRINT B$(I);
230    REM      ENDIF
240          NEXT I
250    REM
260          DATA "S","E","N","S","E"
270          DATA "P","L","A","C","E"
9999         END
```

4. Write a program to sort a list of names into alphabetical order. The list can be typed in from the terminal or read from DATA statements. [*Hint: See Section 8.2, Exercise 11(a).*]

Section 9.4

1. If these variables have the given values

A$ = "APPLE PIE" M$ = "MOTHER" C$ = "CHEVROLET"

what is printed by the following statements?

(a) PRINT MID(M$,1,4)   (b) PRINT MID(M$,4,1)
(c) PRINT LEN(A$)   (d) PRINT LEN(MID(C$,3,5))
(e) PRINT MID(M$,4,3) + MID(A$,6,4)

(f)   PRINT MID(C$,1,LEN(C$))   (g)   PRINT MID(C$,LEN(C$),1)

(h)   PRINT MID(C$,1,3) + MID(C$,4,LEN(C$)-3)

2. What is printed by this program?

```
100   LET A = 2 + 3
110   LET B$ = "2" + "3"
120   LET C$ = "2 + 3"
130   LET D$ = "2" + "+" + "3"
140   PRINT A;B$;C$;D$
9999  END
```

3. In the following program segment:

```
100   INPUT N$
110   PRINT MID(N$, ____, ____)
9999  END
```

Fill in the blanks so that it prints:

(a)   The first letter of the string in N$.

(b)   The last letter of N$.

(c)   The first two letters of N$.

(d)   The last two letters of N$.

(e)   The whole of N$.

4. Show what is printed by each of the following segments.

(a)
```
100   LET X$ = "DIEFFENBACHIA"
110   FOR I = 1 TO LEN(X$)
120        PRINT MID(X$,I,1)
130   NEXT I
9999  END
```

(b)
```
100   LET X$ = "SALPIGLOSSIS"
110   FOR I = 1 TO LEN(X$)
120        PRINT MID(X$,1,I)
130   NEXT I
9999  END
```

(c)
```
100   LET X$ = "NO EVIL DOG WAS I"
110   FOR I = LEN(X$) TO 1 STEP -1
120        PRINT MID(X$,I,1);
130   NEXT I
140   PRINT " T.V."
9999  END
```

(d)
```
100   LET X$ = "*+/-=!?"
110   FOR I = 1 TO LEN(X$)
120        LET B$ = MID(X$,1,I)
130        LET E$ = MID(X$,I+1,LEN(X$)-I)
140        PRINT B$ + E$
150   NEXT I
9999  END
```

5. What is printed by this program when it is executed?

```
100         FOR I = 1 TO 3
110             READ M$,K
120             FOR J = 1 TO K
130                 READ N
140                 PRINT MID(M$,N,1);
150             NEXT J
160             PRINT
170         NEXT I
180     REM
190         DATA "ISN'T",1
200         DATA 1
210         DATA "MATHEMATICS",4
220         DATA 4,7,3,5
230         DATA "A HOT NUMBER",4
240         DATA 9,1,5,3
9999        END
```

6. Show the printout produced by a run of this program.

```
100         LET A$ = "ABCDEFGHIJKLMNOPQRSTUVWXYZ"
110     REM   REPEAT
120             READ C$
130             IF C$ = "*" THEN 220
140             LET K = 0
150     REM     REPEAT
160                 LET K = K+1
170                 LET L$ = MID(A$,K,1)
180                 IF C$ = L$ THEN 200
190             GO TO 150
200             PRINT K;
210         GO TO 110
220     REM
230         DATA "P","E","N","D","R","A","G","O","N","*"
9999    END
```

7. Describe the errors in the following statements.
(a)   IF M$ > N PRINT "HOHO"
(b)   PRINT MID(A$,"N",5)
(c)   LET X$ = "5" + "6"
(d)   FOR B$ = 1 TO LEN(B$)
(e)   LET I$ = 5 + 6
(f)   GO 20
(g)   LET D$ = E$*F$
(h)   DIM $(I)
(i)   DIM N$(10),A(15)
(j)   LET MID(X$,2,6) = "BABIES"
(k)   NEXT L + 1

   (l)   INPUT LEN(X$)
   (m)   LET X$ = "LET X$"
   (n)   IF C$ = * THEN 220

8. Write a program to remove a character from a specified position in a given character string. Here is a typical run:

   RUN
   ENTER CHARACTER STRING? "WE HATE RATS"
   POSITION OF CHARACTER TO BE REMOVED? 4
   MODIFIED STRING: WE ATE RATS
   Ready

   [*Hint: Construct two substrings: one consisting of the beginning of the string up to, but not including, the specified position and the other consisting of the part beyond that position.*]

9. Write a program to read a list of names and print the longest of them. [*Hint: See Section 6.5., Exercise 2(a).*]

10. Write a program to accept a line of text and then, repeatedly, to accept a letter and count the occurrences of that letter in the text. Here is a sample run:

   RUN
   ENTER LINE OF TEXT
   ? "HOLD YOUR HOUR AND HAVE ANOTHER."
   ENTER LETTER TO BE COUNTED (OR STOP)? R
   R OCCURS 3 TIMES
   ENTER LETTER TO BE COUNTED (OR STOP)? STOP
   Ready

   This flowchart may be helpful:

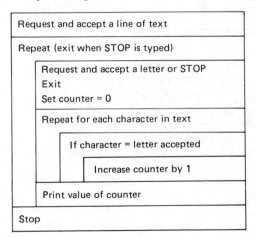

11. (a) When bank checks are printed automatically, some effort is made to minimize the opportunity for forgery. For example, a check-writing machine might write 94.57 as

$$********94DOLLARS\&57CENTS$$

dollars field   cents field

Write a program to convert the decimal representation of any dollars and cents amount to a form similar to that above. Allow a field of 10 characters for the dollar part. Place the digits at the right end of this field and fill the left end with stars. [*Hint: The program will be easier if you store the decimal number accepted from the terminal in a character string variable, not a numerical variable.*]

(b) Modify the program in part (a) so that it puts commas after the "thousands" and "millions" digits if necessary (e.g., ****25,735-DOLLARS&98CENTS).

Section 9.5

1. Write a version of the program developed in this section that will read a list of names from DATA statements and print a list of their initials.

2. Write a program to produce a coded version of a person's name according to the rule described at the beginning of this section. Here is a sample run:

```
RUN
ENTER YOUR NAME? "KITCHEN, JUDITH R."
YOUR CODE IS KTJDR
Ready
```

3. Write a program to accept a (first) name and construct a nickname out of it, according to the following rule. Find the first consonant following the first vowel in the name. Drop the part of the name to the right of this consonant, double the consonant, and add Y. A typical run:

```
RUN
WHAT'S YOUR NAME? FRANCIS
HI FRANNY! HOW'S YOUR LOVE LIFE?
Ready
```

[*Hint: FRANCIS → FRAN → FRANN → FRANNY. The effects are*

often strange, to say the least; for example, CHARLES becomes CHARRY.]

4. (a) Write a program that will accept a line of text and then print it with the words in order, but the letters of each word in reverse order. For example:

RUN
TEXT? "EVE SAW NO LIVE RATS"
REVERSED: EVE WAS ON EVIL STAR
Ready

Here is a flowchart for the program:

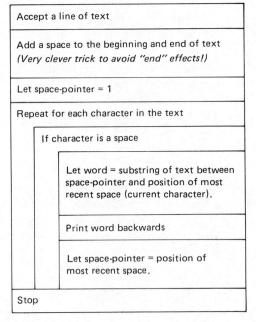

[*Hint: This program will do strange things to punctuation. You should modify the program slightly so that it does at least preserve the final period.*]

(b) Write a program that will accept a line of text and print the words in reverse order but the letters of each word in correct order. [*Hint: This program can be produced by a fairly simple modification of the answer to (a).*]

5. (a) Write a program to translate a one-line English sentence into Pig Latin. [*Hint: Remember, to translate into Pig Latin, move the initial letter of each word to the end and add AY; for example, SHE LOVES ME becomes HESAY OVESLAY EMAY.*]

(b) Write a second program to translate Pig Latin into English.

Section 9.6

1. Show what is printed when each of the following program segments is executed.

(a)
```
100        LET T$ = "A"
110   REM  REPEAT
120             READ A$
130             IF A$ = "*" THEN 160
140             LET T$ = T$ + A$
150        GO TO 110
160        PRINT T$
170        DATA "B","C","D","*"
9999       END
```

(b)
```
100        LET T$ = "A"
110   REM  REPEAT
120             READ A$
130             IF A$ = "*" THEN 160
140             LET T$ = A$ + T$
150        GO TO 110
160        PRINT T$
170        DATA "B","C","D","*"
9999       END
```

(c)
```
100        LET T$ = "A"
110   REM  REPEAT
120             READ A$
130             IF A$ = "*" THEN 160
140             LET T$ = A$ + T$ + A$
150        GO TO 110
160        PRINT T$
170        DATA "B","C","D","*"
9999       END
```

(d)
```
100        LET T$ = "A"
110   REM  REPEAT
120             READ A$
130             IF A$ = "*" THEN 160
140             IF T$ = T$ + A$ + T$
150        GO TO 110
160        PRINT T$
170        DATA "B","C","D","*"
9999       END
```

2. Complete the translation into BASIC of the program developed in this section. What is the disadvantage of using #, or any other symbol for that matter, as an end-of-line marker?

3. Rewrite the program of this section so that the text is stored in an array T$, each line in a separate component. [*Hint: The first line is stored in*

T$(1), the second in T$(2), and so on. This approach is necessary on a system that supports character string arrays but limits the number of characters that can be stored in a string variable.]

4.   Write a program to print form letters requesting overdue bills. The form letter itself should be read from DATA statements into a string variable or string array. The information on the individuals to whom the letter is to be sent should be entered using INPUT statements. Arrange the spacing so that each letter starts on a separate sheet of paper. Use this sample run as a guide.

```
RUN
TO PRODUCE FORM LETTERS, TYPE INFO. AS REQUESTED
TO STOP, TYPE 'STOP' IN RESPONSE TO 'FIRST NAME?'
FIRST NAME? CECIL
FAM. NAME? TETON
STREET?"24 COTTONDALE LANE"
CITY?"BATON ROUGE"
STATE & ZIP?"LA 70008"
BILL? 240.45

                                      SWEENEY'S SEXE SHOPPE
                                      PARADISE ROW
                                      CINNCINCITY, OH 00000
         CECIL TETON
         24 COTTONDALE LANE
         BATON ROUGE
         LA 70008

         DEAR CECIL:
              IN REVIEWING OUR RECORDS WE FIND THAT YOU
         HAVE AN OUTSTANDING BILL OF $240.45. WE ARE SURE
         THAT THIS IS AN OVERSIGHT ON YOUR PART. HOWEVER,
         WE WOULD LIKE TO ADVISE YOU THAT THE NEXT NOTICE YOU
         RECEIVE WILL NOT BE MAILED IN A PLAIN BROWN WRAPPER.
         YOU WOULDN'T WANT THAT, CECIL, WOULD YOU?
              PLEASE MAIL THAT CHECK AT YOUR EARLIEST
         CONVENIENCE.

                                      YOUR FRIENDS AT SWEENEY'S

         FIRST NAME? RED
         FAM. NAME? RIDINGHOOD
         etc.
```

[*Hint: The advantage of having the letter in DATA statements is that it is more easily changed. Place special markers in the text of the form letter to indicate where the name, address, and so on, are to be inserted (you might use FFFF to indicate the first name, NNNN for the family name, etc.); then the program should replace every occurrence of each marker with the actual information for each individual addressed. For example, "- - - WOULDN'T WANT THAT, FFFF, WOULD - - -" is changed to "- - - WOULDN'T WANT THAT, CECIL, WOULD - - -" for CECIL TETON.]*

5. Write a program that will accept a piece of text (more than one line) and then, repeatedly, accept a word and count the occurrences of that word in the text. For example:

```
RUN
ENTER TEXT (TO STOP, TYPE *STOP* ON A LINE BY ITSELF)
? "A SWEET LITTLE DICKIE-BIRD SAT IN THE TREE."
? "HE HOPPED, HE SKIPPED, SO MERRY HE WAS!"
? *STOP*
ENTER WORD TO BE COUNTED (TO STOP, TYPE "*STOP*")
? A
A APPEARS 1 TIME(S).
? HE
HE APPEARS 3 TIME(S).
? *STOP*
Ready
```

[Hint: See Section 9.4, Exercise 10. Note that the program should count words, not just character strings. For example, when counting HE, it must not include the HE in THE. Words, in general, have blanks on either side of them. Have the program add blanks to the word to be counted after it has been typed in (e.g., " HE "). The ends and beginnings of lines will give you trouble, as will the punctuation, so have the program remove all punctuation from the text and use a blank space as an end-of-line marker instead of #.]

6. Write a program that will accept a piece of text (more than one line) and then print the average length of the words in the text as well as a table showing the percentages of words of specific lengths. For example, a typical run:

```
RUN
ENTER TEXT (TO STOP, TYPE *STOP* ON A LINE BY ITSELF).
? "A SWEET LITTLE DICKIE-BIRD SAT ON A BOUGH."
? "HE HOPPED, HE SKIPPED, SO MERRY WAS HE."
? *STOP*
AVERAGE WORD LENGTH 3.9375
PERCENTAGE WORD COUNT:
```

```
WORDS OF
            1 LETTER   12.5   %
            2 LETTERS 31.25  %
            3 LETTERS 12.5   %
            4 LETTERS 0   %
            5 LETTERS 18.75  %
            6 LETTERS 12.5   %
            7 LETTERS 6.25   %
            8 LETTERS 0   %
            9 LETTERS 0   %
           10 OR MORE 6.25   %
Ready
```

[*Hint: See Exercise 5 for suggestions on the preparation of the text for processing.*]

Chapter

10

Functions
and Subroutines

10.1 FUNCTIONS

In earlier chapters we have discussed a number of functions [INT(X), TAB(X), LEN(X$), MID(X$,I,J)] and others have appeared briefly in exercises and examples [e.g., SQR(X), the square root function, and ABS(X), the absolute value of X]. A function is, in a sense, a program within a program—one that performs a specific calculation.

Examples

1.
```
100   PRINT "ENTER THE BASE AND HEIGHT OF A RIGHT TRIANGLE"
110   INPUT X,Y
120   LET P = X*X+Y*Y
130   LET H = SQR(P)
140   PRINT "THE HYPOTENUSE HAS LENGTH"; H
9999  END
```

2.
```
100   PRINT "ENTER A POSITIVE VALUE";
110   INPUT P
120   LET I = INT(P)
130   PRINT "THE INTEGER PART OF "; P; "IS"; I
9999  END
```
■

All functions follow the same pattern. They accept one or more values [e.g., MID(X$,I,J) requires three values]. They then perform operations on these values and return a result. The process by which this result is calculated is not seen by the user. The usefulness of functions is twofold: (1) they perform operations that would otherwise be hard to do in a program, and (2) they hide messy calculations from the user, calculations which, if seen, would not add to an understanding of the overall program.

Examples

1. INT(X) performs an operation that would be quite complicated to program otherwise (see Section 10.1, Exercise 4).
2. TAB(X) doesn't return a value in the normal sense. In its simplest applications it causes a sequence of X spaces to be printed. For example,

```
100   PRINT TAB(X); "*"
```

replaces

```
100   FOR I = 1 TO X
110      PRINT " ";
120   NEXT I
130   PRINT "*"
```

3. SQR(X) [or SQRT(X) on some systems] is an interesting case. Clearly, SQR(X) is equivalent to $X \wedge (0.5)$. The difference is that SQR(X) is calculated by a much faster process which does not generalize to arbitrary exponents. ∎

Most versions of BASIC provide a number of different functions. Here is a table of some of the more popular ones:

Function	Description
INT(X)	Greatest integer that is less than or equal to X
ABS(X)	Absolute value of X
SGN(X)	Sign of X (–1 if X is negative, 0 if X is zero, 1 if X is positive)
SQR(X)	Square root of X
EXP(X)	Exponential function (e^x, where e = 2.71828 . . .)
LOG10(X)	Common logarithm of X (base 10)
LOG(X)	Natural logarithm of X (base e)
SIN(X)	Sine of X (where X is in radians)

Function	Description
COS(X)	Cosine of X (X in radians)
TAN(X)	Tangent of X (X in radians)
RND or RND(X)	Number chosen at random from the range between 0 and 1
TAB(X)	Moves print head of terminal to the (X + 1)st character position measured from the left-hand margin
LEN(X$)*	Number of characters in the string X$
MID(X$,I,J)*	Substring of X$ consisting of J characters, starting with the Ith character of X$

Not available on some systems.

Experiment with these. The usefulness of many of them is restricted to scientific calculations. One exception, however, is the function RND(X), whose peculiar behavior is discussed in Chapter 12.

10.2 USER-DEFINED FUNCTIONS

Many useful functions are missing from the foregoing list; for example, there is no function that rounds numerical values to two decimal places, nor one to calculate monthly mortgage payments given the size of the loan. Clearly, there is a limit to the number of functions that can be provided by a computer system. Every technical field has its own specialized calculations and operations, so that a complete list of all functions, each of which is considered useful in at least one field, would reach into the hundreds.[†] The solution that BASIC adopts (in common with most other computer languages) is to provide the facilities for users to define their own functions.

Look at the following program segment, which calculates the tax in schedule SE of the U.S. federal income tax forms.

```
100    REM   CALCULATE SOCIAL SECURITY SELF-EMPLOYMENT TAX
110    REM
120          PRINT "ENTER S.E. INCOME";
130          INPUT S
140          LET T = S*0.081
150    REM
160    REM   ROUND TAX TO NEAREST CENT
170    REM
180          LET T = INT(T*100+0.5)/100
190          PRINT "S.E. TAX = "; T
```

[†]One reason that BASIC provides primarily scientific functions is that its designers were mathematicians.

```
9999        END
RUN
ENTER S.E. INCOME? 5037.50
S.E. TAX = 408.04
Ready
```

The expression

```
INT(T*100+0.5)/100
```

holds no mysteries. However, suppose that you were writing a program to do *all* the calculations necessary to fill out your tax returns. In such a program there would be numerous percentage calculations, after each of which, for the purposes of printout, the result would have to be rounded to two decimal places. Now, although this calculation is not complicated, it would be helpful to reduce the clutter in the program by hiding the calculation in a "black box." This is done in BASIC by defining a function to do that specific calculation. For example:

```
100     REM   FUNCTION TO ROUND TO 2 DEC. PLACES
110           DEF FNR(X) = INT(X*100+0.5)/100
120     REM   CALCULATE SOCIAL SECURITY SELF-EMPLOYMENT TAX
130     REM
140           PRINT "ENTER S.E. INCOME";
150           INPUT S
160           LET T = S*0.081
170     REM
180     REM   ROUND TAX TO NEAREST CENT
190     REM
200           LET T = FNR(T)
210           PRINT "S.E. TAX ="; T
9999          END
RUN
ENTER S.E. INCOME? 5037.50
S.E. TAX = 408.04
Ready
```

FNR is an example of a user-defined function. In line 110, the statement

```
DEF FNR(X) = INT(X*100+0.5)/100
```

defines the calculation performed by FNR on a value X. Note that X is not an actual variable; it is a place marker which shows where the values will be inserted when the function is used. Later in the program, in line 200,

```
LET T = FNR(T)
```

the function FNR is applied to the variable T. When executing this statement, the computer refers to the definition in line 110, then replaces the marker X by the variable T and performs the calculation. Thus line 200 is equivalent to

```
LET T = INT(T*100+0.5)/100
```

By the way, we could tidy the program further by combining the tax calculation and the rounding in line 160:

```
LET T = FNR(S*0.081)
```

Introducing the function FNR is hardly worth the effort for just one calculation. However, in a full-scale tax program, where such rounding would be performed many times, the elimination of this irritating little calculation could enhance the clarity of the program.

Example

```
100 REM ROUNDING FUNCTION
110     DEF FNR(X) = INT(X*100+0.5)/100
120 REM
130     PRINT "ENTER A NUMBER";
140     INPUT A
150     LET R = FNR(1/A)
160     LET S = FNR(A^0.5)
170     LET T = FNR(1/(A^0.5))
180     PRINT "TO TWO DECIMAL PLACES"
190     PRINT "RECIPROCAL =";R
200     PRINT "SQUARE ROOT =";S
210     PRINT "RECIPROCAL OF ROOT =";T
9999    END


RUN

ENTER A NUMBER? 7
TO TWO DECIMAL PLACES
RECIPROCAL = .14
SQUARE ROOT = 2.65
RECIPROCAL OF ROOT = .38

Ready
```

Experiment with this. Try changing the definition of FNR. ∎

Here are the technical details on user-defined functions. The name of a user-defined function (**function name**) consists of the letters FN followed immediately by a letter.

Examples

Typical valid function names:

FNA; that is, FN followed by A
FNY; FN followed by Y

The following are examples of names that would be illegal on most systems:
FUNKY, FNROUND, FNAA, FN-B, FN3, FN R.   ∎

The list of values on which the function acts (its **argument list**) follows
the function name. They are enclosed in parentheses, and if there is more
than one **argument**, they are separated by commas.

Examples

```
FNR(X)
FNB(X,Y,Z)
FNQ(A,B)
```
                                                                    ∎

Incidentally, most systems put a limit on the number of values that may
appear in the argument list. Many small systems allow no more than a single
argument, whereas larger ones may allow as many as five.

Before a function can be used, it must be defined. A **function definition
statement** has the following form:

line number   DEF   *function name (argument list) = expression*

where the expression describes the action of the function on its arguments.
Once a function has been defined, it can be used anywhere that the expression which defines it can be used. For example, in expressions in LET statements, IF statements, PRINT statements, and FOR statements, and even in
the definition of other functions.

Examples

1.   DEF FNQ(A) = A^3 + A^2 + A + 1

   This represents the cubic polynomial

$$q(a) = a^3 + a^2 + a + 1$$

Here is another representation of the same function:

```
DEF FNQ(A) = ((A + 1)*A + 1)*A + 1
```

2.
```
DEF FNP(X) = X*(1 + 7/100)
```

This function calculates the total payment on an item costing X dollars, when the sales tax is 7%.

3.
```
DEF FNP(X,Y) = X*(1 + Y/100).
```

This is more general than the previous one. The sales tax, Y%, is included as an argument of the function. As some systems will not permit a function with two arguments, here is another approach that should work on any system.

```
DEF FNP(X) = X*(1 + Y/100)
```

Notice that Y is not in the argument list. It is a true variable and must be given a value before the function can be used. Here are two program segments which show the difference between these approaches.

```
100    REM  SALES TAX                100    REM  SALES TAX
110         DEF FNP(X,Y) = X*(1+Y/100)    110         DEF FNP(X)=X*(1+Y/100)
120         PRINT "ENTER COST";        120         PRINT "ENTER COST";
130         INPUT C                     130         INPUT C
140         LET P = FNP(C,7)            140         LET Y = 7
150         PRINT "PAYMENT IS $"; P     150         LET P = FNP(C)
9999        END                         160         PRINT "PAYMENT IS $"; P
                                        9999        END
```

These segments perform identically. The disadvantage of the second is that the variable Y is committed to holding the value of the tax percentage, whereas in the first the Y in the definition is a dummy variable and thus in no way commits one to the use of Y for that purpose in the body of the program.

4.
```
DEF FNR(Z) = INT(Z*100+0.5)/100
DEF FNP(X,Y) = FNR(X*(1+Y/100))
```

One user-defined function can appear in the definition of another. You will notice that FNP(X,Y) is gotten by substituting X*(1+Y/100) for Z in FNR(Z). That is, FNP(X,Y) is effectively

$$((X*(1+Y/100)*100)+0.5)/100$$

a bit of a mouthful!

```
5.    100          DEF FNF(C) = C*9/5 + 32
      110          PRINT "ENTER YOUR TEMPERATURE IN CELSIUS";
      120          INPUT C
      130          IF NOT (FNF(C) > 98.6) THEN 150
      140              PRINT "SICK!"
      150    REM   END IF
      160          IF NOT (FNF(C) < = 98.6) THEN 180
      170              PRINT "HEALTHY!"
      180          END IF
      9999         END
```

When the function is used it doesn't matter whether the variable name is the same as, or different from, the dummy argument in the definition.   ∎

Some systems allow functions to accept string variables as arguments as well as produce results which are strings. If a function returns a value that is a character string, its name should be followed by a dollar sign ($).†

Examples

1.   `DEF FND(X$,Y$) = LEN(X$) - LEN(Y$)`

This function returns a numerical value, the difference in the lengths of the strings X$ and Y$.

2.   `DEF FNF$(X$) = MID(X$,1,1)`

This returns a string, the first character in X$.

3.   `LET A$ = "ABCDEFGHIJKLMNOPQRSTUVWXYZ"`
      `DEF FNL$(N) = MID(A$,N,1)`

This function produces the Nth letter in the alphabet. More correctly, it returns the Nth character in the string stored in A$. A safer, although more clumsy definition is

`DEF FNL$(N) = MID("ABCDEFGHIJKLMNOPQRSTUVWXYZ",N,1)`   ∎

---

†Notice that MID(X$,I,J) is not consistent with this policy. Some versions of BASIC use the more consistent MID$(X$,I,J) instead.

10.3 SUBROUTINES

Some versions of BASIC allow lengthy function definitions, spread over many lines of code. In fact, they may permit the use of IF-THEN statements and FOR-NEXT loops when defining a function, so that the definition becomes a complete program in itself. However, this is the exception rather than the rule and, even in a system that provides such glittering machinery, there is a limitation which is inherent in the way functions are used in BASIC. Functions are designed to be used in BASIC expressions, for example,

```
LET Y = (L + FNR(A))/FNR(B)
```

Because of this, a function must return a single value, a number, or a character string. It cannot return a collection of different values simultaneously. For example, the value produced by a function cannot be a list or an array. On the other hand, the argument that functions are useful for hiding messy calculations holds even more strongly when the calculations involve large amounts of data which have to be processed simultaneously. For example, the calculation or printing of tables of values, the sorting of lists, and the printing of game board patterns for computer games are all procedures that return large quantities of information or produce complicated output. A function would not be the appropriate tool for this kind of problem.

Most programming languages handle such tasks by means of what are called **subroutines**. In a similar way to functions, subroutines provide a means by which lengthy or complex operations can be shunted off to one side so as not to disturb the logical flow of the main program. They can be thought of as footnotes containing the technical details that would otherwise clutter the program. Subroutines in BASIC are, unfortunately, rather primitive when compared with functions. Even so, they can be useful tools. Here is a familiar friend rewritten using a subroutine.

```
100    REM   CALCULATE SOCIAL SECURITY SELF-EMPLOYMENT TAX
110    REM
120          PRINT "ENTER S.E. INCOME";
130          INPUT S
140          LET T = S*0.081
150    REM
160    REM   ROUND TO NEAREST CENT
170          GOSUB 1000
180          PRINT "S.E. TAX ="; T
190          STOP
200    REM
```

```
1000   REM   SUBROUTINE TO ROUND T TO NEAREST CENT
1010           LET T = INT(T*100+0.5)/100
1020           RETURN
```

```
1030   REM
9999           END
```

The boxed section, lines 1000–1020, is the subroutine and

```
GOSUB 1000
```

is the statement that **calls** the subroutine. Let's trace the execution of this program segment in order to see how the subroutine is used.

Suppose that 4053.00 is typed in response to statements 120 and 130. This value is stored in S and at line 140 the tax, T, is computed to be 328.293. The REM statements are ignored by the system, so the next line to be executed is

```
170   GOSUB 1000
```

This causes control to jump to line 1000. The REM statement there is ignored and in line 1020 the tax is rounded to two decimal places so that the variable T now contains 328.29. The next instruction

```
1020   RETURN
```

causes control to return to where the flow was interrupted by GOSUB 1000, that is, to

```
180   PRINT "S.E. TAX = "; T.
```

The rounded value is printed out and execution is complete. Oh, by the way, the statement

```
190   STOP
```

is just there to stop the program from falling into the subroutine by accident. It indicates the end of the main program.

STOP behaves like an END statement. When it is reached, it causes execution of the program to stop. Unlike END, however, STOP can appear anywhere in a program and, in fact, a program can contain more than one STOP statement. The statement GO TO 9999 where line 9999 is

```
9999   END
```

can always be replaced by STOP.

The following diagram indicates the flow of control and shows some snapshots of the workspace as execution proceeds.

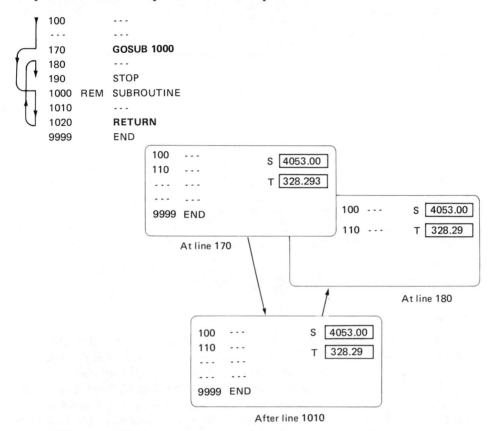

```
100        - - -
- - -      - - -
170        GOSUB 1000
180        - - -
190        STOP
1000  REM  SUBROUTINE
1010       - - -
1020       RETURN
9999       END
```

At line 170

At line 180

After line 1010

This example has probably raised a number of questions in your mind, the first of which may well be "why bother?" Well, it is a little like using an axe to cut your toenails, but bear in mind that it was intended as a simple example, not a realistic one. A more serious question is: Why introduce the new statements GOSUB and RETURN when the whole thing could have been handled with GO TO's?

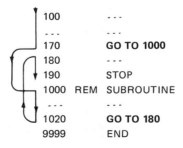

```
100        - - -
- - -      - - -
170        GO TO 1000
180        - - -
190        STOP
1000  REM  SUBROUTINE
- - -      - - -
1020       GO TO 180
9999       END
```

The full advantage of GOSUB and RETURN does not appear unless a subroutine is called repeatedly from different points in the program, as in the following segment:

```
100  REM  DEMONSTRATION OF GOSUB
110       PRINT "ENTER A NUMBER";
120       INPUT A
130  REM
140       LET X = 1/A
150       GOSUB 1000
160       LET R = X
170  REM
180       LET X = A^0.5
190       GOSUB 1000
200       LET S = X
210  REM
220       LET X = 1/(A^0.5)
230       GOSUB 1000
240       LET T = X
250  REM
260       PRINT "TO TWO DECIMAL PLACES"
270       PRINT "RECIPROCAL =";R
280       PRINT "SQUARE ROOT =";S
290       PRINT "RECIPROCAL OF ROOT =";T
300       STOP
310  REM
1000 REM  SUBROUTINE TO ROUND TO 2 DECIMAL PLACES
1010              X = INT(X*100+0.5)/100
1020      RETURN
1030 REM
9999      END
```

Suppose that the program is run and the value 6 is entered at line 120. The reciprocal, 0.166667, is stored in X and at line 150 control jumps to the subroutine. After X has been rounded to 0.17, the RETURN statement restores control to line 160, where the rounded value is placed in R. Next, the square root of 6, 2.44949, is calculated and the subroutine is called again at line 190, after which processing resumes at line 200. The final call to the subroutine occurs at line 230, where the value $1/\sqrt{6} = 0.408248$ is rounded. Following this the program continues uninterrupted from line 240 to the end. The following diagram shows the flow of control:

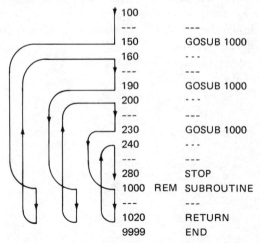

```
       100
       ---          ---
       150          GOSUB 1000
       160          - - -
       ---          ---
       190          GOSUB 1000
       200          - - -
       ---          ---
       230          GOSUB 1000
       240          - - -
       ---          ---
       280          STOP
       1000   REM   SUBROUTINE
       ---          ---
       1020         RETURN
       9999         END
```

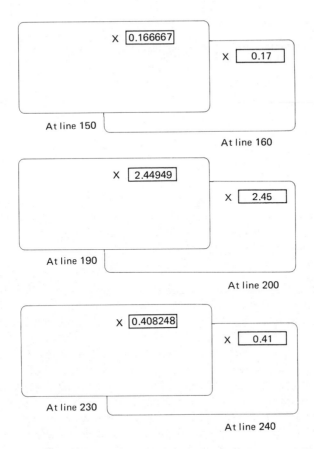

Try replacing the GOSUB and RETURN statements in this program with GO TO statements. You will find that it is impossible. The GOSUB statement is a GO TO "with memory." It looks before it leaps and "remembers" the point from which it is jumping. When the RETURN statement is reached, it causes a branch back to the statement following the most recent GOSUB.

From the example that we have just discussed you will see that the variables in BASIC subroutines are true variables, not dummy ones. Before each jump to the subroutine, the value to be rounded was placed in X. On each return, it had to be dumped out into another variable (R, S, and T, respectively) to free X for the next trip. The variable X was used like a bucket for the transmission of data to and from the subroutine.

Here is an example of a less trivial subroutine:

Example

```
300        LET A = 3.2
310        LET B = -5.9
320        LET C = 0.9
330 REM SOLVE EQUATION A*X^2 + B*X + C = 0
340        GOSUB 1000
```

```
350       PRINT "ROOTS ARE";R1;"AND";R2
990       STOP
1000 REM SUBROUTINE TO SOLVE QUADRATIC EQUATION
1010 REM OF FORM A*X^2 + B*X + C = 0
1020 REM
1030            LET D = B*B - 4*A*C
1040            IF D<0 THEN 1070
1050                 LET R1 = (-B + SQR(D))/(2*A)
1060                 LET R2 = (-B - SQR(D))/(2*A)
1070 REM        END IF
1080      RETURN
1090 REM
9999      END
```

The data transmitted to the subroutine consist of the coefficients of the equation. These are stored in A, B, and C. The roots are returned in R1 and R2. To be complete, the routine should indicate whether or not the roots exist. This information is provided by the quantity D, known as the discriminant.[†] So, in fact, three values are returned: R1, R2, and D. ■

A warning: Because the variables in subroutines, unlike those in functions, are true variables, you must be careful that you don't accidentally use a variable in a subroutine which has already been committed to a different purpose in the main program.

BASIC does not require that one give a name to a subroutine or that one list the variables used by it. However, if a program is to be readable, it is most important that this information, in the form of REMARKS, be included on each subroutine that is used. You should provide sufficient documentation at the beginning of a subroutine, as well as at the points where it is called, so that anyone (this could be you, a month or two later) who wishes to understand the program can see what purpose each subroutine serves and exactly what information passes between it and the main program. I can assure you, from bitter experience, that it is all worth the effort. Here is an example of more systematic documentation applied to our perennial example.

Example:

A segment of the self-employment tax program:

```
140       LET T = S*0.081
150 REM
160 REM CALL: ROUND TO TWO DECIMAL PLACES
170 REM VALUES: T        RETURNED: T
180       GOSUB 1000


1000 REM SUBROUTINE:
1010 REM ROUND TO TWO DECIMAL PLACES
```

[†] If D < 0, the equation has no real roots.

```
1020 REM VALUES: T        RETURNED: T
1030            T = INT(T*100 + 0.5)/100
1040      RETURN
1050 REM
9999     END                                          ■
```

The following represents a reasonably simple convention which is adequate
for most situations. It can be modified if more description is required.

At the point at which the subroutine is called, that is, at the GOSUB
statement, include

```
- - -       - - - -
ee  REM  CALL: short description of subroutine
ff  REM  VALUES: variable-list-1      RETURNED: variable-list-2
gg       GOSUB qq
- - -       - - -
```

Then at the beginning of the subroutine:

```
- - -       - - -
nn       STOP
pp  REM
qq  REM  SUBROUTINE:
rr  REM  short description of subroutine
ss  REM  VALUES: variable-list-1      RETURNED: variable-list-2
- - -                  the statements which
- - -                  constitute the subroutine
- - -       RETURN
- - -       - - -
```
(*ee,ff,* and so on, stand for line numbers).

Variable-list-1 contains those variables that transmit values to the subroutine
and *variable-list-2* those that return results to the main program. By the way,
it is easier to identify the subroutine with the calls to it if the format of the
REMARKs before the GOSUBs and those at the beginning of the subroutine
itself are identical.

Examples

1.   Here is a subroutine that does not return a value.

```
- - -       - - -
720      REM  CALL: PRINT A ROW OF STARS
730      REM  VALUES: N    RETURNED: NONE
740           GOSUB 2000
- - -       - - -
```

```
- - -            - - -
- - -            - - -
- - -            - - -
2000  REM  SUBROUTINE:
2010  REM  PRINT A ROW OF STARS
2020  REM  VALUES: N       RETURNED: NONE
2030            FOR I = 1 TO N
2040               PRINT "*";
2050            NEXT I
2060            PRINT
2070          RETURN
- - -
```

2. A short description of the variables is often helpful, even if they have already been described at the beginning of the main program:

```
- - -            - - -
370            INPUT B,C
380            LET A = 1
390   REM  CALL: SOLVE QUADRATIC EQUATION
400   REM  VALUES: A,B,C = COEFFS
410   REM  RETURNED: R1, R2 = ROOTS; D = DISCRIMINANT
420            GOSUB 1000
430            IF D < 0 THEN 450
440               PRINT R1, R2
450   REM  ENDIF
- - -            - - -
- - -            - - -
1000  REM  SUBROUTINE:
1010  REM  SOLVE QUADRATIC EQUATION
1020  REM  VALUES: A,B,C = COEFFS
1030  REM  RETURNED: R1, R2 = ROOTS; D = DISCRIMINANT
1040            LET D = B*B – 4*A*C
1050            IF D < 0 THEN 1080
1060              LET R1 = (–B + SQR(D))/(2*A)
1070              LET R2 = (–B – SQR(D))/(2*A)
1080  REM       ENDIF
1090            RETURN
- - -            - - -
```

3. A program may contain more than one subroutine and one subroutine may call another.

```
- - -            - - -
490   REM  PRINCIPAL AND INTEREST
500            LET P = 2500
510            LET I = 9.25
```

```
520    REM   CALL: YEAR-END BALS., INTEREST COMPOUNDED QUARTERLY
530    REM   VALUES: P,I      RETURNED: B(1), . . . , B(50)
540          GOSUB 1000
- - -        - - -
- - -        - - -
880          STOP
890    REM
1000   REM   SUBROUTINE:
1010   REM   YEAR-END BALS., INTEREST COMPOUNDED QUARTERLY
1020   REM   VALUES: P,I      RETURNED: B(1), . . . , B(50)
1030         LET Q = (1 + I/400) ^4
1040         FOR N = 1 TO 50
1050           LET X = P*(Q^N)
1060   REM     CALL: ROUND TO 2 DEC. PLACES
1070   REM       VALUES: X    RETURNED: X
1080           GOSUB 2000
1090           LET B(N) = X
1100         NEXT N
1110         RETURN
1120   REM
2000   REM   SUBROUTINE:
2010   REM   ROUND TO 2 DEC. PLACES
2020   REM   VALUES: X      RETURNED: X
2030          LET X = INT(X*100+0.5)/100
2040          RETURN
2050   REM
9999          END                                              ■
```

One last comment: Subroutines should be placed at the end of the program, where they are out of the way but easy to find if needed. Make sure that you protect them by putting a STOP statement in front of the first one (or a GOTO to branch around them to the END):

```
100    ┌─────────────────┐
       │ Main            │
       │ program         │
       └─────────────────┘
- - -    STOP (or GOTO 9999)
       ┌─────────────────┐
- - -  │ Subroutine      │
       ├─────────────────┤
- - -  │ Subroutine      │
       └─────────────────┘
- - -    - - -
       ┌─────────────────┐
- - -  │ Data            │
       │ statements      │
       └─────────────────┘
9999     END
```

If you do not do this, then at the end of the program the system will attempt to execute the first subroutine as though it were part of the main program, with unpredictable results.

10.4 PROGRAM DEVELOPMENT USING SUBROUTINES

The power of subroutines lies in their ability to set complicated manipulations to one side. The appearance of a GOSUB in a program is equivalent to saying to the reader: "At this point we must do the following calculations, the details of which are not essential to an understanding of the program's overall structure. If you wish to see them, you will find them listed below."

This approach to subroutines is a very powerful conceptual tool when it comes to program development. The design of a large program can be a daunting and difficult project. We have already discussed the value of structured design in program development. Well, subroutines and functions have an important part to play here, too.

The overall structure of a program can often be seen more clearly if the details of certain calculations are temporarily overlooked. In fact, one may be able to develop the rest of the program without knowing exactly how one is going to tackle them. As the program develops, GOSUBs can be inserted at the points where the calculations are needed and later the corresponding subroutines can be written. Various versions of the routines can be tested and, in fact, improvements can be made at any time without having to rewrite the whole program. This technique of developing the general structure of a program, before filling the details, is referred to as **top-down programming**.

It is easier to illustrate the power of this approach with an example than to explain it, so we will end this chapter by developing a major project using subroutines.

10.5 A PROGRAM TO PLAY TIC-TAC-TOE

We will write a program to enable the computer to play tic-tac-toe against a human opponent. (Well, I suppose the opponent could even be another machine!) Our program will not be very sophisticated but, by using subroutines, we will design it so that it could easily be modified or improved at a later date.

Here is a preliminary description:

```
┌──────────────────────────────────────────────────┐
│  Describe game and procedures for play             │
├──────────────────────────────────────────────────┤
│  Repeat (exit when player or machine wins          │
│  or there is a draw)                               │
│   ┌────────────────────────────────────────────┐  │
│   │  Player makes move                          │  │
│   ├────────────────────────────────────────────┤  │
│   │  Check for win or draw                      │  │
│   ├────────────────────────────────────────────┤  │
│   │  Machine makes move                         │  │
│   ├────────────────────────────────────────────┤  │
│   │  Check for win or draw                      │  │
│   └────────────────────────────────────────────┘  │
├──────────────────────────────────────────────────┤
│  Stop                                              │
└──────────────────────────────────────────────────┘
```

and here is what the game might look like:

```
RUN
THIS IS THE GAME OF TIC-TAC-TOE. WE WILL
PLAY ON A GAME BOARD NUMBERED AS FOLLOWS:

           1  !  2  !  3
           -  +  -  +  -
           4  !  5  !  6
           -  +  -  +  -
           7  !  8  !  9

YOU PLAY WITH X'S, I'LL USE O'S. TO PLAY,
YOU MUST ENTER THE NUMBER OF AN AVAILABLE
POSITION ON THE BOARD. REMEMBER, A LINE OF
THREE X'S (OR O'S) HORIZONTALLY, VERTICALLY,
OR DIAGONALLY, CONSTITUTES A WIN.

YOUR MOVE? 3

              !     !  X
           -  +  -  +  -
              !     !
           -  +  -  +  -
              !     !

MY MOVE:

           O  !     !  X
           -  +  -  +  -
              !     !
           -  +  -  +  -
              !     !
```

YOUR MOVE? <u>7</u>

```
O !    ! X
- + - + -
  !   !
- + - + -
X !   !
```

MY MOVE:

```
O ! O ! X
- + - + -
  !   !
- + - + -
X !   !
```

YOUR MOVE? <u>5</u>

```
O ! O ! X
- + - + -
  ! X !
- + - + -
X !   !
```

YOU WIN. THANKS FOR A GOOD GAME.

Well, I told you it wouldn't be very sophisticated!

With this as a goal, we can refine the design of the program. We must have some way of storing the moves that have been made. A simple way to do this is to use a character string array:

B$(1) B$(2) B$(3)   B$(4) B$(5) B$(6)   B$(7) B$(8) B$(9)

☐ ☐ ☐   ☐ ☐ ☐   ☐ ☐ ☐

first row   second row   third row

At the beginning this will contain the positions

| 1 | | 2 | | 3 | | 4 | | 5 | | 6 | | 7 | | 8 | | 9 |

Before the first move, these numbers will be replaced by spaces, which will, in turn, be replaced by X's and O's as the game progresses. For example, the winning board pattern above, would be stored as:

| O | | O | | X | | ☐ | | X | | ☐ | | X | | ☐ | | ☐ |

We'll worry about how to print out this information later. Meanwhile, here is a refinement of the original flowchart:

Describe game and print game board (B$)
Clear game board for play
Repeat (exit when player (X) or machine (O) wins or there is a draw)
Request player's move
Accept move (N)
Store move ("X" in B$(N))
Print game board (B$)
Check for a win or draw
Exit
Machine chooses move
Store move ("O" in B$(N))
Print game board (B$)
Check for a win or draw
Exit
Print final message
Stop

Now some of the blocks in this chart are very simple (e.g., "Describe game" and "Accept move"), whereas others (e.g., "Machine chooses move" and "Check for a win or a draw") are more challenging. We'll translate whatever comes easily and defer the nasty bits to subroutines. Notice the use of a variable, W, to indicate a win or a draw in the next flowchart:

PRINT "THIS IS THE GAME OF TIC-TAC-TOE. WE WILL" PRINT "PLAY ON A GAME BOARD NUMBERED AS FOLLOWS"
LET B$(1) = "1" LET B$(2) = "2" --- LET B$(9) = "9"
Call subroutine to print game board

```
PRINT "YOU PLAY WITH X'S. I'LL USE O'S. TO PLAY"
PRINT "YOU MUST ENTER THE NUMBER OF AN AVAILABLE"
PRINT "POSITION ON THE BOARD. REMEMBER, A LINE OF"
PRINT "THREE X'S (OR O'S) HORIZONTALLY, VERTICALLY"
PRINT "OR DIAGONALLY, CONSTITUTES A WIN."
```

```
CLEAR THE BOARD:
FOR I = 1 TO 9
    LET B$(I) = " "
NEXT I
```

Repeat (exit when player (X) or machine (O) wins or there is a draw)

> ```
> PRINT "YOUR MOVE";
> INPUT N
> STORE MOVE:
> LET B$(N) = "X"
> ```
>
> Call subroutine to print game board
>
> Call subroutine to check for a win or a draw. (It will return a value in a variable W: 0 = continue play, 1 = draw, 2 = machine wins, 3 = player wins)
>
> Exit
>
> Call subroutine to choose machine's move (N)
>
> ```
> STORE MOVE:
> LET B$(N) = "O"
> ```
>
> ```
> PRINT "MY MOVE:"
> ```
>
> Call subroutine to print game board
>
> Call subroutine to check for a win or a draw (win/draw returned in W)
>
> Exit

If W = 1

> ```
> PRINT "A DRAW.";
> ```

If W = 2

> ```
> PRINT "I WIN.";
> ```

If W = 3
PRINT "YOU WIN.";
PRINT " THANKS FOR A GOOD GAME."
STOP
Subroutines to be inserted here

Once we include the GOSUBs and the documentation, the main program will be complete apart from the relatively routine business of translating the REPEAT and IF blocks. Let's include the GOSUB linkages before turning our attention to the subroutines themselves. To do this we have to decide what values must travel between the main program and each of its subroutines. The first routine called prints the game board. For this, all that is required is the array B$; no values are returned. The routine that checks for a win or draw must be given the current status of the game, the array B$, and the latest move, N. It will return the win/draw information in the variable W. And finally, the routine that chooses the machine's move must be given the status of the game, B$, and must return a move in N. Incorporating this information into the main program produces the following:

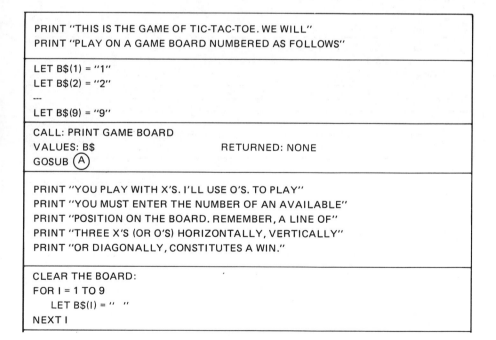

```
PRINT "THIS IS THE GAME OF TIC-TAC-TOE. WE WILL"
PRINT "PLAY ON A GAME BOARD NUMBERED AS FOLLOWS"
```

```
LET B$(1) = "1"
LET B$(2) = "2"
---
LET B$(9) = "9"
```

```
CALL: PRINT GAME BOARD
VALUES: B$                    RETURNED: NONE
GOSUB (A)
```

```
PRINT "YOU PLAY WITH X'S. I'LL USE O'S. TO PLAY"
PRINT "YOU MUST ENTER THE NUMBER OF AN AVAILABLE"
PRINT "POSITION ON THE BOARD. REMEMBER, A LINE OF"
PRINT "THREE X'S (OR O'S) HORIZONTALLY, VERTICALLY"
PRINT "OR DIAGONALLY, CONSTITUTES A WIN."
```

```
CLEAR THE BOARD:
FOR I = 1 TO 9
    LET B$(I) = "  "
NEXT I
```

Repeat (exit when W > 0)

> PRINT "YOUR MOVE";
> INPUT N
> STORE MOVE:
> LET B$(N) = "X"
>
> ---
>
> CALL: PRINT GAME BOARD
> VALUES: B$ RETURNED: NONE
> GOSUB (A)
>
> ---
>
> CALL: CHECK FOR WIN OR DRAW
> VALUES: B$, N   RETURNED: W
> GOSUB (B)
>
> ---
>
> Exit
>
> ---
>
> CALL: MACHINE MAKES MOVE
> VALUES: B$ RETURNED: N
> GOSUB (C)
>
> ---
>
> STORE MOVE:
> LET B$(N) = "O"
>
> ---
>
> PRINT "MY MOVE:"
>
> ---
>
> CALL: PRINT GAME BOARD
> VALUES: B$ RETURNED: NONE
> GOSUB (A)
>
> ---
>
> CALL: CHECK FOR WIN OR DRAW
> VALUES: B$, N   RETURNED: W
> GOSUB (B)
>
> ---
>
> Exit

If W = 1

> PRINT "A DRAW.";

If W = 2

> PRINT "I WIN.";

If W = 3

> PRINT "YOU WIN.";

PRINT " THANKS FOR A GOOD GAME."
STOP

Ⓐ SUBROUTINE:
PRINT GAME BOARD
VALUES: B$ RETURNED: NONE

> Subroutine code here

RETURN

Ⓑ SUBROUTINE:
CHECK FOR WIN OR DRAW
VALUES: B$, N   RETURNED: W

> Subroutine code here

RETURN

Ⓒ SUBROUTINE:
MACHINE MAKES MOVE
VALUED: B$ RETURNED: N

> Subroutine code here

RETURN

END

We have passed the first major hurdle. The main program, an empty chassis, is complete and the subroutines, the working parts, are yet to be written. The next step is to build these parts and test all the components before they are assembled into the finished product. We will turn later to a discussion of testing, but first let's get the subroutines written.

Printing the game board is not really hard. A little ingenuity is required to design a convincing tic-tac-toe board, but the subroutine itself is just a collection of PRINT statements.

SUBROUTINE:
PRINT GAME BOARD
VALUES: B$ RETURNED: NONE

```
PRINT B$(1);"!";B$(2);"!";B$(3)
PRINT " - + - + - "
PRINT B$(4);"!";B$(5);"!";B$(6)
PRINT " - + - + - "
PRINT B$(7);"!";B$(8);"!";B$(9)
```

RETURN

Checking for a win or a draw is rather tedious. The solution given here does not take any clever shortcuts. It just checks each of the eight winning patterns (the three rows, three columns, and two diagonals) in turn.

The numbers of the positions in the rows, columns, and diagonals are read from DATA statements. This way we can use a FOR-NEXT loop to save on the number of IF statements. The only problem is that the data must be reread after every move. As you know, this is not normally possible, as the information in DATA statements can only be read once. After all the data has been read, the next READ statement causes an "OUT OF DATA" message. This problem can be avoided by using the **RESTORE** statement. The first READ following a RESTORE statement will start reading from the top of the data list again. Thus RESTORE allows one to reread the DATA statements as often as required. There are dangers to this approach, though. DATA statements cannot be used anywhere else in the program without running the risk of complete chaos. Luckily these will be the only ones we will need.

```
SUBROUTINE:
CHECK FOR WIN OR DRAW
VALUES: B$, N                           RETURNED: W

     (W = 0, CONTINUE PLAY; W = 1, DRAW;
     W = 2, MACHINE WINS; W = 3, PLAYER WINS)

     INITIALLY, ASSUME A DRAW:
     LET W = 1

     NOT A DRAW, IF ANY POSITION IS STILL BLANK:

     FOR I = 1 TO 9

         If B$(I) = " "

             LET W = 0

     NEXT I

     CURRENT MARKER (X OR O):
     LET M$ = B$(N)

     CHECK FOR WIN:
     RESTORE

     FOR I = 1 TO 8

         READ A,B,C
```

```
          If (B$(A) = M$) AND (B$(B) = M$) AND (B$(C) = M$)

                 LET W = 2

       NEXT I

       IF A WIN, THEN MACHINE WINS
       UNLESS PLAYER MADE CURRENT MOVE:

       If (W = 2) AND (M$ = "X")

          LET W = 3

    RETURN
    DATA: WINNING PATTERNS
    DATA 1,2,3
    DATA 1,4,7
    DATA 1,5,9
    DATA 2,5,8
    DATA 3,5,7
    DATA 3,6,9
    DATA 4,5,6
    DATA 7,8,9
```

The final subroutine, MACHINE MAKES MOVE, is the one that gives the program its character. We can design into it the most sophisticated strategies known for playing tic-tac-toe, or we can make it simple and dumb. To keep this chapter at a reasonable length, we'll take the chicken's way out and design it to make legal but mindless moves. If you want to try your hand at a better solution, see Section 10.7, Exercise 4.

```
    SUBROUTINE:
    MACHINE MAKES MOVE
    VALUES: B$              RETURNED: N

       FIND FIRST AVAILABLE BLANK SPACE:
       LET N = 1

       Repeat (exit when B$(N) = " ")

             EXIT
             LET N = N + 1

    RETURN
```

Notice that if all the positions on the board are filled, this routine will attempt to test B$(10). However, the subroutine CHECK FOR WIN OR DRAW will stop the game before this can happen. This situation is not ideal because an incorrectly written routine for CHECK FOR WIN OR DRAW may cause this routine to misbehave. Can you redesign MACHINE MAKES MOVE so that the search for a blank space stops at B$(9)?

Well, the project is almost finished. All that remains is the final translation into BASIC and testing. Here is the completed program:

```
100 REM TITLE: TIC-TAC-TOE GAME
110 REM PROGRAMMER: A. KITCHEN              DATE: 25-JUL-81
120 REM VARIABLES:
130 REM          B$(1),...,B$(9) = GAME BOARD POSITIONS
140 REM          N = CURRENT MOVE
150 REM          M = CURRENT MARKER (X OR O)
160 REM          W = WIN/DRAW/CONTINUE PLAY (SEE THE
170 REM                SUBROUTINE "CHECK FOR WIN OR DRAW")
180 REM          I = FOR-NEXT LOOP COUNTER
190 REM          A,B,C = ROW, COL, OR DIAGONAL POSITIONS
200 REM PROGRAM:
210     DIM B$(9)
220     PRINT "THIS IS THE GAME OF TIC-TAC-TOE. WE WILL"
230     PRINT "PLAY ON A GAME BOARD NUMBERED AS FOLLOWS:"
240     LET B$(1) = "1"
250     LET B$(2) = "2"
260     LET B$(3) = "3"
270     LET B$(4) = "4"
280     LET B$(5) = "5"
290     LET B$(6) = "6"
300     LET B$(7) = "7"
310     LET B$(8) = "8"
320     LET B$(9) = "9"
330 REM CALL: PRINT GAME BOARD
340 REM VALUES: B$         RETURNED: NONE
350     GOSUB 1000
360     PRINT "YOU PLAY WITH X'S. I'LL USE O'S. TO PLAY"
370     PRINT "YOU MUST ENTER THE NUMBER OF AN AVAILABLE"
380     PRINT "POSITION ON THE BOARD. REMEMBER, A LINE OF"
390     PRINT "THREE X'S (OR O'S) HORIZONTALLY,VERTICALLY"
400     PRINT "OR DIAGONALLY, CONSTITUTES A WIN."
410 REM CLEAR THE BOARD
420     FOR I = 1 TO 9
430         LET B$(I) = " "
440     NEXT I
450 REM REPEAT
460         PRINT "YOUR MOVE";
470         INPUT N
480 REM     STORE MOVE:
490         LET B$(N) = "X"
500 REM     CALL: PRINT GAME BOARD
510 REM     VALUES: B$         RETURNED: NONE
520         GOSUB 1000
530 REM     CALL: CHECK FOR WIN OR DRAW
540 REM     VALUES: B$,N       RETURNED: W
550         GOSUB 2000
560         IF W > 0 THEN 710
570 REM     CALL: MACHINE MAKES MOVE
580 REM     VALUES: B$         RETURNED: N
590         GOSUB 3000
600 REM     STORE MOVE:
```

```
610                     LET B$(N) = "0"
620                     PRINT "MY MOVE:"
630 REM                 CALL: PRINT GAME BOARD
640 REM                 VALUES: B$        RETURNED: NONE
650                     GOSUB 1000
660 REM                 CALL: CHECK FOR WIN OR DRAW
670 REM                 VALUES: B$,N      RETURNED: W
680                     GOSUB 2000
690                     IF W > 0 THEN 710
700                     GO TO 450
710 REM END REPEAT
720     IF NOT (W = 1) THEN 740
730                 PRINT "A DRAW!";
740 REM END IF
750     IF NOT (W = 2) THEN 770
760                 PRINT "I WIN!";
770 REM END IF
780     IF NOT (W = 3) THEN 800
790                 PRINT "YOU WIN!";
800 REM END IF
810     PRINT " THANKS FOR A GOOD GAME!"
820     STOP
830 REM
1000 REM SUBROUTINE:
1010 REM PRINT GAME BOARD
1020 REM VALUES: B$        RETURNED: NONE
1025                PRINT
1030                PRINT B$(1);"!";B$(2);"!";B$(3)
1040                PRINT "-+-+-"
1050                PRINT B$(4);"!";B$(5);"!";B$(6)
1060                PRINT "-+-+-"
1070                PRINT B$(7);"!";B$(8);"!";B$(9)
1075                PRINT
1080     RETURN
1090 REM
2000 REM SUBROUTINE:
2010 REM CHECK FOR WIN OR DRAW
2020 REM VALUES: B$,N   RETURNED: W
2030 REM (W = 0, CONTINUE PLAY; W = 1, DRAW;
2040 REM  W = 2, MACHINE WINS; W = 3, PLAYER WINS.)
2050 REM            INITIALLY, ASSUME A DRAW:
2060                LET W = 1
2070 REM            NOT A DRAW IF ANY POSITION IS BLANK:
2080                FOR I = 1 TO 9
2090                     IF NOT (B$(I) = " ") THEN 2110
2100                          LET W = 0
2110 REM                 END IF
2120                NEXT I
2130 REM            CURRENT MARKER (X OR 0):
2140                LET M$ = B$(N)
2150 REM            CHECK FOR A WIN:
2160                RESTORE
2170                FOR I = 1 TO 8
2180                     READ A,B,C
2190                     IF NOT (B$(A) = M$) THEN 2230†
2200                     IF NOT (B$(B) = M$) THEN 2230
2210                     IF NOT (B$(C) = M$) THEN 2230
2220                          LET W = 2
2230 REM                 END IF
```

†IF NOT ((BR(A) = M$) AND (B$(B) = M$) AND (B$(C) = M$)) THEN 2230 is too long for the line when indented. This is equivalent; see Appendix V.

```
2240              NEXT I
2250 REM         IF A WIN, THEN MACHINE WINS
2260 REM         UNLESS PLAYER MADE CURRENT MOVE:
2270             IF NOT ((W = 2) AND (M$ = "X")) THEN 2290
2280                 LET W = 3
2290 REM         END IF
2300     RETURN
2310 REM DATA: WINNING PATTERNS
2320     DATA 1,2,3
2330     DATA 1,4,7
2340     DATA 1,5,9
2350     DATA 2,5,8
2360     DATA 3,5,7
2370     DATA 3,6,9
2380     DATA 4,5,6
2390     DATA 7,8,9
2400 REM
3000 REM SUBROUTINE:
3010 REM MACHINE MAKES MOVE
3020 REM VALUES: B$        RETURNED: N
3030 REM         FIND FIRST AVAILABLE SPACE:
3040             LET N = 1
3050 REM         REPEAT
3060                 IF B$(N) = " " THEN 3090
3070                 LET N = N + 1
3080             GO TO 3050
3090     RETURN
3100 REM
9999 END
```

Of course, the machine has very little chance of winning with this program. The one positive thing that can be said for it, though, is that someone who plays a few rounds against it will quickly lose any fear of computers. Anything that dumb can't be all bad!

10.6   SUBROUTINE TESTING

Subroutines should always be thoroughly tested before they are attached to the main program. It is so much easier to look for errors in a short segment of code than in a long program. This is not only because there are fewer statements to check, but also because the logic of a single subroutine is simpler than that of the whole program.

This testing business may sound like an onerous chore. In fact, it is not difficult at all. Suppose that we wish to check the last subroutine of the tic-tac-toe game. We write a simple test program which calls just this one subroutine:

```
          ⎛ 10    REM   TEST SUB: MACHINE MAKES MOVE
          ⎜ 20          PRINT "ENTER B$";
Test      ⎜ 30          FOR I = 1 TO 9
program   ⎨ 40             INPUT B$(I)
          ⎜ 50          NEXT I
          ⎜ 60          GOSUB 3000
          ⎜ 70          PRINT "N ="; N
          ⎝ 80          STOP
Sub-      ⎛ 3000  REM   SUBROUTINE:
routine   ⎜ 3010  REM   MACHINE MAKES MOVE
to be     ⎨ - - -        - - -
tested    ⎝ 3100         RETURN
            3110  REM
            9999         END
```

The test program doesn't have to be beautiful; you'll be the only one who
will ever have to see it. All that is required is that it request the values that
are to be transmitted to the subroutine and that it print the values returned.
For example, the test program above asks for a typical game board pattern,
the array B$, to be typed in. It then calls the subroutine, after which it
prints out N, the move chosen.

Example

```
RUN
ENTER B$
? 0
? X
? " "
? X
? " "
? " "
? " "
? " "
? " "
N = 3
Ready
```

Enter blanks in quotes; otherwise, they may be ignored by your system.   ■

This way one can check that the subroutine is handling all possible game
situations, as it is supposed to, by feeding it various states of play and seeing
how it responds.

A program of this form is all that is needed to test any subroutine:

INPUT values to be sent to subroutine, that is, the variables listed after "VALUES:".[†]
GOSUB (A)
PRINT data returned from subroutine, that is, the variables listed after "RETURNED:".[†]
STOP

(A) Subroutine
   to
     be
       tested.

END

Once the subroutine is working correctly, it can be copied into its proper position in the main program.

By the way, copying the subroutine takes time and there is always the chance that you will introduce errors into a perfect subroutine as you retype it. So here is a way of testing it "in situ." Suppose that you have written the main program and also have the subroutine in its correct position following the program. Place the test program in front of the main program by using lower line numbers for its statements (for this reason it is a good idea to start all major programs no lower than line 100). When you type RUN the test program will be executed first, then the STOP statement will terminate the run before the main program is reached.

Example

```
            10      REM  TEST SUB: MACHINE MAKES MOVE
            20            PRINT "ENTER B$"
            30            FOR I = 1 TO 9
Test        40              INPUT B$(I)
program     50            NEXT I
            60            GOSUB 3000
            70            PRINT "N = "; N
            80            STOP
```

[†]If the subroutine does not request (or return) data, the INPUT (respectively, PRINT) section of the test program can be omitted. For example, the test program for the "PRINT GAME BOARD" subroutine will not include a PRINT section, as this subroutine does not return data.

```
          ⎧ 100    REM   TITLE TIC-TAC-TOE GAME
          │ 110    REM   PROGRAMMER: A. KITCHEN          DATE: 25-JUL-81
Main      │ - - -
program   │ 820          STOP
          ⎩ 830    REM


First two ⎧ - - -
          │ - - -
subroutines⎩ - - -

          ⎧ 3000   REM   SUBROUTINE:
          │ 3010   REM   MACHINE MAKES MOVE
          │ 3020   REM   VALUES: B$          RETURNED: N
Sub-      │ - - -
routine   │ - - -
to be     ⎩ 3100         RETURN
tested      3110   REM
            9999         END
```

The performance of this example is identical to that of the previous one. After the testing is complete, the lines containing the test program can be deleted.   ∎

Our discussion presupposes that the main program is correct. This is hardly a valid assumption unless the program has also been tested. This testing can be handled by a simple extension of the approach we have just described. We replace all the subroutines with test routines that allow us to monitor the performance of the main program.

Example

Here is the test subroutine that replaces the routine "CHECK FOR WIN OR DRAW":

```
2000   REM   SUBROUTINE:
2010   REM   CHECK FOR WIN OR DRAW
2020   REM   VALUES: B$, N      RETURNED: W
2030         PRINT "SUB: CHECK FOR WIN OR DRAW."
2040         PRINT "B$ = ";
2050         FOR I = 1 TO 9
2060           PRINT B$ (I):"/";
2070         NEXT I
2080         PRINT
2090         PRINT "N = "; N
```

```
2100            PRINT "ENTER W";
2110            INPUT W
2120         RETURN
```

When the subroutine is called by the main program, it will produce something like this:

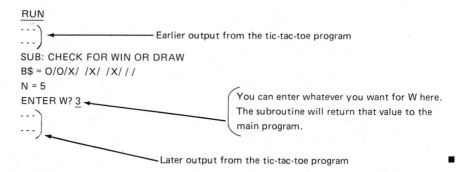

Every subroutine should be replaced with a routine that prints the values transmitted from the main program and allows the programmer to type in the values to be returned to it.

Suppose that we replace the other two subroutines of the tic-tac-toe program with similar code. When the program is executed, each GOSUB statement will cause the name of the corresponding subroutine to be printed, as well as the data transmitted to it. We will then be able to play "subroutine" and type in the values to be returned to the main program. In this way we can monitor the data sent to each subroutine and, by typing appropriate values, test how the program responds to its subroutines. For instance, using the example above, we could test the program's logic by observing its response to each possible value of W (0 = continue play, 1 = draw, 2 = machine wins, 3 = player wins).

10.7 WHY SUBROUTINES? A SUMMARY

The tic-tac-toe program illustrates how subroutines can help to organize program development as well as make the resulting code more readable. A shorter program could possibly have been written if we had dispensed with some of the subroutine calls. On the other hand, the modularity of our program means that we can read the code to the level of detail that we choose. If one just reads the main program and ignores the subroutines, one gets an overview of the procedure. If one wants to understand the details of how a given part is handled, one can read the appropriate subroutine.

Another advantage is that subroutines can be modified or replaced by improved versions with little danger of disturbing the overall logic of the program. For example, a more sophisticated version of "MACHINE MAKES MOVE" would be a welcome improvement in the tic-tac-toe game.

Here are some other suggestions for improvements. It is easy for the user to cheat, just by typing a position that is already filled. The program could be modified by replacing the statement INPUT N with a subroutine that checks the legality of a move and requests a new value if necessary. We could also allow the user to decide who should start first. Both of these require modifications to the main program and here the advantage of subroutines is seen in another light. With so much of the calculation handled by subroutines, the logic of the main program is clear and simple. Thus changes can be made relatively easily and without disturbing other unrelated parts of the program.

Section 10.1

1. If the variables X, Y, and Z$ have the values

    X = 3.83   Y = -2.75   Z$ = "WHIPPER SNAPPERS"

   what is printed when each of these statements is executed?
   (a) PRINT ABS(Y)   (b) PRINT SGN(-Y)
   (c) PRINT INT(X + Y)   (d) PRINT SQR(INT(X) + 1)
   (e) PRINT INT(X + ABS(Y))   (f) PRINT INT(X) + INT(ABS(Y))
   (g) PRINT SGN(Y)*Y   (h) PRINT (SQR(X))^2
   (i) PRINT ABS(INT(Y))   (j) PRINT TAB(LEN(Z$));Z$
   (k) PRINT LEN(MID(Z$,3,7))   (l) PRINT MID(Z$,INT(X),INT(X) + 1)
   (m) PRINT MID(Z$,LEN(Z$)/2,LEN(Z$)/2)

2. Write short program segments to enable you to experiment with the
   following expressions.
   (a) X/ABS(X) for any values of X
   (b) X/SGN(X) for any values of X
   (c) SQR(X) - X^0.5 for positive X
   (d) LOG(EXP(X)) for any values of X
   (e) EXP(LOG(X)) for positive X
   (f) LOG(X)/LOG(2) for X = 1, 2, 4, 8, 16, 32, 64
   (g) LOG(X)/LOG(10) for X = 1, 10, 100, 1000, 10000, 100000
   (h) (COS(X))^2 + (SIN(X))^2 for X = -1, -0.9, -0.8, . . . , 1

3. Show what is printed by each of the following programs.
   (a) ```
        100   LET X = 0.6
        110   FOR I = 1 TO 10
        120   LET Y = INT(X*I)/I
        130   PRINT Y
        140   NEXT I
        9999   END
        ```
   (b)  ```
        100          LET X = 256
        110    REM   REPEAT
        120             PRINT X
        130             IF X <= 2 THEN 9999
        140             LET X = SQR(X)
        150          GO TO 110
        9999         END
        ```

4. (a) Write a program that will perform the same operation as ABS(X)
       without using the function ABS.

(b) Write a program that will perform the same operation as INT(X) for positive X. [*Hint: Needless to say, the program should not use INT. Here is a suggestion: Count up from zero until you get the first whole number that exceeds X; use this to calculate INT(X).*]

(c) Write a program that will perform the same operation as INT(X) for any value of X. [*Hint: ABS(X) and SGN(X) may be useful here.*]

5. Write a program segment that doesn't use the TAB function, but whose performance is identical to this one:

```
100   PRINT "TYPE YOUR NAME";
110   INPUT N$
120   PRINT "TYPE YOUR PLACE OF BIRTH";
130   INPUT B$
140   PRINT
150   PRINT "NAME";TAB(40);"PLACE OF BIRTH"
160   PRINT N$;TAB(40);B$
9999  END
```

[*Hint: Line 150 is easy but line 160 is a little more challenging.*]

Section 10.2

1. Given the definitions

```
DEF FNS(X) = X^2 + 1
DEF FNR(X) = 1/X
```

and the variable assignments T = 3, X = 4, describe what is printed by the following statements.

(a) PRINT FNS(T) (b) PRINT FNR(X+1)
(c) PRINT 1/FNR(1.35) (d) PRINT FNS(X^2)
(e) PRINT FNR(0.1) + FNR(0.2) + FNR(0.4)
(f) PRINT FNR(T)*FNS(T) (g) PRINT FNR(FNS(T))

2. Given the definition

```
DEF FNI$(I) = MID("0123456789",I+1,1)
```

describe what is printed by the following statements.

(a) FNI$(0) (b) FNI$(7)
(c) FNI$(3) + FNI$(5) (d) FNI$(3 + 5)

3.   What is printed by each of the following program segments when it is executed?

(a)
```
100   DEF FNV(X) = X + 1
110   FOR A = 0 TO 2 STEP 0.2
120      PRINT FNV(A);
130   NEXT A
9999  END
```

(b)
```
100   DEF FNW(R) = (R^2 - 1)/(R -1)
110   FOR B = 0 TO 2 STEP 0.2
120      PRINT FNW(B);
130   NEXT B
9999  END
```

(c)
```
100            DEF FNR(X) = 1/X
110   REM  REPEAT
120            READ A
130            LET B = FNR(A)
140            PRINT FNR(B)
150         GO TO 110
160         DATA 4.5, 7.2, 3.9, 1.8, 8.5
9999        END
```

(d)
```
100            DEF FNL$(N$) = MID(N$,LEN(N$),1)
110   REM  REPEAT
120            READ N$
130            PRINT FNL$(N$)
140            IF FNL$(N$) = "*" THEN 9999
150         GO TO 110
160         DATA "*ABCD","D*ABC","CD*AB","BCD*A","ABCD*"
9999        END
```

4.   Show the printout produced by the execution of each of these program segments.

(a)
```
100   DEF FNR(X) = INT(X*T + 0.5)/T
110   LET Y = 9.4567
120   FOR I = -1 TO 4
130      LET T = 10^I
140      LET Z = FNR(Y)
150      PRINT Z
160   NEXT I
9999  END
```

(b)
```
100   DEF FNR(X,T) = INT(X*T + 0.5)/T
110   LET T = 9.4567
120   FOR I = -1 TO 4
130      LET X = 10^I
140      LET Z = FNR(T,X)
150      PRINT Z
160   NEXT I
9999  END
```

5. Write a definition of a user-defined function FNF(X) which returns the fractional part of a positive number [e.g., PRINT FNF(2.97) produces 0.97]. What does your function produce when applied to a negative number?

6. (a) Write a definition of a user-defined function that returns a string consisting of the first N characters of a string X$.
    (b) Write a definition of a function that returns a string consisting of the last N characters of a string X$. [*Hint: You may use MID and LEN in these definitions.*]

7. (a) Write a definition for a function, FNR(N), which returns the right-most digit of a positive integer N [e.g., FNR(795) returns the value 5]. What does this function do to negative numbers? real numbers?
    (b) Write a program that accepts a positive integer and then uses the function defined in part (a) to print the digits of the integer in reverse order. A sample run:

```
RUN
INTEGER? 576
DIGITS IN REVERSE ORDER: 6  7  5
Ready
```

    (c) Can you modify the program so that it prints the integer obtained by reversing the digits? For example:

```
RUN
INTEGER? 576
INTEGER REVERSED: 675
Ready
```

8. (a) Using the formula

$$\text{Monthly payment} = \frac{\left(\dfrac{\text{interest}}{1200}\right)\text{loan}}{1 - \left(\dfrac{\text{interest}}{1200} + 1\right)^{-12(\text{years})}}$$

    write a definition for a function, FNM(I), which calculates the monthly payments on a \$1 loan at *I%* interest for a 25-year mortgage.
    (b) Write an assignment statement that uses this function to calculate the monthly payments on a loan of \$*L* at *I%* for a 25-year mortgage.
    (c) Write a program that uses the function from part (a) to print a table showing monthly payments for 25-year mortgages on loans

of $20,000 through $50,000 in increments of $5000, with interest rates ranging from 12.5 through 13.5% in steps of 0.25%.

Section 10.3

1.   Show what is printed by each of the following, and in each case trace the values of the specified variables; that is, show their values after the execution of every statement.

(a)
```
100             LET A = 1
110             GOSUB 1000
120             GOSUB 2000
130             GOSUB 2000
140             GOSUB 1000
150             GOSUB 2000
160             STOP
1000  REM   SUBROUTINE:
1010              LET X  = 3*A
1020              PRINT X
1030              RETURN
2000  REM   SUBROUTINE:
2010              LET A = 3*A
2020              PRINT A
2030              RETURN
9999              END
```
Trace A and X.

(b)
```
100             READ C,P
110             READ D,Q
120             LET X = C
130             LET Y = P
140     REM   CALL: X PLUS Y PERCENT
150     REM   VALUES: X,Y      RETURNED: Z
160             GOSUB 1000
170             LET W = Z
180             LET X = D
190             LET Y = Q
200     REM   CALL: X PLUS Y PERCENT
210     REM   VALUES: X,Y      RETURNED: Z
220             GOSUB 1000
230             LET W = W + Z
240             PRINT W
250             STOP
1000  REM   SUBROUTINE:
1010  REM   X PLUS Y PERCENT
1020  REM   VALUES: X,Y      RETURNED: Z
1030              LET Z = X*(1 + Y/100)
1040              RETURN
```

```
2000        DATA 39.45, 7
2010        DATA 94.50, 3
9999        END
```

Trace X, Y, and Z.

(c)
```
100         FOR I = 1 TO 4
110             LET J = 5 - I
120             LET K = 2*I + 1
130             GOSUB 1000
140         NEXT I
150         STOP
1000  REM  SUBROUTINE:
1010            FOR L = 0 TO K - 1
1020                PRINT J + L;
1030            NEXT L
1040            PRINT
1050            RETURN
9999        END
```

Trace J, K, and L.

(d)
```
100         LET A = 4
110         LET X = 1
120   REM  REPEAT
130   REM      CALL: ITERATION STEP
140   REM      VALUES X, A      RETURNED: X
150             GOSUB 1000
160             PRINT X
170             LET E = X*X - A
180             IF ABS(E)<0.001 THEN 200
190         GO TO 120
200         STOP
1000  REM  SUBROUTINE:
1010  REM  ITERATION STEP
1020  REM  VALUES: X, A      RETURNED: X
1030            LET X = (X + A/X)/2
1040            RETURN
9999        END
```

Trace A, X, and E.

(e)
```
100         LET A$ = "******"
110         FOR I = 1 TO 4
120             GOSUB 1000
130         NEXT I
140         STOP
1000  REM  SUBROUTINE:
1010            FOR J = 1 TO I
1020                PRINT MID(A$,1,J)
1030            NEXT J
1040            RETURN
9999        END
```

Trace the value of MID(A$,1,J).

2. Identify which of the following statements contain errors. Describe the errors.

    (a) GO TO SUBROUTINE: AVERAGE OF LIST

    (b) FOR I9 = B9 TO E9 STEP S9

    (c) DEF FNC(X) = SQR(1 - FND(X))

    (d) LET FNZ(X) = X*(1 - X)

    (e) CALL: ROUNDING TO NEAREST CENT

    (f) LET Z$ = X + Y$

    (g) GOS UB1000

    (h) LET Y = FUN(A + 4)

    (i) PRINT A(I$)

    (j) RETURN 180

3. Rewrite this program segment:

```
100   PRINT "TO CALCULATE THE QUOTIENTS, A/B AND"
110   PRINT "B/A, OF A PAIR OF NUMBERS A AND B"
120   PRINT "ENTER THE PAIR HERE";
130   INPUT A,B
140   LET Q1 = A/B
150   LET Q2 = B/A
160   LET Q1 = INT(Q1*100 + 0.5)/100
170   LET Q2 = INT(Q2*100 + 0.5)/100
180   PRINT "QUOTIENTS ARE";Q1;"AND";Q2;"TO 2 DEC. PLACES."
9999  END
```

using these subroutines:

```
1000  REM  SUBROUTINE:
1010  REM  CALC. QUOTIENT
1020  REM  VALUES: X,Y       RETURNED: Q
1030            LET Q = X/Y
1040          RETURN
2000  REM  SUBROUTINE:
2010  REM  ROUND TO N DECIMAL PLACES
2020  REM  VALUES: X,N       RETURNED: Y
2030            LET T = 10^N
2040            LET Y = INT(X*T + 0.5)/T
2050          RETURN
```

4. Fill in the bodies of these subroutines.

    (a)
```
1000  REM  SUBROUTINE:
1010  REM  FIND LARGER OF TWO NUMBERS
1020  REM  VALUES: X,Y       RETURNED: L
              ┌──────────────┐
              └──────────────┘
1999          RETURN
```

(b)
```
1000  REM  SUBROUTINE:
1010  REM  SUM A LIST OF NUMBERS
1020  REM  VALUES: N,A(1),...,A(N)      RETURNED: S

1999        RETURN
```

5. Write a subroutine which, given an integer N, will return the quotient, Q, and remainder, R, on division by 2 (e.g., for N = 27, Q = 13, and R = 1).

6. Write a subroutine to print two columns of numbers C(1), . . . , C(N) and D(1), . . . , D(N) under the headings A$ and B$, respectively. The routine should print a row of stars under the headings and a vertical line of stars to separate the two columns. The documentation is as follows:

```
1000  REM  SUBROUTINE:
1010  REM  PRINT A TWO COLUMN TABLE
1020  REM  VALUES: A$, B$, N, C(1),...,C(N),D(1),...,D(N)
1030  REM  RETURNED: NONE
```

7. (a) Write a subroutine to calculate factorial N (N!) for any positive integer, N. [*Hint: N! is the product of all the integers from 1 to N; for example, 5! = (1)(2)(3)(4)(5) = 120.*]

   (b) Write a program to calculate the sum

$$1! + 2! + 3! + \ldots + N!$$

   given a positive integer N. Use the subroutine from part (a).

8. (a) Write a subroutine, REORDER X AND Y, which accepts two integers, X and Y, and exchanges their values if necessary, so that on return X is less than or equal to Y. The subroutine should also accept and return a value E, which is set to 1 if an exchange takes place.

   (b) The technique BUBBLE SORT, discussed in Section 8.2, Exercise 12(a), sorts a list of numbers into increasing order. Unfortunately, it is not very efficient. One problem is that the list is often completely sorted long before the program is finished. This is because there is no way of testing to see if the job is complete. The following flowchart describes a more efficient version of bubble sort:

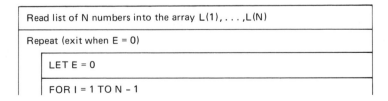

Read list of N numbers into the array L(1),...,L(N)
Repeat (exit when E = 0)
LET E = 0
FOR I = 1 TO N – 1

```
        Exchange L(I) and L(I+1), if necessary
        (Call subroutine REORDER X AND Y)
    NEXT I

    Exit

PRINT sorted list
Stop
```

Using this flowchart and the subroutine from part (a), write an improved bubble sort program.

9. (a) Write a subroutine that accepts a single character and then returns its numerical value if it is a digit, and the value **9999** otherwise. Its heading should read:

```
1000  REM  SUBROUTINE:
1010  REM  CHARACTER TO DIGIT CONVERSION
1020  REM  VALUES: N$      RETURNED: N
```

   (b) Write a program that calculates the numerical value of a character string consisting of a sequence of digits (e.g., "9375" is converted to the integer 9375). A message should be printed if any of the characters in the string is not a digit.

   (c) Write a program that calculates the numerical value of a character string consisting of a sequence of digits, an optional decimal point, and preceded by an optional sign (e.g., "14.72" or "-.55" or "231").

   [*Hint: Use the subroutine from part (a) in parts (b) and (c). This technique is useful if one is designing a program to allow both character string and numerical input, for example, to accept numerical data as well as commands such as HELP and STOP.*]

10. (a) Write a subroutine that accepts a single-digit number and returns the character ("0", "1", "2", etc.) which represents it.

   (b) Write a program that accepts a positive integer and prints the string of characters which represent it.

   (c) Write a program that accepts a real number and prints the character string which represents it.

   [*Hint: Use subroutine (a) in both (b) and (c). These programs may seem rather silly. However, they open the way to techniques for producing more satisfying numerical output. For example, the string "49.5" can be easily modified to produce "$49.50", whereas the best we can produce from the numerical value 49.5 is $ 49.5.*]

11. (a) To shuffle a list, cut it in half and then alternate the items from the two halves to produce a new list. For example,

1, 2, 3, 4, 5, 6, 7, 8, 9, 10

is cut to give:

1, 2, 3, 4, 5   and   6, 7, 8, 9, 10

and then these are interwoven to produce

1, 6, 2, 7, 3, 8, 4, 9, 5, 10.

Write a subroutine that will accept a list consisting of an even number of items and return it shuffled.

(b) Write a program to accept a list containing an even number of items and repeatedly shuffle it, using the subroutine from part (a). The program should print the list after each shuffle. Experiment with lists of different lengths. Is the list eventually shuffled back into its original order? If so, how many shuffles does this take?

Section 10.4

No exercises.

Section 10.5

1. Using the MID function, or its equivalent, to read characters from the string "123456789", rewrite the following segment of the tic-tac-toe program

```
240  LET B$(1) = "1"
250  LET B$(2) = "2"
       - - -
320  LET B$(9) = "9"
```

so that it only takes three or four lines.

2. Rewrite the subroutine CHECK FOR WIN OR DRAW so that the winning positions do not have to be reread from DATA statements every time the subroutine is called. [*Hint: At the beginning of the program store them in an 8 by 3 matrix.*]

3. Rewrite the tic-tac-toe program so that it does not use character string arrays. [*Hint: Store the game board positions and moves in a single*

variable instead of an array, and modify it by means of MID or its equivalent.]

4.   Rewrite the tic-tac-toe program so that no string variables are used. [*Hint: Store "0" and "X" coded, say, as 1 and –1, and empty positions as 0. Make sure that, from the point of view of the user, the external appearance of the game does not change. By the way, it may be easier to eliminate the first call to PRINT GAME BOARD and print the positions directly from the main program.*]

5.   (a) Write a subroutine to print a calendar for any month, given the name of the month, the day of the week it begins on (Sun. = 1, Mon. = 2, etc.), and the number of days in the month:

```
1000  REM  SUBROUTINE:
1010  REM  ONE MONTH CALENDAR
1020  REM  VALUES: M$,B,L       RETURNED: NONE
```

The calendar should be printed in a 6 by 7 grid:

SUN	MON	TUE	WED	THR	FRI	SAT

with the name of the month centered above it. [*Hint: See the subroutine PRINT GAME BOARD for ideas.*]

(b) Write a program to print the calendar for a whole year. Read the information for each month from DATA statements, for example,

```
DATA "JANUARY",5,31
DATA "FEBRUARY",1,28
etc.
```

(c) It is possible to calculate the calendar for any year in the past or future. Investigate how this is done, then write a program that accepts a year and a month and prints the calendar for that month.

6.   (a) Write a program to monitor and update the charge account records

for a small business. It must perform the following procedures at the user's request:

(1) LIST: List all account names and balances.

(2) UPDATE: Accept a name and a new balance. If the name is on the list of accounts, the routine should change the value of the current balance to the new balance; otherwise, it should print an error message.

Here is a structured plan for the program:

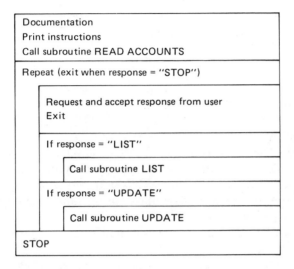

Documentation
Print instructions
Call subroutine READ ACCOUNTS

Repeat (exit when response = "STOP")

    Request and accept response from user
    Exit

    If response = "LIST"

        Call subroutine LIST

    If response = "UPDATE"

        Call subroutine UPDATE

STOP

Subroutine: READ ACCOUNTS

Read number of records

Repeat for every record

    Read account name and balance into list (use two arrays to hold the list)

RETURN

Subroutine: LIST

Print headings "NAME" and "BALANCE"

Repeat for every entry in list of accounts

    Print name and balance

RETURN

Subroutine: UPDATE
Request and accept name and new balance
Repeat for every entry in list of accounts
If name = name on list
Replace balance by new balance RETURN
Print message indicating name is not on list RETURN

DATA statements

[*Hint: The subroutine LIST should show all new balances entered by UPDATE at the time that it is run. Notice that UPDATE has two RETURN statements; this is perfectly legal.*]

(b)   Add one or more of the following options to the procedures that the user may request:

(3)   VERIFY: Accept a name and print the current balance for this account.

(4)   ADD: Accept a new account name and balance and append this name and balance to the end of the account list.

[*Hint: The system does not have to check whether this account duplicates one already on the list; the user can check that by requesting LIST. The new record must be available to LIST, UPDATE, and VERIFY.*]

(5)   DELETE: Accept an account name and remove this record (name and balance) from the list of accounts.

7.   (a)   Write a program to print a list of all the numerical palindromes (i.e., numbers that read the same backward and forward) which lie in a given range. A typical run:

```
RUN
THIS PROGRAM LISTS THE PALINDROMES, X,
WHICH LIE IN THE RANGE A <= X <= B
ENTER VALUES FOR A AND B? 19500, 20500
PALINDROMES IN THIS RANGE:
19591    19691    19791    19891    19991
20002    20102    20202    20302    20402
Ready
```

Here is part of a structured plan for the program:

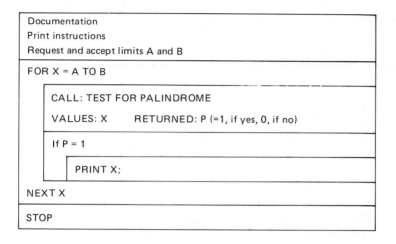

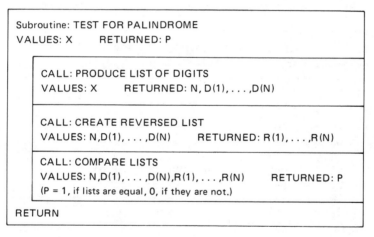

[*Hint: Section 10.2, Exercise 7, will be of help in developing the subroutine PRODUCE LIST OF DIGITS. The last two subroutines can be combined, and the array R eliminated, with some savings in space and efficiency.*]

(b)   You will find that the program in part (a) produces strange results if you specify a range that includes numbers with more than six digits (actual limit varies from system to system). This is because very large numbers are not represented exactly on the computer. Design a program that will handle numbers with as many as 10 digits. [*Hint: Part (b) is definitely more difficult. You will have to use string variables to enter numbers this large. One approach is then to convert to numerical values and store each value in two*

variables (e.g., store 1493507194 as 14935 and 07194). Section
10.3, Exercises 9 and 10, may be useful.]

8. Write a program to accept a decimal number less than 1000, representing a sum of money in dollars, and print that quantity in words. Here is a structured flowchart sketching the form of the program.

Accept a decimal number ≥ 0 with no more than two decimal places.
Split number into dollars (integer part) and cents (from fractional part).
Let value = dollars Call subroutine: TRANSLATE VALUE INTO WORDS PRINT "DOLLARS AND";
Let value = cents Call subroutine: TRANSLATE VALUE INTO WORDS PRINT "CENTS"
STOP

Subroutine: TRANSLATE VALUE INTO WORDS VALUES: value   RETURNED: NONE
If value = 0
PRINT "NO";
If value > 0
Break value into its constituent digits (hundreds, tens, units)   Call subroutine: CONVERT DIGITS TO WORDS
RETURN

When writing the subroutine CONVERT DIGITS TO WORDS, follow these guidelines:

(1) If the hundreds digit is not zero and either the tens or the units digit is not zero, then the word "HUNDRED" must be followed by "AND"; otherwise, not.

(2) If the tens digits equals 1, then convert tens and units combined to one of the following: "TEN", "ELEVEN", . . . , "NINETEEN"; otherwise, convert tens and units separately.

Examples:

200	TWO HUNDRED DOLLARS AND NO CENTS
171.15	ONE HUNDRED AND SEVENTY ONE DOLLARS AND FIFTEEN CENTS

1.05   ONE DOLLARS AND FIVE CENTS *(sic)*

0   NO DOLLARS AND NO CENTS

[*Hint: Note that the printing of the numerical values as words is actually done by the subroutine CONVERT DIGITS TO WORDS.*]

9.   Write a program to allow someone to play the game of Hexapawn against the computer.

     Hexapawn is played on a tic-tac-toe board. Each player has three men (pawns) which move like pawns in the game of chess; they can be moved forward toward the opponent's end of the board, one square at a time. The players take turns making a move. There are two legal moves: a pawn may move directly ahead one square if that square is empty or it may move diagonally ahead to capture an opposing pawn.

Legal:

Illegal:

The starting position is

     To win, you must either reach your opponent's end of the board with one of your men, capture all his men, or force him into a position where he has no legal moves available to him. There is always a winner. [*Hint: Use a top-down structured approach, deferring the more difficult parts to subroutines. As in the tic-tac-toe game, choosing the machine's move and checking for a win will be the hardest. Be sure to check that the user's moves are legal. When handling the machine's moves, write the simplest subroutine that will make legal, but not necessarily intelligent moves. You can build in strategy later, if you wish, but keep it simple at first. For a discussion of this game, and for more ideas, read Martin Gardiner's article, "How to Build a Game-Learning Machine and then Teach It to Play and to Win" in the March 1962 issue of* Scientific American.]

10.   In the game of Nim, three piles of matches are placed on a table, then two players take turns removing any number of matches, but at least one, from any one of the piles. Matches can only be removed from one

pile, but a different pile can be chosen for each move. The one who takes the last match loses.

Write a program to play Nim. [*Hint: First,* design a simple program *that makes legal moves but applies no strategy. You can then attempt to refine it. This game has a relatively simple strategy for winning; see* The Master Book of Mathematical Recreations *by Fred Schuh, Dover Publications.*]

Section 10.6

1. For each of the following subroutines, write a test program that calls it. Use this test program to investigate its behavior. In each case, can you describe what it is that the subroutine does?

    (a)
    ```
    1000  REM  SUBROUTINE:
    1010  REM  MYSTERY
    1020  REM  VALUES: N        RETURNED: S
    1030           LET S = 1
    1040           LET J = INT(N/2)
    1050           FOR I = 2 TO J
    1060              LET K = INT(N/I)*I
    1070              IF NOT (N = K) THEN 1090
    1080                 LET S = S + I
    1090  REM         ENDIF
    1100           NEXT I
    1110        RETURN
    ```

    (b)
    ```
    1000  REM  SUBROUTINE:
    1010  REM  SECRET
    1020  REM  VALUES: N     RETURNED: P
    1030           LET P = 1
    1040           LET S = SQR(N)
    1050           FOR I = 2 TO INT(S)
    1060              IF N <> INT(N/I)*I THEN 1080
    1070                 LET P = 0
    1080  REM         ENDIF
    1090           NEXT I
    1100        RETURN
    ```

    (c)
    ```
    1000  REM  SUBROUTINE:
    1010  REM  STRANGE
    1020  REM  VALUES: N, A(1), ... , A(N), B(1), ... , B(N)
    1030  REM  RETURNED: C(1), ... ,C(N)
    1040           FOR I = 1 TO N
    1050              LET C(I) = 0
    1060              LET K = B(I)
    1070              IF (K > N) OR (K < 1) THEN 1090
    ```

```
1080                    LET C(I) = A(K)
1090  REM        ENDIF
1100            NEXT I
1110         RETURN
```

2. For each of the following program segments, write a test subroutine to handle the subroutine call, as described in this section. Use the subroutine to test the behavior of the program and determine what it does.

(a)
```
100         PRINT "HOW MANY VALUES";
110         INPUT N
120         PRINT "ENTER EACH VALUE AFTER QUESTION MARK"
130         FOR I = 1 TO N
140            INPUT A(I)
150         NEXT I
160  REM   CALL: SORT INTO INCREASING ORDER
170  REM   VALUES: N, A(1), . . . , A(N)      RETURNED: A(1), . . . , A(N)
180         GOSUB 1000
190         LET L1 = INT(A(1))
200         LET L2 = INT(A(2))
210         FOR I = L1 TO L2
220            LET B = 0
230            FOR J = 1 TO N
240               IF I < A(J) THEN 270
250               LET B = B + 1
260            NEXT J
270            PRINT I,B
280         NEXT I
290         STOP
```
The lines 230–260 are marked with a brace and a † symbol.

(b)
```
100         LET S$ = " "
110         PRINT "ENTER ONE LINE OF TEXT"
120         INPUT T$
130         PRINT "ENTER A CHARACTER STRING WHICH APPEARS IN THE
            TEXT";
140         INPUT A$
150         PRINT "ENTER A SECOND CHARACTER STRING";
160         INPUT B$
170         LET C = LEN(A$) – LEN(B$)
180         IF NOT (C <= 0) THEN 200
190            LET B$ = MID(B$,1,LEN(A$))
200  REM   ENDIF
210         IF NOT (C > 0) THEN 250
220            FOR I = 1 TO C
230               LET B$ = B$ + S$
240            NEXT I
250  REM   ENDIF
```

---

†An example of a loop with two exits. We have met this kind of construction before.

```
260  REM  CALL: REPLACE 1ST OCCURRENCE OF A$ IN T$ BY B$
270  REM  VALUES: A$,B$,T$      RETURNED: T$
280       GOSUB 1000
290       PRINT T$
300       STOP
```

Section 10.7

1. Modify the tic-tac-toe program so that the user has the option not to have the instructions printed. Have it print DO YOU WANT INSTRUC-TIONS (Y OR N)? and then act accordingly.

2. Modify the tic-tac-toe program so that it checks the user's moves to see if they are legal. It should reject an illegal move and request that the user type in another. [*Hint: Check that the move is in the range 1 to 9 and also that the position chosen is not occupied.*]

3. Modify the tic-tac-toe program so that it allows the user to choose who goes first.

4. Write an improved version of the subroutine MACHINE MAKES MOVE. Designing perfect game-playing programs can be a very difficult business. However, in many games simple strategies can be developed which improve the chances of winning, even though they do not lead to perfect games. Here is such a strategy for tic-tac-toe:

   (1) Move first and pick the center square.
   (2) Play to win: If two of your men are in a given row, column, or diagonal and the third position is empty, fill it.
   (3) Play to block: If two of your opponent's men are in a given row, column, or diagonal and the third position is empty, fill it.
   (4) If there is a choice between "play to win" and "play to block," choose the former, of course.

   Don't hesitate to add further refinements to this routine.

Chapter

11

Files

11.1 LONG-TERM STORAGE

In Chapter 8 we developed a program to update the records for a beer can collection. Unfortunately, from a practical point of view, the program was not very useful. Any changes that were made to the records while the program was running were erased when it was stopped. The problem was that the information about the cans was in arrays stored in the computer's memory. As you know, data stored in memory are held there only temporarily. Memory is repeatedly being cleared as new programs are written and executed.

We have already discussed the use of magnetic tape and disks for the permanent storage of programs. There is no reason why such media should not be used for the long-term storage of data too. To magnetic tape, for example, there is no apparent difference between programs and data. They are both just sequences of letters, digits, and other characters coded into interminable streams of little magnetic blips.†

Another compelling reason for finding an alternative storage medium is that computer memory is relatively expensive and therefore usually limited in capacity. The customer data required by a large corporation may run to millions of records, and this amount of data far exceeds the space available in even the largest computer memory. Here magnetic tape and magnetic disks come to the rescue as extensions of memory. Although it takes considerably longer to store and retrieve data from tape and disks, their capacity is virtually unlimited and they are relatively cheap.‡ Large-scale storage devices of this kind are often referred to as **mass storage**.

---

†A boring life, being a tape!
‡Mind you, "cheap" really is relative. A disk drive can still cost more than the family car.

Unless the computer system you are using is large, there will probably be just one mass storage device available to you. On this you will save programs as well as data. On a very small microcomputer system the device will probably be a cassette tape recorder, but on anything larger it is more likely to be a disk drive. Throughout the rest of this chapter we will assume that the storage medium available to us is magnetic disk. For some discussion of tape storage, see Appendix I.

11.2   FILES AND FILE NAMES

If many programs and different groups of data are to be stored together on the same device, there has to be some way of keeping them apart. You don't store flour and sugar in the same jar and then expect to be able to put just sugar in your coffee.

This problem is solved by collecting related data records together into what is called a **file.** We have already come in contact with this concept in Section 4.6, where we discussed how to save programs in long-term storage. By this stage you have probably saved a number of programs. Each of these was stored in a file. We refer to these files as **program files,** to distinguish them from **data files,** which contain, need I say, data! Each program is identified by a name. That way the correct program can be retrieved and executed when required. This name is, in fact, the name of the file that contains the program. The same thing is required of data files.

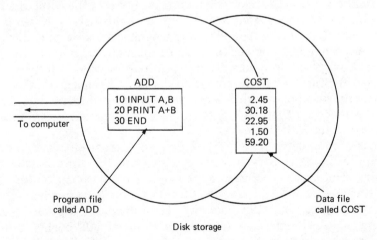

Disk storage

Every file, whether a program or a data file, must be identified by a name. Most systems require that the name be a short string of alphanumeric characters. Usually, the name is limited to no more than six or eight letters and/or numbers.

Examples

Typical file names:

R2D2	TEXT	CUSTAC
DATA1	ITMTBL	7777
ERRORS	MAXVAL	FILEA

Possibly illegal file names:

INVENTORY	(too long for many systems)
SH*T	(character * not allowed)
FILE A	(that goes for the space character, too)

File names, when restricted in length, can be a little cryptic. Does ITMTBL stand for "itemtable" or "initial time table" or, perhaps, "individual tomato bowl"? The name 7777 looks rather silly; it doesn't appear to mean anything at all. Give files names that indicate their contents. This can be quite a challenge, given the restrictions. ∎

11.3 FILES: A SIMPLE EXAMPLE

Before we embark on a detailed discussion of files and their uses, let's look at an example of file handling. This will provide us with an introduction to the properties of files and the programs that access† them.

Here is a short program segment, written in DEC BASIC-PLUS, which establishes a file called TINY and places three numbers in it:

```
100   REM  TITLE: WRITING IN A FILE
110        OPEN "TINY" AS FILE 1
120        LET A = 1.23
130        LET B = 45.67
140        LET C = 8.9
150        PRINT #1, A
160        PRINT #1, B
170        PRINT #1, C
180        CLOSE 1
9999       END
```

Here is a run of this program.

```
RUN
Ready
```

---

†There he goes again, another awful verb! . . . His Wife.

Nothing appears to happen. However, this does not mean that nothing *has* happened. In fact, those weird PRINT statements

```
PRINT #1, A
PRINT #1, B
PRINT #1, C
```

caused the contents of the variables A, B, C to be printed in the file TINY. We have no visible evidence of this because the process occurred inside the system, but we can picture the file as looking like this:

TINY

```
1.23
45.67
8.9
```

The purpose of the unfamiliar statements in this program should not be hard to guess. First, the statement in line 110

```
OPEN "TINY" AS FILE 1
```

appears to associate the number 1 with the file TINY, because from this point on, the name TINY never reappears, but the number 1 pops up with monotonous regularity. For example:

```
PRINT #1, A
```

causes the contents of the variable A to be placed in file 1, that is, in the file TINY, and

```
CLOSE 1
```

"closes" file 1, or TINY. It is not exactly clear what that means but we will discuss the exact purpose of OPEN and CLOSE in Section 11.4.

Meanwhile, let's continue the example. As soon as the execution of the program segment above has been completed, the file TINY is established and contains the values 1.23, 45.67, and 8.9. This file will remain in storage indefinitely, with its contents unchanged. Programs can be written to read the data from TINY without hurting the file and, in fact, the only way TINY can be changed is by writing another program to store other data in it or by issuing a command to delete the whole file. The following program segment retrieves the data stored in TINY and prints them out at the terminal:

```
100   REM  TITLE: READING FROM A FILE
110        OPEN "TINY" AS FILE 1
120        INPUT #1, X
130        INPUT #1, Y
140        INPUT #1, Z
150        PRINT X,Y,Z
160        CLOSE 1
9999       END
```

Assuming that data have already been stored in the file by running the previous segment, execution of this segment produces the following printout:

```
RUN
1.23              45.67              8.9
Ready
```

Tracing the program, line by line, we see that line 110 identifies TINY as file 1 and that the next three statements,

```
INPUT #1, X
INPUT #1, Y
INPUT #1, Z
```

accept values from file 1 and store them in the variables X, Y, and Z. The PRINT statement (without #1) causes these values to be printed at the terminal. Finally, the CLOSE statement tells the system that communication between the program and file 1 is complete.

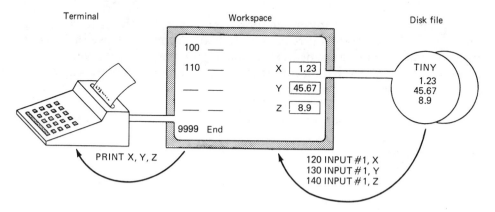

Notice the similarity between INPUT #1 and PRINT #1 on the one hand and INPUT and PRINT on the other. Once a file has been opened, the system handles it rather like a terminal. A program can send data out to a file

(PRINT #) or receive data from one (INPUT #). It is most important to understand that a file is not part of a program; it is external in the way that the keyboard is. In particular, it does not matter that different variables were used for the same data in the two programs (A, B, C in the first; X, Y, Z in the second). Variables are part of the program, not the file. The file itself contains only a list of numbers, with no names attached to them. You can think of it as an invisible terminal to which you have no direct access.

11.4 AN OVERVIEW OF FILE HANDLING

The procedures that are followed when using a data file can be broken into three major steps.

1. *OPEN:* A link must be established between the program and the file. This is referred to as **opening** the file. The process includes the assignment of a number to the file. This **channel number** (or **file number**) provides a compact and flexible way of referring to the file within the program. More than one file may be opened by the same program and each file will be distinguished by a different channel number.
2. *READ OR WRITE:* Once the file is opened, the transfer of data between the file and the program can take place.
3. *CLOSE:* After all communication between the program and the file is complete, the file is **closed.** Various housekeeping operations are performed (about which we need know nothing) and the link between the program and the file is disconnected.

The procedures are not unlike those which one goes through when making a phone call. When you telephone someone, you don't use their name. Instead, you establish a connection by dialing the number of the line to their home or office. For the duration of the call, communication is made via this line. When you are finished, you break the connection, so you won't be overcharged, by placing the receiver back on its cradle.

It is important that you understand file handling in these very general terms because (here comes the bad news, well, hardly *news* by now) no two versions of BASIC handle files in quite the same way[†]. However, in all cases the procedures can be broken down into the three steps given. In this chapter we discuss the DEC BASIC-PLUS approach to files. In Appendix IV you will find a table comparing file handling in a number of different versions of BASIC. If you follow the guidelines established in this chapter and in the appendix, you will find that it is relatively easy to translate a program having

[†] I'm going out on a limb here, but I'm confident that it is a strong one.

access to files in one version of BASIC so that it will run on a system that uses a different dialect. In particular, you should be able to translate the examples in this chapter so that they run on your system.

11.5 OPENING AND CLOSING A FILE

Let's take a second look at the example in Section 11.3. Here are the two program segments that handled the file for TINY:

```
(A)  100   REM  WRITING IN A FILE      (B)  100   REM  READING FROM A FILE
     110        OPEN "TINY" AS FILE 1        110        OPEN "TINY" AS FILE 1
     120        LET A = 1.23                 120        INPUT #1, X
     130        LET B = 45.67                130        INPUT #1, Y
     140        LET C = 8.9                  140        INPUT #1, Z
     150        PRINT #1, A                  150        PRINT X,Y,Z
     160        PRINT #1, B                  160        CLOSE 1
     170        PRINT #1, C                  9999       END
     180        CLOSE 1
     9999       END
```

The action of the OPEN statement is not quite the same in each case. At the time that (A) was run, the file didn't exist. The OPEN statement created TINY and the rest of the program stored data in it. When we ran segment (B) the file TINY already existed, so the OPEN statement just established a channel between the file and the program.

With this insight we will give a formal description of the OPEN statement. Its general form is as follows:

line number OPEN "file name" AS FILE channel number

This statement associates a channel number with the file having the given file name and prepares the file for data transfer. If a file with this name does not exist, then one is created first.

The channel number is used in all subsequent references. Therefore, the OPEN statement *must* appear in the program before the first file access (PRINT # or INPUT #).

Example

```
- - -
200  OPEN "ACCNTS" AS FILE 1
210  OPEN "INVENT" AS FILE 2
- - -
```

■

It is often useful to be able to open more than one file at a time. Of course, each file must have a different channel number. Every system puts a limit on the number of files that can be open simultaneously. Many provide at least eight channels and some even more.

The form of the CLOSE statement is

line number   CLOSE   *channel number*

This closes the communication channel between the program and the file most recently associated with that channel number by an OPEN statement. Every file opened by a program must be closed before the program ends.

Example

```
- - -          ) files not open here
200   OPEN "ACCNTS" AS FILE 1
210   OPEN "INVENT" AS FILE 2
- - -          ) both files open here
850   CLOSE 1
860   CLOSE 2
9999  END
```
■

It is sometimes necessary to close a file and then reopen it within the same program. We will talk later about the implications of this.

Example

```
- - -
180   OPEN "TEMP" AS FILE 1
- - -          ) TEMP open here
530   CLOSE 1
- - -          ) TEMP closed here
590   OPEN "TEMP" AS FILE 1
- - -          ) TEMP open for second time
760   CLOSE 1
- - -
9999  END
```
■

11.6   READING AND WRITING

Once a file is open, data can be written in it using the PRINT # statement or read from it by means of INPUT #. The form of the PRINT # statement is as follows:

line number PRINT *# channel number, variable*

This causes the contents of the variable to be stored (or written) in the file associated with the given channel number. The first PRINT # statement, after the OPEN statement for the same file, will place a value at the beginning of the file. Each subsequent PRINT # will put a value in the file immediately after the previous one.

Example

```
. . .
100  OPEN "LOVE" AS FILE 1
110  LET L$ = "JUDITH"
120  PRINT #1, L$
130  LET L$ = "SAMANTHA"
140  PRINT #1, L$
150  LET L$ = "NELLIE"
160  PRINT #1, L$
- - -
```

The file LOVE at successive points in the program:

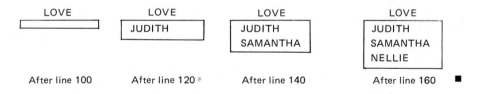

LOVE	LOVE	LOVE	LOVE
	JUDITH	JUDITH SAMANTHA	JUDITH SAMANTHA NELLIE
After line 100	After line 120	After line 140	After line 160 ■

It is most important to understand that the writing of data always starts at the beginning of the file. Thus, if a program opens a file that already contains data and then writes new values in the file, the previous contents of the file are erased and replaced by the current data.

Example

When this program segment is run:

```
100   OPEN "SQUARES" AS FILE 1
110   FOR I = 1 TO 5
120     LET S = I*I
130     PRINT #1, S
```

```
140    NEXT I
150    CLOSE 1
9999   END
RUN
Ready
```

it produces this file:

SQUARES

```
1
4
9
16
25
```

If we then proceed to run the following:

```
100    OPEN "SQUARES" AS FILE 1
110    LET S = 36
120    LET T = 49
130    PRINT #1, S
140    PRINT #1, T
150    CLOSE 1
9999   END
```

The file will become

SQUARES

```
36
49
```

The INPUT # statement has the form

line number   INPUT # *channel number, variable*

When a file is opened with the given channel number, the first INPUT # statement causes the first value in the file to be stored in the given variable. The next INPUT # accepts the second value from the file, and so on. The values are read from the file in the same order in which they were stored there. If, at any time, the data in the file are exhausted, the next INPUT # statement that attempts to read the file produces an error message.

Example

Suppose that the file BIRDS contains the following values:

```
        BIRDS
    ┌──────────────┐
    │ TOUCAN       │
    │ PUFFBIRD     │
    │ ANTWREN      │
    │ QUETZAL      │
    │ MOTMOT       │
    │ HOATZIN      │
    └──────────────┘
```

Then this segment:

```
100          OPEN "BIRDS" AS FILE 1
110   REM  REPEAT
120              INPUT #1, B$
130              PRINT B$
140          GO TO 110
150          CLOSE 1
9999         END
```

produces the following run:

```
RUN
TOUCAN
PUFFBIRD
ANTWREN
QUETZAL
MOTMOT
HOATZIN
End of File
Ready                                                        ■
```

A file from which data are being read behaves like a sequence of DATA statements. Values in the file can be read one after the other until there is nothing left. The message END OF FILE corresponds to the OUT OF DATA error associated with READ and DATA statements.

The INPUT # statement has no effect on the data in the file. Thus a file may be read and reread repeatedly without destroying its contents. If a file is to be reread within the same program, it must first be closed and then reopened. This is similar in effect to the RESTORE statement when reading from DATA statements.

Example

Using our old friend SQUARES:

SQUARES

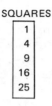

```
1
4
9
16
25
```

the program segment

```
100    OPEN "SQUARES" AS FILE 1
110    INPUT #1, A
120    INPUT #1, B
130    INPUT #1, C
140    PRINT A,B,C
150    CLOSE 1
160    OPEN "SQUARES" AS FILE 1
170    INPUT #1, D
180    INPUT #1, E
190    PRINT D,E
200    CLOSE 1
9999   END
```

produces this output:

```
RUN
1         4         9
1         4
Ready
```

After the file is closed and reopened in lines 150 and 160, the next item to be read is the first in the file (i.e., 1, not 16).   ■

When a file is opened, the system establishes a pointer (the **file pointer**) which points to the beginning of the file. After each file access (PRINT # or INPUT #) the pointer is moved ahead to the position immediately following the item just written or read. If the operation most recently performed was PRINT #, the pointer indicates the current end of the file. (The file is extended each time data are written in it.) If the operation was INPUT #, the pointer indicates the next item in the file. Closing and reopening a file therefore has the effect of restoring the pointer to the beginning of the file.

Examples

The following program segments illustrate the properties of the file-handling instructions:

1.

```
100  REM  CREATE FILE:
110       OPEN "EGGS" AS FILE 1
120       FOR I = 1 TO 9
130           READ E$
140           PRINT #1, E$
150       NEXT I
160       CLOSE 1
170  REM  READ FILE:
180       OPEN "EGGS" AS FILE 1
190       FOR I = 1 TO 9
200           INPUT #1, E$
210           PRINT E$
220       NEXT I
230       CLOSE 1
240  REM  DATA:
250       DATA "BENEDICT", "BOILED", "CODDLED"
260       DATA "DEVILED", "DRIED", "FREID"
270       DATA "GOLDENROD", "MORNAY", "SHIRRED"
9999      END
```

RUN

```
BENEDICT
BOILED
CODDLED
DEVILED
DRIED
FREID
GOLDENROD
MORNAY
SHIRRED
```

Ready

Lines 100 through 150 create the file EGGS, store the values "BENE-DICT", "BOILED", and so on, in it, and then close it. In line 180 EGGS is reopened, so that the pointer is returned to the beginning of the file. The second part of the program then reads the data from the file and prints them at the terminal.

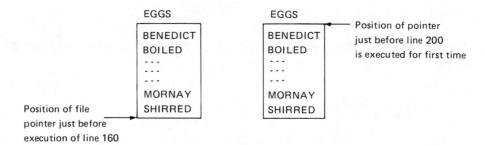

Position of file
pointer just before
execution of line 160

2. The following program is similar except that the file is not closed and reopened before the program attempts to read from it.

```
100   REM  CREATE FILE:
110        OPEN "EGGS" AS FILE 1
120        FOR I = 1 TO 9
130           READ E$
140           PRINT #1, E$
150        NEXT I
160   REM  READ FILE:
170        FOR I = 1 TO 9
180           INPUT #1, E$
190           PRINT E$
200        NEXT I
210        CLOSE 1
220   REM  DATA:
230        DATA "BENEDICT", "BOILED", "CODDLED"
240        DATA "DEVILED", "DRIED", "FREID"
250        DATA "GOLDENROD", "MORNAY", "SHIRRED"
9999       END
RUN
End of File
Ready
```

BAD

After the data have been written in EGGS, the pointer is not returned to the beginning of the file. The first time line 180 is executed it tries to read the item following "Shirred" but there is nothing there, so an error occurs.

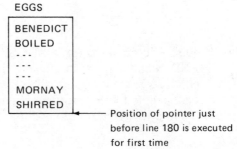

Position of pointer just
before line 180 is executed
for first time

3.   The sixth item in the file EGGS is misspelled. It should, of course, be FRIED. Suppose that we try to write a program to correct this. One approach might be to read the first five items, with the sole purpose of moving the file pointer ahead, then to rewrite the sixth item:

```
100         OPEN "EGGS" AS FILE 1
110   REM   MOVE AHEAD PAST FIRST FIVE ITEMS:
120         FOR I = 1 TO 5
130             INPUT #1, E$
140         NEXT I
150   REM   REPLACE 6TH ITEM:
160         LET E$ = "FRIED"
170         PRINT #1, E$
180         CLOSE 1
9999        END
```

BAD

On some systems this may succeed, but on many the seventh, eighth, and ninth items will be lost. Even the approach of rewriting the whole end of the file is not guaranteed to work in all versions of BASIC.

4.   The approach illustrated by the following program is guaranteed to produce a corrected version, FRSHEG, of the file EGGS on any system.

```
100         OPEN "EGGS" AS FILE 1
110         OPEN "FRSHEG" AS FILE 2
120         FOR I = 1 TO 9
130             INPUT #1, E$
140             IF NOT (E$ = "FREID") THEN 160
150                 LET E$ = "FRIED"
160   REM       END IF
170             PRINT #2, E$
180         NEXT I
190         CLOSE 1
200         CLOSE 2
9999        END
```

Each item in turn is read from EGGS into the variable E$ and then written in the file FRESHEG, except for the string "FREID", which is replaced by "FRIED" before being transferred.   ■

The approach taken in the last example may look heavy handed, but in fact, it has much to recommend it. The uncorrected file, EGGS, still exists, so that if some accident or mistake were to occur while we were attempting to correct it, there would be very little harm done and we could just try again. The introduction of a **backup** file can be very reassuring when using large data files. In the real world, files tend to be huge. Replacing such a file if it is accidentally destroyed can be a very costly business.

Referring again to the example above: once we are confident that all went well, we can delete the file EGGS and change the name of FRSHEG to EGGS. All systems provide commands for such operations. A typical sequence might go as follows:

KILL "EGGS" ●   (delete the file EGGS)
NAME "FRSHEG" AS "EGGS" ●   (change the name of the file FRSHEG to EGGS)

There is a lesson to be drawn from the examples in this section. While a file is open, do not mix the operations that are performed on it. Perform *either* PRINT # operations *or* INPUT # operations, *but do not apply both to the same file.* For example, if you wish to write in a file and then read from it, you must first close the file and then reopen it before attempting to read. By the way, this does not preclude opening two files and reading from one while writing in the other, as in the last example. This is a perfectly acceptable and very useful procedure.

11.7   SEQUENTIAL FILES

The files we have been discussing are examples of the simplest type of data file, one in which the data are stored as a list, that is, as a sequence of values placed one immediately after the other. Such files are called **sequential files.**

Examples

Sequential files:

NAMES	PRIMES
RONNIE	2
JOHNNY	3
DICKY	5
LYNDY	7
JIMMY	11
FRANKIE	13
TEDDY	17
HERBIE	19
DWIGHT	23
ABE	29
GEORGE	31
	37
	41

There are just two operations that can be performed on sequential files.

1. A list of values can be written in the file, each value being placed right after the one before.

2. The values stored in the file can be read from it one by one, starting with the first. This operation does not change the contents of the file.

More sophisticated files allow for the selective reading and writing of values at any position in the file. Such files are called **random access files.** For simplicity we will continue to concentrate our discussion on sequential files, so in this chapter the word "file" when used without any qualification will mean "sequential file."

Sequential files are not always very efficient. For example, if a business has its customer accounts stored in a sequential file, the only way to update an individual record is to read all the records out of the file, make the change, and then write all the records back into the file (the actual process is illustrated in the last example of the preceding section). With a random access file, on the other hand, the particular record can be retrieved from the file and changed in one operation. The great advantage of sequential files, however, is their simplicity. Because they are so simple, they tend to be more reliable than other files. Further, everything that can be done with more sophisticated files can be handled, although perhaps more laboriously, by sequential files. Let's discuss some techniques for handling them.

Suppose that we want to write a program to find the sum of a list of numbers stored in a file. The trouble is that if we don't have a way of controlling it, the computer will read values from the file until it produces the END OF FILE error message. This will cause the program to stop immediately, so that we will not be able to print the total. The problem can be handled just as we handled the identical problem with DATA statements in an earlier chapter. Either we put a dummy value (an **end-of-file flag**) at the end of the file and use a REPEAT loop, which is stopped when the flag is read, or we write the length of the data list as the first item in the file and then use a FOR-NEXT loop to read out the values.

Examples

1. The file STATS contains the following data: 10.45, 2074.0, 79.3, 145.45, 94.0, 87.02, 398.6, followed by the flag 9999.

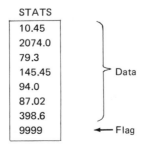

This program segment will sum the contents of STATS, apart from the flag, 9999.

```
100    REM   TITLE: SUM  FILE  STATS  (REPEAT VERSION)
110          OPEN "STATS" AS FILE 1
120          LET S = 0
130    REM   READ DATA, STOP WHEN FLAG IS REACHED
140    REM   REPEAT
150              INPUT #1, A
160              IF A = 9999 THEN 190
170              LET S = S+A
180          GO TO 140
190          PRINT "SUM OF DATA IN FILE STATS IS"; S
200          CLOSE 1
9999         END
RUN
SUM OF DATA IN FILE STATS IS 2888.82
Ready
```

2.   In this case, the first item in STATS is a count of the remaining values.

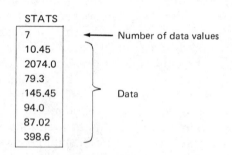

```
100    REM   TITLE: SUM  FILE  STATS  (FOR-NEXT VERSION)
110          OPEN "STATS" AS FILE 1
120          LET S = 0
130    REM   READ DATA COUNT
140          INPUT #1, N
150    REM   READ DATA VALUES
160          FOR I = 1 TO N
170              INPUT #1, A
180              LET S = S+A
190          NEXT I
200          PRINT "SUM OF DATA IN FILE STATS IS"; S
210          CLOSE 1
9999         END
RUN
SUM OF DATA IN FILE STATS IN 2888.82
Ready
```

The disadvantage of the first approach is that 9999 itself cannot appear as a bona fide data value. The disadvantage of the second approach is that one has to know, ahead of time, how many values are going to be put in the file, and this is not always convenient. Well, no point in complaining, one just has to learn to compromise.

The nice thing about a data file is that, once it is established, it can be used by many different programs. The effort involved in writing a program to use a file often has little to do with the size of the file. In fact, there is a tendency, once a large body of data is stored, to feel that one might as well write programs to use it. In this sense, computers are self-perpetuating; they begin to manufacture their own work. Large data files spawn families of programs: among others, housekeeping programs (to establish, to edit, and to add data to the file) as well as programs that use the data.[†] The file STATS, for example, had to be created and filled with data before it could be used.

Example

This program segment allows the user to place data, including the flag 9999, in the file STATS:

```
100    REM  TITLE: PUT DATA IN FILE STATS
110          OPEN "STATS" AS FILE 1
120          PRINT "ENTER VALUES TO BE STORED IN THE"
130          PRINT "FILE STATS. TO STOP, ENTER 9999."
140    REM  REPEAT
150            INPUT A
160            PRINT #1, A
170            IF A = 9999 THEN 190
180          GO TO 140
190          CLOSE 1
9999         END
RUN
ENTER VALUES TO BE STORED IN THE
FILE STATS. TO STOP, ENTER 9999.
? 93.44
? 40.51
- - -
? 101.01
? 9999
Ready
```

STATS
93.44
40.51
- - -
101.01
9999

[†]From this point of view, it is arguable whether the computer is really a laborsaving device. It may, in fact, be *labor producing.*

Notice that the exit from the REPEAT loop occurs *after* PRINT #1, A. The flag 9999 serves two purposes. It stops the REPEAT loop and also becomes the end-of-file flag. ∎

After a file has been established, its contents should be proofread and corrected before they are used. In the rest of this section we will discuss a program to perform this task on the file STATS.

One way to handle this editing job is first to establish a backup file, say TEMP, into which we copy the contents of STATS, then to read each value out of the file TEMP, correct it, if necessary, and transfer it back to STATS. When we are done, STATS will contain the corrected list, while the original contents of STATS will now be in TEMP. The advantage of this approach is that it effectively corrects STATS, rather than producing a new file to hold the corrected data. TEMP can be deleted when no longer needed. Here is a structured flowchart to help you understand the program.

```
Open STATS and a temporary file TEMP
Copy the contents of STATS into TEMP
Close STATS and TEMP
─────────────────────────────────────────────────
Open STATS and TEMP
─────────────────────────────────────────────────
Repeat (exit when end-of-file flag is read from TEMP)
    Read item from TEMP
    ───────────────────────────────────────────
    Exit
    ───────────────────────────────────────────
    Display it at the terminal
    Ask if user wishes to change value
    ───────────────────────────────────────────
    If answer is yes
        Accept new value for this item
    ───────────────────────────────────────────
    Write item in STATS
Write flag in STATS
Close STATS and TEMP
Stop
```

Note: We've assumed that STATS is organized with the end-of-file flag, 9999. The program is as follows:

```
100 REM TITLE: PROGRAM TO EDIT THE FILE STATS
110 REM PROGRAMMER: A. KITCHEN          DATE: 5-JUN-81
120 REM
130 REM VARIABLES:
140 REM          A = VALUE FROM FILE STATS
150 REM          Q = RESPONSE (Y OR N)
```

```
160 REM FILES:
170 REM          STATS = DATA FILE TO BE EDITED
180 REM          TEMP = BACK-UP FILE
190 REM PROGRAM:
200 REM COPY STATS INTO TEMP:
210     OPEN "STATS" AS FILE 1
220     OPEN "TEMP" AS FILE 2
230 REM REPEAT
240             INPUT #1,A
250             PRINT #2,A
260             IF A = 9999 THEN 280
270     GO TO 230
280     CLOSE 1
290     CLOSE 2
300 REM RETURN DATA TO STATS, MAKING CORRECTIONS:
310     PRINT "EDITING PROGRAM FOR FILE STATS."
320     PRINT
330     PRINT "AS EACH VALUE IS PRINTED, TYPE Y (CHANGE)"
340     PRINT "OR N (LEAVE AS IS)."
350     PRINT "TYPE CORRECTION IN RESPONSE TO 'VAL?'"
360     PRINT
370     OPEN "STATS" AS FILE 1
380     OPEN "TEMP" AS FILE 2
390 REM REPEAT
400             INPUT #2,A
410             IF A = 9999 THEN 510
420             PRINT A;
430             INPUT Q$
440             IF NOT (Q$ = "Y") THEN 470
450                     PRINT "VAL";
460                     INPUT A
470 REM         END IF
480             PRINT
490             PRINT #1,A
500     GO TO 390
510 REM PRINT END-OF-FILE FLAG IN STATS
520     PRINT #1,A
530     CLOSE 1
540     CLOSE 2
9999    END
```

Notice the inclusion of a brief description of the two files in the documentation at the beginning of the program.

Suppose that STATS looks like this initially:

STATS

STATS
93.44
40.51
597
20.3
96.67
101.01
9999

After the following run:

RUN
EDITING PROGRAM FOR FILE STATS.

AS EACH VALUE IS PRINTED, TYPE Y (CHANGE)
OR N (LEAVE AS IS).
TYPE CORRECTION IN RESPONSE TO 'VAL?'

93.44 ? <u>N</u>

40.51 ? <u>N</u>

597 ? <u>Y</u>
VAL? <u>59.7</u>

20.3 ? <u>N</u>

96.67 ? <u>Y</u>
VAL? <u>69.67</u>

101.01 ? <u>N</u>
Ready

the contents of STATS and TEMP are as follows:

STATS	TEMP
93.44	93.44
40.51	40.51
59.7	597
20.3	20.3
69.67	96.67
101.01	101.01
9999	9999

This program could easily be modified to handle other files. In fact, on some systems it may be possible to write the OPEN statement with a character string variable in place of the file name, as follows:

```
210   OPEN F$ AS FILE 1
```

This would allow the user to enter the file name in response to an INPUT statement.

```
195   PRINT "WHAT FILE DO YOU WISH TO EDIT";
197   INPUT F$
```

Unfortunately, this option is not generally available in BASIC. Experiment to see if your system supports it.

11.8 THE TROUBLE WITH RECORDS

In earlier chapters we have seen that the information processed by computers is not always obliging enough to arrange itself into simple lists of names or numbers. Its structure invariably is more complicated. In fact, the bread and butter of many of the programs that we have discussed has been lists of records, where each record is a collection of various different data items (or fields).

Example

You should be quite familiar with the concept of a record by now. Here is yet another example:

Early Automobiles

Make	Year	City	State
Selden	1879*	Rochester	NY
Duryea	1893	Springfield	MA
Haynes	1894	Kokomo	IN
Olds	1897	Lansing	MI
Winton	1898	Cleveland	OH
Knox	1899	Springfield	MA
Kelsey	1899	Chestnut Hill	PA
- - -	- - -	- - -	- - -
- - -	- - -	- - -	- - -

*I'm claiming a little too much for Rochester and Mr. Selden. This is the date of the patent application. The engine was built in 1877. The first and only model was not built until 1904.

One might imagine that a file containing the list from this example could be handled with statements like this:

PRINT #1, M$,Y,C$,S$

and this:

INPUT #1, M$,Y,C$,S$

where M$ reads the make, Y the year, and so on. Unfortunately, although this kind of statement (or something like it) is legal in many dialects of BASIC, it does not always produce the results one would hope for. On one system these statements (or their equivalent) may work perfectly, whereas on another, data in a file created by

```
PRINT #1, M$,Y,C$,S$
```

cannot be retrieved by

```
INPUT #1, M$,Y,C$,S$
```

The problem has to do with the way in which a particular system reads a collection of values that has been written in a file by a single PRINT statement. On some systems, INPUT will read such values only if they are separated by commas, which, therefore, must be placed in the file by the PRINT statement, for example,

```
PRINT #1, M$;",";Y;",";"C$;",";S$
```

Others don't require this.

The moral to be drawn from this is: If you want to save yourself headaches when using files to store lists of records, do not do it this way. In fact, *never write more than one item in a file or read more than one from it in one statement.* The following two program segments illustrate the recommended approach.

Example

1. Program to store information about early automobiles in the file OLDCAR:

```
100 REM TITLE: STORE AUTO DATA IN FILE OLDCAR
110     OPEN "OLDCAR" AS FILE 1
120 REM WRITE THE RECORD COUNT IN THE FILE
130     READ K
140     PRINT #1,K
150     FOR I = 1 TO K
160 REM        READ A RECORD FROM A DATA STATEMENT:
170            READ M$,Y,C$,S$
180 REM        WRITE THE RECORD IN THE FILE:
190            PRINT #1,M$
200            PRINT #1,Y
210            PRINT #1,C$
220            PRINT #1,S$
230     NEXT I
240     CLOSE 1
300 REM DATA:
310 REM        NUMBER OF RECORDS:
320     DATA 7
330 REM        RECORD = MAKE, YEAR, CITY, STATE:
340     DATA "SELDEN",1879,"ROCHESTER","NY"
350     DATA "DURYEA",1893,"SPRINGFIELD","MA"
```

```
360      DATA "HAYNES",1894,"KOKOMO","IN"
370      DATA "OLDS",1897,"LANSING","MI"
380      DATA "WINTON",1898,"CLEVELAND","OH"
390      DATA "KNOX",1899,"SPRINGFIELD","MA"
400      DATA "KELSEY",1899,"CHESTNUT HILL","PA"
9999     END
```

Visualize the file OLDCAR like this:

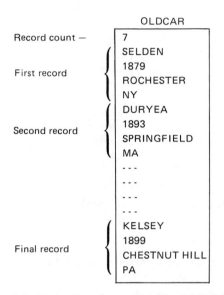

2. Program to read information from the file OLDCAR.

```
100 REM TITLE: READ DATA FROM THE FILE OLDCAR
110      OPEN "OLDCAR" AS FILE 1
120 REM READ RECORD COUNT FROM FILE
130      INPUT #1,K
140      PRINT "MAKE","YEAR","CITY","STATE"
150      PRINT
160      FOR I = 1 TO K
170 REM          READ RECORD FROM FILE:
180              INPUT #1,M$
190              INPUT #1,Y
200              INPUT #1,C$
210              INPUT #1,S$
220 REM          PRINT RECORD AT THE TERMINAL:
230              PRINT M$,Y,C$,S$
240      NEXT I
250      CLOSE 1
9999     END
```

By the way, a file of records using an end-of-file flag instead of a record count should always end with a complete dummy record.

Example

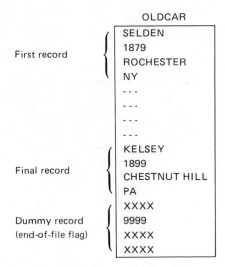

Try modifying the programs above to create and read OLDCAR using an end-of-file flag.

11.9   FILES WITHOUT TEARS: SOME GUIDELINES

This section summarizes the suggestions made in this chapter. As you will see if you read Appendix IV, BASIC files are a tower of Babel. Each version of BASIC says it all in a different way. However, in every version, file handling can be broken into these three steps:

1.   Opening the file
2.   Writing in the file or reading from it
3.   Closing the file

Bearing this in mind, you can translate the programs in this chapter into any of the dialects listed in the table in Appendix IV, by looking up the corresponding statements for each of the three steps.

The following guidelines will help to guarantee that your programs will work no matter what system it is you are using.

Guidelines for Files

1.   Once a file is opened, a program may write in it or read from it, but not both.

Example

```
100  OPEN "FUZZY" AS FILE 1
- - -
150  PRINT #1, A
160  INPUT #1, A
- - -
200  CLOSE 1
- - -
```

BAD

2. To change the mode of interaction with a file from read to write or write to read, the file must first be closed and then reopened.

Example

```
100  OPEN "FUZZY" AS FILE 1
- - -  - - -
130  PRINT #1, A                    }  Write data in the file
- - -  - - -
160  CLOSE 1
170  OPEN "FUZZY" AS FILE 1
- - -  - - -
190  INPUT #1, A                    }  Read data from the file
- - -  - - -
230  CLOSE 1
- - -  - - -
```

3. Only one value should be written in a file at a time (one per PRINT statement). The same rule applies to reading from a file.

Example

This is not recommended:

```
140  PRINT #1, A,B
```

This is OK:

```
140  PRINT #1, A
150  PRINT #1, B
```

BAD

4. When writing a character string into a file, be sure that it does not contain embedded commas or apostrophes. Commas are often treated as

data separators and apostrophes are equivalent to quotations on some systems.

Example

This:

BAD

```
170   LET A$ = "'HI!' HE BAWLED."
180   PRINT #1, A$
```

is dangerous. You may find that, on reading this item out of the file, all you get back is HI! ∎

Chapter 11: EXERCISES

Section 11.1

1. Read your system manuals for information on the types of mass storage devices available to you.

Section 11.2

1. Read the sections of your manuals that describe the conventions for naming files on your system. There is wide variation. For example, if your system has more than one mass storage device, the file name you use may have to include a code to indicate which device the file is stored on.

Section 11.3

1. Experiment with these two program segments:

```
100   REM  PROGRAM: TEST A            100   REM  PROGRAM: TEST B
110        OPEN "WEE" AS FILE 1        110        OPEN "WEE" AS FILE 1
120        PRINT "ENTER 3 NUMBERS";    120   REM  READ VALUES FROM WEE
130        INPUT X,Y,Z                 130   REM  PRINT THEM AT TERMINAL
140   REM  WRITE THEM IN WEE           140        INPUT #1,X
150        PRINT #1, X                 150        PRINT X
160        PRINT #1,Y                  160        INPUT #1,Y
170        PRINT #1,Z                  170        PRINT Y
180        CLOSE 1                     180        INPUT #1,Z
9999       END                         190        PRINT Z
                                       200        CLOSE 1
                                       9999       END
```

(a) What happens if you run TEST B before you ever run TEST A? [*Hint: If you have already run TEST A, you can get the same effect by deleting file WEE before running TEST B. KILL "WEE" or KILL WEE will do this on many systems.*]

(b) Run TEST A twice, entering different data each time; then run TEST B. What happens?

(c) Run TEST A, then run TEST B twice in succession. Is there any difference between the two runs of TEST B?

(d)   In TEST A change line 130 to

```
130  INPUT X,Y
```

and delete line 170. Now run TEST A and then TEST B. What happens? Can you explain the behavior you observe?

2.   Experiment with these segments:

```
100   REM  PROGRAM: CREATE JOT        100   REM  PROGRAM: CHECK JOT
110        OPEN "JOT" AS FILE 1       110        OPEN "JOT" AS FILE 1
120        READ A,B                   120        INPUT #1,A
130        PRINT #1,A                 130        PRINT A
140        PRINT #1,B                 140        INPUT #1,B
150        CLOSE 1                    150        PRINT B
160        DATA 111,222               160        CLOSE 1
9999       END                        9999       END


100   REM  PROGRAM READ-WRITE         100   REM  PROGRAM: WRITE-READ
110        OPEN "JOT" AS FILE 1       110        OPEN "JOT" AS FILE 1
120        INPUT #1,A                 120        LET A = 444
130        PRINT A                    130        PRINT #1,A
140        LET B = 333                140        INPUT #1,B
150        PRINT #1,B                 150        PRINT B
160        CLOSE 1                    160        CLOSE 1
9999       END          .            9999       END
```

(a)   Run CREATE JOT, then READ–WRITE, then finally CHECK JOT. What is the output from these runs?

(b)   Run CREATE JOT, then WRITE–READ, then CHECK JOT. What is printed this time? Can you give an explanation for what you observe? [*Hint: The behavior will vary from system to system. For this reason, the writing of programs of the form of READ–WRITE and WRITE–READ, which mix input and output operations on a file, is NOT RECOMMENDED PRACTICE.*]

Section 11.4

1.   Read the section on file handling in the BASIC manual for your system and identify the statement types that handle opening a file, closing it, reading from a file, and writing in one. Make a careful note of the forms that these statements take and keep it at hand as you read this chapter. With a little practice, you should have no trouble translating the ex-

amples so that they work on your system. You may find Appendix IV helpful in making the translation.

Section 11.5

1. Redo Section 11.3, Exercise 2 with the following versions of READ–WRITE and WRITE–READ.

100	REM PROGRAM: READ – WRITE		100	REM PROGRAM: WRITE – READ
110	OPEN "JOT" AS FILE 1		110	OPEN "JOT" AS FILE 1
120	INPUT #1,A		120	LET A = 444
130	PRINT A		130	PRINT #1,A
140	CLOSE 1		140	CLOSE 1
150	OPEN "JOT" AS FILE 1		150	OPEN "JOT" AS FILE 1
160	LET B = 333		160	INPUT #1,B
170	PRINT #1,B		170	PRINT B
180	CLOSE 1		180	CLOSE 1
9999	END		9999	END

Do you notice any change in behavior?

2. (a) What happens when a program opens a new file (one that previously didn't exist) and immediately reads from it?
    (b) What happens when a program opens a file that already has data in it and immediately writes data in it? [*Hint: If in doubt, experiment!*]

Section 11.6

1. Suppose that the file NUMB has these contents:

NUMB

12
34
56
78
91
23
45
67
89

before each of the following program segments is run. Describe each run and the contents of NUMB after the run is complete.

(a)
```
100    OPEN "NUMB" AS FILE 1
110    FOR I = 1 TO 5
120       PRINT #1,I
130    NEXT I
140    CLOSE 1
9999   END
```

(b)
```
100    OPEN "NUMB" AS FILE 1
110    FOR I = 1 TO 5
120       INPUT #1,X
130       PRINT X
140    NEXT I
150    CLOSE 1
9999   END
```

(c)
```
100    OPEN "NUMB" AS FILE 1
110    FOR I = 1 TO 4
120       INPUT #1,X
130       PRINT X
140    NEXT I
150    FOR I = 1 TO 5
160       PRINT #1,I
170    NEXT I
180    CLOSE 1
9999   END
```

(d)
```
100    OPEN "NUMB" AS FILE 1
110    FOR I = 1 TO 4
120       INPUT #1,X
130       PRINT X
140    NEXT I
150    CLOSE 1
160    OPEN "NUMB" AS FILE 1
170    FOR I = 1 TO 5
180       PRINT #1,I
190    NEXT I
200    CLOSE 1
9999   END
```

(e)
```
100    OPEN "NUMB" AS FILE 1
110    FOR I = 1 TO 5
120       PRINT #1,I
130    NEXT I
140    FOR I = 1 TO 4
150       INPUT #1,X
160       PRINT X
170    NEXT I
180    CLOSE 1
9999   END
```

(f)
```
100    OPEN "NUMB" AS FILE 1
110    FOR I = 1 TO 5
120       PRINT #1,I
130    NEXT I
140    CLOSE 1
150    OPEN "NUMB" AS FILE 1
160    FOR I = 1 TO 4
170       INPUT #1,X
180       PRINT X
190    NEXT I
200    CLOSE 1
9999   END
```

(g)
```
100    OPEN "NUMB" AS FILE 1
110    FOR I = 1 TO 5
120       PRINT #1,I
130    NEXT I
140    FOR I = 6 TO 9
150       PRINT #1,I
160    NEXT I
170    CLOSE 1
9999   END
```

(h)
```
100    OPEN "NUMB" AS FILE 1
110    FOR I = 1 TO 5
120       PRINT #1,I
130    NEXT I
140    CLOSE 1
150    OPEN "NUMB" AS FILE 1
160    FOR I = 6 TO 9
170       PRINT #1,I
180    NEXT I
190    CLOSE 1
9999   END
```

[*Warning: The segments in parts (c) and (e) are NOT RECOMMENDED PRACTICE. It is not advisable to mix read and write operations while a file is open.*]

2. If the file ONE contains the list 231, 132, 321, 213, 312, what does file TWO contain after each of the following segments is executed?

(a)
```
100   OPEN "ONE" AS FILE 1
110   OPEN "TWO" AS FILE 2
120   FOR I = 1 TO 5
130       INPUT #1,X
140       PRINT #2,X
150   NEXT I
160   CLOSE 1
170   CLOSE 2
9999  END
```

(b)
```
100   OPEN "ONE" AS FILE 1
110   OPEN "TWO" AS FILE 2
120   FOR I = 1 TO 5
130       INPUT #1,X
140   NEXT I
150   FOR I = 1 TO 5
160       PRINT #2,X
170   NEXT I
180   CLOSE 1
190   CLOSE 2
9999  END
```

(c)
```
100   DIM X(5)
110   OPEN "ONE" AS FILE 1
120   OPEN "TWO" AS FILE 2
130   FOR I = 1 TO 5
140       INPUT #1,X(I)
150   NEXT I
160   FOR I = 1 TO 5
170       PRINT #2,X(I)
180   NEXT I
190   CLOSE 1
200   CLOSE 2
9999  END
```

(d)
```
100   DIM X(5)
110   OPEN "ONE" AS FILE 1
120   FOR I = 1 TO 5
130       INPUT #1,X(I)
140   NEXT I
150   CLOSE 1
160   OPEN "TWO" AS FILE 2
170   FOR I = 1 TO 5
180       PRINT #2,X(I)
190   NEXT I
200   CLOSE 2
9999  END
```

3. What is in the file FIBSEQ after the following program segment is run if initially it contains the sequence 1, 1, 2, 3, 5, 8, 13, 21, 34, 55?

```
100   DIM A(10)
110   OPEN "FIBSEQ" AS FILE 1
120   FOR I = 1 TO 10
130       INPUT #1, A(I)
140   NEXT I
150   CLOSE 1
160   FOR I = 2 TO 10
170       LET A(I) = A(I) + A(I-1)
180   NEXT I
190   OPEN "FIBSEQ" AS FILE 1
200   FOR I = 1 TO 10
210       PRINT #1,A(I)
220   NEXT I
230   CLOSE 1
9999  END
```

4.   Given the following four program segments:

```
100  REM  PROG 1                      100  REM  PROG 2
110       OPEN "LETUS" AS FILE 1      110       OPEN "LETUS" AS FILE 1
120       FOR I = 1 TO 8              120       OPEN "TEMP" AS FILE 2
130          READ A$                 130       FOR I = 1 TO 8
140          PRINT #1, A$             140          INPUT #1, Y$
150       NEXT I                      150          IF Y$ ="Z" THEN LET Y$ ="A
160       CLOSE 1                     160          PRINT #2,Y$
170       DATA "J","X","Z","Q"        170       NEXT I
180       DATA "W","Z","R","Q"        180       CLOSE 1
9999      END                         190       CLOSE 2
                                      9999      END


100  REM  PROG 3                      100  REM  PROG 4
110       OPEN "TEMP" AS FILE 1       110       OPEN "LETUS" AS FILE 1
120       OPEN "LETUS" AS FILE 2      120       FOR I = 1 TO 8
130       FOR I = 1 TO 8              130          INPUT #1, B$
140          INPUT #1,Z$              140          PRINT B$
150          PRINT #2,Z$              150       NEXT I
160       NEXT I                      160       CLOSE 1
170       CLOSE 1                     9999      END
180       CLOSE 2
```

What happens to the file LETUS when these programs are run in the order specified? Delete the file TEMP before each group of runs (KILL "TEMP" or the appropriate command for your system).

(a)   PROG 1, PROG 4
(b)   PROG 1, PROG 2, PROG 4
(c)   PROG 1, PROG 3, PROG 4
(d)   PROG 1, PROG 2, PROG 3, PROG 4
(e)   PROG 1, PROG 2, PROG 3, PROG 1, PROG 4

5.   Identify which of the following statements contain errors. Describe the errors.

(a)   OPEN FILE "CRAZY"
(b)   DATA 2;5;7
(c)   LET "COOKIE" = FILE 1
(d)   OPEN NAILFILE AS FILE 2
(e)   READ 1,P,Q
(f)   DEF FN(X) = 2*X–1
(g)   INPUT #,X
(h)   GO TO END
(i)   CLOSE "DOOR"
(j)   INPUT FILE 1,B$
(k)   FOR I = 1 STEP 10
(l)   PRINT #1,A
(m)   FILE: MOOCOW
(n)   REM CLOSE FILE 2
(o)   LET B$ + " " = B$

6.   (a)   Write a program to read the data from these statements.

```
1000  REM  DATA: RECORD = NAME,AGE
1010       DATA "NORMA",23
1020       DATA "MAVIS",43
```

```
1030        DATA "DOREEN",39
1040        DATA "MAUDE",6
1050        DATA "ALEXINA",27
1060        DATA "DELIA",15
1070        DATA "MAUREEN",37
1080        DATA "PATIENCE",86
1090        DATA "HERMIONE",53
1100        DATA "PHOEBE",62
1110        DATA "ANNABELLE",31
1120        DATA "CLAUDINE",47
```

and store the list of names in one file, NAME, and the ages in a second file, AGE.

(b) Write a program that reads the two files NAME and AGE and prints the following table:

NAME	AGE
NORMA	23
MAVIS	43
etc.	etc.

Write both of these programs without using arrays.

7. Modify example (4) in Section 11.6 so that it will accept, from the terminal, the name of any egg dish that is listed in the file EGGS and also the name of a new dish. It should, then, read the file EGGS and transfer the contents of EGGS into FRSHEG, with the old dish replaced by the new. What does your program do if the first dish entered is not in EGGS?

8. (a) Write a program to accept 20 items (numbers or character strings, whichever you prefer) from the terminal and store them in a file, LIST.

(b) Write a program to read the data from this file, sort them into order (numerical or alphabetical), and return them to the file. [*Hint: Use one of the sorting techniques developed in earlier exercises.*]

(c) Rewrite the program in part (b) so that the sorted list is placed in a second file, ORDLST, and the original list is left in LIST as a backup. [*Hint: In parts (b) and (c) you may use arrays. When writing programs that handle files, it is helpful to write simple supporting programs which will print the contents of each file at the terminal. Most systems provide special commands to perform this function, but it doesn't hurt to write your own routines anyway. You may need them as part of a package later.*]

9. (a) Write a program to read 20 items from a file SHFFLE and store the first 10 in one file, CUT1, and the rest in a second, CUT2.

[*Hint: First you'll have to write a program to put the values in SHFFLE.*]

(b)   Write a program to read values alternately from CUT1 and CUT2, first an item from CUT1 then one from CUT2, and so on, and write the resulting list in SHFFLE. [*Hint: Do not use arrays.*]

(c)   If you repeatedly run first the program in part (a), then the one from part (b), you will shuffle the list in SHFFLE in exactly the way described in Section 10.3, Exercise 11. How could you modify this pair of programs so that it can handle lists of any length? [*Hint: To monitor the progress of the shuffle, you will find it helpful to write a program that prints the contents of SHFFLE.*]

Section 11.7

1.   Write a program to store data in the file STATS so that STATS contains an initial record count rather than an end-of-file flag. Write a second program to read the data from this version of STATS. Test these programs with different amounts of data. [*Hint: See the discussion of the two forms of organization for the sequential file STATS in this section.*]

2.   Write a program to accept a number and then search for that number in the file STATS and delete it. You can choose to do this for either the end-of-file form or the record count form of STATS. After a run of this program, STATS should contain the updated list and file TEMP, the old version. [*Hint: If your program handles STATS with a record count structure, be sure to change the value of the count in the updated file.*]

3.   Write a program to accept any number of values and add them to the end of the file STATS. When finished, STATS should contain the updated list and TEMP the old one. As in Exercise 2, either structure for the file STATS may be used. [*Hint: Do not use arrays in this program.*]

4.   Write a program that reads a list of numbers, ending with the flag 9999, from a file RUPOS and replaces all the negative ones with 0. The final list should be in RUPOS, the original in TEMP.

5.   It is often necessary to establish a file that can be updated as new data are received. Such a file demands a program that will add data to it. The structure of this update program will be simpler if we can assume that there are data already in the file when it is executed. But, then, how do we get started? The solution is to write a special "creation" program which is run before any data are written in the file. The approach varies depending on whether the file is to have an end-of-file flag or a record count.

(a)   Write a file maintenance "package" for a file CURDAT which is organized with an end-of-file flag. The package should consist of three programs:

(1) CREATE FILE, which opens CURDAT and stores just the end-of-file flag in it

(2) UPDATE FILE, which accepts a value and adds it to the end of CURDAT,

(3) LIST FILE, which lists the contents of CURDAT

[*Hint: Programs UPDATE FILE and LIST FILE should NOT treat the empty file (i.e., CURDAT containing just an end-of-file flag) as a special case.*]

(b) Write a similar maintenance "package" for CURDAT, where, this time, the file is organized using a record count instead of an end-of-file flag. In this case, CREATE FILE should store a record count of 0 as the first and only item in CURDAT. This value will be increased as items are added to CURDAT by the program UPDATE FILE.

6. (a) Write a program to accept an integer, N, and establish a file, AR-RAY, containing N zeros preceded by the record count, N.

(b) Write a program to accept an integer, I, in the range $1 \leqslant I \leqslant N$, and a value, V, and then replace the Ith item in the file, ARRAY, with the contents of V. [*Hint: For the purposes of this exercise, the record count, N, is not considered to be one of the items in the file; that is, I indicates the position of an item AFTER the record count.*]

(c) Write a program to accept an integer, I, in the range $1 \leqslant I \leqslant N$ and print the value of the Ith item in the file ARRAY at the terminal. [*Hint: Write the programs in parts (b) and (c) without using arrays.*]

(d) This exercise illustrates how, by designing appropriate programs or subroutines, a file can be made to behave like an array, A(1), A(2), . . . , A(N). The value of this would be realized if we were required to process an array that was too large to be stored in memory. We could put the data in a file and use subroutines based on these programs to store and retrieve values from it. We would gain almost unlimited space at the cost of speed, as the process of reading a value from a file is much slower than that of retrieving it from a variable in memory. Write statements or program segments to perform the operations on an ordinary array, A(1), A(2), . . . , which correspond to the operations on the file ARRAY described in (a), (b), and (c).

7. A file LIST is to contain a list of values preceded by a number, N, which indicates how many values are in the list.

(a) Write a program that creates the file LIST and places in it an empty list, that is, one with no items in it.

(b) Write a program to accept an integer, I, and a value, V, and to add the value to the list immediately following the Ith item. If $I \leqslant 0$, then V is to be inserted at the beginning of the list; if $I \geqslant N$, then it is placed at the end. [*Hint: For these purposes, the record count, N, is NOT part of the list. However, don't forget to change the value of N to reflect the size of the new list.*]

(c) Write a program to accept an integer, I, and delete the Ith item in the list. If $I \leqslant 0$ or $I > N$, the program should do nothing.

8. (a) Suppose that ORDER is a file which contains a list of numbers in increasing order terminated by a flag 9999. Write a subroutine INSERT IN ORDER, which will accept a number, X, and will insert it in the file ORDER in its correct place in the ordering. Here is a flowchart for the subroutine.

SUBROUTINE:
INSERT IN ORDER
VALUES: X, ORDER   RETURNED: ORDER
Open files ORDER and TEMP Copy contents of ORDER into TEMP Close ORDER and TEMP Open ORDER and TEMP
Repeat (exit when item > X or item = end-of-file flag)

Read item from TEMP
    Exit
    Write item in ORDER

Write X in ORDER
Repeat (exit when item = end-of-file flag)

Write item in ORDER
    Exit
    Read item from TEMP

Close ORDER and TEMP
Stop

[*Note: The file ORDER has been included in the argument list for the subroutine. In a sense, it behaves like a variable, an array perhaps! It transmits data to the subroutine and returns data modified by it. The file TEMP does not appear in the list because it is only used as a tool within the subroutine.*]

(b) Here is a sorting method, **insertion sort,** which uses the subroutine INSERT IN ORDER to sort a list stored in the file DATFIL. Write a program from this flowchart.

```
Create ORDER (Open it, stuff an end-of-file flag in it, close it)
Open DATFIL

Repeat (exit when end of file DATFIL)

    Read X from DATFIL
    Exit
    Call subroutine INSERT IN ORDER

Close DATFIL
Open DATFIL and ORDER
Copy contents of ORDER into DATFIL
Close DATFIL and ORDER
Stop
```

[*Hint: This method is at its fastest when DATFIL is originally in reverse order. However, it is very slow. After all, look at the overhead. Each time INSERT IN ORDER is called, the files ORDER and TEMP are opened and closed twice and the contents of ORDER are read out and then written back into it.*]

9. The advantage of the sorting method described in Exercise 8 is that it uses very little memory. In fact, at any time during execution no more than two items from the list to be sorted are in memory at the same time. On the other hand, the **bubble sort** method, as described in Section 8.2, Exercise 11(a) and Section 10.3, Exercise 8(b), sorts a list stored in an array in memory. Write a program to sort a file using bubble sort, but without using arrays.

10. ORDONE and ORDTWO are two files that contain lists of numbers in increasing order. Write a program that will read the contents of these files and write them into a third file ORDER in such a way that the combined list is in increasing order, too. [*Hint: You should NOT dump the two lists into the file ORDER and then sort it, nor should you use arrays. Read each successive value from either ORDONE or ORDTWO in such a way as to transfer the smallest value remaining in both lists directly to the end of the list in ORDER. The program should only have to read the two files ORDONE and ORDTWO once. This process is referred to as* **merging**.]

11. The Sieve of Eratosthenes: The following method for finding prime numbers was known to the Greeks:

Make a list of consecutive integers, starting with 2, until you get tired:

2 3 4 5 6 7 8 9 10 11 12 13 14 15 16 17 18 19 20 21 22 23 24 25 26 27 28 29 30

Now beginning at 2, set every second integer in the list, other than 2 itself, to zero. In other words, strike out the multiples of 2:

2 3 0 5 0 7 0 9 0 11 0 13 0 15 0 17 0 19 0 21 0 23 0 0 0 27 0 29 0

Next, find the first nonzero entry after 2, namely 3, and set every third integer following it to zero:

2 3 0 5 0 7 0 0 0 11 0 13 0 0 0 17 0 19 0 0 0 23 0 25 0 0 0 29 0

Continue this, each time starting with the next remaining nonzero entry and setting its multiples to zero:

2 3 0 5 0 7 0 0 0 11 0 13 0 0 0 17 0 19 0 0 0 23 0 0 0 0 0 29 0

You'll notice that by the time we have zeroed the multiples of 5 we have eliminated all the nonprimes (composite numbers) below 30. In fact, to find all primes up to any integer, N, we only have to eliminate the multiples of integers $\leqslant$ SQR(N). I'll leave you to figure out the reason for that.

Write a program that uses this method to find all primes less than or equal to an integer, N, specified by the user. Store the integers 2 through N in a file PRIMES, then repeat the process described above until PRIMES contains just prime numbers and zeros. Finally, print a list of the nonzero entries from the file. Do all this without using arrays.

Section 11.8

1. Rewrite the programs of this section to handle the file OLDCAR, using an end-of-file flag instead of a record count.

2. All the techniques developed in the preceding section apply equally well to files with more complex record structure. Write programs to do the following:
    (a) Accept the make of an automobile and then search for its record in the file OLDCAR and print it at the terminal.
    (b) Accept the make of an automobile and delete its record from OLD-CAR.
    (c) Accept a complete record (make, year, city, state) and add it to the end of OLDCAR.
    (d) Sort the file OLDCAR alphabetically by make.
    (e) Accept a complete record and insert it in its correct place in the sorted file OLDCAR.

[*Hint: You can organize the file using either an end-of-file flag or a record count. In fact, if you have the stamina, you should attempt these exercises with OLDCAR organized both ways. Here are some more records for use in the exercises: King, 1896, Detroit, MI; Ford, 1896, Detroit, MI; Riker, 1900, Elizabethport, NJ.*]

3. The beer can records program of Section 8.3 was the first program we discussed that exposed a serious weakness of computer memory—its unsuitability for long-term storage. Rewrite the beer can program using a file BEERCN to store the current state of the list. Handle it in the following two different ways. In both cases you'll have to write another program to put the records in BEERCN initially.

   (a) Read records into the arrays from the file BEERCN rather than from DATA statements. Then, at the end of the program, write the updated contents of the arrays back into the file. [*Hint: In this version, the code of the original program will be essentially unchanged, apart from additions at the beginning and end.*]

   (b) Rewrite the program completely so that no arrays are used at all. [*Hint: Model this program on the techniques used in the editing programs for the files EGGS and STATS, discussed in Sections 11.6 and 11.7.*]

4. (a) Rewrite the program in Section 10.5, Exercise 6(a), which handles the charge accounts for a small business, so that it reads all the records from a file, ACCNTS, instead of from DATA statements, and then returns the updated records to the file.

   (b) The use of files allows one to simplify the structure of many programs, enabling them to be broken up into a number of shorter ones. We can get the same effect as is given by the program in part (a) by rewriting the three subroutines READ ACCOUNTS, LIST, and UPDATE as separate programs. Write the following set of programs:

   > READ ACCOUNTS: reads the initial account data from DATA statements into the file ACCNTS
   >
   > LIST: lists the contents of the file ACCNTS
   >
   > UPDATE: modifies the balance of a selected record in ACCNTS

   (c) Add the programs VERIFY, ADD, and DELETE, which perform the operations described in Section 10.5, Exercise 6(b), on the file ACCNTS.

5. (a) Write a set of programs to update a sorted file of charge account records, MASTER. Each record in this file should consist of at

least an account name (or account number) and a current balance, and the records should be sorted so that the names (or account numbers) are in order. Here are the programs:

DAILY TRANSACTIONS: Accepts payments and charges against various accounts and adds these records to a temporary file, the transaction file, TRANS. Each record in this file should consist of, at least, an account name (or account number) and a payment (–) or charge (+).

SORT TRANSACTIONS: Sorts the records in the file TRANS by name (or account number), using any of the sorting techniques discussed in earlier exercises.

UPDATE MASTER: Reads each record from TRANS, updates the corresponding master record in MASTER, and then deletes the contents of TRANS so that it is ready to receive the next day's transactions.

[*Hint: Because both TRANS and MASTER are sorted files, this last program can be handled with essentially one pass through MASTER. For simplicity, assume that no more than one transaction is listed for any one account in TRANS.*]

(b) Modify UPDATE MASTER so that it is protected against incorrectly entered transactions. It should ignore a record in TRANS if the corresponding record in MASTER is missing. Have it print an error message and then continue with the processing of the remainder of TRANS.

(c) It is realistic to expect that some account holders may make more than one transaction during a day. Write a program to consolidate the file TRANS, once it has been sorted, so that there is just one record for each account listed. [*Hint: See Section 6.5, Exercise 3, for a solution to a similar kind of problem. Of course, to test this program, you must drop the restriction that TRANS contain no more than one record per account.*]

(d) Write a program to add new master records, stored in order in a file NEWACC, to the MASTER file. [*Hint: The technique required is described in Section 11.7, Exercise 10.*]

6. A country hotel has 20 rooms, numbers 101–112 on the first floor and 201–208 on the second. Each room is capable of holding up to two paying guests. The rates are $47 for double occupancy and $31 for single. A file GUESTS is used to keep track of the assignment of guests to rooms for the current night. It contains a record for each room, consisting of:

room number, name of guest, number occupying room, paid

(paid = 0 if the room is prepaid, 1, if it is to be paid for at checkout time). When a room is vacant, its record looks like this:

Room	Guest	Number	Paid
104	XXXX	0	0

Write three programs to manage this file:

CHECK-IN: Given a name and the number of guests registering under this name, this program will search the file for sufficient rooms for the party. It will print the room numbers and the total charge for the night and will request whether payment is to be now or at checkout. It will then update the file, GUESTS, accordingly.

CHECKOUT: Given a name, this program will vacate all rooms registered to this name in the file GUESTS, and will print the charge and request payment, if they are not prepaid.

ROOMS: On request, this program will print either a guest list showing, for each name listed, the number in the party and the room numbers assigned to that name, or a list of the vacant rooms.

[*Hint: CHECK-IN will assign the minimum number of rooms necessary, no matter what the size of the party; thus a party of two will get one room, a party of three will get two, and so on.*]

7. Creating an index for a book is one of those tedious sorting procedures which the computer can handle so well. To make an index, one first has to read the book (unless one can persuade the computer to do this, too), recording each key word or phrase, and the page on which it appears, in a file. This file will consist of a list of records, each of the form: word (or phrase), page number. The next step is to sort the records so that the words are listed alphabetically and, finally, to print the index. Notice that printing the index is not trivial, as there may be more than one reference to the same word:

POISONS	149
POISONS	275
POISONS	783
POKER	522
POLAR	435

and these references must be consolidated:

POISONS	149,275,783
POKER	522
POLAR	435

Incidentally, the page references for each word should be in numerical order, but this will happen automatically if the file was established by reading the book from beginning to end.

Write these programs:

CREATE INDEX: to establish a file, INDEX, for the storage of records of the form: character string, integer

UPDATE INDEX: to add records to the end of INDEX

SORT INDEX: to sort the records in INDEX alphabetically on the character string field.

PRINT INDEX: to print out the sorted version of INDEX in the form described above.

Section 11.9

No exercises.

Chapter

12

Chance Events: The RND Function

12.1 THE VALUE OF RANDOMNESS

You may remember that dull little program which introduced Chapter 5. It was a game, of sorts: the user had to guess a secret number. Unfortunately, the number had been fixed by the programmer ahead of time so that the game had very limited appeal. It could certainly be improved if the computer had some way of choosing a new secret number each time the game was played.

There are many situations in programming where an arbitrary choice of numbers or some other random response would be useful. Most computer games require an element of unpredictability in order to be interesting (e.g., a random scattering of Klingon spaceships or unpredictable movements of unfriendly monsters). An important area of computer science, referred to as **modeling and simulation,** attempts to develop programs that imitate certain aspects of real-life situations. For example, there are simulation programs that attempt to mirror such diverse phenomena as the operation of checkout lines at a supermarket, the behavior of the world economy, the life cycle of a lake, the performance of a new aircraft, the behavior of weather patterns, and so on. Many of these phenomena have elements of randomness which must, therefore, be built into the programs that model them.

A very simple example of a project which could be improved by adding some unpredictability is that of designing a program to set and grade mathematics quizzes. A project of this type appeared as an exercise in Section 5.4. However, there the exercises were stored in DATA statements, so that to produce a different quiz required that these statements be rewritten. How much easier and more flexible the program would be if the computer itself made up a new quiz each time it was executed.

BASIC provides the tool to handle such things: the function RND.[†] Before we discuss this function, I should warn you that its behavior may seem a little unnatural at first. Be reassured that it is not the product of the fevered brain of a madman. It has been designed to provide maximum flexibility in as simple a form as possible. Unfortunately, this means that at times we will have to do some clever engineering in order to make it do exactly what we want.

12.2   THE FUNCTION RND

Try running the following program a number of times:

```
100   RANDOMIZE
110   LET A = RND
120   PRINT A
9999  END
```

Here is a sampling of runs produced by my machine:

RUN	RUN	RUN
0.459851	0.920857	0.271483
Ready	Ready	Ready

While you are at it, try these, too.

Examples

1.
```
100   RANDOMIZE
110   PRINT RND
120   PRINT RND
130   PRINT RND
9999  END
```

[†]I pronounce it "rund."

```
RUN
0.872126
0.284054
0.331485
Ready
```

2.
```
100          RANDOMIZE
110   REM  REPEAT
120             LET A = RND
130             PRINT A,
140          GO TO 110
9999         END
RUN
0.17434      0.574779     0.843091     0.551034     0.245385
0.335364     0.680153     0.741671     0.03642      0.180473
0.409011     etc.
```
■

Your system will produce similar output, but the numbers will not be the same as those listed here. Furthermore, each time you run these programs you will get different values. After you have run them a few times, you should be convinced that the numbers they produce are quite arbitrary, not very useful looking perhaps, but apparently random.

The RND function has the following property: each time it is called (used) it picks a value at random from the range between 0 and 1. More precisely, each value of RND is a decimal fraction which is greater than or equal to 0 and less than 1. We can denote the range of RND as follows:

$$0 \leqslant RND < 1$$

Furthermore, every number in this range is equally likely to be picked and, if RND is used more than once in the same program, successive values do not depend on the previous ones chosen.[†]

The RND function does not require an argument, although on some systems one may be included.

[†]In practice, unfortunately, RND falls short of this ideal. First, the actual range of possible values for RND is limited by the method used to store numbers in the computer's memory. All systems limit the number of digits that can be stored. For example, on my system the limit is six, so that RND actually picks from the range

$$0.000000, 0.000001, 0.000002, \ldots, 0.999998, 0.999999$$

A second weakness is that RND doesn't actually pick numbers at random. It uses a system for calculating them which just appears to be random. For this reason, RND is referred to as a pseudo-random number generator. Although this distinction is important in some applications, it will be safe for us to ignore it here.

Example

Try these programs on your system:

```
100   RANDOMIZE      100   RANDOMIZE      100   RANDOMIZE
110   LET A = RND    110   LET A = RND(0)  110   LET X = 1
120   PRINT A        120   PRINT A        120   LET A = RND(X)
9999  END            9999  END            130   PRINT A
                                          9999  END
```

On many systems they will have an identical effect. On others, however, different values for the argument X in the statement

```
LET A = RND(X)
```

will cause the value of RND(X) to be picked from a different range of numbers. Remember, your best guide in such a situation (although not necessarily the most readable) is the BASIC language manual for your system[†]   ■

Before we find out what RND can do for us, we should discuss the statement RANDOMIZE, which, until now, has lurked in the shadows. If RANDOMIZE is left out of a program containing RND, then every time the program is executed the same sequence of numbers will be produced.

Example

```
110   PRINT RND
120   PRINT RND
130   PRINT RND
9999  END
RUN                   RUN                   RUN
0.374198              0.374198              0.374198
0.183062              0.183062              0.183062
0.641953              0.641953              0.641953
Ready                 Ready                 Ready          ■
```

Each call to the function RND chooses the next in a fixed sequence of random numbers. If the statement RANDOMIZE is omitted from the program, RND will always start at the beginning of this sequence. However, when RANDOMIZE is included before the first call to RND, the sequence is started at an arbitrary point. This starting point is determined by a variable quantity,

---

[†]The description of RND given in this chapter is the one used by ANSI minimal BASIC, the national standard. Unfortunately, many BASICs require the form RND(X), which is not standard and, further, each system interprets X in a different way. Beware!

for example the time of day at which the program is executed, to ensure that each run produces different numbers.

Of course, RANDOMIZE is necessary, if one wants unpredictability, but being able to remove it temporarily in order to get predictable random numbers† is helpful when developing and debugging a program that uses RND. On the whole, make a point of including RANDOMIZE as one of the first statements in any program that employs RND.

12.3 USING RND

Well, what is this RND function good for? First, notice that it can be used anywhere that other functions can be used.

Example

The following are all legal:

```
LET X = 10*RND
PRINT INT(6*RND) + 1
IF RND < 0.5 THEN 420
```

as is this one:

```
DEF FNH = INT(100*RND)
```

A user-defined function does not require an argument (or variable list). ■

The only trouble is that it is not quite clear what statements like these actually do. Try running the following program:

```
100         RANDOMIZE
110    REM  REPEAT
120            LET A = 10*RND
130            PRINT A
140         GO TO 110
9999        END
```

---

†This may seem like a contradiction in terms. The concept of randomness is a subtle one. In everyday terms, something is random if it is unpredictable. However, suppose that one chose a list of numbers by some random process (e.g., by drawing them out of a hat) and then memorized this list. Are the numbers still random? You might feel that, to you at least, they no longer are. However, the statistician would say that the list is just as random now as it ever was and he would demonstrate its randomness by showing that the distribution of numbers in it does not follow any regular pattern. Randomness is really a property of a sequence of values and not a description of the way in which they are chosen.

A typical run might look like this:

```
RUN
 7.84312
 4.47298
 6.99205
 1.73436
 0.84838
 4.23956
 2.43554
 - - -
```

The expression 10*RND causes all the values produced by RND to be multiplied by 10. In the run above, RND must have chosen the sequence

$$0.784312, 0.447298, 0.699205, \text{etc.}$$

which, on multiplication by 10, became

$$7.84312, 4.47298, 6.99205, \text{etc.}$$

In brief, as RND generates numbers in the range

$$0 \leqslant RND < 1$$

the values of 10*RND fall in the range

$$0 \leqslant 10*RND < 10$$

Here is a more interesting example:

```
100         RANDOMIZE
110   REM   REPEAT
120            LET A = INT(10*RND)
130            PRINT A;
140         GO TO 110
9999        END
RUN
4   0   9   5   7   2   2   3   8   ...
...     etc.
```

The function INT, as we know, chops off the fractional part of the numbers 10*RND. For example, if RND produces 0.432379, then 10*RND becomes 4.32379 and INT(10*RND) is 4. Here is the sequence of steps that may have occurred to produce the output above (remember, this is a guess, as we have no way of resurrecting the actual values that RND produced).

RUN	10*RND	INT(10*RND)
0.432379	4.32379	4
0.097756	0.97756	0
0.960154	9.60154	9
0.534641	5.34641	5
- - -	- - -	- - -

Thus INT(10*RND) chooses values at random from the set of integers {0, 1, 2, 3, 4, 5, 6, 7, 8, 9}. Notice that 10 is never chosen because RND is always less than 1. In fact, the largest possible value it can choose is something like 0.999999, and in that case INT(10*RND) takes on its largest value, which is 9. A careful study of INT(10*RND) will show that each of the values 0, 1, 2, 3, 4, 5, 6, 7, 8, and 9 is equally likely to be picked. In other words, a long run of the program above will produce roughly equal numbers of 0's, 1's, 2's, and so on, although the order in which they appear will be random.

With some fiddling we can use RND to pick integers from any range. For example, what expression is needed in order to pick a number at random from the set {0, 1, 2, 3, 4, 5, 6, 7, 8, 9, 10}? the set {1, 2, 3, 4, 5, 6, 7, 8, 9, 10}? The answers are INT(11*RND) and INT(10*RND) + 1, respectively. Experiment by putting these expressions in line 120 of the program above.

In general, if N is a positive integer, the expression

INT(N*RND)

will pick integers at random from the collection

{ 0, 1, 2, 3, . . . , N-1 }

and the expression

INT(N*RND) + 1

will select them from

{ 1, 2, 3, 4, . . . , N }

Each integer in either of these ranges is equally likely to be picked.

Example

1. Suppose that we want to write a program which simulates the tossing of a coin. The program should choose to print, at random, either HEADS or TAILS in such a way that each is equally likely to occur. If we use the number 0 to represent HEADS and 1 for TAILS, then this problem is the same as picking a number at random from the pair $\{0,1\}$. This can be handled by INT(2*RND). The idea is illustrated by the following segment:

```
100        RANDOMIZE
110        PRINT "I TOSS THE COIN AND"
120        PRINT "IT COMES UP ";
130        LET T = INT(2*RND)
140        IF (T <> 0) THEN 160
150            PRINT "HEADS."
160   REM  ENDIF
170        IF (T <> 1) THEN 190
180            PRINT "TAILS."
190   REM  ENDIF
9999       END
```

Here is a typical run:

```
RUN
I TOSS THE COIN AND
IT COMES UP TAILS.
Ready
```

2. Here is an approach to the coin-tossing problem which avoids the use of INT. The function RND is equally likely to choose any number between 0 and 1 ($0 \leqslant$ RND < 1). So half the time it will pick numbers less than 0.5 and the other half numbers greater than or equal to 0.5. For this reason the following segment has the same effect as the one in example 1.

```
100        RANDOMIZE
110        PRINT "I TOSS THE COIN AND"
120        PRINT "IT COMES UP ";
130        LET T = RND
140        IF T > = 0.5 THEN 160
150            PRINT "HEADS."
160   REM  ENDIF
170        IF T < 0.5 THEN 190
180            PRINT "TAILS."
190   REM  ENDIF
9999       END
```

It is important to remember that RND calculates a new value every time it is called. The following example shows the dangers of forgetting this.

Example

This program segment:

```
100        RANDOMIZE
110        PRINT "I TOSS THE COIN AND"
120        PRINT "IT COMES UP ";
130        IF RND > = 0.5 THEN 150
140            PRINT "HEADS."
150  REM  ENDIF
160        IF RND < 0.5 THEN 180
170            PRINT "TAILS."
180  REM  ENDIF
9999       END
```

BAD PROGRAM

could produce this run:

```
RUN
I TOSS THE COIN AND
IT COMES UP
Ready
```

Why? What other forms can the output from this program take?   ■

Numbers are not the only things that can be chosen at random. RND can be used to select components of arrays as well as to pick letters and substrings from character strings. The following two examples illustrate these techniques. Analyze them carefully.

Examples

1.
```
100 REM TITLE: ANIMAL CROSS-BREEDING
110        DIM B$(12),E$(12)
120        RANDOMIZE
130        FOR I = 1 TO 12
140            READ B$(I),E$(I)
150        NEXT I
160 REM REPEAT
170                LET K = INT(12*RND) + 1
180                LET L = INT(12*RND) + 1
190            PRINT B$(K);E$(L)
200        GO TO 160
210 REM DATA:
220        DATA "SPAR","ROW"
230        DATA "HIPPO","POTAMUS"
```

```
240        DATA "ELE","PHANT"
250        DATA "CHIP","MUNK"
260        DATA "RAC","COON"
270        DATA "PHEA","SANT"
280        DATA "BUTTER","FLY"
290        DATA "GI","RAFFE"
300        DATA "KANGA","ROO"
310        DATA "RHINO","CEROS"
320        DATA "RAB","BIT"
330        DATA "BA","BOON"
9999       END
```

```
RUN

RABCOON
HIPPOSANT
RHINORAFFE
SPARROW
RHINOPOTAMUS
BAMUNK
CHIPSANT
RHINOROW
HIPPOPHANT
SPARBOON
PHEAROO
RHINOPHANT
PHEACEROS
BAPOTAMUS
RACSANT
RABFLY
```

2.
```
100 REM TITLE: THREE LETTER WORDS
110        RANDOMIZE
120        LET C$ = "BCDFGHJKLMNPQRSTVWXYZ"
130        LET V$ = "AEIOU"
140 REM REPEAT
150                LET I = INT(21*RND) + 1
160                LET J = INT(5*RND) + 1
170                LET K = INT(21*RND) + 1
180                LET B$ = MID(C$,I,1)
190                LET M$ = MID(V$,J,1)
200                LET E$ = MID(C$,K,1)
210                LET W$ = B$ + M$ + E$
220                PRINT W$;" ";
230        GO TO 140
9999       END
```

Run this program and see what it does.   ■

Both the examples above require certain string-handling facilities which are not provided on every system. In most cases IF blocks and subroutines can be used to handle these problems, although such an approach produces longer and more complicated programs. The following example uses randomly chosen comments, as well as a random secret number, to liven up the number guessing game.

Example

```
100 REM GUESSING GAME
110     RANDOMIZE
120     LET N = INT(20*RND) + 1
130     PRINT "I'M THINKING OF A NUMBER BETWEEN ONE"
140     PRINT "AND TWENTY. CAN YOU GUESS IT";
150 REM REPEAT
160             INPUT G
170             IF G = N THEN 300
180 REM         MACHINE INTERJECTS ENCOURAGEMENT:
190             LET R = INT(3*RND)
200             IF R <> 0 THEN 220
210                 PRINT "MISSED I'M AFRAID! GUESS AGAIN";
220 REM         END IF
230             IF R <> 1 THEN 250
240                 PRINT "BAD LUCK! HERE'S ANOTHER CHANCE";
250 REM         END IF
260             IF R <> 2 THEN 280
270                 PRINT "SORRY, THAT'S NOT IT! TRY ONCE MORE";
280 REM         END IF
290     GO TO 150
300     PRINT "YOU'RE A MIND READER! YOU GO IT!"
9999    END
```
■

So far we have concentrated on generating positive whole numbers by combining RND with INT. However, our choice is not limited to these. Here, for example, is an expression:

$$INT((N - M + 1)*RND) + M$$

which will generate any set of consecutive integers:

$$\{ M, M+1, M+2, \ldots, N-1, N \}$$

Example

The statement LET K = INT(11*RND) - 5 chooses numbers from the set $\{ - 5, -4, -3, -2, -1, 0, 1, 2, 3, 4, 5 \}$. ■

Suppose that we wanted to generate not just integers but decimal fractions. Suppose, for example, that we wanted to pick numbers at random from $\{0.5, 0.6, 0.7, 0.8, 0.9, 1.0, 1.1, 1.2, 1.3, 1.4, 1.5, 1.6, 1.7, 1.8, 1.9, 2.0, 2.1, 2.2, 2.3\}$. Notice that this set is just the set of integers $\{5, 6, 7, 8, 9, 10, 11, 12, 13, 14, 15, 16, 17, 18, 19, 20, 21, 22, 23\}$, all divided by 10. The expression

$$INT((23-5+1)*RND) + 5$$

that is

$$INT (19*RND) + 5$$

will choose numbers at random from the set of integers above, so

$$(INT(19*RND) + 5)/10$$

will choose numbers from the original set of decimal fractions.
  In general, the statement

$$LET X = (INT(((B-A)*10 + 1)*RND) + A*10)/10$$

will generate numbers, X, which lie in the range $A \leqslant X \leqslant B$ and can be represented with up to one digit to the right of the decimal (i.e., one decimal place). The statement

$$LET X = (INT(((B-A)*100 + 1)*RND) + A*100)/100$$

does the same with up to two decimal places.

Example

```
100 REM MULTIPLICATION EXERCISE
110     RANDOMIZE
120     LET A = (INT(900*RND) + 100)/10
130     LET B = (INT(900*RND) + 100)/10
140     PRINT "WHAT IS THE PRODUCT OF";A;"AND";B;
150     INPUT P
160     IF NOT (P = A*B) THEN 180
170         PRINT "CORRECT ANSWER. WELL DONE!"
180 REM END IF
190     IF NOT (P <> A*B) THEN 220
200         PRINT "SORRY, THE ANSWER IS";A*B;"."
210         PRINT "BETTER LUCK NEXT TIME!"
220 REM END IF
9999    END


RUN

WHAT IS THE PRODUCT OF 35.3 AND 72 ? 2521.4
SORRY, THE ANSWER IS 2541.6 .
BETTER LUCK NEXT TIME!

Ready
```

Can you identify the range of values from which the numbers for this exercise are being chosen?   ∎

Once one steps beyond the bounds of simple experiments, such as shooting craps with perfect dice and tossing perfect coins, one quickly comes to realize that the various outcomes of an experiment do not usually occur with equal frequency. For example, if each time one drove to the store, one had an even chance of being killed or of surviving, the supermarkets would be rather empty places. In reality, the chance of dying is very small and of returning home unscathed is correspondingly large. The next example illustrates one technique for handling the problem of unequal frequencies.

Example

Suppose that we wish to write a program to simulate the roll of a loaded die (one of a pair of dice!), that is, one where, in a long series of throws, the values 1, 2, 3, 4, 5, and 6 do not occur with equal frequency. Let's assume that the score 1 occurs slightly more often and 6 with less frequency than we would expect. In fact, let's suppose that

1 occurs 3/12 of the time
2 occurs 1/6 of the time
3 occurs 1/6 of the time
4 occurs 1/6 of the time
5 occurs 1/6 of the time
6 occurs 1/12 of the time

Rewriting the frequencies so that they have a common denominator:

Score	Frequency of Occurrence
1	3/12
2	2/12
3	2/12
4	2/12
5	2/12
6	1/12

we notice that the frequencies add up to 1. This is as it should be. After all, at every throw (i.e., 12/12 of the time) one of the six numbers has to appear.

Now we can view the experiment from a different perspective. Suppose that we put 12 balls in a jar, numbered as follows:

① ① ① ② ② ③ ③ ④ ④ ⑤ ⑤ ⑥

then the likelihood of picking a given number from the jar is the same as the likelihood that this same number will show when the biased die is thrown. For example, there are three balls in the jar with the number 1 stamped on them, so that there is a 3 in 12 (or 3/12) chance of picking a 1. This is the same as the chance of scoring a 1 when the die is thrown.

We can, therefore, imitate a throw of the die by simulating the choice of a ball. The latter can be handled as follows. Use an array of dimension 12 to represent the 12 numbered balls:

1	1	1	2	2	3	3	4	4	5	5	6
D(1)	D(2)	D(3)	D(4)	D(5)	D(6)	D(7)	D(8)	D(9)	D(10)	D(11)	D(12)

(D for die, of course!)

Then, to pick a ball (or throw the die), all we have to do is choose a component of the array, D, at random. The following program segment illustrates the technique.

```
100   REM   THROWING A BIASED DIE
110         DIM D(12)
120         RANDOMIZE
130         FOR I = 1 TO 12
140            READ D(I)
150         NEXT I
160         PRINT "I THROW THE DIE AND"
170         PRINT "THE SCORE IS";
180         LET J = INT(12*RND) + 1
190         PRINT D(J)
200   REM
210         DATA 1,1,1,2,2,3,3,4,4,5,5,6
9999        END
```

I could go on and on, adding more examples of ways to use the function RND, but your patience is probably wearing thin and, besides, it is much better for you to experiment for yourself. The next section contains my Parthian shot.

12.4 PROGRAMMING PROJECT: GAMBLING ON π†

Random numbers and gambling may seem very far removed from the kind of exact manipulations that are required to calculate a mathematical quantity

---

†This section presupposes a rudimentary knowledge of analytic geometry.

such as π. This project shows that the relationship is closer than one might think.

Imagine the following experiment: Draw a large square on the ground and inside it draw a circle that touches its sides. Then, take a bucket of small pebbles, stand back and start throwing them in the general direction of the square, being careful not to aim at any particular part of the figure. When you are done, you count the number of pebbles that landed in the square and also how many of these ended up inside the circle.

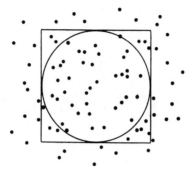

If you have been completely random in the way you threw the pebbles, every part of the square had an equal chance of being hit. So the ratio

$$\frac{\text{number of pebbles in the circle}}{\text{number of pebbles in the square}}$$

should be approximately equal to

$$\frac{\text{area of the circle}}{\text{area of the square}}$$

and the agreement should be better the larger the number of pebbles thrown.

Let's calculate the second ratio. Suppose that the radius of the circle equals R; then the sides of the square will be $2R$.

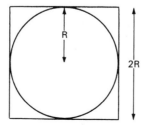

The area of the circle is $\pi R^{2\dagger}$ and that of the surrounding square is $(2R)^2 = 4R^2$. So that:

$$\frac{\text{area of the circle}}{\text{area of the square}} = \frac{\pi R^2}{4R^2} = \frac{\pi}{4}$$

We conclude, therefore, that $\pi/4$ is approximately equal to

$$\frac{\text{number of pebbles in the circle}}{\text{number of pebbles in the square}}$$

or

$$\pi \approx 4\left(\frac{\text{number of pebbles in the circle}}{\text{number of pebbles in the square}}\right)^{\ddagger}$$

In this way, the data from the pebble game can be used to get an estimate of the value of π.

The throwing of the pebbles is the weak point in this experiment. It is hard not to focus on the center of the figure and, thereby, favor the circle, so that the estimate for π is too large. The RND function can do a better job of this than a human being can. It is not seduced by the circle's perfect figure. So let's write a program to do this experiment for us.

Our method will be as follows. We will use RND to pick points at random from the square. The program will check each one to see whether it lies inside the circle and will keep track of the total number of points picked, N, as well as the number, C, which fall in the circle. Then it will calculate an estimate, P, of π by the formula

$$P = 4*C/N$$

Here is a preliminary description of the program:

Ask user how many points are to be picked from the square
Accept user's response (N)
Set counter (C), for points falling in the circle, to zero

---

†Remember that π or pi is the ratio of the circumference to the diameter of a circle.
$^\ddagger \approx$ means "approximately equal to."

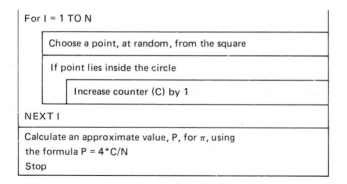

```
For I = 1 TO N

    Choose a point, at random, from the square

    If point lies inside the circle

        Increase counter (C) by 1

NEXT I

Calculate an approximate value, P, for π, using
the formula P = 4*C/N
Stop
```

The only part of the program that requires much discussion is the body of the FOR-NEXT loop. We must develop a method for generating random points in the square and a formula for testing whether these points lie inside the circle. Notice that the radius of the circle does not appear anywhere in the calculations, so we can choose its value to suit our convenience. We'll take the radius to be 1.

Half the battle in solving many a programming problem is finding the best mathematical vocabulary with which to describe it. In this case, the language of analytic geometry provides simple descriptions of the circle and the square. If we draw two perpendicular axes through the center of the circle, then the coordinates $(X, Y)^\dagger$ of a point P on its circumference:

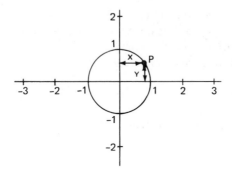

†Remember that the X-coordinate (Y-coordinate) of a point, P, is its perpendicular distance from the vertical (horizontal) axis.

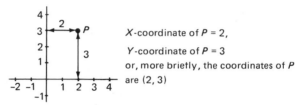

X-coordinate of $P = 2$,

Y-coordinate of $P = 3$
or, more briefly, the coordinates of P
are (2, 3)

satisfy the relation

$$X^2 + Y^2 = 1$$

Those that lie inside the circle satisfy

$$X^2 + Y^2 < 1$$

and those outside

$$X^2 + Y^2 > 1$$

Example

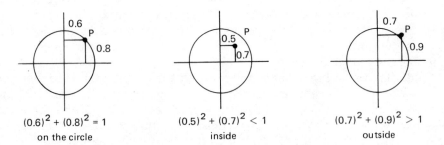

$$(0.6)^2 + (0.8)^2 = 1$$
on the circle

$$(0.5)^2 + (0.7)^2 < 1$$
inside

$$(0.7)^2 + (0.9)^2 > 1$$
outside ∎

If we interpret "the point lies inside the circle" as meaning "inside and not on the circumference," then this sentence can be rephrased as "the coordinates (X, Y) of the point satisfy $X^2 + Y^2 < 1$." Similarly, the coordinates (X, Y) of a point in the square satisfy

$$-1 < X < 1 \quad \text{and} \quad -1 < Y < 1$$

if we interpret "in" in the same strict sense.

Example

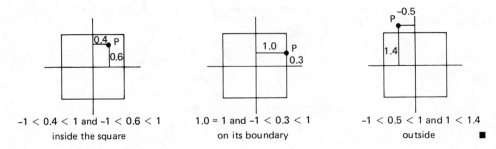

$-1 < 0.4 < 1$ and $-1 < 0.6 < 1$
inside the square

$1.0 = 1$ and $-1 < 0.3 < 1$
on its boundary

$-1 < 0.5 < 1$ and $1 < 1.4$
outside ∎

To choose a point at random from the square, all we have to do is pick two numbers, strictly between –1 and 1, to be its coordinates. The statements

```
LET X = 2*RND – 1
LET Y = 2*RND – 1
```

will generate values satisfying $-1 \leqslant X < 1$ and $-1 \leqslant Y < 1$. These are not quite the ranges we want, but we can handle that by discarding the value –1, if it should be generated, and picking the next value. Here is a translation of the FOR-NEXT loop:

```
FOR I = 1 TO N

    GENERATE THE COORDINATES OF A PT. IN THE SQUARE

    Repeat (exit when –1 < X)

        LET X = 2*RND –1

        Exit

    Repeat (exit when –1 < Y)

        LET Y = 2*RND – 1

        Exit

    DOES PT. LIE INSIDE CIRCLE?

    If X*X + Y*Y < 1

        LET C = C + 1

NEXT I
```

The construction of the rest of the program offers no difficulty. Here is a final version:

```
100 REM TITLE: ESTIMATION OF PI USING RANDOM NUMBERS
110 REM PROGRAMMER: A. KITCHEN          DATE: 7-JUL-81
120 REM VARIABLES:
130 REM        N = NUMBER OF POINTS CHOSEN FROM SQUARE
140 REM        C = NUMBER OF POINTS LYING IN CIRCLE
150 REM        X = X-COORDINATE OF POINT IN SQUARE
160 REM        Y = Y-COORDINATE OF POINT IN SQUARE
170 REM PROGRAM:
180     RANDOMIZE
190     PRINT "IN THIS PROGRAM, POINTS ARE CHOSEN AT"
200     PRINT "RANDOM FROM A SQUARE. THE FRACTION"
210     PRINT "OF THESE FALLING IN THE INSCRIBED"
220     PRINT "CIRCLE IS THEN USED TO ESTIMATE PI."
```

```
230        PRINT "HOW MANY POINTS ARE TO BE CHOSEN";
240        INPUT N
250        LET C = 0
260        FOR I = 1 TO N
270 REM           GENERATE POINT IN THE SQUARE:
280 REM           REPEAT
290                    LET X = 2*RND - 1
300                     IF -1 < X THEN 320
310               GO TO 280
320 REM           REPEAT
330                    LET Y = 2*RND - 1
340                     IF -1 < Y THEN 360
350               GO TO 320
360 REM           DOES POINT LIE INSIDE CIRCLE?
370               IF NOT (X*X + Y*Y < 1) THEN 390
380                    LET C = C + 1
390 REM           END IF
400        NEXT I
410        LET P = 4*C/N
420        PRINT "OF THE";N;"POINTS CHOSEN,";C;"FELL"
430        PRINT "INSIDE THE CIRCLE, GIVING AN ESTIMATE"
440        PRINT "OF";P;"FOR THE VALUE OF PI."
9999       END
```

Here is a typical run:

```
RUN

IN THIS PROGRAM, POINTS ARE CHOSEN AT
RANDOM FROM A SQUARE. THE FRACTION
OF THESE FALLING IN THE INSCRIBED
CIRCLE IS THEN USED TO ESTIMATE PI.
HOW MANY POINTS ARE TO BE CHOSEN? 5000
OF THE 5000 POINTS CHOSEN, 3919 FELL
INSIDE THE CIRCLE, GIVING AN ESTIMATE
OF 3.1352 FOR THE VALUE OF PI.

Ready
```

The peculiarity of this program is that, although the estimate of π does get better as more points are chosen, no two estimates will be exactly the same, even if the same number of points is used in both cases. The reason is, of course, that the points are random, so that the exact value of C/N is unpredictable. This is an example of what is called a **Monte Carlo method** (named after the gambling casinos of Monte Carlo in Monaco, the "Las Vegas" of Europe). Monte Carlo methods are numerical techniques that use random numbers and the principles of games of choice to calculate mathematical and physical quantities. There are faster and more accurate ways of calculating π. However, Monte Carlo methods can sometimes be used in situations where other approaches would be difficult or impossible to use, so they have a well-established, although minor role to play in the field of numerical calculation.

Chapter 12: EXERCISES

Section 12.1

No exercises.

Section 12.2

1. What kind of behavior do you observe if you run each of the following segments repeatedly?

(a)
```
100   RANDOMIZE
110   PRINT RND
120   PRINT RND
9999  END
```

(b)
```
100   PRINT RND
110   RANDOMIZE
120   PRINT RND
9999  END
```

(c)
```
100   PRINT RND
110   PRINT RND
120   RANDOMIZE
9999  END
```

(d)
```
100   REM  REPEAT
110        LET A = RND
120        RANDOMIZE
130        PRINT A
140        GO TO 100
9999       END
```

2. Experiment by running these program segments a number of times.

(a)
```
100        RANDOMIZE
110        LET C = 0
120        FOR I = 1 TO 10000
130          LET X = RND
140          IF X >= 0.5 THEN 160
150            LET C = C + 1
160   REM   ENDIF
170        NEXT I
180        PRINT "RND WAS BELOW 0.5";C;"TIMES OUT OF 10000."
9999       END
```

In the long run, does RND appear to pick values above and below 0.5 with equal likelihood? [*Hint: In other words, is the median of these values approximately 0.5? For a definition of the median, see Section 8.2, Exercise 12(b).*]

(b)
```
100   RANDOMIZE
110   LET S = 0
120   FOR I = 1 TO 10000
130     LET X = RND
140     LET S = S + X
150   NEXT I
```

```
160   LET M = S/10000
170   PRINT "THE AVERAGE OF 100000 VALUES OF RND IS";M;"."
9999  END
```
Is the average value always close to 0.5?

3.   Experiment with this program, entering different values for X.

```
100   RANDOMIZE
110   PRINT "#";
120   INPUT X
130   FOR I = 1 TO 20
140     PRINT RND(X);
150   NEXT I
9999  END
```

Do different values of X appear to change the behavior of RND(X)? If so, what effect do they have? Before committing yourself to an answer, confirm your conjecture by running the program repeatedly for different values of X. [*Hint: On some systems the argument X has no effect on RND; on others it does. Do sufficient experimentation to pin down exactly what is happening. Of course, you can always take the easy way out and look at the manuals.*]

Section 12.3

1.   Describe precisely the sets of numbers from which these expressions pick values.

(a) 20*RND   (b) INT(20*RND)
(c) INT(20*RND)/10   (d) INT(20*RND)/20
(e) INT(RND/10)*10   (f) INT(5*RND)*10
(g) INT(10*RND)*5   (h) INT(41*RND) – 1
(i) INT(6*RND) + 7   (j) (INT(17*RND) + 21)/100
(k) 0.1*RND + 0.5   (l) (INT(10*RND))^2
(m) 3^(INT(5*RND))

2.   Write expressions to pick numbers at random from these sets.

(a) {1, 2, 3, 4, 5, 6, 7}
(b) {0, 1, 2, 3}
(c) {95, 96, 97, 98, 99}
(d) {5, 10, 15, 20, 25}
(e) {1, 3, 5, 7, 9, 11, 13, 15, 17}
(f) {1.7, 1.8, 1.9, 2.0, 2.1, 2.2, 2.3}
(g) {0.25, 0.26, 0.27, 0.28, 0.29, 0.30}
(h) {–7, –6, –5, –4, –3, –2, –1, 0, 1, 2, 3}
(i) {1, 8, 27, 64, 125, 216}
(j) {1, 2, 4, 8, 16, 32, 64, 128, 256, 512, 1024}

3. In each case, write a program segment that will pick a value at random from the given set.
   (a) {1, 2, 3, 5, 8, 13, 21, 34, 55, 89, 144}
   (b) {"MISERABLE", "MOURNFUL", "MOROSE", "MOPISH", "MELANCHOLIC"}

4. (a) Write a program segment that will pick numbers at random from the set {1, 2, 3, 4, 5, 6, 7, 8, 9, 10}

   in such a way that, on average, each of the numbers 1, 2, 3, 4, 5 is picked three times as often as any of 6, 7, 8, 9, or 10.
   (b) Write a program segment that will pick words from the set {"ADEQUATE", "GOOD", "EXCELLENT", "QUINTESSENTIAL"} in such a way that "GOOD" occurs only half as often as "ADEQUATE", "EXCELLENT" half as often as "GOOD", and so on.

5. (a) Write a program to generate a list of at least 200 numbers, using the expression

   INT(11*RND)

   Run the program a number of times and keep tallies of the number of times each value generated appears in the list. Use this to check the randomness of RND: Does each value appear with approximately equal frequency? [*Hint: You can save a lot of work by having the computer keep the tallies for you. See Section 8.3 for the technique.*]
   (b) Write a program to generate a list of at least 200 numbers, using the expression

   INT(10*RND + 0.5)

   As in part (a), run the program and keep a record of the number of repetitions of each value picked. Do parts (a) and (b) produce the same range of values? Do you notice any differences in the frequencies of values produced by the two programs? If so, can you explain why?

6. (a) Write a program to toss a die (plural: dice) as many times as the user requires. It should keep track of the number of 1's, 2's, 3's, 4's, 5's, and 6's scored. Have it print these results as a bar chart. Verify that all scores appear with approximately equal frequency over the long run. [*Hint: See Section 7.5, Exercise 3, for a description of bar charts. You will need to scale your results down by a factor of 10, or 100, depending on the number of throws, in order to fit each bar on one line.*]
   (b) Write a program to throw two dice and keep tallies of the combined scores. Can you explain why this produces different results

from picking numbers at random from the set {2, 3, 4, . . . , 11, 12}? If you are not convinced that there is a difference, write a program to do the latter, too, and compare.

7. The Game of Craps: Write a program to simulate the throw of dice in the game of craps. The program should keep throwing until either you win or you lose. The rules are as follows:

   (1) If you shoot a "natural," 7 or 11, you win.
   (2) If you shoot "craps," 2, 3, or 12, you lose.
   (3) If you shoot 4, 5, 6, 8, 9, 10, that number becomes your "point." Throw until you make your point again or you shoot 7. If you make your point, you win; if you shoot 7, you lose.

   The program should print your throws until either you win or lose. It should repeat the game as often as you wish. For example:

   ```
   RUN
   THE GAME OF CRAPS:
   WANT TO SHOOT? Y
   6 2 11 9 4 6 YOU WIN!
   WANT TO SHOOT? Y
   2 YOU LOSE!
   WANT TO SHOOT? N
   Ready
   ```

8. Suppose that we have analyzed a sample of English text and have calculated approximate frequencies for the characters appearing in it (apart from punctuation). The following table summarizes our results:

Character	Average Repetitions per 125 Characters of Text	Character	Average Repetitions per 125 Characters of Text
Space	25	M	2
Apostrophe	2	N	6
A	9	O	8
B	2	P	2
C	2	Q	1
D	4	R	6
E	12	S	4
F	2	T	6
G	3	U	4
H	2	V	2
I	9	W	2
J	1	X	1
K	1	Y	2
L	4	Z	1

Generate nonsense "sentences" of between 60 and 80 characters, using characters picked at random according to these frequencies. [*Hint: I cheated! The frequencies printed here, apart from those for the space and apostrophe, were actually copied from my SCRABBLE board. You could produce your own statistics by counting the character frequencies in a chapter of a book by your favorite author. However, don't forget to count spaces; after all, they make the text readable by dividing it into words.*]

9. Write a program to deal a bridge hand, that is, 13 cards from a standard deck of 52. At the very least, each card in the hand should be printed as a letter (S, H, D, C) and a number (1–13), but you might try polishing up the output so that it prints the suits and the face cards in words, maybe even sorting the hand into suits. [*Hint: Internally, you can use the number 1 through 52 to represent the deck: 1–13 for spades, 14–26 for hearts, 27–39 for diamonds, and 40–52 for clubs. Beware: You must not deal the same card twice. Keep a running record of the cards chosen so far, so that you can discard duplicates.*]

10. (a) Write a program that will generate an arithmetic quiz, using random numbers. It should accept the student's answers, check them, and then print out the student's grade. A simple solution to this exercise would involve a program that sets 10 multiplication problems. However, a classier version might involve a choice in the number of questions, choice in the difficulty of the problems, mixtures of addition, subtraction, multiplication, and division (beware of division by zero), and so on.

    Give the grade as a percentage, rounded to the nearest integer. Remember to explain everything very clearly to the student, who is probably young, with little or no experience with computers.

    (b) Create a file MTH001 containing a class list for the course MTH 001. Write a program to generate arithmetic quizzes for this class, administer them, and store the students' grades in the file. The program should request the student's name before administering the quiz. If he or she has already taken it, a message to this effect should be printed and the program should stop immediately. Otherwise, the program should allow the student to take the quiz and should store the grade in the file.

    Write a program to allow the instructor to review the class list to check on grades and on those who haven't taken the quiz yet.

11. (a) Write a program to generate a file of 1000 random integers in the range 10,000 to 30,000. Such a file is useful as data for testing the performance of programs: for example, sorting programs. [*Hint: Make this file as big as possible; big data banks are more likely to expose differences of speed in competing programs. If you have room, increase the size of the file to 5000 numbers.*]

    (b) If you have already written more than one sorting program, you can use this file to compare the speed with which they sort. For a reliable comparison, you should test them repeatedly on a number of different lists. [*Hint: Such a test does not, in fact, tell the whole story. Some sorting techniques are better at sorting lists where there are relatively few inversions of order; others perform quite poorly in this case but excel with extremely jumbled lists. Their performance has to be judged in terms of the use to which you plan to put them.*]

(c) The principle behind statistical sampling is to estimate properties of a large population by picking a small number of members of the population at random and measuring those same properties for this sample. Statistical theory then states that these values can be used, with a certain degree of confidence, as estimates of the properties of the population as a whole. This, roughly, is the idea behind those predictions made by the television networks when they estimate the outcome of an election with only 20% of the vote tallied.

Write a program to pick 40 numbers at random from the file in part (a) and calculate their average and standard deviation. Run this program a number of times. Compare the values you get with the average and standard deviation for the whole file; you better write a program to calculate that. Apply this program to the file after it has been sorted by one of the programs in part (b). Do you notice any appreciable change in the sample average? [*Hint: Picking 40 numbers at random from a file is not as easy as it might, at first, sound. Here is a suggestion: Pick 40 integers at random from the range 1 to 1000, sort this list into increasing order, then use the sorted list to help pick numbers from the file. For a definition of standard deviation, see Section 4.5, Exercise 9.*]

Section 12.4

1. Write program segments to pick points at random from the regions given.
   (a) $1 \leqslant X < 2, -1 \leqslant Y < 0$
   (b) $-2 < X < 2, -2 < Y < 2$
   (c) $0 < X < 1, -2 < Y < 3$
   (d) $0 \leqslant X \leqslant 1, 0 \leqslant Y \leqslant 1$
   (e) $0 < X, 0 < Y$, and $X + Y < 1$
   (f) $X^2 + Y^2 \leqslant 4$
   (g) $-1 < X < 1, 0 < Y < X^2$

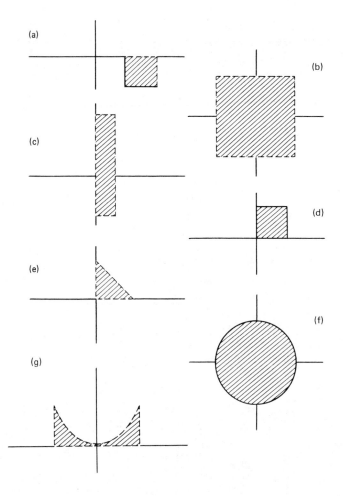

[*Hint: The dashed lines indicate that that part of the boundary is not included in the region. It is fairly easy to pick points at random from a rectangle of the form $a \leqslant X < b$, $c \leqslant Y < d$. For any other region, find a rectangle of this form which encloses the region and pick points from this rectangle. Throw away those that don't fall within the region.*]

2. Modify the program developed in this section so that it picks 20,000 points in groups of 1000 and prints a table showing the cumulative totals of all points picked and all points falling inside the circle, for every 1000 generated. The table should also print the successive estimates of π corresponding to these totals.

3. Use the Monte Carlo method to estimate the areas of these figures.

(a) The triangle $0 < X$, $0 < Y$, and $X + Y < 1$. Enclose it in the square $0 < X < 1$, $0 < Y < 1$.

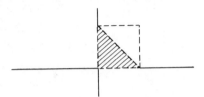

(b) The region $-1 < X < 1$, $0 < Y < 1 - X^2$, under the parabola $Y = 1 - X^2$. Enclose it in the rectangle $-1 < X < 1$, $0 < Y < 1$.

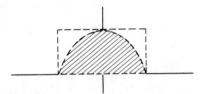

(c) The region $X^{2/3} + Y^{2/3} < 1$. The curve $X^{2/3} + Y^{2/3} = 1$ is called the astroid.

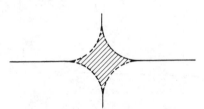

(d) The region $1 < X < A$, $0 < Y < 1/X$, where A is a fixed value picked by the user. This is the area under a section of the graph of $Y = 1/X$. Enclose it in the rectangle $1 < X < A$, $0 < Y < 1$. Compare the value you get for various A with the value of $\text{LOG}(A)$, for the same values of A.

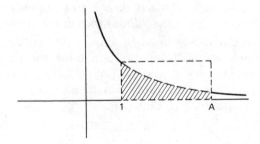

4. Kasje is played by two players with three dice. The aim is to throw certain scoring patterns and, further, to throw a better one than your opponent. The scoring throws, called kasjes, are (4, 1, 1), (4, 1, 2), (4, 1, 3), (4, 1, 4), (4, 1, 5), and (4, 1, 6). (4, 1, 6) is a better kasje than (4, 1, 5), (4, 1, 5) better than (4, 1, 4) and so on. Each player is allowed two throws in order to make his score, but not all the dice are thrown on the second try. If no 4 appears on the first throw [e.g., (2, 6, 1)], all three are thrown again; if 4 appears on the first throw but not 1 [e.g., (5, 4, 3)], the 4 is kept and the other two dice are thrown; if a 4 and a 1 appear on the first throw, the player may choose whether or not to risk throwing the third die to improve his kasje.

   When both players have thrown, the one with a kasje wins. However, if they both have scored, the game goes to the better kasje. Furthermore, the combination (4, 4, 4) wins over everything else, provided that it is gained in just one throw. If neither player gains a kasje or their scores are equal, the result is a draw.

   Write a program to play Kasje against the computer. Have the computer simulate the throw of dice for both players and, for simplicity, always have it play second.

   [*Hint: It should make the second throw for itself or its opponent automatically, unless the first throw is the combination (4, 1, ?). If the user throws this, the computer should give him or her the option to throw the third die or stand pat. If the machine throws (4, 1, ?), it should decide whether to throw the third die on the basis of its opponent's score. This is a simplified version of the game. For more on Kasje, see* The Master Book of Mathematical Recreations, *Fred Schuh, Dover Publications.*]

5. It is standard practice, when printing prose, to give a uniform appearance to each page by spacing the text so that every line ends exactly on the right-hand margin. Of course, certain lines, titles, paragraph ends, and special displays, are left untouched. This process is known as **right justification.**

   (a) Write a program to accept a piece of text and print it right-justified, according to the following procedure. Find the length of the longest line in the text, then fill the remaining lines with sufficient extra blanks to bring their lengths up to the maximum. Insert the extra blanks randomly between words in the line, but not before the first or after the last.

   [*Hint: For the techniques of text manipulation, see Section 9.6. You must protect title lines and the like from this surgery. You might, perhaps, end them with a special character.*]

   (b) Here is a more ambitious project. Write a program to accept text and then print it organized into 70 character lines, right-justified except for titles and ends of paragraphs. Words should not be broken by the end of a line.

[*Hint: The program will have to adjust each end-of-line marker, forward or backward, to make the line length as close as possible to, but not over, 70 characters. Then the line will have to be randomly padded with extra spaces.*]

6.   (a)   A drunk is standing on the end of a pier, which has railings down the sides but not at the end. It is 10 steps to the safety of the dock.

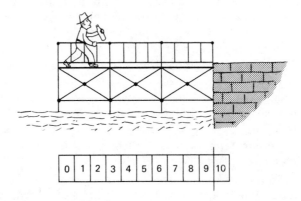

This man is "100 proof" drunk and has a 50/50 chance of staggering either backward or forward one step on each step he takes. What are his chances of falling off the end of the pier? They are more than 50%. Suppose that he performs this trick every night. On those nights in which he does make it to the dock, how many steps does he take, on average?

One way to get at least approximate answers to these questions is to perform the experiment. You can do it yourself, without getting drunk, by tossing a coin to decide whether to step forward or backward. Even better is to simulate it on the computer. Write a program to do this experiment.

(b)   Change the program in order to experiment with a "50 proof" drunk, one who steps forward twice as often as he steps back. What does the increased purposefulness of this man do to his chances of taking a swim? his average number of steps to safety?

(c)   Try other values for the likelihood of stepping forward. Change the length of the pier. What do these changes do to the outcome? [*Note: These experiments are examples of what statisticians call* **random walk.** *Two- and three-dimensional analogs of this process are used to model diffusion processes in physics. One well-known phenomenon accessible to this approach is that of Brownian motion, the random movement of microscopic particles suspended in liquid, produced by molecular collisions.*]

7.   You walk into your bathroom in the dead of night and hear a cock-roach skittering across the floor. You want to kill him, but the light doesn't work. So you must catch him in the dark.

Your bathroom floor has 10 rows of 15 tiles each, like this:

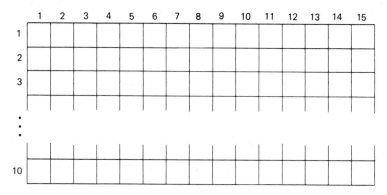

The cockroach is on one of the tiles. You try to get him by stepping on the correct one. Each time you stomp and miss, he moves to an adjacent tile.

Possible moves for cockroach:

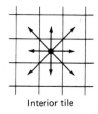
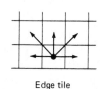

Interior tile   Edge tile   Corner tile

However, your friendly computer has a special bug sensor. If you type the row and column positions of the tile you have just stomped, it will tell you how many moves have occurred since the cockroach last visited that tile. Your score is the number of stomps before you squash him. Write a program to play this game. [*Hint: Use RND to generate the bug's moves; store the past history of its moves in a 10 by 15 matrix. Design the instructions to be clear and concise. Also, give the user the option to skip them. To speed up the response and make the game as exciting as possible, the output surrounding each move should be as brief as possible. Tune the game for maximum interest by making the room bigger or smaller and by experimenting with different floor plans.*]

Chapter 13

Computers
and Computing

13.1 INTRODUCTION

It is not necessary to know how an automobile works in order to drive one and, to a certain extent, the same is true of the computer and programming. The computer is an infinitely more complicated and intricate machine than the automobile and an explanation of its internal working is something we will not even attempt. However, it is possible for us to place this invention in historical perspective and that we will do.

In the last 40 years the computer has grown from an immense programmable scientific calculator to a processor of information, in the most general sense of this term. It is used to analyze, sort, correct, create, monitor, transmit, receive, encode, decode, and so on, information in the form of numbers, lists, text, electrical signals, visual images, sounds, movement, and so on. To say that it has grown is misleading. As the computer has become more powerful, it has shrunk from an instrument weighing tons to a portable device of not much more than 20 pounds. However, the true computer revolution has probably hardly begun. It may completely change the way that society views the machine and the uses to which it is put. Our use of the computer is still fairly clumsy, but it has outgrown its infancy as an exclusively scientific instrument to where it can be found in such diverse applications as data processing, the handling of airline reservations, supermarket checkout, the controlling of special effects for movies, arcade games, talking language translators, and control devices in automobile engines and household appliances. I believe that it is destined to become such an integral part of our lives that it will be as ever-present and as unnoticed as light switches and electric outlets are today.

13.2 COMPUTING BEFORE THE INDUSTRIAL REVOLUTION

Although the history of the computer, as we understand the term, reaches back only a little over 40 years,[†] human beings appear to have made instruments to help them with mathematical calculations from the earliest days of recorded civilization. Some were aids to memory; others provided assistance in computation.

From prehistoric times come the remains of notched tally sticks and knotted cords. These were apparently used to keep livestock records and as aids in counting. With increasing trade and the rise of a merchant class grew the need to calculate costs and make change. Out of this need came the counting table or abacus,[‡] a stone slab engraved with lines on which the four arithmetical operations (addition, subtraction, multiplication, and division) could be performed with pebbles.[§] A portable version of this early calculating machine, which substituted a wooden frame holding beads threaded onto rods for the table and its pebbles, traveled east to China and Japan, where it is still in common use. In the hands of an expert, it is a very fast machine.

One of the earliest mechanical calculators, an adding machine, is attributed to the great French mathematician, Blaise Pascal (1623–1662). Pascal, when he was about 20 years old, designed one for his father, a government official, to help him in performing tax calculations. In those days arithmetic was not considered a necessary part of an educated person's training. For example, neither Samuel Pepys[‖] nor, surprisingly, Gottfried Leibnitz[#] were taught to multiply as children, and both attempted to master it in later life.

Leibnitz's deficiency in arithmetic led him to improve on Pascal's "Machine Arithmetique" and, by 1673, he had produced a four-function calculator (addition, subtraction, multiplication, and division). Unfortunately, the machine was not very reliable. Leibnitz cannot be blamed for this; it was

---

[†]This rather unfairly discounts the pioneering work of Charles Babbage, but as we shall see, his contribution was seen to be important only in retrospect and had little direct effect on the pioneers of the 1940s.

[‡]Originally a sand-covered slab on which drawings were done, the ancient geometer's substitute for scratch paper.

[§]Calculi (Latin), whence the term "calculate."

[‖]1633–1703, English diarist and Secretary to the Admiralty.

[#]1646–1716, Gottfried Wilhelm von Leibnitz, mathematician, the codiscoverer with Isaac Newton of the calculus.

just that his design was beyond the rather meager engineering skills of the time. This struggle between ideas and technology occurs more than once in the history of computing. As we will see, it worked against Charles Babbage in the nineteenth century, but, on the other hand, the tide has been with the computer engineers of the last 40 years.

Although the machines of Pascal and Leibnitz are well known early prototypes of the mechanical calculator, they were not the first. It is one of the sad accidents of history that the first record of such a machine was lost until 1957, when it was discovered among the papers of Johannes Kepler. The inventor, Wilhelm Schickard, a fellow astronomer of Kepler, wrote to him in 1623 describing the machine in great detail.[†] Unfortunately, it was destroyed in a fire before it could be completed and Schickard himself perished in a plague a few years later, so his invention was lost to the world for over three centuries.

Refinements of the Pascal–Leibnitz machine were developed by others in subsequent years and, in fact, until the advent of the electronic hand-held calculator, devices built on these principles were the standard mechanical tools for anything but the most sophisticated calculations.[‡]

13.3 BABBAGE'S ANALYTICAL ENGINE

No major advances occurred in computing technology until the nineteenth century, when an Englishman, Charles Babbage (1791–1871), conceived and developed—at least in principle—the first programmable computer. This feat is particularly impressive when it is realized that Babbage had a grasp of the principal components and procedures associated with the modern computer over 100 years before any further attempts were made to build one.

Babbage moved in the center of the intellectual life of nineteenth-century England and his interests were immensely broad. He produced inventions and published papers and books in a number of fields, ranging from the design of medical equipment and diving gear, through railroad engineering, to efficiency studies of the postal service. For 12 years he held a professorship in mathematics at the University of Cambridge.[§] For all these accomplishments, he seems to have been a particularly unhappy and driven man. Over the years he became a slave to one overwhelming passion, to build a universal calculator. His principal claim to fame nowadays rests on his attempt, eventually unsuccessful, to complete this machine.

To be precise, he designed two machines. His first, the "Difference

---

[†] Great enough detail for a modern replica to be built and Schickard's claims for it verified.

[‡] We are ignoring that faithful friend of the engineer, the slide rule, which also dates from the seventeenth century. This too has, in the last 10 years, become an historical curiosity.

[§] He does not seem to have taken this duty particularly seriously, as there is no record of his ever having given a single lecture during his tenure there.

Engine," was more limited in scope, although still ambitious for its day. It was designed for the purpose of calculating and printing mathematical and nautical tables. These tables were, at that time, calculated by hand. This was tediously slow work and the resulting tables were not noted for their accuracy. For this reason the British government was persuaded, in 1823, to support his work. After many crises and stops and starts, the project finally died in 1842, when the government declared that it was no longer interested. The limitations of the technology of the time and Babbage's irascible personality both played a part in the failure of this project, but it also seems likely that he had lost interest in the Difference Engine because by 1833 he had already begun to lay the groundwork for the project that was to haunt him for the rest of his life. This he called the "Analytical Engine."

He was inspired by the Jacquard loom, a modification of the weaver's loom, which had been invented about 30 years earlier. On this machine patterns could be woven of an intricacy almost impossible to reproduce by hand. The lifting of the warp was "programmed" by a sequence of punched cards which allowed selected threads to be raised while the others stayed in place, so that the shuttle could pass between them.[†] Babbage realized that this same idea could be used to direct the operations of a calculating engine and, also, that data could be introduced into the machine in the same way. The uncanny foresight of this idea is shown by the fact that, until very recently, programs and data were introduced into almost every large system by means of punched cards.

Babbage realized that, besides the calculator part (which he called the "mill"), the machine needed a memory (Babbage's name for it, the "store," is still the preferred term in Britain) to save intermediate values produced during calculations. In one stroke, he encompassed all the major components of the modern computer:

1. The mill, which read the instructions and performed the calculations, present-day jargon refers to it as the **central processing unit**
2. The store, where numerical values were stored (Babbage's notes are unclear but it does not appear that he ever intended to store instructions here as well)
3. Program input, using punched cards
4. Data input using punched cards, and output onto cards or by means of a printer

The instructions punched on the cards were determined more by the

[†]As the pattern of threads to be lifted changed at almost every pass of the shuttle, the task would have been too complicated to do by hand. The Jacquard loom was popular in nineteenth-century America. Examples of Jacquard woven coverlets are still to be found in antique stores and attics. These coverlets displayed patriotic or floral motifs and were often done in two colors so that one face was the negative of the other—giving a summer and a winter side.

linkages that controlled the machine than by any attempt to mirror English or the language of mathematics. However, he anticipated the need for iteration (REPEAT loops) and branching (IF blocks).

The machine was an elaborate concoction of gears and drive shafts— completely mechanical—to be driven, like a grandfather clock, by falling weights. Unfortunately, this machine, too, was doomed. It was never completed, although Babbage continued to work on it sporadically until his death.[†]

The need for such a machine was not perceived by most of his contemporaries. Although the Analytical Engine promised great accuracy, it would not have been a great deal faster than a good human calculator. Perhaps, considering the nature of the science of that era, such accuracy was seen as more of a luxury than a necessity. There was a rather similar reaction in 1950 to the development of the electronic computer, when scientists estimated that no more than 10 computers would be required to fulfill all the computing needs of the United States for many years to come. No one knows how many machines are currently in operation, but it is known to exceed 1 million.

Some effort was made to continue what Babbage had started, but his work eventually dropped from public notice, forgotten until it was rediscovered on the eve of the computer revolution of the 1940s. This is not to say that more and more powerful calculating equipment was not developed. In fact, succeeding years produced a great range of sophisticated machines, each designed to do a specific type of scientific calculation (e.g., harmonic and differential analyzers) or business data processing operation (e.g., tabulators, sorters, collators). However, the idea of a general-purpose machine, which could be programmed to handle any kind of calculation or data processing problem, does not seem to have been considered again until just before World War II.

13.4   THE DATA PROCESSING REVOLUTION

Before we begin the recent history of computing, we will return to the late nineteenth century to pick up another thread in the tale.

As the United States grew in size and population, the effort and time required for the decennial census demanded by the constitution became monumental. During work on the 1880 census, John Shaw Billings, who was in charge of the analysis of the data, mentioned to an assistant, Herman Hollerith, that he felt there ought to be a way of mechanizing the tabulation

---

[†]He was assisted in this by Augusta Ada, Countess of Lovelace, the gifted daughter of the poet Byron, who was herself a mathematician.

of the census returns. One version of the story has him suggesting that such equipment might use the punched-card principle of the Jacquard loom.

In any case, Hollerith took upon himself the development of machinery to tally census data. By 1887, prototypes had been constructed, and by 1889 (in good time for the next census), he had already been able to test his invention on mortality statistics from the city of Baltimore. His equipment was chosen for the 1890 census and with it the analysis of the data was completed in just three years (it had been estimated that, without Hollerith's automatic tabulators, the 1890 census would not have been completed by 1900, the time of the next census).

Hollerith's machinery used cards, on each of which were punched the vital statistics of an individual. These cards were punched by hand at local offices and then sent to the central office, where they were placed one by one into a tabulating machine. The machine sensed the holes electrically and then advanced counters corresponding to the punched holes. In this way, simultaneous counts were made of the total population, number of foreign-born, number of males, females, children, and so on. As well as the tabulator, Hollerith designed a sorting machine which worked on a similar principle. The so-called IBM, or Hollerith, cards we use today are direct descendants of the 1890 census cards, even down to the cut-off corner, although the originals were only the size of a dollar bill in order to take advantage of existing equipment.

The success of the American experiment caught the attention of census takers in Europe, and the Tabulating Machine Company, which Hollerith established in 1896, flourished. Later Hollerith was to sell his company and it was a descendant of this corporation which, in 1924, became International Business Machines (IBM) under the guidance of Thomas J. Watson. The business world soon realized the suitability of tabulating equipment for its data processing needs and the ensuing demand was to build a number of major corporations, among them, of course, IBM itself.

In the late 1920s the astronomer Leslie John Comrie was the first person to apply tabulating equipment to scientific calculation, in the construction of tables of the moon's position. This was, in a sense, a turning point. Babbage's goal, the mechanization of scientific calculation, and Hollerith's, the mechanization of data processing, were converging. Eventually, it was to be seen that both these goals could be achieved by the same machine—a general-purpose information processor—the modern computer.

13.5 THE BIRTH OF THE ELECTRONIC COMPUTER

By the 1930s Babbage's pioneering work had been forgotten by scientists working in numerical computation. There is a little irony in the fact that

Babbage's dream should first be realized by a man who had never heard his name.

In 1938, a small mechanical computer, the Z1, which read its instructions from paper tape, was built by a German, Konrad Zuse. As the Z1 did not perform reliably, Zuse, with the help of Helmut Schreyer, worked on the development of an electronic version, and in 1941, the first fully operational program-controlled computer, the Z3, was working. Zuse and Schreyer, unfortunately, suffered a fate similar to Schickard and Babbage. Most of their work was destroyed in the war and a lack of funds prevented them from realizing their goal of a larger, more powerful, machine. The war, of course, put a complete blanket on news from Germany, so researchers in the United States and England labored in ignorance of developments there.

Meanwhile, similar developments were taking place in the United States, with one difference—major government and industrial support was forthcoming. In 1937, Howard Aiken, a graduate student in physics at Harvard who was working on some particularly difficult numerical calculations proposed that IBM punched-card and tabulating equipment could be combined under the direction of a paper tape controller to produce a powerful automatic calculator. Aiken collaborated with IBM engineers to build the Automatic Sequence Controlled Calculator, which has come to be known as the Harvard Mark I. This machine was first put into operation in 1944 and became the first program-controlled computer in the United States. Like Zuse's machine, it was largely mechanical in operation and therefore very slow by modern standards.†

Around the same time, George R. Stibitz at the Bell Telephone Laboratories began to investigate the use of telephone relays in the building of calculating equipment. By 1946 his group had produced a program-controlled machine. This read data and instructions from punched paper tape and, like the Harvard machine, was quite slow.

There is no doubt that there comes a time when an idea is ripe for the picking, and when this happens it is hard to sort one's way through all the separate and simultaneous discoverers. This is particularly true of the computer. Around 1840 the idea was there, but neither the need nor the technical know-how really existed. By 1940 the need and the technology were there and the idea just seems to have sprouted everywhere, at various levels of sophistication.

John V. Atanasoff, a professor at what is now Iowa State University, became impressed with the reaction time of electronic circuitry‡ and began to investigate the processing of data by electronic means. He apparently had a prototype running by 1940. His machine was a special-purpose calculator designed explicitly for solving systems of linear equations and so does not

---

†Aiken estimated it to be about 100 times faster than a manual calculator.
‡Principally the vacuum tube.

qualify as the first general-purpose electronic computer. Its importance lies in the fact that Atanasoff's ideas influenced John W. Mauchly.[†] Mauchly was also aware of the developments at Bell Labs and by 1942 he had become deeply interested in the idea of using electronic components to build a high-speed computer.

By 1943, a group including Mauchly, J. Presper Eckert, and Herman H. Goldstine was assembled at the University of Pennsylvania to develop a high-speed electronic calculator for the war effort, principally to produce ballistics tables.[‡] Out of this group came, in 1946, the Electronic Numerical Integrator and Calculator, ENIAC. This machine was a step backward in some ways, as it was programmed by means of plugboards, something like an old telephone exchange, by which the circuits to perform the individual arithmetical operations and logical decisions were physically wired in sequence to produce a program for the complete calculation. Programming was, therefore, an incredibly tedious and lengthy process. It often took days just to complete the wiring. However, the speed of the machine once it was programmed was truly stupendous. The Harvard Mark I took about 3 seconds to perform the multiplication of two 10-digit numbers. ENIAC took a thousandth of that time, 0.003 second (3 milliseconds). Built with over 18,000 vacuum tubes, it was the first programmable electronic computer. The ENIAC experiment was immensely successful and with modifications it remained in use until 1955.

The difficulties involved in changing the programs on the ENIAC, as well as its limited data storage capacity,[§] led to the idea of expanding internal memory and storing programs in the same area as the data. Before ENIAC was completed, a proposal for a faster and more flexible computer, whose instructions could be stored electronically, was developed. The draft report on this machine, EDVAC (Electronic Discrete Variable Arithmetic Computer) was submitted by John L. von Neumann in 1945. Von Neumann (1903-1957), a mathematician who is considered one of the giants of twentieth-century science, is often credited with having invented the stored program concept. Although the details on this matter are not clear, it is certainly true that he was the first to see the power of this idea and to see computing as a logical process rather than as a part of engineering. His insights into the problems of computer design have had a significant influence on the direction of computer science since those early years.

Let's take a moment to discuss why the idea of storing instructions in

---

[†]In a patent suit in the early 1970s, Atanasoff was awarded prior discovery of the principles of electronic computing over Eckert and Mauchly.

[‡]These tables incorporated information on the size and weight of shells, the power of the explosive charge that drove them, wind speed and direction, and so on, to give angles of elevation and direction for the firing of large guns.

[§]Over 300 constant values could be set up by means of switches before the execution of a program, but no more than 20 variables could be stored while a program was running.

memory, as opposed to executing them directly from tape or cards, has been such an important one. First of all, it certainly produces faster execution times because, with the instructions stored internally, the machine is not continually reading the tape or cards, a relatively slow process. Also, the repetition of segments of code (REPEAT loops) is much easier to handle when all the code is in memory. However, the most important effect of the idea, historically, was to free computer designers from the absolute distinction between instructions and data. We see the effects of this in modern programming languages in two ways. First, instructions can be changed. We saw, in Chapter 10, that the destination of the RETURN statement depends on where its subroutine was called from. As stored in the memory of the computer, the RETURN statement contains a variable part.[†] It is, in a sense, GO TO X, where the value of X may be changed during the execution of the program. Second, a program can be considered to be data. This idea was crucial to the development of languages such as BASIC, which are not the natural languages of computers. Programs written in such a language must be translated into **machine language** (the internal switching codes which control the circuits of the computer) before they can be executed. For this, they must be treated as data and fed to a special program that performs the translation.

To return to the EDVAC, it was completed in 1951 and can truly be considered the prototype of the modern computer. In the words of Mauchly, what he called an "EDVAC-type machine" had: "(1) an extensive internal memory; (2) elementary instructions, few in number, to which the machine will respond; and (3) the ability to store instructions as well as numerical quantities in the internal memory, and to modify instructions so stored in accordance with other instructions."[‡] Those "elementary instructions" form what is now called machine language. By extensive memory he meant "memory, accessible at electronic speeds, of the order of a thousand numbers each of perhaps 10 digits." This is a very small memory by modern standards even for a home computer.

The EDVAC was not the first stored program machine to be completed. In England, computing equipment was being developed concurrently with the American effort and scientists there were well aware of von Neumann's draft report on EDVAC. The British response to this was EDSAC (Electronic Delay Storage Automatic Calculator), completed two years earlier than EDVAC in 1949.

Von Neumann, meanwhile, had gone on to become the major force in the development of a refinement of the EDVAC concept. This computer, the IAS or von Neumann machine, was completed in 1952 at the Institute for Advanced Study at Princeton. Von Neumann's reports on the development of this machine served the scientists and engineers of the time as a textbook in computer design.

[†]This fact is masked by the form of the RETURN statement in BASIC.

[‡]J. W. Mauchly, "Preparation of problems for EDVAC-type machines," Proceedings of a Symposium on Large Scale Digital Calculating Machinery, 1947.

The completion of the IAS machine marked the end of the first phase of computer development. From that point on, the universities would begin to leave the construction business, and would also cease to be the major users of computing equipment. Computer building was about to become a lucrative commercial endeavor.

13.6 THE SUCCEEDING GENERATIONS

In 1946, Eckert and Mauchly had formed a company to design and build computers. In 1950, their company was taken over by Remington Rand, which itself was soon to become part of the Sperry Rand Corporation. In 1951, the company delivered its first product, a UNIVAC-1, to the Census Bureau and by 1954, the first computer to be devoted purely to business data processing, another UNIVAC-1, had been installed at a General Electric plant in Kentucky. However, IBM was not far behind. Their collaboration with Aiken on the Harvard Mark I had brought them into the computer business quite early, and they soon developed their own machine, the 701. This was followed quickly by a number of other models, including the IBM 650, a relatively inexpensive machine. This machine pulled computing into the assembly line age. By the end of 1955, well over 100 of these machines were in operation and IBM had accepted orders for another 750.

The early electronic computers used vacuum tubes. The tubes required large amounts of power, generated quantities of heat, and had short lifetimes (ENIAC, with its 18,000 tubes, blew about one a day). In 1948, the transistor was invented and the timing could not have been better. By the time this device was commercially available, the computer had outgrown its teething pains. Transistors require very little power. They are very reliable and, above all, small, so computers rapidly became more reliable and economical to run as well as smaller and more powerful. These second-generation, solid-state machines dominated the market through the early 1960s. However, with the unveiling of IBM's System/360 family in 1964, the so-called third generation of machines was born. These machines started the trend toward increased miniaturization with their **integrated circuit chips** (microscopic transistor-based circuits on wafers of silicon smaller than a postage stamp). Miniaturization has continued at a reckless pace and shows little sign of slowing. At the present time, the circuitry for a computer more powerful than ENIAC can be put onto a chip of silicon no more than one-fourth of an inch square.

The birth of what is now called the **microcomputer** was really an accident. In 1972, an integrated chip manufacturer, Intel, was left with an apparently useless product on their hands, the 8008 chip. They had designed this chip for Display Terminals Corporation, to be used in the control of a video display terminal. The 8008 performed correctly but was too slow, so they dumped it on the market. By accident, someone stumbled on the fact that this chip could be used for general-purpose computing and the microcomputer age had begun. A year later, Intel introduced an improvement, the 8080 microprocessor chip, and other companies began to jump on the bandwagon. Currently, there are many different microprocessor chips available. Among the most popular are the Z80 (used in the TRS-80 microcomputer), the 6502 (in the Apple computer), and the 6800 (used by Southwest Technical Products Corporation).

The first microcomputers were sold as kits, the feeling being that such equipment would be of interest only to a small coterie of computer buffs. However, it quickly became apparent that the demand was wider than this, and numerous small companies sprang up overnight to manufacture microcomputers and supporting equipment (peripherals). Now this is a thriving industry with computer stores in most larger cities, so much so that even as venerable an old giant as IBM is stooping to catch a little of the action with its "IBM Personal Computer."

By the mid-1970s, reliable home computer systems were available for around $1000. Now there are some small systems which sell for less than $300. At the other end of the scale, very large machines have not really dropped in price, but the power and capacity per dollar of investment has increased dramatically. For example, the average large system in 1960 might have had memory space for 150,000 characters, with room for perhaps 10 to 50 million characters in mass storage (usually, magnetic tapes). In 1980, for the same cost one could have a system with over 50 million characters of main memory and practically unlimited secondary storage. Meanwhile, the processing time for one computer instruction has dropped from about 5 microseconds (5 millionths of a second) in 1960 to about 5 nanoseconds (5 billionths of a second) in 1980.

13.7 THE DEVELOPMENT OF PROGRAMMING LANGUAGES

Along with the growth in the use of computing equipment (**hardware** is the current term) has gone the development of more sophisticated ways of communicating instructions and data to the computer.

The early computers received their instructions coded on punched paper tape or, like ENIAC, had them wired in on plugboards. The advantage of plugboard programming was that the instructions could be executed at electronic speeds, whereas the use of paper tape slowed the speed of execution to the rate at which instructions could be read from the tape. Through the 1950s and 1960s the most popular vehicle for entering instructions and data was the punched card, probably because of IBM's dominance of the field. The fact that the instructions could be stored in memory compensated for the relative slowness of the card reader so that the actual execution of the program was not compromised. Of course, this advantage is realized only if the program, once stored, is used over and over again.

It was becoming quite clear, however, that the real bottleneck in computing occurred in the writing and debugging of the programs. The instructions given to the machine took the form of coded switching patterns for its internal circuits, what is called **machine language.** The codes were different for each make of computer and, although the card and tape punching equipment was designed so that numbers could be typed in to produce the machine instructions, program coding was still a forbidding task involving the memorization of long strings of digits. The reading and debugging of these programs was very difficult, so that programming was slow and demanded highly trained technicians.

Many researchers began to realize that, for programming to be done quickly and efficiently, the instructions should be easy to remember and the programmer should be able to read and check the code rapidly for errors. A number of experimental codes were developed and by 1954, IBM had sponsored a committee headed by John Backus to design a scientific language for programming, using mathematical notation instead of machine codes. In 1957, the first version of this language, FORTRAN,[†] was commercially available. In Europe similar developments gave rise to the language ALGOL.[‡] FORTRAN has gone through many revisions, the latest being FORTRAN-77, but still preserves the style of its original version and therefore qualifies as the oldest currently available computing language. BASIC,[§] designed in 1963–1964 at Dartmouth College by John Kemeny and Thomas Kurtz, was developed from FORTRAN as a language for teaching the elements of programming. It still holds center stage as the most popular introductory language, but is challenged by such languages as APL[‖] and Pascal.[#] COBOL,[††] first offered commercially in 1961, was designed by a committee from the universities, business, and government for use in general data processing. Here the requirement was that programs be readable by nonscientists, so COBOL programs use English words and phrases instead of mathematical notation.

All the above are examples of **higher-level languages.** Their syntax is intended to make them readable by human beings, in contrast to machine languages, which are designed for machines. Of course, this description begs the question: How on earth does the machine execute a program in a language like FORTRAN or BASIC? The answer is that the program first has to be

[†]**FOR**mula **TRAN**slation.
[‡]**ALGO**rithmic **L**anguage.
[§]**B**eginner's **A**ll-purpose **S**ymbolic **I**nstruction **C**ode.
[‖]**A** **P**rogramming **L**anguage.
[#]In honor of Blaise **PASCAL.**
[††]**CO**mmon **B**usiness-**O**riented **L**anguage.

translated into machine language before the computer can run it. Who does the translating? The computer of course! This sounds impossible, like lifting oneself up by one's bootstraps. In fact, the manufacturer of the machine provides a program written in machine language, which can take instructions written, say, in FORTRAN and translate them into machine language. Such a program is called a **compiler**. A compiler takes as its data the original FOR-TRAN program (the **source code**) and produces a machine language transla-tion (the **object code**). Each compiler is designed to translate programs in just one language. For example, on a system that runs both FORTRAN and COBOL programs, there must be two compilers, one for each language.

Once a FORTRAN program has been compiled (or translated), the compiler is saved on magnetic disk or tape and the machine translation of the FORTRAN code can be executed. Thus, running a program is a two-step process (actually there is a third step, which we will ignore):

1.   The program is translated into machine language.
2.   The resulting machine language program is executed.

The first step may take a long time if the program is a big one, but once the program is translated it can be saved in its machine language form and run whenever it is required.

BASIC programs, however, are usually handled in a slightly different way. It was decided, at an early stage in the development of this language, that the two-step compiler process would be somewhat confusing to a beginner and would slow down the feedback from mistakes, so necessary when learning a new skill.

Suppose that you have written a BASIC program and typed RUN. A program called an **interpreter** reads each statement of the BASIC program in turn, translates it into machine code, and immediately executes this code before moving on to the next statement. Thus the two steps, translation and execution, are performed simultaneously.

The advantage of this approach is that it is simple for the user—just type in the instructions and RUN! The disadvantages are:

1.   The interpreter has to stay in memory while the program is running, and so takes up valuable space.
2.   As translation and execution are combined, the BASIC program runs much slower than a corresponding FORTRAN program, translated by a compiler ahead of time.

On a modern machine, with large memory capacity and a high-speed processer, these disadvantages are hardly noticeable, particularly since most BASIC programs are written by beginners and so tend to be small.

To summarize, we have seen that language translators for higher-level languages take two forms: compilers, which translate programs into machine code for later execution, and interpreters, which translate and execute programs statement by statement. FORTRAN and COBOL are compiler languages and BASIC is most often handled by an interpreter. In fact, in many of the popular microcomputers the BASIC interpreter is a permanent part of the machine, residing in a special memory called **read-only memory** (ROM).

13.8 THE SOFTWARE CRISIS

The programs supplied with a computing system are referred to as **software** to distinguish them from the equipment itself—the hardware. As well as compilers and interpreters, the manufacturer will supply other software: programs to control card readers, and punches, line printers, terminals, tape drives, disk drives, and ones to help schedule the jobs (the user programs, etc.) to be run on the system. This collection of programs is referred to as the **operating system** for the computer. We mentioned **time sharing** in the first chapter (remember that this is a method by which a number of users can run programs on a system simultaneously). The scheduling problems for a multiuser system of this type involve the most intricate timing of interruptions to programs and rapid swapping of code and data between memory and the disk. Such operating systems are among the most complex objects ever designed.

As well as the operating system and the language translators, the manufacturer may provide other programs for editing and sorting files, and performing general housekeeping functions. Packages of application programs are available: programs to do statistical analysis, routines to calculate values of specialized mathematical functions, plot graphs, word processing programs, games—the list is almost inexhaustible. Many of these will be written in higher-level languages; FORTRAN is one of the most popular for this.

The software contributes to making the computer a flexible and powerful tool. In fact, without all these programs the computer would be practically useless, just a box of electronic junk. So, software is just as important as the hardware and, what is more, just as expensive. As hardware gets cheaper and more powerful, the true limitation on computing power has become clear. Human beings cannot write reliable software fast enough to take advantage of the power of the machines they are building. Major computer users are finding that their computing budgets are being swallowed up by the costs of software development and maintenance, and the major part of this cost is going toward the checking and correcting of programming errors.

It is this software crisis which, in the last 10 years, has led to the popularization of the concepts of **structured programming** and **top-down program development**—in other words, to attempts to establish a systematic science of program writing. New languages have been developed (e.g., Pascal, designed by Nicklaus Wirth in Switzerland), old languages have been given face lifts (e.g., FORTRAN-77) and more systematic approaches to the writing of programs in the old unimproved languages are being adopted (REPEAT and IF blocks and structured flowcharts, as discussed in this text). The verdict is not in on these and other more experimental ideas, but all evidence points to the fact that we still haven't found our way out of the software jungle. Computer science is still waiting for new ideas that will point the way to better methods of controlling computers.

13.9 A QUICK LOOK UNDER THE HOOD

The modern computer is a beast of infinite variety, from huge machines, the **mainframes,** with storage for millions of characters and awesome power, through the **minicomputers,** more modest machines with sufficient power to service a small business or a college, down to the **microcomputers,** small low-priced desktop models suitable for home computing. Computers are often linked together in what is called a **network,** so that they can share common programs and data. Sometimes minis or micros will serve a large mainframe, handling small jobs themselves but passing major ones back to the master computer.

In spite of their diversity, computers have not really changed their organizational structure radically since the days of EDVAC and the IAS machine. Every computer contains the following units:

1. A **central processing unit (CPU)** consisting of a **control unit,** which interprets the machine instructions and directs the functioning of the computer, and an **arithmetic and logic unit** (ALU), which performs all calculations and makes logical tests
2. An internal memory for storing programs and data
3. Input and output devices: terminals, card readers, punches, line printers, plotters, disk and tape drives

We will take a brief look at a typical microcomputer to get a feeling for how the major components are organized.

If we open the computer cabinet, we will find that it contains a power supply and a number of parallel circuit boards. These boards are not fixed permanently into the cabinet. You will find that they can be removed quite easily. Each board has up to 100 electrical contacts projecting from its in-board edge which plug into a slot in the back plane of the computer. They actually make connection with a set of signal lines (called the **bus**) which allow information and signals to be sent from one part of the computer to another. The bus runs the length of the back plane and—here is the beauty of the concept—to add more memory or expand the computer in other ways, essentially all that has to be done is to plug more boards into the bus. Every board has access to the signals on the bus and can place signals on it, too. So the bus is, as its name suggests, public transport for moving information from one part of the computer to another.

Let's look at the individual boards. Each one is encrusted with black plastic rectangles of various sizes. A closer inspection will show that each of these rectangles is plugged into a socket on the board by means of anywhere from 8 to 40 pins. These units are called **DIPs (dual in-line packages)** and they contain the integrated circuit chips that constitute the computer.

One board holds a particularly large 40-pin DIP, about 2 inches long. This board is the **processor board,** and the 40-pin DIP contains the **micro-processor chip,** which is the heart of the computer. The large package belies its contents. The actual size of the chip is about one-fourth of an inch square. The package only has to be this big in order to hold all 40 connector pins. The microprocessor is essentially the CPU (central processing unit) of the computer plus a small number of very high speed memory locations called **registers,** which help to improve the performance of the computer.

Other boards contain regular arrays of smaller chips; these are the **memory boards.** Each chip contains a small amount of storage and there may be as many as 32 of them to a board.

For each **peripheral device** (terminal, tape recorder, disk drive, etc.) there will be a board called an **interface board,** which controls it. Schematically, the computer looks like this (the double-headed arrows indicate the flow of information):

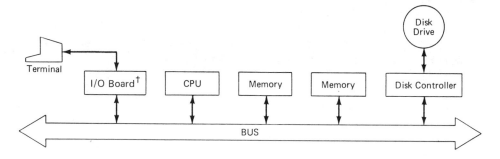

Boards can be added to provide extra facilities: for example, more memory can be added, a controller board for a printer, a board to provide high-resolution graphics, a music synthesizer, a speech synthesizer, and so on.

As the microprocessor chips in most home computers do not vary much in performance, there is a tendency to measure the power of a microcom-

†I/O means input/output.

puter by the amount of memory it has. Memory capacity is given in terms of the number of characters it can hold. The unit of storage occupied by one character is referred to as a **byte**. Thus a memory of 1000 bytes has room for 1000 characters. Most quantities in computer science seem to be measured in powers of 2, and memory is no exception.[†] It is measured in multiples of 2^{10}, which is 1024 or approximately 1000 and is written as K.[‡] Thus 32K bytes of memory indicates a capacity of over 32,000 characters (32×2^{10} = 32,768, to be exact). A minimum amount of memory for any useful work is 4K bytes. However, the normal range is 16K to 32K bytes. At the other extreme, the internal structure of most microprocessors limits the amount of memory that can be used to a maximum of 64K, unless special tricks are played.

As we discussed in an earlier section, many small systems have a BASIC interpreter permanently resident in a special type of memory, called **read-only memory** or **ROM**. Information in read-only memory cannot be erased and so is permanently stored. Software stored in ROM is often called **firmware**, to indicate its permanence.

Other systems, particularly those with built-in disk drives, must load the BASIC interpreter from the disk before a program can be run. This may sound like an inconvenience, but, in fact, it gives more flexibility to the system. As the interpreter is not a permanent resident, it can be replaced by other language translators if required so that the system is not tied to just one language.

Long-term storage on the cheapest microcomputer systems is handled by means of a cassette tape recorder. However, storage and loading of programs is a slow process and work with files is very limited.

The most popular and cheapest type of disk storage is the **floppy disk**. It consists of a small rectangular unit with a "mail slot" in the front, the **disk drive**. The floppy disk itself, a small flexible plastic disk about 5 inches in diameter and sealed in a protective sleeve, is pushed into the slot. The surface of the disk has a magnetic coating, and information is coded on it using the same principle as magnetic tape. The drive, which is connected to a disk controller board in the computer, rotates the disk when commanded and reads information from it or writes it on it. These operations are handled by the operating system through the disk controller board.

A single floppy disk has a capacity of around 150K bytes. For more mass storage extra drives can be added. Larger and faster disk storage systems are also available. These are, however, much more expensive.

Although we have only covered the microcomputer, the discussion should give you some idea of the physical structure of a computing system—

[†]This is related to the fact that the internal arithmetic of a computer is binary, or baze 2, arithmetic. This is not a matter of great importance to a BASIC programmer. However, note that in this connection, a byte is by definition eight binary digits or bits.

[‡]K, said "kay" as in "thirty-two kay," is derived from the suffix kilo—representing 1000.

but remember, such is the rate of development of computer hardware that some details will already be out of date by the time you read this.

13.10   THE COMPUTER IN SOCIETY

The computing field, these days, is a very exciting one. The applications of this device are limited only by our own imaginations. Its limitations arise from our limitations. It can be put to good uses, ones that genuinely save work or make a positive contribution to society (e.g., airline reservations systems, computerized weather forcasting, automation of telephone equipment), to silly ones (computerized dating services, biorhythm calculations), and destructive ones (weapon controllers, data banks on dissidents and political activists). The computer is a tool, a very reliable and efficient one, and, as a tool, is morally neutral. It should not be blamed for our excesses.

One of the greatest dangers in the current use of the machine as a data processor is that it tends to have the same deadening effect on individual initiative as the most inflexible bureaucracy. We have all had the experience of being told by a bank or a department store that "this cannot be done, because it won't go through the computer" or "the computer will reject it." It is important to understand that this inflexibility is not an unavoidable side effect of the use of computers. It is not a quality of the computer, but arises out of the philosophy of the programmers who design the software and of the companies who use the equipment. Our goal should be to allow the computer to function as the flexible tool that it truly is.

We should hope that future generations will see the computer, like the pen and the printing press, as being an instrument by which human beings have extended their intellectual reach and improved the quality of their lives.

Appendix

I

Two Case Studies:
The TRS-80
and Apple
Microcomputer
Systems

In the text we discussed a multiuser system, BASIC-PLUS, running under the RSTS-E time-sharing system on a DEC PDP-11 minicomputer. Although the PDP-11 computers are not large when compared with some of the systems to be found in big universities and businesses, they are representative of large machine style, at least from the point of view of someone programming in BASIC.

In this appendix we try to show the other end of the spectrum by discussing two popular microcomputer systems. Tandy Radio Shack and Apple Computer produce systems of equal power and provide similar ranges of enhancements and gadgets. However, in order to illustrate the diversity of systems that run BASIC, we will discuss a limited Radio Shack system which uses a cassette tape recorder for mass storage and a more well-appointed Apple system with a "floppy" disk drive.

We will find that the dialects of BASIC provided on the two machines are not that different in power. However, the disk-based system is definitely more flexible, as far as the management of programs is concerned, and a little closer in style to the DEC system. Incidentally, neither Radio Shack Model III BASIC nor Applesoft BASIC conform completely to the standard for minimal BASIC set by the American Standards Institute in 1978.

The descriptions given below are not intended to be exhaustive introductions to the two systems. They are meant to give you a feeling for the differences between these machines and the DEC system featured in the text.

PART 1   The TRS-80 Model III
with cassette tape storage

1.   The System

The TRS-80 Model III microcomputer has provision for the insertion of two disk drives in its main cabinet. However, to illustrate the use of a cassette tape drive for long-term storage we will discuss an economy model without these enhancements. The system consists of two major components. They are:

The Computer: This looks like a television set with a typewriter keyboard sprouting from it. To the right of the screen there is space for the addition of two disk drives, which, we will assume, are not in place.

The Cassette Tape Recorder: This is an ordinary tape recorder. It will be used for the long-term storage of programs and data.

The computer and the recorder are plugged into standard electrical outlets and are connected together by means of a short cable.

2.   Logging In and Out

Once the system is set up, the power-up (log-in) procedure is very simple: turn on the POWER switch under the right-hand edge of the keyboard. After a few seconds, the message

    CASS? _

will appear on the screen. Do not type anything, just press the ENTER key. The computer will respond with

    MEMORY SIZE? _

Once again, just press the ENTER† key. The computer responds

```
RADIO SHACK MODEL III BASIC
(c) '80 TANDY
READY
—
```

We have no need, at this time, for the options offered by CASS? and MEM-ORY SIZE?, so we will ignore them. Information on them can be found in the Model III Reference Manual. The following example summarizes the complete procedure.

Example

Turn on power:

```
CASS? ●
MEMORY SIZE? ●
RADIO SHACK MODEL III BASIC
(c) '80 TANDY
READY
⟩ _                                                          ■
```

You can now start writing BASIC programs!

At the end of a session on the computer, all you have to do is switch off the power. If you have been using the cassette recorder, press the STOP button on that device, too.

3.   Entering a BASIC Program

Begin by typing NEW and pressing ENTER:

```
⟩ NEW ●‡
READY
⟩ _
```

This clears your workspace in preparation for entering a program. Notice that whenever the computer completes its response, it prints ⟩ _ on the next line. The symbol ⟩ is a prompt character. It indicates that the computer is ready to accept a command (NEW, RUN, LIST, etc.) or a BASIC statement. Type your response right after it. You will notice that the other char-

---

†This key corresponds to the RETURN key discussed in the text and is used in the same way. We will use the same notation for it, ●

‡We continue the convention of underlining what is typed by the user.

acter, _, the **cursor,** moves ahead as you type. It indicates the position at which the next character you type will be entered on the screen.

Programs are entered, executed, and listed much as described in the text. Here is a typical session.

Example

```
) NEW  ●
READY ●
) 10     LET I = 1 ●
) 20     LET B$ = "BANG!" ●
) 30     PRINT I, I + 1; I + 2; B$ ●
) 9999  END ●
) RUN ●
1  2  3  BANG!
READY
) LIST ●
10     LET I = 1
20     LET B$ = "BANG!"
30     PRINT I; I + 1; I + 2; B$
9999  END
READY
) _
```

■

4.   Making Corrections

As in most versions of BASIC, a line can be changed by retyping it. However, one advantage of the video screen is the ease with which corrections can be made within a line (before ENTER has been pressed). When the key, ← , is hit, it erases the character immediately to the left of the cursor from the screen and from memory.

Example

Suppose that you make a mistake while typing a line:

```
) 240   LEM P = _
```

Press ← five times. The display will look like this:

```
) 240 LE _
```

Now complete the line:

```
) 240 LET P = 3.14159 ●
) _
```

■

5.   Stopping a Runaway Machine

If you wish to regain control of the machine while it is running or listing a program or if it is behaving abnormally, press the BREAK key. This should produce the response

```
READY
) __
```

In certain situations this may not work. If that is the case, press the orange RESET button. Be warned, however, that this will lose the program currently in memory and so should be used only in emergencies.

6.   Saving and Retrieving Programs

The mass storage device for this system is the cassette tape recorder. First make sure that:

1.   The tape recorder is plugged into an electrical outlet and is connected to the computer.
2.   You have loaded a tape cassette into the machine.
3.   The tape counter on the recorder is set to zero (we will assume that the cassette is a fresh one).

Each program saved on the tape is identified by a one-character name (a letter or a digit). Suppose that you have a program in your workspace which you wish to save under the name B. Put the recorder in RECORD mode. If it is correctly plugged into the computer, nothing should happen. Now type

```
) CSAVE "B" ●        (Cassette SAVE)
```

The recorder will begin to copy the program onto the tape. When the transfer is complete, the tape will stop and

```
READY
) __
```

will appear on the screen. Write the program name and the value of the tape counter on the cassette. If you want to save another program later, you will have to advance the tape beyond the end of this one (use the tape counter as a guide) before trying to save the second one. Also, make sure that each program saved has a different one-character name.

Suppose, now, that you want to retrieve a program, J, stored on the cassette tape. Insert the cassette in the recorder and make sure that it is rewound to the beginning. Press the PLAY button on the recorder and type

```
) NEW ●
```

to clear the workspace and then

⟩ <u>CLOAD "J"</u>●

The recorder will start to play (only the computer "hears" the "sound") and the computer will search for the program, J, on the tape. As each program stored on the tape is passed, its name will appear in the upper right-hand corner of the video screen.

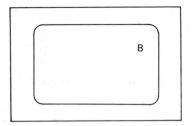

When the program, J, is reached, two stars appear. The right-hand one blinks as every 64th character is read from the tape.

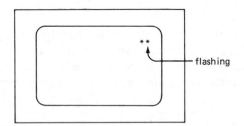

When loading is complete, the tape will stop and the screen will display

READY
⟩ __

You can now run, list, or edit the program.

If at any time during the transfer the star should stop flashing, the loading process must be repeated. Consistent trouble loading programs indicates problems with the cassette recorder. Things to look for: the volume setting is incorrect (see the Model III Reference Manual), or the read/write head on the recorder is dirty or in need of demagnetization.

There is no command for deleting programs from a tape. The only way to delete a program is to write another on top of it. The safest thing to do is to save just one program on each side of the tape.

7.   Limitations of the Video Screen

The size of the screen is a limitation of the video unit. It has room to display 16 lines, each no more than 64 characters long. This restriction is only on the number of lines that can be viewed at a time, not on the length of the programs that can be written. It does mean, however, that one can only look at segments of the code. Typing LIST for a long program is practically useless. The lines of code stream by and disappear off the top of the screen as new ones are printed at the bottom (this is referred to as scrolling). This problem can be handled by a modification of the LIST command.

Example

To display lines 370 through 480 of the program currently in the workspace, type:

```
LIST 390 – 480  ●
```

The machine responds with, say:

```
390  REM  REPEAT
400            READ N$,F,M
410            IF N$ = "****" THEN 600
420            LET I = INT((F/M)+0.5)
430            PRINT N$,I
440            IF NOT (I <= 4000) THEN 480
450               PRINT "X"
460               LET T1 = T1 + I
470               LET C1 = C1 + 1
480  REM      ENDIF
READY
) _                                                        ■
```

This modification of LIST is available on many BASIC systems.

Incidentally, the display can be temporarily frozen, while running or listing a program, by pressing the SHIFT key and typing @ (SHIFT/ @). To resume execution (or the listing) hit any key; it doesn't matter which one. This process of halting and continuing the printout can be repeated as often as you like.

The video screen does not provide as wide an output field as most printing terminals. In particular, when using the comma in a PRINT statement, only four fields, each 16 characters wide, are available.

Example

```
) 10   PRINT 1,2,3,4,5,6,   ●
) 9999   END ●
) RUN ●
1                2                3                4
5                6
READY
) __
```

This means that some of the examples and exercises in the book will have to be modified to run on this system. Tables should consist of no more than four columns, unless the TAB function is used. Also, if you don't want a table to scroll past you as the program is run, you should restrict it to about 12 rows of data.

8.   The Model III BASIC Dialect

In general, you should not have much trouble running examples from the text on the TRS-80 microcomputer. There are some differences, though, and these, together with other comments, are presented below, by chapter.

Chapter 2: The character [is used to denote exponentiation instead of ^. That is, 2[3 means 2^3 (= 8).

Chapter 5: Model III BASIC allows the use of both forms of the IF statement:

> IF *relation* THEN *line-number*
> IF *relation* THEN *statement*

and the logical operators NOT, AND, and OR.

Chapter 9: A character string variable may contain a maximum of 255 characters. Model III BASIC supports character string arrays as well. However, one peculiarity of this BASIC is that a special block of memory space must be set aside for character string storage. This is done as follows:

```
100   CLEAR 500
```

This statement sets aside storage for up to 500 characters, which can be spread between any number of variables. Any program that uses string variables should begin with the CLEAR statement. Make sure that adequate storage is set aside for all string variables used; otherwise, you will get an Out of String Space error (OS) when you run the program. When the computer is turned on, a CLEAR 50 is performed automatically.

Example

```
- - -
200  CLEAR 1500
210  DIM T$(25)
- - -
```

This provides sufficient storage for each component of T$ to contain up to 60 characters. If other string variables are used in the program as well, more storage may have to be set aside.   ■

The MID function takes the form

```
MID$(X$,I,J)
```

but otherwise is identical in performance to the function discussed in Chapter 9. Everything else in this chapter is valid for Model III BASIC.

Chapter 11: File handling with the cassette drive is quite limited. First of all, data files are not named; therefore, there is no way of distinguishing two files on the same tape other than by their positions on the tape—so don't try! Store one file to a side of tape. On this system only one file can be open at a time.

Files are opened and closed by hand. Assuming that the tape recorder has power and is connected to the computer, a file is opened by pressing the appropriate buttons on the recorder:

to OPEN for writing in the file—press PLAY and RECORD
to OPEN for reading from the file—press PLAY

The close operation is similar:

to CLOSE the file—press REWIND to rewind the tape, then STOP

Writing in the file is then handled by the statement

```
PRINT #-1, variable
```

and reading from it by

```
INPUT #-1, variable
```

The principal difficulty in dealing with a Model III cassette tape file is the fact that the file cannot be opened or closed by the computer. The way to handle this is to have the program tell the user what to do and then stop until the operation is complete. The following example illustrates the technique:

Example

Here is a program segment, written in DEC BASIC-PLUS, which stores two numbers in a file and then reads them from it:

```
200    OPEN "CONST" AS FILE 1
210    LET P = 3.14159
220    LET E = 2.71828
230    PRINT #1,P
240    PRINT #1,E
250    CLOSE 1
260    OPEN "CONST" AS FILE 1
270    INPUT #1,P
280    INPUT #1,E
290    PRINT P,E
300    CLOSE 1
9999   END
RUN ●
 3.14159      2.71828
Ready
```

Here is the same segment rewritten for the TRS-80.

```
200         CLEAR 100
210         READ W$,R$,C$
220         PRINT "PRESS TAPE RECORDER BUTTONS WHEN PROMPTED."
230         PRINT "THEN PRESS ENTER, TO CONTINUE."
240         PRINT W$              }
250         INPUT Z$                open file to write, then continue
260         LET P = 3.14159
270         LET E = 2.71828
280         PRINT #-1,P
290         PRINT #-1,E
300         PRINT C$               }
310         PRINT R$                 close file, then open to read,
320         INPUT Z$                 then continue
330         INPUT #-1,P
340         INPUT #-1,E
350         PRINT P,E
360         PRINT C$               }
370         INPUT Z$                 close the file
380    REM  OPEN AND CLOSE PROCEDURES
```

```
390        DATA "PRESS PLAY AND RECORD."
400        DATA "PRESS PLAY."
410        DATA "PRESS REWIND, THEN STOP."
9999       END                                          ■
```

Z$ is a dummy variable that plays no part in the program. The statement
INPUT Z$ is used to stop the program so that the user can open or close
the file. When he is finished he enters a blank string into Z$ (just presses
ENTER) to allow the program to continue. The RUN looks like this:

```
) RUN ●
PRESS TAPE RECORDER BUTTONS WHEN PROMPTED,
THEN PRESS ENTER TO CONTINUE.
PRESS PLAY AND RECORD.
? ●
PRESS REWIND, THEN STOP.
PRESS PLAY
? ●
  3.14159      2.71828
PRESS REWIND, THEN STOP.
? ●
READY
) _
```

Chapter 12: The RANDOMIZE statement is written

```
RANDOM
```

in Model III BASIC and the RND function described in this chapter is written

```
RND(0)
```

The argument of this function must be 0 if it is to perform exactly as RND
does. Other values for the argument produce different effects.

PART 2: Applesoft BASIC on the Apple II
with "floppy" disk storage and DOS[†]

1. The System

The Apple II system consists of three units.

The Keyboard Computer Unit: This looks like a typewriter that has
suffered radical surgery. It consists of the keyboard alone, without any

[†]Disk Operating System.

printing mechanism. In fact, there is more here than meets the eye, as the whole computer is hidden in this unit.

The Video Display: A special television monitor can be bought for this purpose or a good-quality television set may be used, provided that it is linked to the computer through a unit (RF modulator) which modifies the computer signal to make it palatable to the set.

The Apple Disk II "Floppy" Disk Drive: This unit stores programs and data on 5-inch-diameter disks which look like small phonograph records. The disks are, in fact, coated with the material that is used on magnetic tape and the information is stored on them in the same way, as patterns made up of tiny magnetized regions. An extra piece of circuitry (the controller card) has to be slotted into the computer unit so that it can handle the disk drive. The disks provide mass storage in a more convenient form than tape. The principal advantage is speed of access. Information can be read from any place on a disk with equal ease. The disk provides what is called **random access storage**. Tape storage, on the other hand, is sequential: a program at the end of the tape cannot be read until all the information preceding it has been wound past the recorder's read head.

Unlike the tape recorder, which has to be worked by hand, the disk is operated by the computer. The programs that do this are themselves stored on the disk. This package of programs is known as the disk operating system (DOS). Before you can use a new disk, you must copy DOS onto it from a master disk, which is kept solely to produce such clones.

2.   Logging In and Out

Make sure that the whole system is plugged together and that all three units have power. Take a disk that is a copy of the master disk, place it carefully in the disk drive and close the door. The disk is enclosed in a black plastic sleeve. Disk and sleeve together are pushed into the slot on the front of the disk drive. The manufacturer's manuals describe the correct way to do this.

Turn on the power switch on the back of the keyboard unit. A light on the keyboard, labeled POWER, indicates that the system is on. The disk drive's IN USE light will go on[†] and clicking and whirring sounds will be heard. When the noise stops and the IN USE light goes out, a message will appear on the video screen:

```
SLAVE DISK 5           8-20-81
APPLE DOS VERSION 3.3  A. KITCHEN
 ]□
```

[†]Never attempt to remove the disk when the IN USE light is on.

The system is now "up" and ready to go. The Applesoft prompt symbol is] and the cursor is a flashing square, □. In the examples given here, as before, ● represents the RETURN key.

When you have finished using the computer, make sure that the disk drive is not in operation (the IN USE light should be off), then switch off the power and remove the disk. Don't leave disks in the disk drive for extended periods when the computer is not being used. The disks must be stored away from extreme heat and from sources of magnetic fields (transformers, electric motors, magnets, etc.)

3. Entering a BASIC Program

To clear the workspace in preparation for writing a BASIC program, type NEW and press the RETURN key:

```
]NEW ●
]□
```

Notice that this system does not print READY. The prompt,], is the only indication you get that your command has been obeyed.

Entering, running, and listing of programs are all done in the standard way.

Example

```
]NEW ●
]10    LET I = 1 ●
]20    LET B$ = "BANG!" ●
]30    PRINT I;I + 1;I + 2;B$ ●
]9999  END ●
]RUN ●
123BANG!
]LIST ●
10    LET I = 1
20    LET B$ = "BANG!"
30    PRINT I;I + 1;I + 2;B$
9999  END
]□                                                          ■
```

Notice the output from this program. Applesoft BASIC treats numbers and character strings alike; neither are surrounded by spaces.

4. Making Corrections

Again, BASIC statements can be corrected by retyping them. Also, just as with the TRS-80 microcomputer, corrections can be made to a line, before the RETURN key is hit, by erasing characters with the ← key and retyping.

5. Stopping a Runaway Machine

On this system the emergency procedure is CTRL/C: hold down the control key (CTRL) and type the letter C. If this doesn't work, repeat CTRL/C and then hit RETURN.

6. Saving and Retrieving Programs

The disk drive is the mass storage device on this system. Unlike the cassette recorder of the TRS-80 system, control of the disk is completely automatic. In fact, its behavior is closer to the RSTS-E time-sharing system discussed at the end of Chapter 4.

Suppose that you wish to save a program currently in the workspace. You must give it a name in order to identify it among your disk files. This is done at the time you save the program: type SAVE, followed by the program name.

Example

A program to play backgammon is in computer memory. This command:

```
] SAVE BACKGAMMON ●
] □
```

will store a copy of it on the disk, under the name BACKGAMMON.   ■

A program name must begin with a letter. However, it can be up to 30 characters long and any printing characters other than the comma (,) can be used.

To copy a program from the disk to the memory of the computer, type LOAD, followed by its name.

Example

The program STANDARD DEVIATE:2 is stored on the disk. This command:

```
] LOAD STANDARD DEVIATE:2 ●
] □
```

stores a copy in your workspace.   ■

To erase a program from the disk, type DELETE followed by the name.

Example

```
] DELETE TIC TAC DOUGH ●
]□
```

removes the program TIC TAC DOUGH from the disk, but it has no effect
on the program currently in your workspace.   ■

7.   Limitations of the Video Screen

The output from the Apple II computer is displayed up to 24 lines at a
time, with no more than 40 characters per line. The same restrictions, of
course, apply here as apply to the TRS-80. The LIST command offers the
same option, that of printing just a segment of the program at a time.

Example

```
] LIST 390-480 ●
390  REM  REPEAT
400            READ N$,F,M
410            IF N$ = "****" THEN 600
420            LET I = INT((F/M)+0.5)
430            PRINT N$,I
440            IF NOT(I < =4000) THEN 480
450              PRINT "X"
460              LET T1 = T1 + I
470              LET C1 = C1 + 1
480  REM    ENDIF
]□
```
                                                                          ■

Again, some examples and exercises will have to be tailored to fit the
screen. You will also have to be cautious about the amount of indenting you
do for REPEAT and IF blocks. Don't skip it—it makes programs more readable—but limit it to two or three spaces.

8.   The Applesoft BASIC Dialect

This version of BASIC is similar to TRS-80 Model III and to the one in
the text. However, there are a few differences. Here is a review of the most
important features.

Chapter 5: Applesoft BASIC allows both the jumping and nonjumping
forms of the IF statement, just as Model III BASIC does. It also allows the
use of the logical operators NOT, AND, and OR.

Chapter 7: TAB(0) causes a tab to the 255th position!

Chapter 9: String variables may contain up to 255 characters, and string arrays are supported as well. Unlike Model III BASIC, it is not necessary to set aside storage space for strings (a CLEAR instruction does exist, but it does not serve the same purpose). The MID function takes the form

```
MID$(X$,I,J)
```

but otherwise string manipulation is handled in the way described in the text.

Chapter 11: The file handling in Applesoft BASIC with the disk operating system is a little idiosyncratic. To gain access to a file on the disk, the program must actually print commands to DOS. Up to three files can be open simultaneously (five if a further command is given).

Names for data files follow the rule described for programs: up to 30 printing characters, beginning with a letter.

An Applesoft BASIC program that handles a disk file should contain the following assignment statement, before the first file is opened:

```
LET D$ = CHR$(4)
```

This stores the nonprinting character, CTRL/D, in the variable D$ (the particular variable used is not important). This character is used to signal to the disk operating system that the program is about to pass a command to it. To illustrate this, here is the beginning of a program that opens a file, NEWSPAPER ROUTE:

```
- - -
200   LET D$ = CHR$(4)
210   PRINT D$; "OPEN NEWSPAPER ROUTE"
- - -
```

The opening of the file is handled by a PRINT statement, but because the output begins with CTRL/D, nothing is printed on the video screen. This command is directed to DOS, not the user.

Here are the open and close statements. To open a disk file, use

```
line-number   PRINT D$; "OPEN file-name"
```

To close it, use

```
line-number   PRINT D$; "CLOSE file-name"
```

Writing in a file and reading from it are then handled in a similar way. For example, to write data in the file NEWSPAPER ROUTE, once it is open, the program must signal that a "write" operation is about to begin:

```
- - -
220   PRINT D$; "WRITE NEWSPAPER ROUTE"
- - -
```

The output from subsequent PRINT statements:

```
- - -
230   PRINT B
- - -
```

is then directed to this file instead of the video screen. When the writing is complete, this statement

```
- - -
240   PRINT D$
- - -
```

restores to the PRINT statement its normal function of printing on the screen. Thus, to write a value in a file, use the sequence

```
nn   PRINT D$; "WRITE file-name"
pp   PRINT variable
qq   PRINT D$
```

(where nn, pp, and qq stand for line numbers).

Example

```
- - -
220   PRINT D$: "WRITE NEWSPAPER ROUTE"
230   PRINT B
240   PRINT D$
- - -
```
■

Reading from a file is handled similarly:

```
nn   PRINT D$; "READ file-name"
pp   INPUT variable
qq   PRINT D$
```

When writing a sequence of values in a file, it is not necessary to repeat the WRITE command. The same is true when reading from a file.

Example

```
- - -
160   PRINT D$: "READ OLDCAR"
170   INPUT M$
180   INPUT Y
190   INPUT C$
200   INPUT S$
210   PRINT D$
220   PRINT M$,Y,C$,S$
- - -
```

} Read record from file

Display it on the screen.

The following example shows the file program discussed in Part 1 of this appendix rewritten for the Apple II system.

Example

```
200    LET D$ = CHR$(4)
210    PRINT D$; "OPEN CONST"
220    LET P = 3.14159
230    LET E = 2.71828
240    PRINT D$; "WRITE CONST"
250    PRINT P
260    PRINT E
270    PRINT D$
280    PRINT D$; "CLOSE CONST"
290    PRINT D$; "OPEN CONST"
300    PRINT D$; "READ CONST"
310    INPUT P
320    INPUT E
330    PRINT D$
340    PRINT P,E
350    PRINT D$; "CLOSE CONST"
9999   END
]RUN ●
3.14159        2.71828
]□
```

If your system has two disk drives, files can be open simultaneously on both disks. A file name should then be followed by

, D1   or   , D2

to designate which disk (drive) it is stored on (or that you wish to have it stored on).

Example

```
210   PRINT D$; "OPEN STATS, D1"
220   PRINT D$; "OPEN TEMP, D2"
```

opens the file STATS on drive 1 and TEMP on drive 2.   ∎

If the extension is missing, the system assumes that the file is on the disk in drive 1; that is, STATS and STATS, D1 indicate the same file.

Chapter 12: There is no RANDOMIZE or RANDOM statement in Applesoft BASIC, and furthermore the RND function must be followed by an argument [e.g., RND(1)]. If this argument is positive (not zero), the function behaves like RND preceded by RANDOMIZE.

Example

This segment in Applesoft BASIC,

```
100    PRINT RND(1)
110    PRINT RND(1)
120    PRINT RND(1)
9999   END
```

behaves like this one in DEC BASIC-PLUS:

```
100    RANDOMIZE
110    PRINT RND
120    PRINT RND
130    PRINT RND
9999   END
```

These will produce different sets of random numbers between 0 and 1 each time they are run.   ∎

Each negative argument produces a fixed value between 0 and 1. This value is the same every time that argument is used. Subsequent calls to RND with positive arguments will produce a repeatable sequence of random numbers.

Example

This segment in Applesoft BASIC:

```
100   PRINT RND(-1)
110   PRINT RND(1)
120   PRINT RND(1)
9999  END
```

will produce the same three random numbers every time it is run.   ■

Appendix

II

Summary of BASIC Used in Text

1. Introduction

The version of BASIC assumed in this book is a subset of the language BASIC-PLUS designed by Digital Equipment Corporation as a time-sharing language for their PDP-11 family of computers. It is an extension of the American National Standard for BASIC (1978)[†]. The enhancements that have been included in the text involve, principally, character string manipulation and file handling. These were not covered in the original standards but are provided in some form or other in most dialects of BASIC currently available. See Appendices III and IV for comparisons of string and file handling in different versions of BASIC.

2. Constants

Numbers or Numerical Constants: These are positive or negative real numbers, or zero. The magnitudes of nonzero numbers are assumed to lie

[†]ANSI minimal BASIC.

in the range 10^{-38} to 10^{38}. However, they are only represented to six significant figures.

Numbers are written in standard decimal format. Negative numbers are preceded by a minus sign. The plus sign is optional in front of positive numbers. The decimal point may be discarded if the number is an integer.

Examples

All these are valid forms for numerical constants:

0.0034	97	97.
-27.94	+3.5	3.5
-400001.		

■

Scientific notation may be used to represent numerical constants. It is a convenient notation for very large and very small values.

Examples

1. $0.000076 = 7.6 \times 10^{-5}$ is written in BASIC as 7.6E-5.
2. $-8.642100 = -8.6421 \times 10^{6}$ is written in BASIC as -8.6421E6.   ■

The letter E stands for " . . . times 10 to the power . . . ".

Character Strings or Character String Constants: Any string of characters enclosed in quotes constitutes a character string constant. Its length is limited only by the physical length of a line.

Examples

1.   "THIS IS A B*L?#1234 CHARACTER STRING CONSTANT"
2.   "S O   I S   T H I S!"   ■

3.   Variables

Type	Notation	Examples
Numerical	Single letter or single letter followed by a digit	K A3
Character string	Single letter followed by a dollar sign	B$
Numerical array	Single letter followed by a single subscript (integer, numerical variable, or expression) enclosed in parentheses	P(3) G(I) F(A + 2*T)

Type	Notation	Examples
Character string array	Same as numerical array, except that initial letter is followed by a dollar sign	N$(T) A$(X) R$(K + N – 1)
Rectangular numerical array	Single letter followed by two subscripts, separated by a comma and enclosed in parentheses	M(7,5) D(I,J) Z(L – M,N)

Each numerical variable and each component of a numerical array is able to store a real number, whose magnitude is in the range 10^{-38} to 10^{38} or is zero, with a precision of six digits. Array subscripts are assumed to be integers. It is the programmer's responsibility to ensure that subscripts which are variables or expressions evaluate to integer values. However, in ANSI minimal BASIC, if a subscript is not an integer, it is rounded to the nearest integer.

Character string variables are assumed to hold at least 72 characters, or at least one line of text. ANSI minimal BASIC only requires that string variables hold 18 characters.

The same letter should not be used for a simple variable and an array name, or for an array and a rectangular array, appearing in the same program. However, the same letter may be used for a numerical and a string variable.

Example

1. This should NOT be done:

```
- - -
200  READ N
- - -
350  LET N(I) = X + T
- - -
```

2. This is OK:

```
- - -
200  READ N
- - -
350  LET N$ = X$ + T$
- - -
```

∎

4.   Operators

Mathematical Operators: These operate on numerical constants, variables, and expressions.

Operator Name	Notation	Examples
Exponentiation	^	A ^ 3
Negative (minus)	–	–7.3
Multiplication	*	X*Y
Division	/	P/2
Addition	+	N + 1
Subtraction	–	A – INT(B)

(It is standard convention to use the same symbol for the negative, –3, as for subtraction, 7 – 5. These are, however, handled as separate operations in BASIC.)

Two operators must not appear adjacent to one another.

Example

The expression A*–K is illegal. It should be written A*(–K).   ∎

When more than one operator appears in an expression, the following rules of precedence are used to determine the order in which the operations are to be performed.

1.   Assuming that the expression contains no parentheses, the operations are performed in the following order:
(a)   Exponentiation   ^
(b)   Negative   –
(c)   Multiplication and division   *,/
(d)   Addition and subtraction   +,–

If two or more operators at the same level in the order of precedence appear in an expression, they are evaluated from left to right.

Example

The operations in 1 + 3*4/2 – 5 are evaluated in this order:

$$1 + 3 * 4 / 2 - 5$$
$$③ \quad ① \quad ② \quad ④$$

That is,

$$1 + 3*4/2 - 5$$
$$1 + 12/2 - 5$$
$$1 + 6 - 5$$
$$7 - 5$$ ∎

2.   If the expression contains parentheses, the part within parentheses is evaluated first, before it is used in further calculations.

Example

In order to evaluate $(7*(3 - 2)^4)^2*3$, the expression $7*(3 - 2)^4$ must be calculated, but this requires the evaluation of $3 - 2$. Thus the order of the operations is

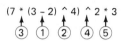

That is,

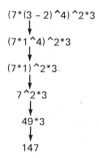

■

It is good practice to add parentheses to expressions if there is any possibility of misinterpretation.

Example

$$2 + 3 + 7 + 9$$

does not require punctuation. On the other hand,

$$(2/3)*7 + 9$$

is the same as

$$2/3*7 + 9$$

but expresses the intention of the programmer more clearly.   ■

Character String Operator: This operates on character string constants, variables, and expressions.

Operator Name	Notation	Example
Concatenation	+	"GOODBYE" + N$

This operator joins character strings end to end.

Example

    "HOPE" + "LESS" + " " + "CASE"

produces

    "HOPELESS CASE"   ■

Relational Operators: These operate on mathematical or character string constants, variables, or expressions. They are used only in IF statements. ANSI minimal BASIC only allows the use of = and <> with character strings.

Operator Name	Notation	Examples
Equal to	=	A$ = "STOP"
Less than	<	J < K
Less than or equal	<=	M + L <= A(I)
Greater than	>	R > INT(X)
Greater than or equal	>=	SQR(B) >= 10
Not equal to	<>	V*M <> I + J

A relation consists of two expressions separated by a relational operator. It is either true or false. Its truth can be tested by means of an IF statement.

Example

The statement

    210   IF J < K THEN 300

means: If the relation "J is less then K" is true, then jump to statement 300; otherwise, advance to the statement immediately following line 210.   ■

Logical Operators: These operate on relations.

Operator Name	Notation	Examples
Logical not (negation)	NOT	NOT(A$ = "LIST")
Logical and	AND	(10 < B) AND (B < 100)
Logical or (inclusive or)	OR	(X = 0) OR (Y = 0)

NOT produces the negation of a relation; that is, NOT (*relation*) is true only when *relation* is false.

Example

    NOT(A$ = "LIST") is the same as A$ <> "LIST"   ■

The logical expression (*relation-1*) AND (*relation-2*) is true only when both *relation-1* and *relation-2* are true.

Example

The expression (10 < B) AND (B < 100) is true only if B lies strictly between 10 and 100, that is, B is both greater than 10 and less than 100.   ∎

The logical expression (*relation-1*) OR (*relation-2*) is true if either *relation-1* or *relation-2* is true and false only when both *relation-1* and *relation-2* are false.

Example

The expression (M = 1) OR (N = 1) is true if M = 1 and N = any value or if M = any value and N = 1.
Note, in particular, that it is true if M = 1 and N = 1.   ∎

The operators AND and OR can be extended to more than two relations.

Examples

1. (L = 1) AND (M = 1) AND (N = 1) is true only if all these relations are true, that is, if all three variables have the value 1.
2. (L = 1) OR (M = 1) OR (N = 1) is true if at least one of these relations is true, that is, if at least one of the variables has the value 1.   ∎

No precedence rules are assumed in the text when the operators NOT, AND, and OR are mixed. Always parenthesize any logical expression involving a mixture of these operators.

5.   Functions

Mathematical Functions: These accept and return numerical values.

Notation	Description
ABS(X)	Absolute value of X
SGN(X)	Algebraic sign of X: –1 if X is negative, 0 if X is zero, +1 if X is positive
INT(X)	Greatest integer less than or equal to X
SQR(X)	Square root of X; on some systems, SQRT(X)
EXP(X)	Value of e^X, where e = 2.71828
LOG(X)	Log of X to the base e = 2.71828, the natural log of X

Notation	Description
LOG10(X)	Log of X to the base 10, the common log of X
SIN(X)	Trigonometric sine of X, where X is in radians
COS(X)	Trigonometric cosine of X, where X is in radians
TAN(X)	Trigonometric tangent of X, where X is in radians
RND	Next in a sequence of random numbers generated by the system; these numbers are in the range $0 \leqslant RND < 1$

Examples

1. INT(3.97) returns 3
2. SGN(-7.5) returns -1
3. The statement PRINT RND,RND,RND will produce something like

   0.437091   0.155269   0.799581   ∎

Print Position Function: This function can be used only in PRINT statements.

Notation	Description
TAB(X)	Moves print head of terminal or cursor through X (or X – 1) spaces from the left margin: the next character is printed in the X + 1st (or Xth) position

TAB(0) should leave print head at left margin. However, on some systems it may produce strange effects.

Example

The statement PRINT TAB(10);"*";TAB(20);"*" produces

   12345678901234567890`1` ← these are not actually printed
            *   *   ∎

Character String Functions: These functions accept string and numerical values and return either string or numerical results.

Notation	Description
MID(X\$,I,J)	Substring of X\$, starting at the Ith character of X\$ and consisting of J characters (Ith through (I+J–1)st character of X\$)
LEN(X\$)	Number of characters, including blank spaces, in the string X\$

Examples

1. MID("MUMBLETY PEG",7,4) returns "TY P"
2. LEN("MUMBLE THE PEG") returns 14   ∎

User-Defined Functions

Notation	Description
FN followed by a letter, followed in turn by an argument, or arguments, enclosed in parentheses	Numerical-valued function Definition is given by a DEF statement
FN followed by a letter and a dollar sign, followed in turn by an argument or arguments enclosed in parentheses	String-valued function Definition is given by a DEF statement

An argument is understood to be either a dummy variable name or a constant, variable, or expression, depending on the context. Arguments may take numerical or character string values. ANSI minimal BASIC allows only numerical arguments and numerical-valued functions.

Examples

1. DEF FNR(X) = INT(X*10 + 0.5)/10
2. DEF FNF$(X$) = MID(X$,1,1)   ∎

6. Statements

This section is not intended as a rigorous description of BASIC syntax. Instead, it is an informal summary of the features discussed in the text.

Each BASIC statement is preceded by a line number and consists of one or more key words plus other optional or variable parts. In the statement descriptions given below the KEYWORDS are capitalized and the *variable parts of the statements* are indicated by italics.

First, here is a brief explanation of the terms used (some of these are described in more detail above):

Term	Description
Array	Array name: a letter or a letter and a dollar sign
Channel-number	Small positive integer (usually 1 or 2)
Constant	Numerical or character string constant
Dimension	Positive integer
Expression	Legal combination of constants, variables, and functions with mathematical or character string operators
File-name	String of from one to six alphanumeric characters
Function	Function name: FN followed by a letter or a letter and a dollar sign

Term	Description
Line-number	Positive integer, normally in the range 1 to 9999
Relation	Relation or logical expression
Simple-variable	Numerical variable (not an array)
Statement	Legal BASIC statement
String-of-characters	Character string not necessarily enclosed in quotes
Variable	Simple variable or a component of an array, either a numerical or character string variable, depending on the context
{ }	Used to enclose optional parts of a statement

Specification and Description

DIM

specifies the size of an array or a rectangular array:

line-number   DIM *array-specification* {, *array-specification* etc.}

where *array-specification* stands for

array (dimension)   or   *array (dimension, dimension)*

More than one array can be specified in a single DIM statement.

Example

    200 DIM N$(100),A(50,50),C(2)

REM

indicates a comment. REM statements are ignored by the computer.

line-number   REM   *string-of-characters*

Example

    100 REM TITLE: PROGRAM TO DRAW MONA LISA

RANDOMIZE

causes the function RND to generate a different sequence of random numbers each time the program is executed:

line-number   RANDOMIZE

Example

```
210  RANDOMIZE
```

■

DEF

indicates the definition of a user-defined function:

line-number DEF *function (variable) = expression*

Example

```
230  DEF FNQ(X) = 1/(X^0.5)
```

■

Calculation

LET

calculates the value of an expression and assigns this value to a variable:

line-number LET *variable = expression*

Examples

1. `430  LET P = A*B`
2. `790  LET B$ = MID(T$,I,1)`
3. `240  LET S(I) = 0`

■

Control

GO TO

causes a jump to the statement with the given line number:

line-number GO TO *line-number*

Example

```
570  GO TO 320
```

■

IF-THEN

(a.) Causes a jump to the given line number if the relation is true, otherwise passes on to the next line of the program.

line-number IF *relation* THEN *line-number*

Examples

1. 420 IF X = 9999 THEN 760
2. 330 IF NOT (B > C) THEN 390   ∎

(b.) Executes the given statement if the relation is true, otherwise passes on to the next line of the program

line-number   IF *relation* THEN *statement*

Example

510 IF A > 0 THEN LET S = S+A   ∎

FOR

begins a FOR/NEXT loop; it specifies initial and final values of the counter (or index) variable and the amount by which the loop is increased or decreased. The loop must end with a NEXT statement:

line-number   FOR *simple-variable* = *expression1* TO *expression2* STEP *expression3*

The step size part can be omitted; then *expression3* is assumed to be 1:

line-number   FOR *simple-variable* = *expression1* TO *expression2*

Of course, *expression1*, *expression2*, and *expression3* must be valid numerical expressions.

Examples

1. 270 FOR Q = 0 TO N + 1 STEP 0.5
2. 400 FOR I = 1 TO 100   ∎

On some systems the FOR/NEXT loop is always executed at least once. Test yours with this segment:

```
100  FOR I = 1 TO 0
110     PRINT I
120  NEXT I
```

NEXT

indicates the end of a loop begun by a FOR statement. The variable in the NEXT statement must be the same as that in its matching FOR statement:

line-number   NEXT *simple-variable*

Example

```
380  NEXT Q
```

■

GO SUB

causes a jump to the given line number. Later, control must be returned to the line following the GOSUB statement by means of a RETURN statement:

line-number GOSUB *line-number*

Example

```
290  GOSUB 1000
```

■

RETURN

causes program control to return to the line following the last GOSUB statement executed:

line-number RETURN

Example

```
1130  RETURN
```

■

Input and Output

INPUT

prints a question mark and stops execution of the program until the user has entered a value (or values). The data are stored in the given variables, then the program continues:

line-number INPUT *variable* {,*variable* etc.}

Variables are separated by commas.

Examples

1. ```
   250  INPUT X
   ```
2. ```
   560  INPUT N$,B,C
   ```

■

READ

reads consecutive values from DATA statements and stores them in the given variables. Variables are separated by commas:

line-number READ *variable* {*,variable* etc.}

Example

710 READ M,X,T$ ∎

DATA

The list of values to be read by READ statements is stored in DATA statements. The data list can be read only once during execution, unless the RESTORE statement is used. Constants listed must be separated by commas:

line-number DATA *constant* {*,constant* etc.}

Examples

1. 950 DATA 500
2. 1200 DATA "CORNFLAKES",110,2,25,0,305 ∎

RESTORE

causes the next READ statement that is executed to return to the beginning of the data list, that is, to read the first item from the first DATA statement. Allows the data list to be read more than once in the same program:

line-number RESTORE

Example

860 RESTORE ∎

PRINT

prints the values of the specified expressions at the terminal. Each consecutive item in the list of expressions must be separated from the others by a comma or a semicolon:

line-number PRINT *expression* {,or; *expression* etc.}

The comma causes the values to be printed in columns; the semicolon prints consecutive values as close together as possible. The TAB function gives greater control over output. At least one system handles PRINT in a non-

standard fashion. North Star BASIC does not allow the semicolon and uses
the comma to pack data items close together. On this system the only way
to print in columns is to use the TAB function.

Examples

1.　500　PRINT X
2.　350　PRINT N - 1;"BOTTLES ON THE WALL";A$;"!"
3.　270　PRINT N$(I),Q(I),B(I),M(I);Y(I)
4.　410　PRINT I;TAB(I*I + 5);"*"　　　　　　　　　■

File Manipulation

OPEN

establishes a linkage between the program and the given file and assigns a
channel number to the file. If the file does not exist at the time of opening,
a file with the given name is created. The OPEN statement must be executed
before the file can be read or written into.

line-number　OPEN *"file-name"* AS FILE *channel-number*

Example

210　OPEN "DEBIT" AS FILE 1　　　　　　　　　■

CLOSE

disconnects the link (channel) between the program and the file with the
given channel number.

line-number　CLOSE *channel-number*

Example

780　CLOSE 1　　　　　　　　　　　　　■

INPUT

accepts the next available value from the file specified and stores it in the
given variable. Values are read from the file consecutively, starting with the
first.

line-number　INPUT # *channel-number, variable*

Example

```
300   INPUT #2,V
```

PRINT #

prints the contents of the variable in the file whose channel number is given. Data are stored in the file consecutively, starting from the beginning of the file.

line-number PRINT *# channel number, variable*

Example

```
510   PRINT #1,N$
```

File handling is not covered by the ANSI standards for minimal BASIC.

Ending

STOP

causes execution to stop:

line-number STOP

Example

```
590   STOP
```

END

causes execution to stop and also indicates the physical end of the program code. END must be the last statement in the program; in other words, it must have a larger line number than any other statement.

line-number END

Example

```
9999   END
```

7. Commands

There are no standard specifications for the commands that are used to handle BASIC programs, as they are not part of the language itself. The following is a representative selection. Some typical variations are listed. On some systems *program-name* may have to be enclosed in quotes.

NEW *program-name* or SCRATCH

clears the workspace and establishes the name of the next program to be written. Some systems do not provide the means to name a program in the workspace; on those systems this is done when the program is saved.

OLD *program-name*, GET *program-name*, or LOAD *program-name*

clears the workspace and transfers a copy of the given program from long-term storage to the workspace.

SAVE or SAVE *program-name*

saves a program in long-term storage under the name already given to it by the NEW command or under the name specified in the SAVE command.

UNSAVE *program-name*, KILL *program-name*, or DELETE *program-name*

erases the given program from long-term storage but not from the workspace. Beware! On some systems the DELETE command is used to delete the program currently sitting in the workspace, not from the disk (all very confusing!)

RUN

causes the program currently in the workspace to be executed.

LIST

causes the code of the program currently in the workspace to be listed.

BREAK key or CTRL-C

To gain control of the system in case of difficulties, press the BREAK key. If this key doesn't exist or doesn't work, try CTRL/C[†] (hold down the

---

[†]If neither of these work, find someone who knows the system or look at the manuals. Don't panic until all else fails!

CONTROL or CTRL key and type the letter C). On some systems it may be necessary to press the RETURN or ENTER key afterward.

This action returns control to the monitor. The monitor is the program that accepts and interprets all the system commands. It will acknowledge the request by printing the system prompt (Ready,], ⟩, etc.) possibly accompanied by a message.

Appendix

III

Character Strings on Other Systems

ANSI minimal BASIC, the national standard for the BASIC language which was set in 1978, requires only the most rudimentary string operations: input, output, the ability to store at least 18 characters in each string variable, and comparison of strings for equality and inequality. Most current versions of the language offer more than this and a few provide a great variety of sophisticated functions for string manipulation. The material in Chapter 9 represents a compromise. It is a fairly conservative extension of the standard, which still provides all the tools necessary to perform most kinds of string manipulation. A large number of popular BASIC dialects provide facilities similar to those described in Chapter 9:

1. Storage capacity of string variables equal to at least one line of input
2. Comparison of strings according to lexicographical ordering, using the operators =, <, >, <=, >=, <>
3. Character string arrays
4. A function to measure the length of a string
5. An operation that joins two strings end to end (concatenation)
6. A function to slice pieces (substrings) from a string

However, there does tend to be a wide variation in the way these are handled.

Storage: The limits for string variable capacity vary widely from a high of over 65,000 characters per variable to a low of about 75. A common limit is 255 characters per variable. Some systems set the capacity of a string variable by means of a DIM statement (e.g., Hewlett-Packard BASIC/1000D, Cromemco BASIC, APF BASIC, Textronix 4050 BASIC, Datapoint BASICPLS); others must CLEAR an area of memory for string storage (e.g., TRS-80 Model III BASIC, Intecolor BASIC).

Ordering: The lexicographical ordering of strings depends on an assumed order for the characters used. Here are the two most common orderings for the space, letters, and the digits:

space abcdefghijklmnopqrstuvwxyzABCDEFGHIJKLMNOPQRSTUVWXYZ0123456789

and

space 0123456789ABCDEFGHIJKLMNOPQRSTUVWXYZabcdefghijklmnopqrstuvwxyz

These orders arise out of the numerical codes that are used to represent characters in the computer. The first ordering occurs on machines that use the Extended Binary Coded Decimal Interchange Code, nicknamed EBCDIC[†] (e.g., IBM, Sperry-Univac, Burroughs Systems, etc.). The second occurs on those which use the American Standard Code for Information Interchange, or ASCII[‡] (e.g., DEC, Hewlett-Packard, Control Data Corp., TRS-80, Apple, etc.). Both these coding systems provide a number code for every printing character and control function on the typical computer terminal. We won't bother to list these here. You should find a full listing of the code used on your machine in the manufacturer's manuals.

Arrays: A few systems do not support character string arrays, at least not in the sense discussed in the text (e.g., Hewlett-Packard BASIC/1000D, Textronix 4050 BASIC, Cromemco BASIC).

Length: Most systems provide the function LEN(X$), as described in Chapter 9.

Concatenation: This operation is usually written X$ + Y$. However, Sperry-Univac's OS/3 BASIC calls it X$ & Y$ and in their VS/9 BASIC it is written as a function, CAT$(X$,Y$). Hewlett-Packard BASIC/1000D does not provide a concatenation operator, but the same effect can be gotten by this sequence of instructions:

```
100  LET I = LEN(X$)
110  LET J = LEN(Y$)
```

[†]Ebsidick.
[‡]Askey.

```
120  LET C$(1,I) = X$
130  LET C$(I+1,I+J) = Y$
```

The string C\$ now contains the concatenation of X\$ and Y\$. Atari BASIC takes a similar approach. The following segment assigns X\$ + Y\$ to C\$:

```
100  LET I = LEN(X$)
110  LET C$ = X$
120  LET C$(I+1) = Y$
```

Substrings: There are as many ways of handling this operation as there are versions of BASIC. Some systems use a function to do the work [e.g., MID(X\$,I,J) of DEC BASIC–PLUS]; others use a kind of array notation [e.g., X\$(I,K) in Hewlett-Packard BASIC/1000D]. The approaches also break down into two classes according to the method used to specify the substring. There are those that give the beginning position of the substring and its length [e.g., DEC's MID(X\$,I,J)] and those that give the beginning and ending positions [e.g., SUB(X\$,I,K) of PRIME BASIC].

Each function or notation in the table below satisfies one or other of these two definitions:

A.　The substring of X\$ consisting of J consecutive characters, beginning at the Ith character of X\$.
B.　The substring of X\$ consisting of all the characters from the Ith up to and including the Kth.

Notice that throughout the table:

I = position of the first character of the substring
J = length of the substring
K = position of the last character of the substring

For example, for the substring "THOCHRO" of "XANTHOCHROID",

The following relation always holds between I, J, and K:

$$K = I + J - 1$$

The last column of the table gives a formula for each system which will produce the same effect as the function MID(X\$,I,J) of Chapter 9.

Comparison of the Substring Operation in a Selection of BASIC Dialects*

Dialect of BASIC	Notation	Definition	Substring of X$ Consisting of J Characters, Starting at the Ith
DEC BASIC-PLUS Harris Extended BASIC	MID(X$,I,J)	A	MID(X$,I,J)
Microsoft BASIC (incl. IBM Personal Computer) TRS-80 Model III BASIC Applesoft BASIC	MID$(X$,I,J)	A	MID$(X$,I,J)
IBM 5100 BASIC	STR(X$,I,J)	A	STR(X$,I,J)
Sperry-Univac UBASIC	CPY$(X$,I,J)	A	CPY$(X$,I,J)
Textronix 4050 BASIC	SEG(X$,I,J)	A	SEG(X$,I,J)
Sperry-Univac VS/9 BASIC	SST$(X$,I,J)	A	SST$(X$,I,J)
DEC RT-11 BASIC Sperry-Univac OS/3 BASIC	SEG$(X$,I,K)	B	SEG$(X$,I,I+J–1)
PRIME Interpretive BASIC	SUB(X$,I,K)	B	SUB$(X$,I,I+J–1)
Cromemco BASIC	X$(I,–J) or X$(I,K)	A B	X$(I,–J) X$(I,I+J–1)
Hewlett-Packard BASIC/1000D North Star BASIC Atari BASIC	X$(I,K)	B	X$(I,I+J–1)
Datapoint BASICPLS	X$(I,K) For Nth component, X$(N), of array X$: X$: X$(N,I,K)	B B	X$(I,I+J–1) X$(N,I,I+J–1)
CDC BASIC version 3	X$(I:K) For Nth component, X$ (N), of array X$: X$(N)(I:K)	B B	X$(I:I+J–1) X$(N)(I:I+J–1)

*This list is not intended to be exhaustive. It is given to illustrate the wide variety of implementations of this operation.

Sequential Files
on Other
Systems

File handling is another operation not covered by the ANSI standards for minimal BASIC. Consequently, there is wide variation in style from one version of BASIC to another. However, the underlying process of opening a file, reading or writing in it, and then closing it are followed by just about every system. The main variations occur in the procedures for opening and closing the file.

Opening a file for writing is really a different process from opening it for reading. When a file is opened for reading, it is assumed to exist and its previous contents are not changed. When it is opened for writing, the old contents (if any) can be considered to have been destroyed. In a sense, opening for writing creates a new file. Many systems distinguish between these two operations. In fact, even in the version discussed in the text, DEC BASIC-PLUS, we can distinguish them if we wish:

Reading: OPEN *"name"* FOR INPUT AS FILE *n*

Writing: OPEN *"name"* FOR OUTPUT AS FILE *n*

Other systems use a separate CREATE instruction for new files (in a sense, files opened for writing).

There are a number of systems that do not have a CLOSE statement.

Files on these systems are automatically closed at the end of a program and, instead of closing and reopening a file in the middle of a program as described in Chapter 11, a rewind or reset operation must be performed to move the file pointer back to the beginning of the file.

Remember that, for trouble-free operation of sequential files, write and read operations should not be mixed while the file is open. To change from writing to reading, or vice versa: Close the file and reopen it (or reset the file pointer if the system has no CLOSE statement). To update a file: *Always rewrite the whole file.* Also, to minimize the problems when converting from one version of BASIC to another, only handle one variable in each "read" or "write" statement.

In the table, we use the following notation:

n = channel number assigned to an open file

The number of files (or channels) that can be open simultaneously varies widely. If you keep n in the range $1 \leqslant n \leqslant 3$, you will be safe on most systems. See Appendix I for a couple of exceptions to this.

name = the file name

Although some systems may allow file names to contain as many as 30 characters, the normal range is 6 to 8 characters. The following guideline will guarantee legal file names on most systems: from 1 to 6 alphanumeric characters, the first one being a letter.

len = file length

On some systems the anticipated length of the file has to be specified in characters or record blocks. See the comments in the table.

var = any numerical or character string variable

Comparison of File Operations in a Selection of BASIC Dialects*

Dialect of BASIC	Open	Close	Read	Write	Comments
DEC BASIC-PLUS, DEC RT-11 BASIC	OPEN "name" AS FILE n	CLOSE n	INPUT #n,var	PRINT #n,var	
Datapoint BASIC	OPEN #n,"name"	CLOSE #n	INPUT #n,var	PRINT #n,var	
APF BASIC	OPEN n,"name"	CLOSE n	READ #n,var	PRINT #n;var	
MicroMike's BaZic	OPEN n, "name"	CLOSE #n	READ #n,var	WRITE #n,var	
Technical Syst. Consultants 6800/6809 BASIC	To write: OPEN NEW "name" AS n / To read: OPEN OLD "name" AS n	CLOSE n	INPUT #n,var	PRINT #n,var	
Sperry-Univac UBASIC	To write: OPEN name FOR OUTPUT AS FILE n / To read: OPEN name FOR INPUT AS FILE n	CLOSE n	INPUT FROM n:var	PRINT ON n:var	
Commodore PET	To write: DOPEN #n, "name",W / To read: DOPEN #n,"name"	DCLOSE #n	INPUT n,var	PRINT n,var	
Oasis Z80 BASIC	To write: OPEN #n:"name", OUTPUT,SEQUENTIAL / To read: OPEN #n:"name", INPUT,SEQUENTIAL	CLOSE #n	INPUT #n:var	PRINT #n:var	
IBM Personal Computer BASIC (Microsoft)	To write: OPEN "name" FOR OUTPUT AS #n / To read: OPEN "name" FOR INPUT AS #n	CLOSE #n	INPUT #n,var	PRINT #n,var	
IBM 5100 BASIC	To write: OPEN n,"name",OUT / To read: OPEN n,"name",IN	CLOSE n	GET n,var	PUT n,var	
Control Data Corp. BASIC version 3	FILE #n="name"	CLOSE #n	INPUT #n,var	PRINT #n,var	
PRIME Interpretive BASIC	DEFINE FILE #n="name"	CLOSE #n	READ #n,var	WRITE #n,var	
Harris Extended BASIC	ASSIGN #n="name" / OPEN #n	CLOSE #n	INPUT #n,var	PRINT #n,var	
Cromemco 16K and 31K BASIC	New file: CREATE "name" / All files: OPEN \n\ "name"	CLOSE\n\	INPUT\n\var	PRINT\n\var	
Atari BASIC	To write: OPEN #n, 8, 0, "D:name" / To read: OPEN #n, 4, 0, "D:name"	CLOSE #n	INPUT #n,var	PRINT #n,var	

Comparison of File Operations in a Selection of BASIC Dialects*

Dialect of BASIC	Open	Close	Read	Write	Comments
Textronix 4050 BASIC with 4907 file manager	New file: CREATE "name", "A", len,0 All files: OPEN "name"; n, "F", string-var	CLOSE n	INPUT #n:var	PRINT #n:var	len = length of file in characters. string-var = a string variable in which the system stores a file status message.
Intecolor Extended Disk BASIC	New file (create): FILE "N", "name", len, 128,1 All files (open): FILE "R", n, "name", 1	FILE "C", n	GET n,var	PUT n,var	len = length of file in 128-character records. The record size and other factors can be changed. See the manuals.
Sperry-Univac OS/3 BASIC	FILE #n:"name"	Implicit close at END. Other times: RESET #n	INPUT #n:var	PRINT #n:var	Channel numbers, n, are assigned in order (1, 2, etc.) to files listed in FILES statement.
Sperry-Univac VS/9 BASIC	FILES name(,name etc.)	Implicit close at END. Other times: SET #n,1	READ #n,var	WRITE #n,var	Channel numbers, n, are assigned in order (1, 2, etc.) to files listed in FILES statement. len = length of file in 128 character records.
Hewlett-Packard BASIC/1000D	New file (given as a command before running program): CREATE name,len All files: FILES name(,name etc.)	Implicit close at END Other times: READ #n,1	READ #n:var	PRINT #n:var	
Applesoft BASIC with DOS with single disk drive	At beginning of program: LET D$=CHR$(4) To open file: PRINT D$;"OPEN name"	PRINT D$;"CLOSE name"	PRINT D$;"READ name" INPUT var PRINT D$	PRINT D$;"WRITE name" PRINT var PRINT D$	
TRS-80 Model III BASIC with cassette tape recorder	To write: Press: PLAY and RECORD buttons on recorder To read: Press PLAY button	Press REWIND Then STOP	INPUT #-1,var	PRINT #-1,var	Only one file can be open at a time.
with single disk drive	To write: OPEN "O", n, "name" To read: OPEN "I", n, "name"	CLOSE #n	INPUT #n,var	PRINT #n,var	

*This is not intended to be exhaustive. It is presented to illustrate the range of different approaches to file handling. The information in the table is taken from the manufacturers' manuals and/or specification sheets. It is only a brief summary of the capabilities of the individual systems. For trouble-free operation of file-handling programs on any new system, you should read the manuals carefully.

Appendix

V

Program
Structure and
Documentation

1. Structured Programming

The most important thing to understand about the art of programming is that, once the control structure of the procedure to be programmed is understood (i.e., the order in which the steps of the calculation are performed, the nature of the decisions that have to be made, and the tasks that have to be repeated), the actual programming process is quite straightforward.

Although the analysis of this flow of control is not always easy, it has been found that the control structure of a procedure can always be described in terms of three fundamental building blocks: SEQUENTIAL, REPEAT, and IF blocks. These blocks are simple enough that the task of translating them into BASIC is an almost mechanical process.

In the text we introduced structured flowcharts as a way of helping us to break programming projects down into these fundamental blocks, in preparation for the final step of translation. Here is a summary of the process of program development:

1. Become completely familiar with the problem to be programmed. Incidentally, you should ask yourself at this stage whether designing a program is the most appropriate way to solve the problem.

2.   Write an informal paragraph describing the goals of the project and how they are to be achieved by the program.

3.   Plan the output of the program *before a single line of code has been written.* This means that the requirements of potential users must be analyzed. Are they infrequent users? Experienced users? Are they specialists in the field addressed by the program? What quantities are required as output?

4.   Analyze the paragraph you wrote in step 2. Break it down into a sequence of separate tasks. Ask yourself these questions:
     (a)   Which tasks have to be repeated? In each case how does the repetition come to a halt?
     (b)   Are there tasks that are performed only under certain conditions? What are the conditions? What happens if the conditions are not satisfied?
     (c)   What is the nature of the data? Will it be needed more than once? How should it be stored?

5.   Rewrite the paragraph. Break it down into blocks to emphasize those tasks which are performed just once (SEQUENTIAL), those which are repeated (REPEAT), and those which are only performed under certain conditions (IF). Try to identify which quantities will be variables in the final program.

6.   Break each task into yet smaller tasks, again identifying them as SEQUENTIAL, REPEAT, or IF blocks. Repeat this refinement until the individual tasks are simple enough that you can translate them into BASIC statements. As each task or group of tasks is translated, it should be tested before being incorporated into the program.

7.   The last steps involve translating the control structures (the REPEAT and IF blocks) into BASIC, adding line numbers, polishing the documentation, and testing the completed program.

2.   The Building Blocks

The advantage of breaking a program into SEQUENTIAL, REPEAT, and IF blocks is that their control structure is very simple, so that

1.   They eliminate unnecessary complexity in programs.
2.   Their translation into BASIC, or any other language for that matter, is easy.

SEQUENTIAL Block: A sequence of tasks (statements) that are performed in order from beginning to end without jumps or repetitions. There are no control statements, so there is nothing to do but to translate the flowchart statements into BASIC.

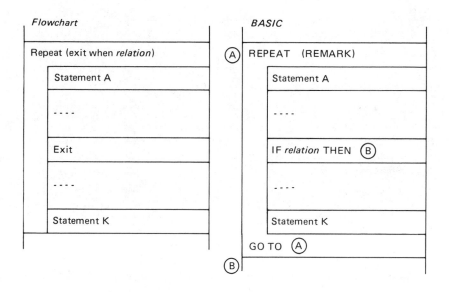

REPEAT Block: A sequence of tasks that is repeated. The repetition is stopped when the specified relation is true.

The FOR/NEXT loop in BASIC is a special case of the REPEAT block.

IF Block: A sequence of tasks that is performed if the given relation is true, and skipped if it is false.

Flowchart | BASIC

If *relation*

  Statement A

  - - - -

  Statement K

IF NOT (*relation*) THEN Ⓒ

  Statement A

  - - - -

  Statement K

Ⓒ ENDIF   (REMARK)

When these blocks are translated into BASIC, Ⓐ , Ⓑ , and Ⓒ become line numbers and REPEAT and ENDIF become REMARKS.

3. IF Blocks Involving AND and OR

Sometimes the condition under which an IF block is executed can be quite complicated, requiring the use of the logical operators AND and OR. This can produce large and unwieldy IF statements. Furthermore, some systems do not provide NOT, AND, and OR, so the following alternatives are sometimes useful, although not quite as neat.

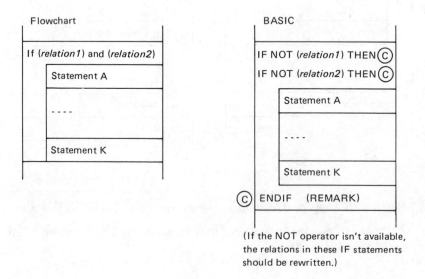

Flowchart | BASIC

If (*relation1*) and (*relation2*)

  Statement A

  - - - -

  Statement K

IF NOT (*relation1*) THEN Ⓒ
IF NOT (*relation2*) THEN Ⓒ

  Statement A

  - - - -

  Statement K

Ⓒ ENDIF   (REMARK)

(If the NOT operator isn't available, the relations in these IF statements should be rewritten.)

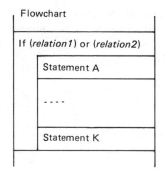

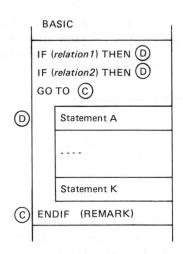

Conditions such as "If (relation1) and (relation2) and (relation3)" can be handled by a simple extension of this approach.

4. Documentation

This section summarizes the guidelines for documentation and program form discussed in the text.

1. Precede the program code with the following information, in REMARK statements:

```
REM TITLE: program title
REM PROGRAMMER: programmer's name   DATE: date on which program was completed
REM DESCRIPTION: a description of the program goals and of its overall design (most
                    important in large programs)
REM VARIABLES: a description of all variables used in the program
REM FILES: a description of the files used by the program
REM PROGRAM:
```

2. Begin the program code with DIM statements, function definitions, and the RANDOMIZE statement, if required.
3. Indent the bodies of all REPEAT and IF blocks. Use REM statements to identify them.
4. Place subroutines immediately after the code for the main program. A STOP statement should be inserted between end of the main program and the beginning of the first subroutine. Document all subroutines, as follows:

```
REM SUBROUTINE:
REM subroutine name or description
```

REM VALUES: *variables and files from main program, required by subroutine*
REM RETURNED: *variables and files changed by subroutine, required by main program*
                    Body of subroutine
    RETURN

and all subroutine calls, as follows:

REM CALL: *subroutine name or description*
REM VALUES: *variables and files from main program, required by subroutine*
REM RETURNED: *variables and files changed by subroutine, required by main program*
    GOSUB *line number*

5.   Place DATA statements at the very end of the program code right
     before the END statement. If the data have a record structure, list one
     record to a DATA statement. Begin the DATA block with a REMARK
     of the following form:

REM DATA: RECORD = *description of record fields*

5.   **Documentation Checklist**

     External

1.   Is the output neat and clear?
2.   Are the printed instructions appropriate for the intended users?
3.   Are suitable prompting messages used with the INPUT statements?
4.   Is every value that is printed by the program explained by a heading or
     a description?

     Internal

1.   Is the program neat and clear?
2.   Have you included the initial documentation?
3.   Have you used both REM statements and indenting to identify REPEAT
     and IF blocks?
4.   Have you used REM statements to give headings to the sections of the
     program, particularly the subroutines?

     Simplicity is a virtue, but if you can't make it simple, at least make it
     clear!
     The primary purpose of a programming language is for communication
     between human beings, so write programs that others can read!
     Take pride in the program itself—not just in what it can do!

Index